✔ KU-314-509

EVERYMAN'S LIBRARY
EDITED BY ERNEST RHYS

POETRY AND
THE DRAMA

SPENSER'S FAERIE QUEENE
WITH AN INTRODUCTION BY
PROFESSOR J. W. HALES
VOL. ONE

THIS IS NO. 443 OF *EVERYMAN'S LIBRARY*. THE PUBLISHERS WILL BE PLEASED TO SEND FREELY TO ALL APPLICANTS A LIST OF THE PUBLISHED AND PROJECTED VOLUMES, ARRANGED UNDER THE FOLLOWING SECTIONS:

TRAVEL ❦ SCIENCE ❦ FICTION
THEOLOGY & PHILOSOPHY
HISTORY ❦ CLASSICAL
FOR YOUNG PEOPLE
ESSAYS ❦ ORATORY
POETRY & DRAMA
BIOGRAPHY
REFERENCE
ROMANCE

IN FOUR STYLES OF BINDING: CLOTH, FLAT BACK, COLOURED TOP; LEATHER, ROUND CORNERS, GILT TOP; LIBRARY BINDING IN CLOTH, & QUARTER PIGSKIN

LONDON: J. M. DENT & SONS, LTD.
NEW YORK: E. P. DUTTON & CO.

POETS ARE THE TRUMPETS WHICH SING TO BATTLE. POETS ARE THE UNACKNOWLEDGED LEGISLATORS OF THE WORLD. SHELLEY

The FAERIE QUEENE

Disposed into Twelve Books Fashioning Twelve Moral Vertues by EDMUND SPENSER

VOLUME I.

LONDON & TORONTO
PUBLISHED BY J·M·DENT
& SONS LTD & IN NEW YORK
BY E·P·DUTTON & CO

First Issue of this Edition . 1910
Reprinted 1912, 1917

INTRODUCTION

"The nobility of the Spensers has been illustrated and enriched by the trophies of Marlborough, but I exhort them to consider *The Faerie Queene* as the most precious jewel of their coronet."—GIBBON.

LIKE all other great works of art, *The Faerie Queene* is intimately and thoroughly associated with the age in which it was written and published. Perhaps, even more than most great works, it is so. For it recalls and reflects its age, not only unconsciously and inevitably, — not only because it cannot help itself, so to speak; for a writer cannot, if he will, sever himself from his time, and so an Elizabethan cannot be other than an Elizabethan, whatever disguise he may assume in the shape of language or form—but also deliberately; it lays itself out of goodwill prepense to perpetuate the image of Elizabethan England. Spenser himself frankly informs us that such a portraiture was intended and designed by him in his famous Epic. Many persons, he says, may fancy that what he writes is but the "abundance of an idle brain," and "painted forgery," and may remind him that he omits to give any geographical definition of his Fairy land. To such criticasters he replies, that after all the terrestrial world is yet imperfectly traversed and known, and the land of Fairy may exist, though no bold navigator has yet discovered it. Are not fresh, unsuspected countries being found and announced every day? But, lest through the dulness of his audience there should be any misconception, he goes on to state explicitly, that in fact his Fairy land is neither more nor less than England itself. Apostrophising Queen Elizabeth, he declares that in the country he depicts, she may confidently recognise her own kingdom. Thus not only indirectly and accidentally but directly and purposefully *The Faerie Queene* describes, after its manner, the England and the Englishmen of Spenser's day. And therefore, if we would fully understand it, the chronology of its composition and of contemporary events is particularly important.

The Faerie Queene—it is a mere fragment (about a quarter)

of what it was intended to be [1]—was not built in a day. The
first three Books took about a decade to write; no doubt
there were long intervals in which Spenser had for one reason
or another to put his *magnum opus* altogether on one side.
The second three Books took some three years. We first
hear of *The Faerie Queene* as already begun in 1580; we know
that the first three Books were completed in or by 1589, and
also that the second three Books were finished in or by 1594.
The evidence for these statements is to be found in the correspondence of Spenser and his friend Gabriel Harvey, in *Colin
Clout's Come Home Again*, and in Sonnet lxxx.

Writing to Harvey from Lord Leicester's House, Strand,
on the 2nd of April 1580, Spenser begs his friend to return
him his *Faerie Queene* that he may go on with it:

" Now my Dreams and Dying Pelican being fully finished (as I partly
signified in my last letters) and presently to be imprinted, I will in hand
forthwith with my *Faery Queene*, which I pray you heartily send me with
all expedition, and your friendly letters and long expected judgment withal,
which let not be short, but in all points such as you ordinarily use and I
extraordinarily desire."

And presently " Hobbinol " delivers himself on the subject
which was evidently so much on Spenser's mind and so little
on his, and delivers himself in a way that might have sup-
pressed Spenser's poetic enterprise altogether, had he not
reserved his independence, or if his own instinct had not made
a pedant's censure of little moment:

" In good faith I had once again nigh forgotten your *Faerie Queene*.
Howbeit, by good chance, I have now sent her home at the last, neither in
better nor worse case than I found her. And must you of necessity have
my judgment of her indeed? To be plain, I am void of all judgment, if
your *Nine Comedies* whereunto, in imitation of Herodotus, you give the
names of the Nine Muses (and in one man's fancy not unworthily) come
not nearer Ariosto's Comedies either for the fineness of plausible elocution,
or the rareness of poetical invention than that Elvish Queen doth to his
Orlando Furioso, which, notwithstanding, you will needs seem to emulate
and hope to overgo, as you flatly professed yourself in one of your last
letters. . . .

Spenser's nine comedies are not extant, so far as is known,
and so we cannot compare them with *The Faerie Queene ;* but

[1] See " A letter of the Author's expounding his whole intention in the
course of this work . . . to the right noble and valorous Sir Walter
Raleigh, Knight ": " By ensample of which excellent poets [Tasso and
Ariosto] I labour to portrait in Arthur, before he was king, the image
of a brave knight perfected in the twelve private moral virtues as Aristotle
hath devised,—the which is the purpose of these first twelve books, which,
if I find to be well accepted, I may be perhaps encouraged to frame the
other part of politic virtues in his person, after that he came to be king."

we shall perhaps not greatly err if we accept Gabriel Harvey's alternative, and believe him to be void of all judgment in the preference he declares for them.

The next mention of *The Faerie Queene* at present observed occurs in Briskett's *Discourse of Civill Life, containing the Ethike part of Morall Philosophie*. This work describes a party of friends met at the author's cottage near Dublin. One is Dr. Long, Primate of Armagh; and Dr. Long did not become Primate of Armagh till the summer of 1584; so that, unless that title is anticipated—the *Discourse* was not published till 1606, and so possibly may have had additions or modifications—the date cannot be earlier than that year; and it certainly cannot be much later, as there is good reason for maintaining that in 1588, if not before, Spenser was well settled at Kilcolman; it was probably that very year. We learn from a speech which Briskett's reports " M. Edmond Spenser late your Lordship's (Lord Arthur Grey of Wilton) Secretary " as making, that *The Faerie Queene* was now well advanced:

" For sure I am that it is not unknown unto you that I have already undertaken a work tending to the same effect [a setting forth of Moral Philosophy] which is in heroical verse under the title of a *Faerie Queene* to represent all the moral virtues. . . . Which work, *as I have already well entered into*, if God shall please to spare me life that I may finish it according to my mind, your wish, M. Briskett, will be in some sort accomplished though perhaps not so effectually as you could desire."

I think we may find ground for supposing that the whole of Book I. and a good half of Book II. were written before he went to Ireland. The identification of Braggadochio with the Duke of Anjou is generally accepted; now, it was early in 1580 that the Duke of Anjou caused so much annoyance, and excited so much disgust; and it is in the early cantos of Book II. of *The Faerie Queene* that Braggadochio is held up to contempt. Moreover, and this fact has, I think, hitherto escaped notice, it is in Canto ix. of Book II. that we first have scenes and allusions that belong to Ireland and Irish experiences. In Stanza 6 we have the first mention of Arthegall, who unquestionably stands for Lord Arthur Grey of Wilton, the special hero of Book V. In Stanza 13 we have certainly a ghastly Irish idyll, painted from the life—such an idyll as he had seen with his own eyes in Glenmalure and elsewhere, and as his *View of the Present State of Ireland* abundantly illustrates. In Stanza 16 he speaks in a simile of " the fens of

Allen," and the gnats that swarm from them at eventide.
And yet again, in Stanza 24 he thus describes a part of the
House of Temperance:

> " Of hewen stone the porch was fairly wrought,
> Stone more of value and more smooth and fine
> Than jet or marble far from Ireland brought."

Certainly in or by 1589 the first three books were finished,
and in that year, as we gather from *Colin Clout's Come Home
Again* (=Spenser's Return)—a poem originally written in
1591 when he was once again domiciled at Kilcolman—he
went with Raleigh to England to have them printed and
published.

Undoubtedly, the reception of his masterpiece greatly
cheered and encouraged him. Even Harvey joined in the
chorus of praise and delight that arose in its honour. And
with a spirit refreshed and renewed the Prince of Poets—
such was the title bestowed on him—set himself to the con-
tinuation of his splendid task; and, enjoying comparative
quiet in the interval between two great rebellions, he succeeded in producing three more books in the years 1591, '92,
'93 and part of '94. The great domestic event, contemporary
with these compositions, was his falling in love with the
lady whom, not, it would seem, without some rebuffs and
despondencies, he at last won to be his wife. And in the Sixth
Book of *The Faerie Queene* he so far gives way to his private
rapture as to introduce his *fiancée* into the midst of the legend
of Sir Calidore. His love-suit and its anxieties, we learn, had
somewhat interfered with the progress of his poem. But at
last the lady accepted his devotion, and presently we hear
that the second three books were completed, and that the
work was, after a breathing space, to be continued with
renewed energy and spirit; see *Amoretti* lxxx., which was
certainly written before the *Epithalamion*, the song that
celebrates his marriage, June 11, 1594.

Two years later, *i.e.*, in 1596, Spenser again visited London,
and these second three books were published, the first three
re-issued with them. No other part of his vast, too vast,
design was ever to be completed. What leisure for poetising
he had in London must have been fully occupied with his
Hymns to Heavenly Love and Beauty, his *Prothalamion*, and
his memorable prose work *A View of the Present State of
Ireland*, on which he evidently spent much labour and care.

And when he returned to Ireland, the clouds of another
rebellion were rapidly gathering. In such deepening dark-
ness it must have been difficult to see to write, so to speak.
Housed in an old castle of the Desmonds, and conspicuously
representing the detestable scheme of English colonisation,
he was exposed to no common danger. The woods that then
grew round Kilcolman were rife with bitter enemies biding
their time. He must often have seen their threatening looks
and heard their furious curses. No wonder he found it hard
to go on singing of the Fairy Queen, or to sing of anything.
Two more cantos and two stanzas of a third seem to be all he
produced after 1594, which—how procured by the publisher
we do not know—were first printed in the first folio edition of
The Faerie Queene in 1609, appearing " both for matter and
form " . . . " to be parcel of some following Book . . . under
the legend of Constancy."

The composition of *The Faerie Queene*, then, as we have it,
extends over a period of some fifteen years, *i.e.*, from 1579 to
1594; and with the English history of this time it very closely
associates itself. It is, in fact, a prolonged pæan to the glory
of England. Had it been completed, the overthrow of the
Spanish Armada would have received its special celebration.
Lords Howard, and Essex, and Hunsdon, and other great
sailors, and soldiers, and statesmen were all to have a place
in his gorgeous pageant. In so much of it as was completed,
the Earl of Leicester, Sir Philip Sidney, Sir Walter Raleigh,
Lord Arthur Grey of Wilton, Sir Francis Walsingham, and
many more of contemporary note and fame move before us
" larger than human," transfigured and glorified. The Red
Cross Knight himself,—what is he, both in his strength and
in his weakness but the idealised Englishman of Spenser's
century? Spenser lived in the midst of events of great
magnitude and of absorbing interest, and in the midst of men
that were equal to occasions so fateful and supreme; and
even in the soarings of his fancy he could not escape from the
excitements and intensities of which the life of the time con-
sisted. He could take up no other themes than the great
world in which he found himself provided. Neither in his
head nor his heart was there room for any other story than
the Elizabethan, with all its terrible hazards, its strange
surprises, its brilliant achievements. He was fascinated and
possessed by it. And so, as we have seen, England becomes
to him a land of fairy, wrapt in a golden mist of chivalry and

romance, populous with knight-errants of divine purpose
and indomitable prowess.

Strangely enough, *The Faerie Queene* has not yet received
any adequate exploration from this point of view, though
there can be little doubt such a study of it would amply
reward the student, casting fresh light on well-known persons
and situations, or, at all events, presenting them in unfamiliar
attitudes and aspects. To the moral allegory, some atten-
tion has been given, but to the historical very little. Years
ago Sir Walter Scott, reviewing in the *Quarterly Review* Todd's
Edition of Spenser, expressed his regret that these historical
allusions had not been more carefully studied, Upton alone
having given them any recognition. " The ingenuity of a
commentator," he writes, " would have been most usefully
employed in deciphering what 'for avoiding of jealous
opinions and misconstructions' our author did not choose to
leave open to the contemporary reader." Of course such a
study is quite distinct from the purely poetic enjoyment of
The Faerie Queene, and is not necessary to any one who cares
merely for the melody of its verse or for its exquisite fanciful-
ness. But no one who wishes to appreciate the work of
Spenser in its entirety, to understand his art as fully as may
be, and to consider his mind as well as his art, no one who
wishes thoroughly to survey and comprehend one of the
masterpieces of English literature from all points of view,
can afford to neglect a field of investigation so large and so
fruitful. Only he who so explores *The Faerie Queene* will
recognise how solidly it is based upon actuality and fact. It
may seem to be one of the most purely aerial of poems, to be
but an estate in cloudland, and to appertain altogether to
the skies; but in very truth its foundations are firmly planted
in the England of Spenser's time, and its fine-woven parapets
and heaven-piercing pinnacles are not mere whiffs and shapes
of mist, but concrete things, however delicately refined and
veiled. This dreamer of dreams was assuredly a very practical
and efficient member of the workaday world; and his visions
are not so unreal and unsubstantial as a careless reader might
think, are not mere airy nothings, but, indeed, subtilised and
spiritual expressions of present and instant realities. They
are the idealisations of actual men and actual deeds; and in
them we see, as in a glass, the great Elizabethan age in all its
fervent, eager movement, with all its hopes and fears, its
passions of love and of hate, its anathemas and its adorations.

It was certainly Spenser's design to make our great war with Spain a central event of his poem, though such a design was not to be carried out, and, probably, had Spenser's circumstances been much more favourable, could not have been carried out, at least with any adequateness. But he undoubtedly set it before him. He distinctly announces it in the 11th Canto of the First Book, when about to describe the battle between St. George and the dragon, he invokes the Muse to gently come into his " feeble breast." And in his sonnet addressed to Lord Howard of Effingham, one of those prefixed to *The Faerie Queene*, he seems to anticipate this promised performance—to write as if it was actually executed in the first three Books, and the Conqueror of the Armada were already duly celebrated.

Upton conjectured that Marinell in some sort represented this famous Lord Howard, but such an identification is scarcely satisfactory. More probably Spenser sanguinely pictures what was so vividly conceived and confidently intended as actually performed. Of his purpose there can be no question. Essex, too, was, and was to be celebrated. But the supreme figure of his poem is she whose name is perpetually on the lips of contemporary poetry, the great queen whom her people idolised, and whom our own time, in spite of many fierce, and even virulent attacks, regards still as one of the greatest English Sovereigns. Under one form or another Queen Elizabeth is almost omnipresent throughout *The Faerie Queene*. Gloriana, Belphœbe, Britomartis, Mercilla—each is none other than Queen Elizabeth.

" In that Fairy Queen," writes Spenser to Raleigh, " I mean glory in my general intention, but in my particular, I conceive the most excellent and glorious person of our sovereign the Queen, and her kingdom in Fairy land. *And yet in some places else I do otherwise shadow her.* For, considering she beareth two persons, the one of a most royal Queen or Empress, the other of a most virtuous and beautiful Lady, this latter part in some places I do express in Belphœbe, fashioning her name according to your own excellent conceipt of Cynthia, Phœbe and Cynthia being both names of Diana."

Thus, that there is a correspondence between Belphœbe and Queen Elizabeth, is no idle conjecture of an over-curious commentator. But, on the other hand, the correspondence must not be pushed too far; we must not insist on identity in all actions and respects. Spenser does not surrender himself to a mere imitation or reflection of a certain set of facts. He retains the right of variation or of addition. In other words, the correspondences between his personæ and living people are not servile; they are general rather than particular.

Queen Elizabeth's arch-enemy, Philip II. of Spain, is more than once suggested or presented to Spenser's readers, though probably his completer portrait was to have been given in the Books that were never written. Unquestionably he is denoted by Gerioneo in the Fifth Book—a Book remarkable for its many unmistakable, and scarcely at all disguised historical allusions. The rhyming argument of Canto X. runs thus:—

> Prince Arthur takes the Enterprise
>   For Belgee for to fight.
> Gerioneo's Seneschall
>   He slayes in Belge's right.

Evidently "Gerioneo's Seneschall" is the Spanish commander in the low countries. And Prince Arthur here, as elsewhere, though perhaps not always, signifies the Earl of Leicester. If it shocks us that such a very second-rate character as Robert Dudley should have served as the original of Spenser's Prince Arthur, we must remember that Spenser saw that handsome but not high-natured nobleman with different eyes from ours, from a very different standpoint, in a very different atmosphere. And so, when in Canto XII. we are told how—

> Artegall doth Sir Burbon aide,
>   And blames for changing shield;
> He with the great Grantorto fights,
>   And slaieth him in field,

the references to Henri Quatre and his change of religion are made sufficiently obvious to the most careless reader. The connection of Duessa and Mary Queen of Scots in Canto IX. was so patent as to give extreme annoyance to James VI. of Scotland. We learn from a letter to Lord Burghley from the English ambassador at Edinburgh that great offence was conceived by the King against Edmund Spenser for publishing in print in the second part of *The Faerie Queene* (*i.e.* in the second three books, published—1596), "some dishonourable effects," as the King deemed, against himself and his mother deceased.

Thus it is clear, in respect of Spenser's material, that, largely as he borrowed from books—especially from the Classics and from the Italians—he borrowed yet more largely from contemporary society and history, and that in his great poem in a very full and special sense he mirrors the events and the personages of his own age. But, of course, such historical interpretations are quite distinct from poetical studies. Obviously, the first duty of a poem is to be poetical, not historical, or ethical, or metaphysical.

Beyond question, what moved Spenser to write was a genuine poetic impulse. As we have seen, his mind was indeed profoundly interested in the great movements of his time; he was a thoroughly intelligent and devoted Protestant; he admired and cultivated "the new learning" with rare ability and fervent delight; he was penetrated and pervaded by a passionate patriotism. But in addition to all these incitements and motives he was actuated by a real creative instinct. He sang because he must, not only because people listened, and there was so much to say. His heart was hot within him; and while he was thus musing, the fire kindled, and at the last he "spake with his tongue." He sang, not because he was learned—an epithet often assigned him by his contemporaries [1]—or an intense votary of the Reformation or the Renascence, but because his imagination longed for outward embodiment, because it must needs give birth to its divine conceptions, because it insisted on relief and deliverance. In other words, Spenser's poetry is a true incarnation of a poetical spirit, not the elaborate effort of a partisan, literary, political, religious.

It is his inexhaustible freshness and abundance of fancy, combined with his astonishing dominion over language and over rime and rhythm, that has won for Spenser his distinguishing title of "the Poets' Poet." The material he uses is sometimes prosaic enough, as especially in the Second Book, in his description of the House of Alma, otherwise the human body, in Canto IX., or in his versification of Geoffrey of Monmouth's *History of the Britons* in the following Canto; but under any and all circumstances, whether he is happy in his immediate subject or not, whatever are the strange tasks he sets himself, or ponderous burdens he undertakes, he never ceases to be a poet, and it can never be forgotten by any capable and appreciative reader that he is a poet. In most great poets there is a certain vein of prose which " crops up " from time to time. No one is wise at all hours, says an old Latin adage; certainly, it is true that no one is poetical at all hours. Instead of flying and soaring according to their

[1] Dryden too remarks: " No man was ever born with a greater genius than Spenser, or had more knowledge to support it."

proper form of movement, we see poets walking, or even crawling, *i.e.*, their speech, in Horace's phrase, becomes "pedestrian." [1] Now, whatever may be Spenser's deficiencies and faults, it seems true that no one ever lived more constantly and fully in the world of imagination than he,— that, though others may have risen higher, no one ever sank out of his empyrean and touched the gross earth less frequently or fatally. " Of all the poets," writes Hazlitt, " he is the most poetical." Whatever we may think of his Fairy land in other respects, there can be no question that it is a province of poetry.

Spenser created a new world, which, from its first appearance in the firmament of literature, had a special charm and fascination for his brother artists, who, generation after generation, delighted to wander in it.

There are several traces in Shakespeare's Plays of his familiarity with Spenser's Poems, and personally they must have been well acquainted, meeting often no doubt at the house of their common friend Lord Essex. Not, however, to insist on imperfectly ascertained relations, no less a person than Milton declared Spenser was his " poetical father "; and without any such declaration we should confidently have inferred this spiritual sonship, so evident is Spenser's influence on Milton's earlier poetry. In the *Areopagitica* also Milton speaks of " our sage and serious Spenser whom I dare be known to think a better teacher than Scotus and Aquinas." Dryden and Pope are by no means poets of the Spenserian type; yet both of them testify their debt and their admiration. With the revival of the imagination in the last century arose a yet warmer enthusiasm for Spenser. Thomson's lines in his *Summer* are highly appreciative as well as discriminating:—

> Nor shall my verse that elder bard forget,
> The gentle Spenser, Fancy's pleasing son,
> Who, like a copious river, pour'd his song
> O'er all the mazes of enchanted ground.

Certainly on what is best of Thomson's work, as on *The Castle of Indolence*, the influence of Spenser is very deeply impressed. Gray found the perusal of Spenser one of his best incentives and excitements, when he wished to cultivate the poetical mood. The air of *The Faerie Queene* seemed to arouse and invigorate his often languid faculties. To Wordsworth,

[1] *See* Hor. *Ep.* 2, i. 251; *Sat.* 2. vi. 17; *A.P.* 95.

Byron, Shelley, Keats, that same air was scarcely less delightful and scarcely less benign.

Amongst our poets Wordsworth was perhaps one of the least susceptible to literary impressions; and yet we see with what grateful joy he submitted himself to the sweet influence of Spenser. Probably the first lines Keats wrote were headed *In imitation of Spenser.* Possibly the power of Spenser over him at that time was to a large extent indirect, that is, was exercised through intermediate writers; but to the end of his life, acting indirectly or directly, it was a determining force. A last century writer, one Dr. Sewell, made the memorable remark that " more poets have sprung from Spenser than all other English writers."

Thus, whatever Spenser's defects, however true it may be that he is wanting in humour, that in archaising his grammar and his vocabulary he " writ no language, that his characters lack at times human interest, and whatever else Zoiluses or even well-meaning and generous critics may urge against him, it remains that to highly sensitive natures he is a poet of exceptional and of sovereign charm, of an inspiration that is singularly full and overflowing, so that—

> Hither, as to their fountain, other stars
> Repairing in their urns draw golden light.

In spite of all his superabundance of fantasy, his want of human substance, and his epic confusions in *The Faerie Queene,* Spenser securely holds one of the chief thrones of English poetry; and around no one of our poetic kings is there gathered a court more remarkable for its selectness, its culture, and its devotion; and on him, as we have mentioned, has been conferred by right divine the significant " style " of the Poets' Poet. As we have seen, from Drayton and Raleigh and many another Elizabethan down to Wordsworth and Keats and many another singer of the nineteenth century, all the poets, with scarcely an exception, rise up and call him blessed. For three hundred years now he has been one of the supreme inspiring influences of our literature. If his work is not perfect, yet it suggests a sense of perfection, that is, it brings vividly before us one visited and possessed by visions of rare loveliness, and striving with no common cunning and no common success to embody them worthily and immortally. And, whatever its imperfection or imperfections as a whole, it contains pictures and passages of incomparable finish and beauty, pictures and passages as nearly perfect as anything that has proceeded from human pen. " The heavenly Una with her milk-white lamb " will remain to the end of time one of the fairest and sweetest figures to be found in books. He who could create so exquisite a being was unquestionably and beyond all protest an artist of the highest order, even though he failed to accomplish any other like achievement. But indeed *The Faerie Queene* abounds in stanzas and in passages of surpassing beauty, and in signs and tokens of a nature haunted and inspired by the very spirit of grace and loveliness.

The Text and Glossary here used are those of Dr. R. Morris, by kind permission of Messrs. Macmillan & Co.

JOHN W. HALES.

1909.

The following is a list of the works of Spenser:—

Shepheard's Calendar, 1st edition, 1579; reproduced in facsimile by Oskar Sommer, 1890; re-edited by Prof. C. H. Herford, 1895; Faerie Queene, 1590 (first 3 books) and 1596; 2nd edition, 1596; Daphnaïda, 1591; Complaints (nine smaller poems), 1591; Colin Clout's Come Home Again, 1595; Amoretti, 1595; Foure Hymns, 1596; Prothalamion, 1596; Prosopopoia, or Mother Hubberd's Tale, 1613 (had appeared in Complaints).

PROSE: Three Letters to Gabriel Harvey, 1580; View of the State of Ireland, in dialogue, written 1596, 1633.

WORKS: First Collected Edition of Works, 1611; Complete Edition with Life, by Grosart, 1882-4.

LIFE: Prefixed to Todd's Edition of Works, 1805; and to Globe Edition (J. W. Hales); by Grosart, see Works; by R. M. Church, English Men of Letters, 1879; Sidney Lee, Great Englishmen of the Sixteenth Century, 1904; W. Tuckwell (Miniature Series of Great Writers), 1906.

To
The most high, mightie, and magnificent
Empresse,
Renowmed for pietie, vertue, and all gratious government,

ELIZABETH,

by the grace of God,
Queene of England, Fraunce, and Ireland,
and of Virginia,
Defendour of the Faith, etc.,
Her most humble servaunt

EDMUND SPENSER,

doth, in all humilitie,
dedicate, present, and consecrate
these his labours,
To live with the eternitie of her fame.

CONTENTS

THE FAERIE QUEENE

A LETTER OF THE AUTHORS,

*Expounding his whole intention in the course of this worke :
which, for that it giveth great light to the reader, for
the better understanding is hereunto annexed.*

To the Right Noble and Valorous
SIR WALTER RALEIGH, KNIGHT.

*Lord Wardein of the Stanneryes, and Her Maiesties
Liefetenaunt of the County of Cornewayll.*

*Sir, knowing how doubtfully all Allegories may be construed,
and this booke of mine, which I have entituled the Faery Queene,
being a continued Allegory, or darke conceit, I haue thought
good, as well for avoyding of gealous opinions and misconstructions, as also for your better light in reading thereof, (being so by
you commanded,) to discover unto you the general intention and
meaning, which in the whole course thereof I have fashioned,
without expressing of any particular purposes, or by accidents,
therein occasioned. The generall end therefore of all the booke
is to fashion a gentleman or noble person in vertuous and gentle
discipline : Which for that I conceived shoulde be most plausible
and pleasing, being coloured with an historicall fiction, the which
the most part of men delight to read, rather for variety of matter
then for profite of the ensample, I chose the historye of King
Arthure, as most fitte for the excellency of his person, being made
famous by many mens former workes, and also furthest from the
daunger of envy, and suspition of present time. In which I have
followed all the antique Poets historicall ; first Homere, who in
the Persons of Agamemnon and Ulysses hath ensampled a good
governour and a vertuous man, the one in his Ilias, the other in
his Odysseis : then Virgil, whose like intention was to doe in
the person of Aeneas : after him Ariosto comprised them both
in his Orlando : and lately Tasso dissevered them againe, and*

I   A

*formed both parts in two persons, namely that part which they in
Philosophy call Ethice, or vertues of a private man, coloured in
his Rinaldo; the other named Politice in his Godfredo. By
ensample of which excellente Poets, I labour to pourtraict in
Arthure, before he was king, the image of a brave knight, perfected
in the twelve private morall vertues, as Aristotle hath devised;
the which is the purpose of these first twelve bookes: which if I
finde to be well accepted, I may be perhaps encoraged to frame the
other part of polliticke vertues in his person, after that hee came
to be king.*

*To some, I know, this Methode will seeme displeasaunt, which
had rather have good discipline delivered plainly in way of precepts,
or sermoned at large, as they use, then thus clowdily enwrapped in
Allegoricall devises. But such, me seeme, should be satisfide
with the use of these dayes, seeing all things accounted by their
showes, and nothing esteemed of, that is not delightfull and pleasing
to commune sence. For this cause is Xenophon preferred before
Plato, for that the one, in the exquisite depth of his judgement,
formed a Commune welth, such as it should be; but the other
in the person of Cyrus, and the Persians, fashioned a governement,
such as might best be: So much more profitable and gratious
is doctrine by ensample, then by rule. So haue I laboured to doe
in the person of Arthure: whome I conceive, after his long educa-
tion by Timon, to whom he was by Merlin delivered to be brought
up, so soone as he was borne of the Lady Igrayne, to have seene
in a dream or vision the Faery Queene, with whose excellent
beauty ravished, he awaking resolved to seeke her out; and so
being by Merlin armed, and by Timon throughly instructed, he
went to seeke her forth in Faerye land. In that Faery Queene I
meane glory in my generall intention, but in my particular I conceive the most excellent and glorious person of our soveraine the
Queene, and her kingdome in Faery land. And yet, in some
places els, I doe otherwise shadow her. For considering she
beareth two persons, the one of a most royall Queene or Empresse,
the other of a most vertuous and beautifull Lady, this latter part
in some places I doe expresse in Belphœbe, fashioning her name
according to your owne excellent conceipt of Cynthia, (Phœbe and
Cynthia being both names of Diana). So in the person of Prince
Arthure I sette forth magnificence in particular; which vertue,
for that (according to Aristotle and the rest) it is the perfection of
all the rest, and conteineth in it them all, therefore in the whole
course I mention the deedes of Arthure applyable to that vertue,
which I write of in that booke. But of the xii. other vertues, I*

make xii. other knightes the patrones, for the more variety of the
history : Of which these three bookes contayn three.

The first of the knight of the Redcrosse, in whome I expresse
Holynes : The seconde of Sir Guyon, in whome I sette forth
Temperaunce : The third of Britomartis, a Lady Knight, in whome
I picture Chastity. But, because the beginning of the whole
worke seemeth abrupte, and as depending upon other antecedents,
it needs that ye know the occasion of these three knights seuerall
adventures. For the Methode of a Poet historical is not such,
as of an Historiographer. For an Historiographer discourseth
of affayres orderly as they were donne, accounting as well the times
as the actions ; but a Poet thrusteth into the middest, even where
it most concerneth him, and there recoursing to the thinges fore-
paste, and divining of thinges to come, maketh a pleasing Analysis
of all.

The beginning therefore of my history, if it were to be told by
an Historiographer should be the twelfth booke, which is the last ;
where I devise that the Faery Queene kept her Annuall feaste xii.
dayes ; uppon which xii. severall dayes, the occasions of the xii.
severall adventures hapned, which, being undertaken by xii.
severall knights, are in these xii. books severally handled and
discoursed. The first was this. In the beginning of the feast,
there presented him selfe a tall clownishe younge man, who falling
before the Queene of Faeries desired a boone (as the manner then
was) which during that feast she might not refuse ; which was
that hee might have the atchievement of any adventure, which
during that feaste should happen : that being graunted, he rested
him on the floore, unfitte through his rusticity for a better place.
Soone after entred a faire Ladye in mourning weedes, riding on a
white Asse, with a dwarfe behind her leading a warlike steed, that
bore the Armes of a knight, and his speare in the dwarfes hand.
Shee, falling before the Queene of Faeries, complayned that her
father and mother, an ancient King and Queene, had bene by an
huge dragon many years shut up in a brasen Castle, who then
suffred them not to yssew ; and therefore besought the Faery
Queene to assygne her some one of her knights to take on him that
exployt. Presently that clownish person, upstarting, desired that
adventure : whereat the Queene much wondering, and the Lady
much gainesaying, yet he earnestly importuned his desire. In
the end the Lady told him, that unlesse that armour which she
brought, would serve him (that is, the armour of a Christian man
specified by Saint Paul, vi. Ephes.) that he could not succeed in
that enterprise ; which being forthwith put upon him, with dewe

furnitures thereunto, he seemed the goodliest man in al that company, and was well liked of the Lady. And eftesoones taking on him knighthood, and mounting on that straunge Courser, he went forth with her on that adventure : where beginneth the first booke, viz.

A gentle knight was pricking on the playne, etc.

The second day there came in a Palmer, bearing an Infant with bloody hands, whose Parents he complained to have bene slayn by an Enchaunteresse called Acrasia ; and therefore craved of the Faery Queene, to appoint him some knight to performe that adventure ; which being assigned to Sir Guyon, he presently went forth with that same Palmer : which is the beginning of the second booke, and the whole subject thereof. The third day there came in a Groome, who complained before the Faery Queene, that a vile Enchaunter, called Busirane, had in hand a most faire Lady, called Amoretta, whom he kept in most grievous torment, because she would not yield him the pleasure of her body. Whereupon Sir Scudamour, the lover of that Lady, presently tooke on him that adventure. But being unable to performe it by reason of the hard Enchauntments, after long sorrow, in the end met with Britomartis, who succoured him, and reskewed his loue.

But by occasion hereof many other adventures are intermedled ; but rather as Accidents then intendments : As the love of Brito- mart, the overthrow of Marinell, the misery of Florimell, the vertuousnes of Belphœbe, the lasciviousnes of Hellenora, and many the like.

Thus much, Sir, I have briefly overronne to direct your under- standing to the wel-head of the History ; that from thence gathering the whole intention of the conceit, ye may as in a handfull gripe al the discourse, which otherwise may happily seeme tedious and confused. So, humbly craving the continuance of your honorable favour towards me, and th' eternall establishment of your happines, I humbly take leave.

23. *January* 1589,
Yours most humbly affectionate,

Ed. Spenser.

VERSES ADDRESSED TO THE AUTHOR

A Vision upon this conceipt of the Faery Queene

ME thought I saw the grave where Laura lay,
Within that Temple where the vestall flame
Was wont to burne; and passing by that way
To see that buried dust of living fame,
Whose tumbe faire love, and fairer vertue kept,
All suddeinly I saw the Faery Queene:
At whose approch the soule of Petrarke wept,
And from thenceforth those graces were not seene;
For they this Queene attended, in whose steed
Oblivion laid him downe on Lauras herse.
Hereat the hardest stones were seene to bleed,
And grones of buried ghostes the hevens did perse:
　　Where Homers spright did tremble all for griefe,
　　And curst th'accesse of that celestiall theife.

Another of the same

The prayse of meaner wits this worke like profit brings,
As doth the Cuckoes song delight when Philumena sings.
If thou hast formed right true vertues face herein,
Vertue her selfe can best discerne to whom they written bin.
If thou hast beauty praysd, let her sole lookes divine
Judge if ought therein be amis, and mend it by her eine.
If Chastitie want ought, or Temperaunce her dew,
Behold her Princely mind aright, and write thy Queene anew.
Meane while she shall perceive, how far her vertues sore
Above the reach of all that live, or such as wrote of yore:
And thereby will excuse and favour thy good will;
Whose vertue can not be exprest, but by an Angels quill.
　　Of me no lines are lov'd, nor letters are of price,
　　Of all which speak our English tongue, but those of thy device.
　　　　　　　　　　　　　　　　　　　　　W. R.

To the learned Shepeheard

Collyn, I see, by thy new taken taske,
　Some sacred fury hath enricht thy braynes,
That leades thy muse in haughty verse to maske,
　And loath the layes that longs to lowly swaynes;
That lifts thy notes from Shepheardes unto kinges:
So like the lively Larke that mounting singes.

Thy lovely Rosolinde seemes now forlorne,
　And all thy gentle flockes forgotten quight:
Thy chaunged hart now holdes thy pypes in scorne,
　Those prety pypes that did thy mates delight;
Those trusty mates, that loved thee so well;
Whom thou gav'st mirth, as they gave thee the bell.

Yet, as thou earst with thy sweete roundelayes
　Didst stirre to glee our laddes in homely bowers;
So moughtst thou now in these refyned layes
　Delight the daintie eares of higher powers:
And so mought they, in their deepe skanning skill,
Alow and grace our Collyns flowing quyll.

And faire befall that *Faery Queene* of thine,
　In whose faire eyes love linckt with vertue sittes;
Enfusing, by those bewties fyers devyne,
　Such high conceites into thy humble wittes,
As raised hath poore pastors oaten reedes
From rustick tunes, to chaunt heroique deedes.

So mought thy *Redcrosse knight* with happy hand
　Victorious be in that faire Ilands right,
Which thou dost vayle in Type of Faery land,
　Elizas blessed field, that *Albion* hight:
That shieldes her friendes, and warres her mightie foes,
Yet still with people, peace, and plentie flowes.

But (jolly shepheard) though with pleasing style
　Thou feast the humour of the Courtly trayne,
Let not conceipt thy setled sence beguile,
　Ne daunted be through envy or disdaine.
Subject thy dome to her Empyring spright,
From whence thy Muse, and all the world, takes light.
　　　　　　　　　　　　　　　　HOBYNOLL.

Fayre Thamis streame, that from Ludds stately towne
Runst paying tribute to the Ocean seas,
Let all thy Nymphes and Syrens of renowne
Be silent, whyle this Bryttane Orpheus playes.
Nere thy sweet bankes there lives that sacred crowne,
Whose hand strowes Palme and never-dying bayes:
Let all at once, with thy soft murmuring sowne,
Present her with this worthy Poets prayes;
For he hath taught hye drifts in shepeherdes weedes,
And deepe conceites now singes in *Faeries* deeds.   R. S.

Grave Muses, march in triumph and with prayses;
Our Goddesse here hath given you leave to land;
And biddes this rare dispenser of your graces
Bow downe his brow unto her sacred hand.
Deserte findes dew in that most princely doome,
In whose sweete brest are all the Muses bredde:
So did that great Augustus erst in Roome
With leaves of fame adorne his Poets hedde.
Faire be the guerdon of your *Faery Queene*,
Even of the fairest that the world hath seene!   H. B.

When stout Achilles heard of Helens rape,
And what revenge the States of Greece devisd,
Thinking by sleight the fatall warres to scape,
In womans weedes him selfe he then disguisde;
But this devise Ulysses soone did spy,
And brought him forth the chaunce of warre to try.

When Spencer saw the fame was spredd so large,
Through Faery land, of their renowned Queene,
Loth that his Muse should take so great a charge,
As in such haughty matter to be seene,
To seeme a shepeheard then he made his choice;
But Sydney heard him sing, and knew his voice.

And as Ulysses brought faire Thetis sonne
From his retyred life to menage armes,
So Spencer was by Sydney's speaches wonne
To blaze her fame, not fearing future harmes;
For well he knew, his Muse would soone by tyred
In her high praise, that all the world admired.

Yet as Achilles, in those warlike frayes,
Did win the palme from all the Grecian Peeres,
So Spenser now, to his immortall prayse,
Hath wonne the Laurell quite from all his feres.
What though his taske exceed a humaine witt,
He is excus'd, sith Sidney thought it fitt.   W. L.

To looke upon a worke of rare devise
The which a workman setteth out to view,
And not to yield it the deserved prise
That unto such a workmanship is dew,
   Doth either prove the judgement to be naught,
   Or els doth shew a mind with envy fraught.

To labour to command a peece of worke,
Which no man goes about to discommend,
Would raise a jealous doubt, that there did lurke
Some secret doubt whereto the prayse did tend;
   For when men know the goodnes of the wyne,
   'Tis needlesse for the hoast to have a sygne.

Thus then, to shew my judgement to be such
As can discerne of colours blacke and white,
As alls to free my minde from envies tuch,
That never gives to any man his right,
   I here pronounce this workmanship is such
   As that no pen can set it forth too much.

And thus I hang a garland at the dore;
Not for to shew the goodness of the ware;
But such hath beene the custome heretofore,
And customes very hardly broken are;
   And when your tast shall tell you this is trew,
   Then looke you give your hoast his utmost dew.   IGNOTO.

VERSES

To the Right honourable Sir Christopher Hatton, Lord high Chauncelor of England, &c.

THOSE prudent heads, that with theire counsels wise
  Whylom the pillours of th' earth did sustaine,
  And taught ambitious Rome to tyrannise
  And in the neck of all the world to rayne,
Oft from those grave affaires were wont abstaine,
  With the sweet Lady Muses for to play:
  So Ennius the elder Africane,
  So Maro oft did Cæsars cares allay.
So you, great Lord, that with your counsell sway
  The burdeine of this kingdom mightily,
  With like delightes sometimes may eke delay
  The rugged brow of carefull Policy,
And to these ydle rymes lend litle space,
Which for their titles sake may find more grace.

To the most honourable and excellent Lord the Earle of Essex. Great Maister of the Horse to her Highnesse, and knight of the Noble order of the Garter, &c.

Magnificke Lord, whose vertues excellent,
  Doe merit a most famous Poets witt
  To be thy living praises instrument,
  Yet doe not sdeigne to let thy name be writt
In this base Poeme, for thee far unfitt:
  Nought is thy worth disparaged thereby;
  But when my Muse, whose fethers, nothing flitt,
  Doe yet but flagg, and lowly learne to fly,
With bolder wing shall dare alofte to sty
  To the last praises of this Faery Queene;
  Then shall it make more famous memory
  Of thine Heroicke parts, such as they beene:
Till then, vouchsafe thy noble countenaunce
To these first labours needed furtheraunce.

9

To the Right Honourable the Earle of Oxenford, Lord high
Chamberlayne of England, &c.

Receive, most Noble Lord, in gentle gree,
    The unripe fruit of an unready wit;
    Which by thy countenaunce doth crave to bee
    Defended from foule Envies poisnous bit.
Which so to doe may thee right well befit,
    Sith th' antique glory of thine auncestry
    Under a shady vele is therein writ,
    And eke thine owne long living memory,
Succeeding them in true nobility:
    And also for the love which thou doest beare
    To th' Heliconian ymps, and they to thee;
    They unto thee, and thou to them, most deare:
Deare as thou art unto thy selfe, so love
That loves and honours thee, as doth behove.

To the right honourable the Earle of Northumberland

The sacred Muses have made alwaies clame
    To be the Nourses of nobility,
    And Registres of everlasting fame,
    To all that armes professe and chevalry.
Then, by like right the noble Progeny,
    Which them succeed in fame and worth, are tyde
    T' embrace the service of sweete Poetry,
    By whose endevours they are glorifide;
And eke from all, of whom it is envide,
    To patronise the authour of their praise,
    Which gives them life, that els would soone have dide,
    And crownes their ashes with immortall baies.
To thee, therefore, right noble Lord, I send
This present of my paines, it to defend.

To the Right Honourable the Earle of Ormond and Ossory

Receive, most noble Lord, a simple taste
    Of the wilde fruit which salvage soyl hath bred;
    Which, being through long wars left almost waste,
    With brutish barbarisme is overspredd:

And, in so faire a land as may be redd,
    Not one Parnassus nor one Helicone,
    Left for sweete Muses to be harboured,
    But where thy selfe hast thy brave mansione:
There, in deede, dwel faire Graces many one,
    And gentle Nymphes, delights of learned wits;
    And in thy person, without paragone,
All goodly bountie and true honour sits.
Such, therefore, as that wasted soyl doth yield,
Receive, dear Lord, in worth, the fruit of barren field.

*To the right honourable the Lord Ch. Howard, Lord high Admiral
    of England, knight of the noble order of the Garter, and one
    of her Majesties privie Counsel, &c.*

And ye, brave Lord, whose goodly personage
    And noble deeds, each other garnishing,
    Make you ensample to the present age
    Of th' old Heroes, whose famous ofspring
The antique Poets wont so much to sing;
    In this same Pageaunt have a worthy place,
    Sith those huge castles of Castilian King,
    That vainly threatned kingdomes to displace,
Like flying doves ye did before you chace;
    And that proud people, woxen insolent
    Through many victories, didst first deface:
    Thy praises everlasting monument
Is in this verse engraven semblably,
That it may live to all posterity.

*To the most renowmed and valiant Lord, the Lord Grey of Wilton,
    knight of the Noble order of the Garter, &c.*

Most Noble Lord, the pillor of my life,
    And Patrone of my Muses pupillage;
    Through whose large bountie, poured on me rife
    In the first season of my feeble age,
I now doe live, bound yours by vassalage;
    Sith nothing ever may redeeme, nor reave
    Out of your endlesse debt, so sure a gage,
    Vouchsafe in worth this small guift to receave,

Which in your noble hands for pledge I leave
  Of all the rest that I am tyde t' account:
  Rude rymes, the which a rustick Muse did weave
  In savadge soyle, far from Parnasso Mount,
And roughly wrought in an unlearned Loome:
The which vouchsafe, dear Lord, your favorable doome.

To the right noble and valorous knight, Sir Walter Raleigh, Lord Wardein of the Stanneryes, and lieftenaunt of Cornewaile

To thee, that art the sommers Nightingale,
  Thy soveraine Goddesses most deare delight,
  Why doe I send this rusticke Madrigale,
  That may thy tunefull eare unseason quite?
Thou onely fit this Argument to write,
  In whose high thoughts Pleasure hath built her bowre,
  And dainty love learnd sweetly to endite.
My rimes I know unsavory and sowre,
To tast the streames that, like a golden showre,
  Flow from thy fruitfull head, of thy love's praise;
  Fitter, perhaps, to thonder Martiall stowre,
When so thee list thy lofty Muse to raise:
Yet, till that thou thy Poeme wilt make knowne,
Let thy faire Cinthias praises be thus rudely showne.

To the right honourable the Lord Burleigh, Lord high Threasurer of England

To you, right noble Lord, whose carefull brest
  To menage of most grave affaires is bent;
  And on whose mightie shoulders most doth rest
  The burdein of this kingdomes governement,
As the wide compasse of the firmament
  On Atlas mighty shoulders is upstayd,
  Unfitly I these ydle rimes present,
  The labor of lost time, and wit unstayd:
Yet if their deeper sence be inly wayd,
  And the dim vele, with which from commune vew
  Their fairer parts are hid, aside be layd,
  Perhaps not vaine they may appeare to you.
Such as they be, vouchsafe them to receave,
And wipe their faults out of your censure grave.   E. S.

To the right honourable the Earle of Cumberland

Redoubted Lord, in whose corageous mind
  The flowre of chevalry, now bloosming faire,
  Doth promise fruite worthy the noble kind
  Which of their praises have left you the haire;
To you this humble present I prepare,
  For love of vertue and of Martiall praise;
  To which though nobly ye inclined are,
  As goodlie well ye shew'd in late assaies,
Yet brave ensample of long passed daies,
  In which trew honor yee may fashioned see,
  To like desire of honor may ye raise,
  And fill your mind with magnanimitee.
Receive it, Lord, therefore, as it was ment,
For honor of your name and high descent.   E. S.

To the right honourable the Lord of Hunsdon, high Chamberlaine to her Majesty

Renowmed Lord, that, for you worthinesse
  And noble deeds, have your deserved place
  High in the favour of that Emperesse,
  The worlds sole glory and her sexes grace:
Here eke of right have you a worthie place,
  Both for your nearnes to that Faerie Queene
  And for your owne high merit in like cace:
  Of which, apparaunt proofe was to be seene,
When that tumultuous rage and fearfull deene
  Of Northerne rebels ye did pacify,
  And their disloiall powre defaced clene,
  The record of enduring memory.
Live, Lord, for ever in this lasting verse,
That all posteritie thy honor may reherse.   E. S.

To the right honourable the Lord of Buckhurst, one of her Majesties privie Counsell

In vain I thinke, right honourable Lord,
  By this rude rime to memorize thy name,
  Whose learned Muse hath writ her owne record
  In golden verse, worthy immortal fame:

Thou much more fit (were leasure to the same)
  Thy gracious Soverains praises to compile,
  And her imperiall Majestie to frame
  In loftie numbers and heroicke stile.
But, sith thou maist not so, give leave a while
  To baser wit his power therein to spend,
  Whose grosse defaults thy daintie pen may file,
  And unadvised oversights amend.
  But evermore vouchsafe it to maintaine
  Against vile Zoilus backbitings vaine.

*To the right honourable Sir Fr. Walsingham, knight, principall
  Secretary to her Majesty, and one of her honourable privy
  Counsell*

That Mantuane Poetes incompared spirit,
  Whose girland now is set in highest place,
  Had not Mecænas, for his worthy merit,
  It first advaunst to great Augustus grace,
Might long perhaps have lien in silence bace,
  Ne bene so much admir'd of later age.
  This lowly Muse, that learns like steps to trace,
  Flies for like aide unto your Patronage,
That are the great Mecænas of this age,
  As wel to al that civil artes professe,
  As those that are inspir'd with Martial rage,
  And craves protection of her feeblenesse:
Which if ye yield, perhaps ye may her rayse
In bigger tunes to sound your living prayse.   E. S.

*To the right noble Lord and most valiaunt Captaine, Sir John
  Norris, knight, Lord president of Mounster*

Who ever gave more honourable prize
  To the sweet Muse then did the Martiall crew,
That their brave deeds she might immortalize
  In her shril tromp, and sound their praises dew?
Who then ought more to favour her than you,
  Moste noble Lord, the honor of this age,
  And Precedent of all that armes ensue?
Whose warlike prowesse and manly courage,

Tempred with reason and advizement sage,
　　Hath fild sad Belgicke with victorious spoile;
　　In Fraunce and Ireland left a famous gage;
　　And lately shakt the Lusitanian soile.
Sith, then, each where thou hast dispredd thy fame,
Love him that hath eternized your name.　　　　E. S.

*To the right honourable and most vertuous Lady the Countesse of
Penbroke*

Remembraunce of that most Heroicke spirit,
　　The hevens pride, the glory of our daies,
　　Which now triumpheth, through immortall merit
　　Of his brave vertues, crownd with lasting baies
Of hevenlie blis and everlasting praies;
　　Who first my Muse did lift out of the flore,
　　To sing his sweet delights in lowlie laies;
　　Bids me, most noble Lady, to adore
His goodly image, living evermore
　　In the divine resemblaunce of your face;
　　Which with your vertues ye embellish more,
　　And native beauty deck with hevenlie grace:
For his, and for your owne especial sake,
Vouchsafe from him this token in good worth to take.
　　　　　　　　　　　　　　　　　　　　　　E. S.

To the most vertuous and beautifull Lady, the Lady Carew

Ne may I, without blot of endlesse blame,
　　You, fairest Lady, leave out of this place;
　　But with remembraunce of your gracious name,
　　Wherewith that courtly garlond most ye grace
And deck the world, adorne these verses base.
　　Not that these few lines can in them comprise
　　Those glorious ornaments of hevenly grace,
　　Wherewith ye triumph over feeble eyes,
And in subdued harts do tyranyse;
　　For thereunto doth need a golden quill,
　　And silver leaves, them rightly to devise;
　　But to make humble present of good will:
Which, whenas timely meanes it purchase may,
In ampler wise it selfe will forth display.　　　E. S.

To all the gratious and beautifull Ladies in the Court.

The Chian Peincter, when he was requirde
  To pourtraict Venus in her perfect hew,
  To make his worke more absolute, desird
  Of all the fairest Maides to have the vew.
Much more me needs, to draw the semblant trew
  Of beauties Queene, the worlds sole wonderment,
  To sharpe my sence with sundry beauties vew,
  And steale from each some part of ornament.
If all the world to seeke I overwent,
  A fairer crew yet no where could I see
  Then that brave court doth to mine eie present,
  That the worlds pride seemes gathered there to bee.
Of each a part I stole by cunning thefte:
Forgive it me, faire Dames, sith lesse ye have not lefte.

                                        E. S.

THE FIRST BOOKE

CONTAYNING THE LEGEND OF THE KNIGHT OF THE RED
CROSSE, OR OF HOLINESSE

I. Lo! I, the man whose Muse whylome did maske,
  As time her taught, in lowly Shephards weeds,
  Am now enforst, a farre unfitter taske,
  For trumpets sterne to change mine Oaten reeds,
  And sing of Knights and Ladies gentle deeds;
  Whose praises having slept in silence long,
  Me, all too meane, the sacred Muse areeds
  To blazon broade emongst her learned throng:
  Fierce warres and faithfull loves shall moralize my song.

II. Helpe then, O holy virgin! chiefe of nyne,
  Thy weaker Novice to performe thy will;
  Lay forth out of thine everlasting scryne
  The antique rolles, which there lye hidden still,
  Of Faerie knights, and fayrest Tanaquill,
  Whom that most noble Briton Prince so long
  Sought through the world, and suffered so much ill,
  That I must rue his undeserved wrong:
  O, helpe thou my weake wit, and sharpen my dull tong!

III. And thou, most dreaded impe of highest Jove,
  Faire Venus sonne, that with thy cruell dart
  At that good knight so cunningly didst rove,
  That glorious fire it kindled in his hart;
  Lay now thy deadly Heben bowe apart,
  And with thy mother mylde come to mine ayde;
  Come, both; and with you bring triumphant Mart,
  In loves and gentle jollities arraid,
  After his murdrous spoyles and bloudie rage allayd.

17

iv. And with them eke, O Goddesse heavenly bright!
    Mirrour of grace and Majestie divine,
    Great Ladie of the greatest Isle, whose light
    Like Phœbus lampe throughout the world doth shine,
    Shed thy faire beames into my feeble eyne,
    And raise my thoughtes, too humble and too vile,
    To thinke of that true glorious type of thine,
    The argument of mine afflicted stile:
    The which to heare vouchsafe, O dearest dread, a-while!

CANTO I

The Patrone of true Holinesse
Foule Errour doth defeate:
Hypocrisie, him to entrappe,
Doth to his home entreate.

I. A gentle Knight was pricking on the plaine,
Ycladd in mightie armes and silver shielde,
Wherein old dints of deepe woundes did remaine,
The cruell markes of many' a bloody fielde;
Yet armes till that time did he never wield.
His angry steede did chide his foming bitt,
As much disdayning to the curbe to yield:
Full jolly knight he seemed, and faire did sitt,
As one for knightly giusts and fierce encounters fitt.

II. And on his brest a bloodie Crosse he bore,
The deare remembrance of his dying Lord,
For whose sweete sake that glorious badge he wore,
And dead, as living, ever him ador'd:
Upon his shield the like was also scor'd,
For soveraine hope which in his helpe he had.
Right faithfull true he was in deede and word,
But of his cheere did seeme too solemne sad;
Yet nothing did he dread, but ever was ydrad.

III. Upon a great adventure he was bond,
That greatest Gloriana to him gave,
(That greatest Glorious Queene of Faery lond)
To winne him worshippe, and her grace to have,
Which of all earthly thinges he most did crave:
And ever as he rode his hart did earne
To prove his puissance in battell brave
Upon his foe, and his new force to learne,
Upon his foe, a Dragon horrible and stearne.

IV. A lovely Ladie rode him faire beside,
Upon a lowly Asse more white then snow,
Yet she much whiter; but the same did hide

Under a vele, that wimpled was full low;
And over all a blacke stole shee did throw
As one that inly mournd, so was she sad,
And heavie sate upon her palfrey slow;
Seemed in heart some hidden care she had,
And by her, in a line, a milkewhite lambe she lad.

v. So pure and innocent, as that same lambe,
She was in life and every vertuous lore;
And by descent from Royall lynage came
Of ancient Kinges and Queenes, that had of yore
Their scepters stretcht from East to Westerne shore,
And all the world in their subjection held;
Till that infernall feend with foule uprore
Forwasted all their land, and them expeld;
Whom to avenge she had this Knight from far compeld.

vi. Behind her farre away a Dwarfe did lag,
That lasie seemd, in being ever last,
Or wearied with bearing of her bag
Of needments at his backe. Thus as they past,
The day with cloudes was suddeine overcast,
And angry Jove an hideous storme of raine
Did poure into his Lemans lap so fast,
That everie wight to shrowd it did constrain;
And this faire couple eke to shroud themselves were fain.

vii. Enforst to seeke some covert nigh at hand,
A shadie grove not farr away they spide,
That promist ayde the tempest to withstand;
Whose loftie trees, yclad with sommers pride,
Did spred so broad, that heavens light did hide,
Not perceable with power of any starr:
And all within were pathes and alleies wide,
With footing worne, and leading inward farr.
Faire harbour that them seems, so in they entered **ar.**

viii. And foorth they passe, with pleasure forward led,
Joying to heare the birdes sweete harmony,
Which, therein shrouded from the tempest dred,
Seemd in their song to scorne the cruell sky.
Much can they praise the trees so straight and hy,
The sayling Pine; the Cedar proud and tall;

The vine-propp Elme; the Poplar never dry;
The builder Oake, sole king of forrests all;
The Aspine good for staves; the Cypresse funerall;

IX. The Laurell, meed of mightie Conquerours
And Poets sage; the Firre that weepeth still:
The Willow, worne of forlorne Paramours;
The Eugh, obedient to the benders will;
The Birch for shaftes; the Sallow for the mill;
The Mirrhe sweete-bleeding in the bitter wound;
The warlike Beech; the Ash for nothing ill;
The fruitfull Olive; and the Platane round;
The carver Holme; the Maple seeldom inward sound.

X. Led with delight, they thus beguile the way,
Untill the blustring storme is overblowne;
When, weening to returne whence they did stray,
They cannot finde that path, which first was showne,
But wander too and fro in waies unknowne,
Furthest from end then, when they neerest weene,
That makes them doubt their wits be not their owne:
So many pathes, so many turnings seene,
That which of them to take in diverse doubt they been.

XI. At last resolving forward still to fare,
Till that some end they finde, or in or out,
That path they take that beaten seemd most bare,
And like to lead the labyrinth about;
Which when by tract they hunted had throughout,
At length it brought them to a hollowe cave
Amid the thickest woods. The Champion stout
Eftsoones dismounted from his courser brave,
And to the Dwarfe a while his needlesse spere he gave.

XII. " Be well aware," quoth then that Ladie milde,
" Least suddaine mischiefe ye too rash provoke:
The danger hid, the place unknowne and wilde,
Breedes dreadfull doubts. Oft fire is without smoke,
And perill without show: therefore your stroke,
Sir Knight, with-hold, till further tryall made."
" Ah Ladie," (sayd he) " shame were to revoke
The forward footing for an hidden shade:
Vertue gives her selfe light through darknesse for to wade."

cf Comus.

XIII. " Yea but " (quoth she) " the perill of this place
    I better wot then you: though nowe too late
    To wish you backe returne with foule disgrace,
    Yet wisedome warnes, whilest foot is in the gate,
    To stay the steppe, ere forced to retrate.
    This is the wandring wood, this *Errours* den,
    A monster vile, whom God and man does hate:
    Therefore I read beware." " Fly, fly ! " (quoth then
    The fearefull Dwarfe) " this is no place for living men."

XIV. But, full of fire and greedy hardiment,
    The youthfull Knight could not for aught be staide;
    But forth unto the darksom hole he went,
    And looked in: his glistring armor made
    A litle glooming light, much like a shade;
    By which he saw the ugly monster plaine,
    Halfe like a serpent horribly displaide,
    But th' other halfe did womans shape retaine,
    Most lothsom, filthie, foule, and full of vile disdaine.

XV. And, as she lay upon the durtie ground,
    Her huge long taile her den all overspred,
    Yet was in knots and many boughtes upwound,
    Pointed with mortall sting. Of her there bred
    A thousand yong ones, which she dayly fed,
    Sucking upon her poisnous dugs; each one
    Of sundrie shapes, yet all ill-favored:
    Soone as that uncouth light upon them shone,
    Into her mouth they crept, and suddain all were gone.

XVI. Their dam upstart out of her den effraide,
    And rushed forth, hurling her hideous taile
    About her cursed head; whose folds displaid
    Were stretcht now forth at length without entraile.
    She lookt about, and seeing one in mayle,
    Armed to point, sought backe to turne againe;
    For light she hated as the deadly bale,
    Ay wont in desert darknes to remaine,
    Where plain none might her see, nor she see any plaine.

XVII. Which when the valiant Elfe perceiv'd, he lept
    As Lyon fierce upon the flying pray,
    And with his trenchand blade her boldly kept

XXVI. That detestable sight him much amazde,
To see th' unkindly Impes, of heaven accurst,
Devoure their dam; on whom while so he gazd,
Having all satisfide their bloudy thirst,
Their bellies swolne he saw with fulnesse burst,
And bowels gushing forth: well worthy end
Of such as drunke her life the which them nurst!
Now needeth him no lenger labour spend,
His foes have slaine themselves, with whom he should
    contend.

XXVII. His Lady, seeing all that chaunst from farre,
Approcht in hast to greet his victorie;
And saide, " Faire knight, borne under happie starre,
Who see your vanquisht foes before you lye,
Well worthie be you of that Armory,
Wherein ye have great glory wonne this day,
And proov'd your strength on a strong enimie,
Your first adventure: many such I pray,
And henceforth ever wish that like succeed it may! "

XXVIII. Then mounted he upon his Steede againe,
And with the Lady backward sought to wend.
That path he kept which beaten was most plaine,
Ne ever would to any byway bend,
But still did follow one unto the end,
The which at last out of the wood them brought.
So forward on his way (with God to frend)
He passed forth, and new adventure sought:
Long way he traveiled before he heard of ought.

XXIX. At length they chaunst to meet upon the way
An aged Sire, in long blacke weedes yclad,
His feete all bare, his beard all hoarie gray,
And by his belt his booke he hanging had:
Sober he seemde, and very sagely sad,
And to the ground his eyes were lowly bent,
Simple in shew, and voide of malice bad;
And all the way he prayed as he went,
And often knockt his breast, as one that did repent.

XXX. He faire the knight saluted, louting low,
Who faire him quited, as that courteous was;

And after asked him, if he did know
Of straunge adventures, which abroad did pas.
"Ah! my dear sonne," (quoth he) "how should, alas!
Silly old man, that lives in hidden cell,
Bidding his beades all day for his trespas,
Tydings of warre and worldly trouble tell?
With holy father sits not with such thinges to mell.

XXXI. "But if of daunger, which hereby doth dwell,
And homebredd evil ye desire to heare,
Of a straunge man I can you tidings tell,
That wasteth all this countrie, farre and neare."
"Of such," (saide he,) "I chiefly doe inquere,
And shall thee well rewarde to shew the place,
In which that wicked wight his dayes doth weare;
For to all knighthood it is foule disgrace,
That such a cursed creature lives so long a space."

XXXII. "Far hence" (quoth he) "in wastfull wildernesse
His dwelling is, by which no living wight
May ever passe, but thorough great distresse."
"Now," (saide the Ladie,) "draweth toward night,
And well I wote, that of your later fight
Ye all forwearied be; for what so strong,
But, wanting rest, will also want of might?
The Sunne, that measures heaven all day long,
At night doth baite his steedes the Ocean waves emong.

XXXIII. "Then with the Sunne take, Sir, your timely rest,
And with new day new worke at once begin:
Untroubled night, they say, gives counsell best."
"Right well, Sir knight, ye have advised bin,"
Quoth then that aged man: "the way to win
Is wisely to advise; now day is spent:
Therefore with me ye may take up your In
For this same night." The knight was well content;
So with that godly father to his home they went.

XXXIV. A litle lowly Hermitage it was,
Downe in a dale, hard by a forests side,
Far from resort of people that did pas
In traveill to and froe: a litle wyde
There was an holy chappell edifyde,

And, lifting up his lompish head, with blame
Halfe angrie asked him, for what he came.
"Hether" (quoth he,) "me Archimago sent,
He that the stubborne Sprites can wisely tame,
He bids thee to him send for his intent
A fit false dreame, that can delude the sleepers sent.

XLIV. The God obayde; and, calling forth straight way
A diverse Dreame out of his prison darke,
Delivered it to him, and downe did lay
His heavie head, devoide of carefull carke;
Whose sences all were straight benumbd and starke.
He, backe returning by the Yvorie dore,
Remounted up as light as chearefull Larke;
And on his litle winges the dreame he bore
In hast unto his Lord, where he him left afore.

XLV. Who all this while, with charmes and hidden artes,
Had made a Lady of that other Spright,
And fram'd of liquid ayre her tender partes,
So lively and so like in all mens sight,
That weaker sence it could have ravisht quight:
The maker selfe, for all his wondrous witt,
Was nigh beguiled with so goodly sight.
Her all in white he clad, and over it
Cast a black stole, most like to seeme for Una fit.

XLVI. Now, when that ydle dreame was to him brought,
Unto that Elfin knight he bad him fly,
Where he slept soundly void of evil thought,
And with false shewes abuse his fantasy,
In sort as he him schooled privily:
And that new creature, borne without her dew,
Full of the makers guyle, with usage sly
He taught to imitate that Lady trew,
Whose semblance she did carrie under feigned hew

XLVII. Thus, well instructed, to their worke they haste;
And, comming where the knight in slomber lay,
The one upon his hardie head him plaste,
And made him dreame of loves and lustfull play,
That night his manly hart did melt away,
Bathed in wanton blis and wicked joy.

Then seemed him his Lady by him lay,
And to him playnd, how that false winged boy
Her chaste hart had subdewd to learne Dame Pleasures toy.

XLVIII. And she her selfe, of beautie soveraigne Queene,
Fayre Venus, seemde unto his bed to bring
Her, whom he, waking, evermore did weene
To bee the chastest flowre that aye did spring
On earthly braunch, the daughter of a king,
Now a loose Leman to vile service bound:
And eke the Graces seemed all to sing,
Hymen Iö Hymen! dauncing all around;
Whylst freshest Flora her with Yvie girlond crownd.

XLIX. In this great passion of unwonted lust,
Or wonted feare of doing ought amis,
He starteth up, as seeming to mistrust
Some secret ill, or hidden foe of his.
Lo! there before his face his Ladie is,
Under blacke stole hyding her bayted hooke;
And as halfe blushing offred him to kis,
With gentle blandishment and lovely looke,
Most like that virgin true which for her knight him took.

L. All cleane dismayd to see so uncouth sight,
And half enraged at her shameless guise,
He thought have slaine her in his fierce despight;
But hastie heat tempring with sufferance wise,
He stayde his hand; and gan himselfe advise
To prove his sense, and tempt her faigned truth.
Wringing her hands, in wemens pitteous wise,
Tho can she weepe, to stirre up gentle ruth
Both for her noble blood, and for her tender youth.

LI. And sayd, " Ah Sir, my liege Lord, and my love,
Shall I accuse the hidden cruell fate,
And mightie causes wrought in heaven above,
Or the blind God that doth me thus amate,
For hoped love to winne me certaine hate?
Yet thus perforce he bids me do, or die.
Die is my dew; yet rew my wretched state,
You, whom my hard avenging destinie
Hath made judge of my life or death indifferently.

LII. " Your owne deare sake forst me at first to leave
My fathers kingdom "—There she stopt with teares;
Her swollen hart her speech seemd to bereave,
And then againe begonne; " My weaker yeares,
Captiv'd to fortune and frayle worldly feares,
Fly to your fayth for succour and sure ayde:
Let me not die in languor and long teares."
" Why, Dame," (quoth he,) " what hath ye thus dismayd?
What frayes ye, that were wont to comfort me affrayd? "

LIII. " Love of your selfe," she saide, " and deare constraint,
Lets me not sleepe, but waste the wearie night
In secret anguish and unpittied plaint,
Whiles you in carelesse sleepe are drowned quight."
Her doubtfull words made that redoubted knight
Suspect her truth: yet since no' untruth he knew,
Her fawning love with foule disdainefull spight
He would not shend; but said, " Deare dame, I rew,
That for my sake unknowne such griefe unto you grew.

LIV. " Assure your selfe, it fell not all to ground;
For all so deare as life is to my hart,
I deeme your love, and hold me to you bound:
Ne let vaine feares procure your needlesse smart,
Where cause is none; but to your rest depart."
Not all content, yet seemd she to appease
Her mournefull plaintes, beguiled of her art,
And fed with words that could not chose but please:
So, slyding softly forth, she turnd as to her ease.

LV. Long after lay he musing at her mood,
Much griev'd to thinke that gentle Dame so light,
For whose defence he was to shed his blood.
At last, dull wearines of former fight
Having yrockt asleepe his irkesome spright,
That troublous dreame gan freshly tosse his braine
With bowres, and beds, and ladies deare delight:
But, when he saw his labour all was vaine,
With that misformed spright he backe returnd againe.

CANTO II

The guilefull great Enchaunter parts
The Redcrosse Knight from Truth:
Into whose stead faire falshood steps,
And workes him woefull ruth.

I. By this the Northerne wagoner had set
His sevenfold teme behind the stedfast starre
That was in Ocean waves yet never wet,
But firme is fixt, and sendeth light from farre
To al that in the wide deepe wandring arre;
And chearefull Chaunticlere with his note shrill
Had warned once, that Phœbus fiery carre
In hast was climbing up the Easterne hill,
Full envious that night so long his roome did fill:

II. When those accursed messengers of hell,
That feigning dreame, and that faire-forged Spright,
Came to their wicked maister, and gan tel
Their bootelesse paines, and ill succeeding night:
Who, all in rage to see his skilfull might
Deluded so, gan threaten hellish paine,
And sad Proserpines wrath, them to affright:
But, when he saw his threatning was but vaine,
He cast about, and searcht his baleful bokes againe.

III. Eftsoones he tooke that miscreated faire,
And that false other Spright, on whom he spred
A seeming body of the subtile aire,
Like a young Squire, in loves and lusty-hed
His wanton daies that ever loosely led,
Without regard of armes and dreaded fight:
Those twoo he tooke, and in a secrete bed,
Covered with darkenes and misdeeming night,
Them both together laid to joy in vaine delight.

IV. Forthwith he runnes with feigned faithfull hast
Unto his guest, who, after troublous sights
And dreames, gan now to take more sound repast;

Whom suddenly he wakes with fearful frights,
As one aghast with feends or damned sprights,
And to him cals; "Rise, rise! unhappy Swaine,
That here wex old in sleepe, whiles wicked wights
Have knit themselves in Venus shameful chaine:
Come, see where your false Lady doth her honor staine."

v. All in amaze he suddenly up start
With sword in hand, and with the old man went;
Who soone him brought into a secret part,
Where that false couple were full closely ment
In wanton lust and leud embracement:
Which when he saw, he burnt with gealous fire;
The eie of reason was with rage yblent,
And would have slaine them in his furious ire,
But hardly was restreined of that aged sire.

vi. Retourning to his bed in torment great,
And bitter anguish of his guilty sight,
He could not rest; but did his stout heart eat,
And wast his inward gall with deepe despight,
Yrkesome of life, and too long lingring night.
At last faire Hesperus in highest skie
Had spent his lampe, and brought forth dawning light;
Then up he rose, and clad him hastily:
The dwarfe him brought his steed; so both away do fly.

vii. Now when the rosy fingred Morning faire,
Weary of aged Tithones saffron bed,
Had spred her purple robe through deawy aire,
And the high hils Titan discovered,
The royall virgin shooke off drousy-hed;
And, rising forth out of her baser bowre,
Lookt for her knight, who far away was fled,
And for her dwarfe, that wont to wait each howre:
Then gan she wail and weepe to see that woeful stowre.

viii. And after him she rode, with so much speede
As her slowe beast could make; but all in vaine,
For him so far had borne his light-foot steede,
Pricked with wrath and fiery fierce disdaine,
That him to follow was but fruitlesse paine:
Yet she her weary limbes would never rest;

I   B

But every hil and dale, each wood and plaine,
Did search, sore grieved in her gentle brest,
He so ungently left her, whome she loved best.

IX. But subtill Archimago, when his guests
He saw divided into double parts,
And Una wandring in woods and forrests,
Th' end of his drift, he praisd his divelish arts,
That had such might over true meaning harts:
Yet rests not so, but other meanes doth make,
How he may worke unto her further smarts;
For her he hated as the hissing snake,
And in her many troubles did most pleasure take.

X. He then devisde himselfe how to disguise;
For by his mighty science he could take
As many formes and shapes in seeming wise,
As ever Proteus to himselfe could make:
Sometime a fowle, sometime a fish in lake,
Now like a foxe, now like a dragon fell;
That of himselfe he ofte for feare would quake,
And oft would flie away.   O! who can tell
The hidden powre of herbes, and might of Magick spel?

XI. But now seemde best the person to put on
Of that good knight, his late beguiled guest:
In mighty armes he was yclad anon,
And silver shield; upon his coward brest
A bloody crosse, and on his craven crest
A bounch of heares discolourd diversly.
Full jolly knight he seemde, and wel addrest;
And when he sate upon his courser free,
Saint George himselfe ye would have deemed him to be.

XII. But he, the knight whose semblaunt he did beare,
The true Saint George, was wandred far away,
Still flying from his thoughts and gealous feare:
Will was his guide, and griefe led him astray.
At last him chaunst to meete upon the way
A faithlesse Sarazin, all armde to point,
In whose great shield was writ with letters gay
Sans foy; full large of limbe and every joint
He was, and cared not for God or man a point.

XIII. Hee had a faire companion of his way,
    A goodly Lady clad in scarlot red,
    Purfled with gold and pearle of rich assay;
    And like a Persian mitre on her hed
    Shee wore, with crowns and owches garnished,
    The which her lavish lovers to her gave.
    Her wanton palfrey all was overspred
    With tinsell trappings, woven like a wave,
    Whose bridle rung with golden bels and bosses brave.

XIV. With faire disport, and courting dalliaunce,
    She intertainde her lover all the way;
    But, when she saw the knight his speare advaunce,
    She soone left off her mirth and wanton play,
    And bad her knight addresse him to the fray,
    His foe was nigh at hand.   He, prickte with pride
    And hope to winne his Ladies hearte that day,
    Forth spurred fast: adowne his coursers side
    The red bloud trickling staind the way, as he did ride.

XV. The knight of the Redcrosse, when him he spide
    Spurring so hote with rage dispiteous,
    Gan fairely couch his speare, and towards ride.
    Soone meete they both, both fell and furious,
    That, daunted with theyr forces hideous,
    Their steeds doe stagger, and amazed stand;
    And eke themselves, too rudely rigorous,
    Astonied with the stroke of their owne hand,
    Doe backe rebutte, and ech to other yealdeth land.

XVI. As when two rams, stird with ambitious pride,
    Fight for the rule of the rich fleeced flocke,
    Their horned fronts so fierce on either side
    Doe meete, that, with the terror of the shocke,
    Astonied, both stand sencelesse as a blocke,
    Forgetfull of the hanging victory:
    So stood these twaine, unmoved as a rocke,
    Both staring fierce, and holding idely
    The broken reliques of their former cruelty.

XVII. The Sarazin, sore daunted with the buffe,
    Snatched his sword, and fiercely to him flies;
    Who well it wards, and quyteth cuff with cuff:

Each others equall puissaunce envies,
And through their iron sides with cruell spies
Does seeke to perce; repining courage yields
No foote to foe: the flashing fier flies,
As from a forge, out of their burning shields;
And streams of purple bloud new die the verdant fields.

XVIII. " Curse on that Cross," (quoth then the Sarazin,)
" That keepes thy body from the bitter fitt!
Dead long ygoe, I wote, thou haddest bin,
Had not that charme from thee forwarned itt:
But yet I warne thee now assured sitt,
And hide thy head." Therewith upon his crest
With rigor so outrageous he smitt,
That a large share it hewd out of the rest,
And glauncing downe his shield from blame him fairly blest.

XIX. Who, thereat wondrous wroth, the sleeping spark
Of native vertue gan eftsoones revive;
And at his haughty helmet making mark,
So hugely stroke, that it the steele did rive,
And cleft his head. He, tumbling downe alive,
With bloudy mouth his mother earth did kis,
Greeting his grave: his grudging ghost did strive
With the fraile flesh; at last it flitted is,
Whither the soules doe fly of men that live amis.

XX. The Lady, when she saw her champion fall
Like the old ruines of a broken towre,
Staid not to waile his woefull funerall,
But from him fled away with all her powre;
Who after her as hastily gan scowre,
Bidding the dwarfe with him to bring away
The Sarazins shield, signe of the conqueroure.
Her soone he overtooke, and bad to stay;
For present cause was none of dread her to dismay.

XXI. Shee turning backe, with ruefull countenaunce,
Cride, " Mercy, mercy, Sir, vouchsafe to show
On silly Dame, subject to hard mischaunce,
And to your mighty wil!" Her humblesse low,
In so ritch weedes, and seeming glorious show,
Did much emmove his stout heroicke heart;

And said, " Deare dame, your sudden overthrow
Much rueth me; but now put feare apart,
And tel both who ye be, and who that tooke your part."

XXII. Melting in teares, then gan shee thus lament,
" The wretched woman, whom unhappy howre
Hath now made thrall to your commandement,
Before that angry heavens list to lowre,
And fortune false betraide me to thy powre,
Was (O! what now availeth that I was?)
Borne the sole daughter of an Emperour,
He that the wide West under his rule has,
And high hath set his throne where Tiberis doth pas.

XXIII. " He, in the first flowre of my freshest age,
Betrothed me unto the onley haire
Of a most mighty king, most rich and sage:
Was never Prince so faithfull and so faire,
Was never Prince so meeke and debonaire;
But ere my hoped day of spousall shone,
My dearest Lord fell from high honors staire
Into the hands of hys accursed fone,
And cruelly was slaine; that shall I ever mone.

XXIV. " His blessed body, spoild of lively breath,
Was afterward, I know not how, convaid,
And fro me hid: of whose most innocent death
When tidings came to mee, unhappy maid,
O, how great sorrow my sad soule assaid!
Then forth I went his woefull corse to find,
And many yeares throughout the world I straid,
A virgin widow, whose deepe wounded mind
With love long time did languish, as the striken hind.

XXV. " At last it chaunced this proud Sarazin
To meete me wandring; who perforce me led
With him away, but yet could never win
The Fort, that Ladies hold in soveraigne dread.
There lies he now with foule dishonour dead,
Who, whiles he livde, was called proud Sans foy,
The eldest of three brethren; all three bred
Of one bad sire, whose youngest is Sans joy;
And twixt them both was born the bloudy bold Sans loy.

XXVI. " In this sad plight, friendlesse, unfortunate,
    Now miserable I, Fidessa, dwell,
    Craving of you, in pitty of my state,
    To doe none ill, if please ye not doe well."
    He in great passion al this while did dwell,
    More busying his quicke eies her face to view,
    Then his dull eares to heare what shee did tell;
    And said, " faire lady, hart of flint would rew
    The undeserved woes and sorrowes, which ye shew.

XXVII. " Henceforth in safe assuraunce may ye rest,
    Having both found a new friend you to aid,
    And lost an old foe that did you molest;
    Better new friend then an old foe is said."
    With chaunge of chear the seeming simple maid
    Let fal her eien, as shamefast, to the earth,
    And yeelding soft, in that she nought gainsaid,
    So forth they rode, he feining seemely merth,
    And shee coy lookes: so dainty, they say, maketh derth.

XXVIII. Long time they thus together traveiled;
    Til, weary of their way, they came at last
    Where grew two goodly trees, that faire did spred
    Their armes abroad, with gray mosse overcast;
    And their greene leaves, trembling with every blast,
    Made a calme shadowe far in compasse round:
    The fearefull shepheard, often there aghast,
    Under them never sat, ne wont there sound
    His mery oaten pipe, but shund th' unlucky ground.

XXIX. But this good knight, soone as he them can spie,
    For the coole shade him thither hastly got:
    For golden Phœbus, now ymounted hie,
    From fiery wheeles of his faire chariot
    Hurled his beame so scorching cruell hot,
    That living creature mote it not abide;
    And his new Lady it endured not.
    There they alight, in hope themselves to hide
    From the fierce heat, and rest their weary limbs a tide.

XXX. Faire seemely pleasaunce each to other makes,
    With goodly purposes, there as they sit;
    And in his falsed fancy he her takes

To be the fairest wight that lived yit;
Which to expresse he bends his gentle wit:
And, thinking of those braunches greene to frame
A girlond for her dainty forehead fit,
He pluckt a bough; out of whose rifte there came
Smal drops of gory bloud, that trickled down the same.

XXXI. Therewith a piteous yelling voice was heard,
Crying, " O! spare with guilty hands to teare
My tender sides in this rough rynd embard;
But fly, ah! fly far hence away, for feare
Least to you hap that happened to me heare,
And to this wretched Lady, my deare love;
O, too deare love, love bought with death too deare!"
Astond he stood, and up his heare did hove;
And with that suddein horror could no member move.

XXXII. At last whenas the dreadfull passion
Was overpast, and manhood well awake,
Yet musing at the straunge occasion,
And doubting much his sence, he thus bespake:
" What voice of damned Ghost from Limbo lake,
Or guilefull spright wandring in empty aire,
Both which fraile men doe oftentimes mistake,
Sends to my doubtful eares these speaches rare,
And ruefull plaints, me bidding guiltlesse blood to
spare?"

XXXIII. Then, groning deep; " Nor damned Ghost," (quoth he,)
" Nor guileful sprite to thee these words doth speake;
But once a man, Fradubio, now a tree;
Wretched man, wretched tree! whose nature weake
A cruell witch, her cursed will to wreake,
Hath thus transformd, and plast in open plaines,
Where Boreas doth blow full bitter bleake,
And scorching Sunne does dry my secret vaines;
For though a tree I seme, yet cold and heat me paines."

XXXIV. " Say on, Fradubio, then, or man or tree."
Quoth then the Knight; " by whose mischievous arts
Art thou misshaped thus, as now I see?
He oft finds med'cine who his griefe imparts,
But double griefs afflict concealing harts,

As raging flames who striveth to suppresse."
" The author then," (said he) " of all my smarts,
Is one Duessa, a false sorceresse,
That many errant knights hath broght to wretchednesse.

xxxv. " In prime of youthly yeares, when corage hott
The fire of love, and joy of chevalree,
First kindled in my brest, it was my lott
To love this gentle Lady, whome ye see
Now not a Lady, but a seeming tree;
With whome, as once I rode accompanyde,
Me chaunced of a knight encountred bee,
That had a like faire Lady by his syde;
Lyke a faire Lady, but did fowle Duessa hyde.

xxxvi. " Whose forged beauty he did take in hand
All other Dames to have exceeded farre:
I in defence of mine did likewise stand,
Mine, that did then shine as the Morning starre.
So both to batteill fierce arraunged arre,
In which his harder fortune was to fall
Under my speare: such is the dye of warre.
His Lady, left as a prise martiall,
Did yield her comely person to be at my call.

xxxvii. " So doubly lov'd of ladies, unlike faire,
Th' one seeming such, the other such indeede,
One day in doubt I cast for to compare
Whether in beauties glorie did exceede:
A Rosy girlond was the victors meede.
Both seemde to win, and both seemed won to bee,
So hard the discord was to be agreede.
Frælissa was as faire as faire mote bee,
And ever false Duessa seemde as faire as shee.

xxxviii. " The wicked witch, now seeing all this while
The doubtfull ballaunce equally to sway,
What not by right she cast to win by guile;
And by her hellish science raisd streight way
A foggy mist that overcast the day,
And a dull blast, that breathing on her face
Dimmed her former beauties shining ray,
And with foule ugly forme did her disgrace:
Then was she fayre alone, when none was faire in place.

XXXIX. " Then cride she out, ' Fye, fye! deformed wight,
        Whose borrowed beautie now appeareth plaine
        To have before bewitched all mens sight:
        O! leave her soone, or let her soone be slaine.'
        Her loathly visage viewing with disdaine,
        Eftsoones I thought her such as she me told,
        And would have kild her; but with faigned paine
        The false witch did my wrathful hand withhold:
        So left her, where she now is turnd to treen mould.

XL.   " Thensforth I tooke Duessa for my Dame,
        And in the witch unweeting joyd long time,
        Ne ever wist but that she was the same;
        Till on a day (that day is everie Prime,
        When Witches wont do penance for their crime,)
        I chaunst to see her in her proper hew,
        Bathing her selfe in origane and thyme:
        A filthy foule old'woman I did vew,
        That ever to have toucht her I did deadly rew.

XLI. " Her neather partes misshapen, monstruous,
        Were hidd in water, that I could not see;
        But they did seeme more foule and hideous,
        Then womans shape man would beleeve to bee.
        Thensforth from her most beastly companie
        I gan refraine, in minde to slipp away,
        Soone as appeard safe opportunitie:
        For danger great, if not assured decay,
        I saw before mine eyes, if I were knowne to stray.

XLII. " The divelish hag by chaunges of my cheare
        Perceiv'd my thought; and, drownd in sleepie night,
        With wicked herbes and oyntments did besmeare
        My body all, through charmes and magicke might,
        That all my senses were bereaved quight:
        Then brought she me into this desert waste,
        And by my wretched lovers side me pight;
        Where now, enclosed in wooden wals full faste,
        Banisht from living wights, our wearie daies we waste."

XLIII. " But how long time," said then the Elfin knight,
        " Are you in this misformed hous to dwell?"
        " We may not chaunge," (quoth he,) " this evill plight,

Till we be bathed in a living well:
That is the terme prescribed by the spell."
" O! how," sayd he, " mote I that well out find,
That may restore you to your wonted well? "
" Time and suffised fates to former kynd
Shall us restore; none else from hence may us unbynd."

xliv. The false Duessa, now Fidessa hight,
Heard how in vaine Fradubio did lament,
And knew well all was true.   But the good knight,
Full of sad feare and ghastly dreriment,
When all this speech the living tree had spent,
The bleeding bough did thrust into the ground,
That from the blood he might be innocent,
And with fresh clay did close the wooden wound:
Then, turning to his Lady, dead with feare her fownd.

xlv. Her seeming dead he fownd with feigned feare,
As all unweeting of that well she knew;
And paynd himselfe with busie care to reare
Her out of carelesse swowne.   Her eyelids blew,
And dimmed sight, with pale and deadly hew,
At last she up gan lift: with trembling cheare
Her up he tooke, (too simple and too trew)
And oft her kist.   At length, all passed feare,
He set her on her steede, and forward forth did beare.

① Fight with Sarazins. Duessa his lady.
② The 2 trees.   Fradubio.

CANTO III

Forsaken Truth long seekes her love,
    And makes the Lyon mylde;
Marres blind Devotions mart, and fals
    In hand of leachour vylde.

I. NOUGHT is there under heav'ns wide hollownesse,
    That moves more deare compassion of mind,
    Then beautie brought t'unworthie wretchednesse
    Through envies snares, or fortunes freakes unkind.
    I, whether lately through her brightnes blynd,
    Or through alleageance, and fast fealty,
    Which I do owe unto all womankynd,
    Feele my hart perst with so great agony,
    When such I see, that all for pitty I could dy.

II. And now it is empassioned so deepe,
    For fairest Unaes sake, of whom I sing,
    That my frayle eies these lines with teares do steepe,
    To thinke how she through guyleful handeling,
    Though true as touch, though daughter of a king,
    Though faire as ever living wight was fayre,
    Though nor in word nor deede ill meriting,
    Is from her knight divorced in despayre,
    And her dew loves deryv'd to that vile witches shayre.

III. Yet she, most faithfull Ladie, all this while
    Forsaken, wofull, solitarie mayd,
    Far from all peoples preace, as in exile,
    In wildernesse and wastfull deserts strayd,
    To seeke her knight; who, subtily betrayd
    Through that late vision which th'Enchaunter wrought,
    Had her abandon.   She, of nought affrayd,
    Through woods and wastnes wide him daily sought;
    Yet wished tydinges none of him unto her brought.

IV. One day, nigh wearie of the yrkesome way,
    From her unhastie beast she did alight;
    And on the grasse her dainty limbs did lay

In secrete shadow, far from all mens sight:
From her fayre head her fillet she undight,
And layd her stole aside.   Her angels face,
As the great eye of heaven, shyned bright,
And made a sunshine in the shady place;
Did ever mortall eye behold such heavenly grace.

v. It fortuned, out of the thickest wood
A ramping Lyon rushed suddeinly,
Hunting full greedy after salvage blood.
Soone as the royall virgin he did spy,
With gaping mouth at her ran greedily,
To have attonce devourd her tender corse;
But to the pray when as he drew more ny,
His bloody rage aswaged with remorse,
And, with the sight amazd, forgat his furious forse.

vi. In stead thereof he kist her wearie feet,
And lickt her lilly hands with fawning tong,
As he her wronged innocence did weet.
O, how can beautie maister the most strong,
And simple truth subdue avenging wrong!
Whose yielded pryde and proud submission,
Still dreading death, when she had marked long,
Her hart gan melt in great compassion;
And drizling teares did shed for pure affection.

vii. " The Lyon, Lord of everie beast in field,"
Quoth she, " his princely puissance doth abate,
And mightie proud to humble weake does yield,
Forgetfull of the hungry rage, which late
Him prickt, in pittie of my sad estate:
But he, my Lyon, and my noble Lord,
How does he find in cruell hart to hate
Her, that him lov'd, and ever most adord
As the God of my life? why hath he me abhord? "

viii. Redounding teares did choke th' end of her plaint,
Which softly ecchoed from the neighbour wood;
And, sad to see her sorrowfull constraint,
The kingly beast upon her gazing stood:
With pittie calmd downe fell his angry mood.
At last, in close hart shutting up her payne,

Arose the virgin, borne of heavenly brood,
And to her snowy Palfrey got agayne,
To seeke her strayed Champion if she might attayne.

IX. The Lyon would not leave her desolate,
But with her went along, as a strong gard
Of her chast person, and a faythfull mate
Of her sad troubles and misfortunes hard:
Still, when she slept, he kept both watch and ward;
And, when she wakt, he wayted diligent,
With humble service to her will prepard:
From her fayre eyes he tooke commandement,
And ever by her lookes conceived her intent.

X. Long she thus traveiled through deserts wyde,
By which she thought her wandring knight shold pas,
Yet never shew of living wight espyde;
Till that at length she found the troden gras,
In which the tract of peoples footing was,
Under the steepe foot of a mountaine hore:
The same she followes, till at last she has
A damzel spyde, slow footing her before,
That on her shoulders sad a pot of water bore.

XI. To whom approching she to her gan call,
To weet if dwelling place were nigh at hand;
But the rude wench her answerd nought at all:
She could not heare, nor speake, nor understand;
Till, seeing by her side the Lyon stand,
With suddeine feare her pitcher downe she threw,
And fled away: for never in that land
Face of fayre Lady she before did vew,
And that dredd Lyons looke her cast in deadly hew.

XII. Full fast she fled, ne ever lookt behynd,
As if her life upon the wager lay;
And home she came, whereas her mother blynd
Sate in eternall night: nought could she say;
But, suddeine catching hold, did her dismay
With quaking hands, and other signes of feare:
Who, full of ghastly fright and cold affray,
Gan shut the dore.   By this arrived there
Dame Una, weary Dame, and entrance did requere:

XIII. Which when none yielded, her unruly Page
With his rude clawes the wicket open rent,
And let her in; where, of his cruell rage
Nigh dead with feare, and faint astonishment,
Shee found them both in darksome corner pent;
Where that old woman day and night did pray
Upon her beads, devoutly penitent:
Nine hundred *Pater nosters* every day,
And thrise nine hundred *Aves* she was wont to say.

XIV. And to augment her painefull penaunce more,
Thrise every weeke in ashes shee did sitt,
And next her wrinkled skin rough sackecloth wore,
And thrise three times did fast from any bitt:
But now, for feare her beads she did forgett:
Whose needlesse dread for to remove away,
Faire Una framed words and count'naunce fitt;
Which hardly doen, at length she gan them pray,
That in their cotage small that night she rest her may.

XV. The day is spent; and commeth drowsie night,
When every creature shrowded is in sleepe.
Sad Una downe her laies in weary plight,
And at her feete the Lyon watch doth keepe:
In stead of rest she does lament and weepe,
For the late losse of her deare loved knight,
And sighes, and grones, and evermore does steepe
Her tender brest in bitter teares all night;
All night she thinks too long, and often lookes for light.

XVI. Now when Aldeboran was mounted hye
Above the shinie Cassiopeias chaire,
And all in deadly sleepe did drowned lye
One knocked at the dore, and in would fare:
He knocked fast, and often curst, and sware,
That ready entraunce was not at his call;
For on his backe a heavy load he bare
Of nightly stelths, and pillage severall,
Which he had got abroad by purchas criminall.

XVII. He was, to weete, a stout and sturdy thiefe,
Wont to robbe churches of their ornaments,
And poore mens boxes of their due reliefe,

Which given was to them for good intents:
The holy Saints of their rich vestiments
He did disrobe, when all men carelesse slept,
And spoild the Priests of their habiliments;
Whiles none the holy things in safety kept,
Then he by conning sleights in at the window crept.

xviii. And all that he by right or wrong could find,
Unto this house he brought, and did bestow
Upon the daughter of this woman blind,
Abessa, daughter of Corceca slow,
With whom he whoredome usd, that few did know,
And fed her fatt with feast of offerings,
And plenty, which in all the land did grow:
Ne spared he to give her gold and rings;
And now he to her brought part of his stolen things.

xix. Thus, long the dore with rage and threats he bett,
Yet of those fearfull women none durst rize,
The Lyon frayed them, him in to lett.
He would no lenger stay him to advize,
But open breakes the dore in furious wize,
And entring is, when that disdainfull beast,
Encountring fierce, him suddein doth surprize;
And, seizing cruell clawes on trembling brest,
Under his Lordly foot him proudly hath supprest.

xx. Him booteth not resist, nor succour call,
His bleeding hart is in the vengers hand;
Who streight him rent in thousand peeces small,
And quite dismembred hath: the thirsty land
Dronke up his life; his corse left on the strand.
His fearefull freends weare out the wofull night,
Ne dare to weepe, nor seeme to understand
The heavie hap which on them is alight;
Affraid least to themselves the like mishappen might.

xxi. Now when broad day the world discovered has,
Up Una rose, up rose the lyon eke;
And on their former journey forward pas,
In waies unknowne, her wandring knight to seeke,
With paines far passing that long wandring Greeke,
That for his love refused deitye.

Such were the labours of this Lady meeke,
Still seeking him, that from her still did flye;
Then furthest from her hope, when most she weened nye.

XXII. Soone as she parted thence, the fearfull twayne,
That blind old woman, and her daughter dear,
Came forth; and, finding Kirkrapine there slayne,
For anguish great they gan to rend their heare,
And beat their brests, and naked flesh to teare:
And when they both had wept and wayld their fill,
Then forth they ran, like two amazed deare,
Halfe mad through malice and revenging will,
To follow her that was the causer of their ill.

XXIII. Whome overtaking, they gan loudly bray,
With hollow houling, and lamenting cry;
Shamefully at her rayling all the way,
And her accusing of dishonesty,
That was the flowre of faith and chastity:
And still, amidst her rayling, she did pray
That plagues, and mischiefes, and long misery,
Might fall on her, and follow all the way,
And that in endlesse error she might ever stray.

XXIV. But, when she saw her prayers nought prevaile,
Shee backe retourned with some labour lost;
And in the way, as shee did weepe and waile,
A knight her mett in mighty armes embost,
Yet knight was not for all his bragging bost;
But subtill Archimag, that Una sought
By traynes into new troubles to have toste:
Of that old woman tidings he besought,
If that of such a Lady shee could tellen ought.

XXV. Therewith she gan her passion to renew,
And cry, and curse, and raile, and rend her heare,
Saying, that harlott she too lately knew,
That causd her shed so many a bitter teare;
And so forth told the story of her feare.
Much seemed he to mone her haplesse chaunce,
And after for that Lady did inquere;
Which being taught, he forward gan advaunce
His fair enchaunted steed, and eke his charmed launce.

XXVI. Ere long he came where Una traveild slow,
    And that wilde champion wayting her besyde;
    Whome seeing such, for dread hee durst not show
    Him selfe too nigh at hand, but turned wyde
    Unto an hil; from whence when she him spyde,
    By his like seeming shield her knight by name
    She weend it was, and towards him gan ride:
    Approaching nigh she wist it was the same;
    And with faire fearefull humblesse towards him shee
        came:

XXVII. And weeping said, " Ah, my long lacked Lord,
    Where have ye bene thus long out of my sight?
    Much feared I to have bene quite abhord,
    Or ought have done, that ye displeasen might,
    That should as death unto my deare heart light:
    For since mine eie your joyous sight did mis,
    My chearefull day is turnd to chearelesse night,
    And eke my night of death the shadow is;
    But welcome now, my light, and shining lampe of blis! "

XXVIII. He thereto meeting said, " My dearest Dame,
    Far be it from your thought, and fro my wil,
    To thinke that knighthood I so much should shame,
    As you to leave that have me loved stil,
    And chose in Faery court, of meere goodwil,
    Where noblest knights were to be found on earth.
    The earth shall sooner leave her kindly skil
    To bring forth fruit, and make eternal derth,
    Then I leave you, my liefe, yborn of hevenly berth.

XXIX. " And sooth to say, why I lefte you so long,
    Was for to seeke adventure in straunge place;
    Where, Archimago said, a felon strong
    To many knights did daily worke disgrace;
    But knight he now shall never more deface:
    Good cause of mine excuse, that mote ye please
    Well to accept, and evermore embrace
    My faithfull service, that by land and seas
    Have vowd you to defend. Now then, your plaint
        appease."

XXX. His lovely words her seemd due recompence
    Of all her passed paines: one loving howre

For many yeares of sorrow can dispence;
A dram of sweete is worth a pound of sowre.
Shee has forgott how many a woeful stowre
For him she late endurd; she speakes no more
Of past: true is, that true love hath no powre
To looken backe; his eies be fixt before.
Before her stands her knight, for whom she toyld so sore.

XXXI. Much like, as when the beaten marinere,
That long hath wandred in the Ocean wide,
Ofte soust in swelling Tethys saltish teare;
And long time having tand his tawney hide
With blustring breath of Heaven, that none can bide,
And scorching flames of fierce Orions hound;
Soone as the port from far he has espide,
His chearfull whistle merily doth sound,
And Nereus crownes with cups; his mates him pledg
around.

XXXII. Such joy made Una, when her knight she found;
And eke th' enchaunter joyous seemde no lesse
Then the glad marchant, that does vew from ground
His ship far come from watrie wildernesse;
He hurles out vowes, and Neptune oft doth blesse.
So forth they past; and all the way they spent
Discoursing of her dreadful late distresse,
In which he askt her, what the Lyon ment;
Who told her all that fell, in journey as she went.

XXXIII. They had not ridden far, when they might see
One pricking towards them with hastie heat,
Full strongly armd, and on a courser free
That through his fiersnesse fomed all with sweat,
And the sharpe yron did for anger eat,
When his hot ryder spurd his chauffed side:
His looke was sterne, and seemed still to threat
Cruell revenge, which he in hart did hyde;
And on his shield *Sansloy* in bloody lines was dyde.

XXXIV. When nigh he drew unto this gentle payre,
And saw the Red-crosse which the knight did beare,
He burnt in fire; and gan eftsoones prepare
Himselfe to batteill with his couched speare.

Loth was that other, and did faint through feare,
To taste th' untryed dint of deadly steele:
But yet his Lady did so well him cheare,
That hope of new good hap he gan to feele;
So bent his speare, and spurd his horse with yron heele.

XXXV. But that proud Paynim forward came so ferce
And full of wrath, that, with his sharphead speare,
Through vainly crossed shield he quite did perce;
And, had his staggering steed not shronke for feare,
Through shield and body eke he should him beare:
Yet, so great was the puissance of his push,
That from his sadle quite he did him beare.
He, tombling rudely downe, to ground did rush,
And from his gored wound a well of bloud did gush.

XXXVI. Dismounting lightly from his loftie steed,
He to him lept, in minde to reave his life,
And proudly said; " Lo! there the worthie meed
Of him that slew Sansfoy with bloody knife:
Henceforth his ghost, freed from repining strife,
In peace may passen over Lethe lake;
When mourning altars, purged with enimies life,
The black infernall Furies doen aslake:
Life from Sansfoy thou tookst, Sansloy shall from thee
   take."

XXXVII. Therewith in haste his helmet gan unlace,
Till Una cride, " O! hold that heavie hand,
Deare Sir, what ever that thou be in place:
Enough is, that thy foe doth vanquisht stand
Now at thy mercy: Mercy not withstand;
For he is one the truest knight alive,
Though conquered now he lye on lowly land;
And, whilest him fortune favourd, fayre did thrive
In bloudy field; therefore, of life him not deprive."

XXXVIII. Her piteous wordes might not abate his rage,
But, rudely rending up his helmet, would
Have slayne him streight; and when he sees his age,
And hoarie head of Archimago old,
His hasty hand he doth amased hold,
And halfe ashamed wondred at the sight:

For the old man well knew he, though untold,
In charmes and magick to have wondrous might,
Ne ever wont in field, ne in round lists, to fight:

XXXIX. And said, " Why Archimago, lucklesse syre,
What doe I see? what hard mishap is this,
That hath thee hether brought to taste mine yre?
Or thine the fault, or mine the error is,
In stead of foe to wound my friend amis? "
He answered nought, but in a traunce still lay,
And on those guilefull dazed eyes of his
The cloude of death did sit.   Which doen away,
He left him lying so, ne would no lenger stay:

XL. But to the virgin comes; who all this while
Amased stands, her selfe so mockt to see
By him, who has the guerdon of his guile,
For so misfeigning her true knight to bee:
Yet is she now in more perplexitie,
Left in the hand of that same Paynim bold,
From whom her booteth not at all to flie:
Who, by her cleanly garment catching hold,
Her from her Palfrey pluckt, her visage to behold.

XLI. But her fiers servant, full of kingly aw
And high disdaine, whenas his soveraine Dame
So rudely handled by her foe he saw,
With gaping jawes full greedy at him came,
And, ramping on his shield, did weene the same
Have reft away with his sharp rending clawes:
But he was stout, and lust did now inflame
His corage more, that from his griping pawes
He hath his shield redeemed, and forth his **swerd he**
    drawes.

XLII. O! then, too weake and feeble was the forse
Of salvage beast his puissance to withstand;
For he was strong, and of so mightie corse,
As ever wielded speare in warlike hand,
And feates of armes did wisely understand.
Eft soones he perced through his chaufed chest
With thrilling point of deadly yron brand,
And launcht his Lordly hart: with death opprest
He ror'd aloud, whiles life forsooke his stubborne brest.

XLIII. Who now is left to keepe the forlorne maid
From raging spoile of lawlesse victors will?
Her faithfull gard remov'd, her hope dismaid,
Her selfe a yielded pray to save or spill:
He now, Lord of the field, his pride to fill,
With foule reproches and disdaineful spight
Her vildly entertaines; and, will or nill,
Beares her away upon his courser light:
Her prayers nought prevaile, his rage is more of might.

XLIV. And all the way, with great lamenting paine,
And piteous plaintes, she filleth his dull eares,
That stony hart could riven have in twaine;
And all the way she wetts with flowing teares;
But he, enrag'd with rancor, nothing heares.
Her servile beast yet would not leave her so,
But followes her far off, ne ought he feares
To be partaker of her wondring woe;
More mild in beastly kind then that her beastly foe.

Una meets Lyon.
Santyey. Kills Archimago dressed as the Knight.
Kills Lyon, comes off Una.

CANTO IV

To sinfull hous of Pryde Duessa
Guydes the faithfull knight;
Where, brothers death to wreak, Sansjoy
Doth chaleng him to fight.

I. Young knight whatever, that dost armes professe,
And through long labours huntest after fame,
Beware of fraud, beware of ficklenesse,
In choice, and chaunge of thy deare-loved Dame;
Least thou of her believe too lightly blame,
And rash misweening doe thy hart remove:
For unto knight there is no greater shame
Then lightnesse and inconstancie in love:
That doth this Redcrosse knights ensample plainly prove.

II. Who, after that he had faire Una lorne,
Through light misdeeming of her loialtie;
And false Duessa in her sted had borne,
Called Fidess', and so supposd to be,
Long with her traveild; till at last they see
A goodly building bravely garnished;
The house of mightie Prince it seemd to be,
And towards it a broad high way that led,
All bare through peoples feet which thether traveiled.

III. Great troupes of people traveild thetherward
Both day and night, of each degree and place;
But few returned, having scaped hard,
With balefull beggery, or foule disgrace;
Which ever after in most wretched case,
Like loathsome lazars, by the hedges lay.
Thether Duessa badd him bend his pace,
For she is wearie of the toilsom way,
And also nigh consumed is the lingring day.

IV. A stately Pallace built of squared bricke,
Which cunningly was without morter laid,
Whose wals were high, but nothing strong nor thick

And golden foile all over them displaid,
That purest skye with brightnesse they dismaid:
High lifted up were many loftie towres,
And goodly galleries far over laid,
Full of faire windowes and delightful bowres:
And on the top a Diall told the timely howres.

v. It was a goodly heape for to behould,
And spake the praises of the workmans witt;
But full great pittie, that so faire a mould
Did on so weake foundation ever sitt:
For on a sandie hill, that still did flitt
And fall away, it mounted was full hie,
That every breath of heaven shaked itt:
And all the hinder partes, that few could spie,
Were ruinous and old, but painted cunningly.

vi. Arrived there, they passed in forth right;
For still to all the gates stood open wide:
Yet charge of them was to a Porter hight,
Cald Malvenú, who entrance none denide:
Thence to the hall, which was on every side
With rich array and costly arras dight.
Infinite sortes of people did abide
There waiting long, to win the wished sight
Of her, that was the Lady of that Pallace bright.

vii. By them they passe, all gazing on them round,
And to the Presence mount; whose glorious vew
Their frayle amazed senses did confound:
In living Princes court none ever knew
Such endlesse richesse, and so sumpteous shew;
Ne Persia selfe, the nourse of pompous pride,
Like ever saw.   And there a noble crew
Of Lords and Ladies stood on every side,
Which with their presence fayre the place much beautifide.

viii. High above all a cloth of State was spred,
And a rich throne, as bright as sunny day;
On which there sate, most brave embellished
With royall robes and gorgeous array,
A mayden Queene that shone as Titans ray,
In glistring gold and perelesse pretious stone;

Yet her bright blazing beautie did assay
To dim the brightnesse of her glorious throne,
As envying her selfe, that too exceeding shone:

IX. Exceeding shone, like Phœbus fayrest childe,
That did presume his fathers fyrie wayne,
And flaming mouthes of steedes, unwonted wilde,
Through highest heaven with weaker hand to rayne:
Proud of such glory and advancement vayne,
While flashing beames do daze his feeble eyen,
He leaves the welkin way most beaten playne,
And, rapt with whirling wheeles, inflames the skyen
With fire not made to burne, but fayrely for to shyne.

X. So proud she shyned in her princely state,
Looking to heaven, for earth she did disdayne,
And sitting high, for lowly she did hate:
Lo! underneath her scornefull feete was layne
A dreadfull Dragon with an hideous trayne;
And in her hand she held a mirrhour bright,
Wherein her face she often vewed fayne,
And in her selfe-lov'd semblance took delight;
For she was wondrous faire, as any living wight.

XI. Of griesly Pluto she the daughter was,
And sad Prosperina, the Queene of helle;
Yet did she thinke her pearelesse worth to pas
That parentage, with pride so did she swell;
And thundring Jove, that high in heaven doth dwell
And wield the world, she claymed for her syre,
Or if that any else did Jove excell;
For to the highest she did still aspyre,
Or, if ought higher were than that, did it desyre.

XII. And proud Lucifera men did her call,
That made her selfe a Queene, and crownd to be;
Yet rightfull kingdome she had none at all,
Ne heritage of native soveraintie;
But did usurpe with wrong and tyrannie
Upon the scepter which she now did hold:
Ne ruld her Realme with lawes, but pollicie,
And strong advizement of six wisards old,
That, with their counsels bad, her kingdome did uphold.

XIII. Soone as the Elfin knight in presence came,
And false Duessa, seeming Lady fayre,
A gentle Husher, Vanitie by name,
Made rowme, and passage for them did prepaire:
So goodly brought them to the lowest stayre
Of her high throne; where they, on humble knee
Making obeysaunce, did the cause declare,
Why they were come her roiall state to see,
To prove the wide report of her great Majestee.

XIV. With loftie eyes, halfe loth to looke so lowe,
She thancked them in her disdainefull wise:
Ne other grace vouchsafed them to showe
Of Princesse worthy; scarse them bad arise.
Her Lordes and Ladies all this while devise
Themselves to setten forth to straungers sight:
Some frounce their curled heare in courtly guise;
Some prancke their ruffes; and others trimly dight
Their gay attyre; each others greater pride does spight.

XV. Goodly they all that knight doe entertayne,
Right glad with him to have increast their crew;
But to Duess' each one himselfe did payne
All kindnesse and faire courtesie to shew,
For in that court whylome her well they knew:
Yet the stout Faery mongst the middest crowd
Thought all their glorie vaine in knightly vew,
And that great Princesse too exceeding prowd,
That to strange knight no better countenance allowd.

XVI. Suddein upriseth from her stately place
The roiall Dame, and for her coche doth call:
All hurtlen forth; and she, with princely pace,
As faire Aurora in her purple pall
Out of the East the dawning day doth call.
So forth she comes; her brightnes brode doth blaze.
The heapes of people, thronging in the hall,
Doe ride each other upon her to gaze:
Her glorious glitterand light doth all mens eies amaze.

XVII. So forth she comes, and to her coche does clyme,
Adorned all with gold and girlonds gay,
That seemed as fresh as Flora in her prime;

And strove to match, in roiall rich array,
Great Junoes golden chayre; the which, they say,
The gods stand gazing on, when she does ride
To Joves high hous through heavens bras-paved way,
Drawne of fayre Pecocks, that excell in pride,
And full of Argus eyes their tayles dispredden wide.

XVIII. But this was drawne of six unequall beasts,
On which her six sage Counsellours did ryde,
Taught to obay their bestiall beheasts,
With like conditions to their kindes applyde:
Of which the first, that all the rest did guyde,
Was sluggish Idlenesse, the nourse of sin;
Upon a slouthfull Asse he chose to ryde,
Arayd in habit blacke, and amis thin,
Like to an holy Monck, the service to begin.

XIX. And in his hand his Portesse still he bare,
That much was worne, but therein little redd;
For of devotion he had little care,
Still drownd in sleepe, and most of his daies dedd:
Scarse could he once uphold his heavie hedd,
To looken whether it were night or day.
May seeme the wayne was very evill ledd,
When such an one had guiding of the way,
That knew not whether right he went, or else astray.

XX. From worldly cares himselfe he did esloyne,
And greatly shunned manly exercise;
From everie worke he chalenged essoyne,
For contemplation sake: yet otherwise
His life he led in lawlesse riotise,
By which he grew to grievous malady;
For in his lustlesse limbs, through evill guise,
A shaking fever raignd continually.
Such one was Idlenesse, first of this company.

XXI. And by his side rode loathsome Gluttony,
Deformed creature, on a filthie swyne.
His belly was upblowne with luxury,
And eke with fatnesse swollen were his eyne;
And like a Crane his necke was long and fyne
With which he swallowed up excessive feast,

For want whereof poore people oft did pyne:
And all the way, most like a brutish beast,
He spued up his gorge, that all did him deteast.

XXII. In greene vine leaves he was right fitly clad,
For other clothes he could not ware for heate;
And on his head an yvie girland had,
From under which fast trickled downe the sweat.
Still as he rode he somewhat still did eat,
And in his hand did beare a bouzing can,
Of which he supt so oft, that on his seat
His dronken corse he scarse upholden can:
In shape and life more like a monster then a man.

XXIII. Unfit he was for any worldly thing,
And eke unhable once to stirre or go;
Not meet to be of counsell to a king,
Whose mind in meat and drinke was drowned so,
That from his frend he seeldome knew his fo.
Full of diseases was his carcas blew,
And a dry dropsie through his flesh did flow,
Which by misdiet daily greater grew.
Such one was Gluttony, the second of that crew.

XXIV. And next to him rode lustfull Lechery
Upon a bearded Gote, whose rugged heare,
And whally eies (the signe of gelosy,)
Was like the person selfe whom he did beare:
Who rough, and blacke, and filthy, did appeare,
Unseemely man to please faire Ladies eye;
Yet he of Ladies oft was loved deare,
When fairer faces were bid standen by:
O! who does know the bent of womens fantasy?

XXV. In a greene gowne he clothed was full faire,
Which underneath did hide his filthinesse;
And in his hand a burning hart he bare,
Full of vaine follies and new fanglenesse:
For he was false, and fraught with ficklenesse,
And learned had to love with secret lookes;
And well could daunce, and sing with ruefulnesse;
And fortunes tell, and read in loving bookes,
And thousand other waies to bait his fleshly hookes.

XXVI. Inconstant man, that loved all he saw,
    And lusted after all that he did love;
    Ne would his looser life be tide to law,
    But joyd weake wemens hearts to tempt, and prove,
    If from their loyall loves he might them move:
    Which lewdnes fild him with reprochfull pain
    Of that foule evill, which all men reprove,
    That rotts the marrow, and consumes the braine.
    Such one was Lechery, the third of all this traine.

XXVII. And greedy Avarice by him did ride,
    Uppon a Camell loaden all with gold:
    Two iron coffers hong on either side,
    With precious metall full as they might hold;
    And in his lap an heap of coine he told;
    For of his wicked pelfe his God he made,
    And unto hell him selfe for money sold:
    Accursed usury was all his trade,
    And right and wrong ylike in equall ballaunce waide.

XXVIII. His life was nigh unto deaths dore yplaste;
    And thred-bare cote, and cobled shoes, hee ware;
    Ne scarse good morsell all his life did taste,
    But both from backe and belly still did spare,
    To fill his bags, and richesse to compare:
    Yet childe ne kinsman living had he none
    To leave them to; but thorough daily care
    To get, and nightly feare to lose his owne,
    He led a wretched life, unto himselfe unknowne

XXIX. Most wretched wight, whom nothing might suffise;
    Whose greedy lust did lacke in greatest store;
    Whose need had end, but no end covetise;
    Whose welth was want, whose plenty made him pore;
    Who had enough, yett wished ever more;
    A vile disease: and eke in foote and hand
    A grievous gout tormented him full sore,
    That well he could not touch, nor goe, nor stand.
    Such one was Avarice, the fourth of this faire band.

XXX. And next to him malicious Envy rode
    Upon a ravenous wolfe, and still did chaw
    Between his cankred teeth a venemous tode,

That all the poison ran about his chaw;
But inwardly he chawed his owne maw
At neighbours welth, that made him ever sad,
For death it was, when any good he saw;
And wept, that cause of weeping none he had;
But when he heard of harme he wexed wondrous glad.

XXXI. All in a kirtle of discolourd say
He clothed was, ypaynted full of eies;
And in his bosome secretly there lay
An hatefull Snake, the which his taile uptyes
In many folds, and mortall sting implyes.
Still as he rode he gnasht his teeth to see
Those heapes of gold with griple Covetyse;
And grudged at the great felicitee
Of proud Lucifera, and his owne companee.

XXXII. He hated all good workes and vertuous deeds,
And him no lesse, that any like did use;
And who with gratious bread the hungry feeds,
His almes for want of faith he doth accuse.
So every good to bad he doth abuse;
And eke the verse of famous Poets witt
He does backebite, and spightfull poison spues
From leprous mouth on all that ever writt.
Such one vile Envy was, that fifte in row did sitt.

XXXIII. And him beside rides fierce revenging Wrath,
Upon a Lion, loth for to be led;
And in his hand a burning brond he hath,
The which he brandisheth about his hed:
His eies did hurle forth sparcles fiery red,
And stared sterne on all that him beheld;
As ashes pale of hew, and seeming ded;
And on his dagger still his hand he held,
Trembling through hasty rage when choler in him sweld.

XXXIV. His ruffin raiment all was staind with blood
Which he had split, and all to rags yrent,
Through unadvized rashnes woxen wood;
For of his hands he had no governement,
Ne car'd for blood in his avengement:
But, when the furious fitt was overpast,

His cruel facts he often would repent;
Yet, wilfull man, he never would forecast
How many mischieves should ensue his heedlesse hast.

xxxv. Full many mischiefes follow cruell Wrath:
Abhorred bloodshed, and tumultuous strife,
Unmanly murder, and unthrifty scath,
Bitter despight, with rancours rusty knife,
And fretting griefe, the enemy of life:
All these, and many evils moe haunt ire,
The swelling Splene, and Frenzy raging rife,
The shaking Palsey, and Saint Fraunces fire.
Such one was Wrath, the last of this ungodly tire.

xxxvi. And, after all, upon the wagon beame,
Rode Sathan with a smarting whip in hand,
With which he forward lasht the laesy teme,
So oft as Slowth still in the mire did stand.
Huge routs of people did about them band,
Showting for joy; and still before their way
A foggy mist had covered all the land;
And, underneath their feet, all scattered lay
Dead sculls and bones of men whose life had gone astray.

xxxvii. So forth they marchen in this goodly sort,
To take the solace of the open aire,
And in fresh flowring fields themselves to sport:
Emongst the rest rode that false Lady faire,
The foule Duessa, next unto the chaire
Of proud Lucifer', as one of the traine:
But that good knight would not so nigh repaire,
Him selfe estraunging from their joyaunce vaine,
Whose fellowship seemd far unfitt for warlike swaine.

xxxviii. So, having solaced themselves a space
With pleasaunce of the breathing fields yfed,
They backe retourned to the princely Place;
Whereas an errant knight in armes ycled,
And heathnish shield, wherein with letters red,
Was writt *Sansjoy*, they new arrived find:
Enflam'd with fury and fiers hardy hed,
He seemd in hart to harbour thoughts unkind,
And nourish bloody vengeance in his bitter mind.

XXXIX. Who, when the shamed shield of slaine Sansfoy
　　　　He spide with that same Faery champions page,
　　　　Bewraying him that did of late destroy
　　　　His eldest brother; burning all with rage,
　　　　He to him lept, and that same envious gage
　　　　Of victors glory from him snacht away:
　　　　But th' Elfin knight, which ought that warlike wage,
　　　　Disdaind to loose the meed he wonne in fray;
　　　　And, him rencountring fierce, reskewd the noble pray.

XL. Therewith they gan to hurtlen greedily,
　　　Redoubted battaile ready to darrayne,
　　　And clash their shields, and shake their swerds on hy,
　　　That with their sturre they troubled all the traine;
　　　Till that great Queene, upon eternall paine
　　　Of high displeasure that ensewen might,
　　　Commaunded them their fury to refraine;
　　　And, if that either to that shield had right,
　　　In equall lists they should the morrow next it fight.

XLI. "Ah dearest Dame," quoth then the Paynim bold,
　　　"Pardon the error of enraged wight,
　　　Whome great griefe made forgett the raines to hold
　　　Of reasons rule, to see this recreaunt knight,
　　　No knight, but treachour full of false despight
　　　And shameful treason, who through guile hath slayn
　　　The prowest knight that ever field did fight,
　　　Even stout Sansfoy, (O who can then refrayn?)
　　　Whose shield he beares renverst, the more to heap disdayn.

XLII. "And, to augment the glorie of his guile,
　　　His dearest love, the faire Fidessa, loe!
　　　Is there possessed of the traytour vile;
　　　Who reapes the harvest sowen by his foe,
　　　Sowen in bloodie field, and bought with woe:
　　　That brothers hand shall dearely well requight,
　　　So be, O Queene! you equall favour showe."
　　　Him litle answerd th' angry Elfin knight;
　　　He never meant with words, but swords, to plead his right:

XLIII. But threw his gauntlet, as a sacred pledge
　　　His cause in combat the next day to try:
　　　So been they parted both, with harts on edge

To be aveng'd each on his enimy.
That night they pas in joy and jollity,
Feasting and courting both in bowre and hall;
For Steward was excessive Gluttony,
That of his plenty poured forth to all:
Which doen, the Chamberlain, Slowth, did to rest them call.

XLIV. Now wheras darkesome night had all displayed
Her coleblacke curtein over brightest skye;
The warlike youthes, on dayntie couches layd,
Did chace away sweet sleepe from sluggish eye,
To muse on meanes of hoped victory.
But whenas Morpheus had with leaden mace
Arrested all that courtly company,
Uprose Duessa from her resting place,
And to the Paynims lodging comes with silent pace.

XLV. Whom broad awake she findes, in troublous fitt,
Fore-casting how his foe he might annoy;
And him amoves with speaches seeming fitt:
"Ah deare Sansjoy, next dearest to Sansfoy,
Cause of my new griefe, cause of my new joy;
Joyous to see his ymage in mine eye,
And greevd to thinke how foe did him destroy,
That was the flowre of grace and chevalrye;
Lo! his Fidessa, to thy secret faith I flye."

XLVI. With gentle wordes he can her fayrely greet,
And bad say on the secrete of her hart:
Then, sighing soft; "I learne that litle sweet
Oft tempred is," (quoth she,) "with muchell smart:
For since my brest was launcht with lovely dart
Of deare Sansfoy, I never joyed howre,
But in eternall woes my weaker hart
Have wasted, loving him with all my powre,
And for his sake have felt full many an heavie stowre.

XLVII. "At last, when perils all I weened past,
And hop'd to reape the crop of all my care,
Into new woes unweeting I was cast
By this false faytor, who unworthie ware
His worthie shield, whom he with guilefull snare
Entrapped slew, and brought to shamefull grave:

Me, silly maid, away with him he bare,
And ever since hath kept in darksom cave,
For that I would not yeeld that to Sansfoy I gave.

XLVIII. " But since faire Sunne hath sperst that lowring clowd,
And to my loathed life now shewes some light,
Under your beames I will me safely shrowd
From dreaded storme of his disdainfull spight:
To you th' inheritance belonges by right
Of brothers prayse, to you eke longes his love.
Let not his love, let not his restlesse spright,
Be unreveng'd, that calles to you above
From wandring Stygian shores, where it doth endlesse
move."

XLIX. Thereto said he, " Faire Dame, be nought dismaid
For sorrowes past; their griefe is with them gone:
Ne yet of present perill be affraid,
For needlesse feare did never vantage none;
And helplesse hap it booteth not to mone.
Dead is Sansfoy, his vitall paines are past,
Though greeved ghost for vengeance deep do grone:
He lives that shall him pay his dewties last,
And guiltie Elfin blood shall sacrifice in hast."

L. " O! but I feare the fickle freakes," (quoth shee)
" Of fortune false, and oddes of armes in field."
" Why, dame," (quoth he) " what oddes can ever bee,
Where both doe fight alike, to win or yield? "
" Yea, but," (quoth she) " he beares a charmed shield,
And eke enchaunted armes; that none can perce,
Ne none can wound the man that does them wield."
" Charmd or enchaunted," answered he then ferce,
" I no whitt reck; ne you the like need to reherce.

LI. " But, faire Fidessa sithens fortunes guile,
Or enimies powre, hath now captived you,
Returne from whence ye came, and rest a while,
Till morrow next that I the Elfe subdew,
And with Sansfoyes dead dowry you endew."
" Ah me! that is a double death," (she said)
" With proud foes sight my sorrow to renew,
Where ever yet I be, my secret aide
Shall follow you." So, passing forth, she him obaid.

CANTO V

The faithfull knight in equall field
Subdewes his faithlesse foe;
Whom false Duessa saves, and for
His cure to hell does goe.

I. THE noble hart that harbours vertuous thought,
And is with childe of glorious great intent,
Can never rest, untill it forth have brought
Th' eternall brood of glorie excellent:
Such restlesse passion did all night torment
The flaming corage of that Faery knight,
Devizing how that doughtie turnament
With greatest honour he atchieven might:
Still did he wake, and still did he watch for dawning light.

II. At last, the golden Orientall gate
Of greatest heaven gan to open fayre;
And Phœbus, fresh as brydegrome to his mate,
Came dauncing forth, shaking his deawie hayre,
And hurld his glistring beams through gloomy ayre.
Which when the wakeful Elfe perceiv'd, streight way,
He started up, and did him selfe prepayre
In sunbright armes, and battailous array;
For with that Pagan proud he combatt will that day.

III. And forth he comes into the commune hall;
Where earely waite him many a gazing eye,
To weet what end to straunger knights may fall.
There many Minstrales maken melody,
To drive away the dull melancholy;
And many Bardes, that to the trembling chord
Can tune their timely voices cunningly;
And many Chroniclers, that can record
Old loves, and warres for Ladies doen by many a Lord.

IV. Soone after comes the cruell Sarazin,
In woven maile all armed warily;
And sternly lookes at him, who not a pin

Does care for looke of living creatures eye.
They bring them wines of Greece and Araby,
And daintie spices fetch from furthest Ynd,
To kindle heat of corage privily;
And in the wine a solemne oth thy bynd
T' observe the sacred lawes of armes that are assynd.

v. At last forth comes that far renowned Queene:
With royall pomp and princely majestie
She is ybrought unto a paled greene,
And placed under stately canapee,
The warlike feates of both those knights to see.
On th' other side in all mens open vew
Duessa placed is, and on a tree
Sansfoy his shield is hangd with bloody hew;
Both those the lawrell girlonds to the victor dew.

vi. A shrilling trompett sownded from on hye,
And unto battaill bad them selves addresse:
Their shining shieldes about their wrestes they tye,
And burning blades about their heades doe blesse,
The instruments of wrath and heavinesse.
With greedy force each other doth assayle,
And strike so fiercely, that they do impresse
Deepe dinted furrowes in the battred mayle:
The yron walles to ward their blowes are weak and fraile.

vii. The Sarazin was stout and wondrous strong,
And heaped blowes like yron hammers great;
For after blood and vengeance he did long:
The knight was fiers, and full of youthly heat,
And doubled strokes, like dreaded thunders threat;
For all for praise and honour he did fight.
Both stricken stryke, and beaten both doe beat,
That from their shields forth flyeth firie light,
And hewen helmets deepe shew marks of eithers might.

viii. So th' one for wrong, the other strives for right.
As when a Gryfon, seized of his pray,
A Dragon fiers encountreth in his flight,
Through widest ayre making his ydle way,
That would his rightfull ravine rend away:
With hideous horror both together smight,

And souce so sore that they the heavens affray;
The wise Southsayer, seeing so sad sight,
Th' amazed vulgar telles of warres and mortall fight.

IX. So th' one for wrong, the other strives for right,
And each to deadly shame would drive his foe:
The cruell steele so greedily doth bight
In tender flesh, that streames of blood down flow;
With which the armes, that earst so bright did show,
Into a pure vermillion now are dyde.
Great ruth in all the gazers harts did grow,
Seeing the gored woundes to gape so wyde,
That victory they dare not wish to either side.

X. At last the Paynim chaunst to cast his eye,
His suddein eye flaming with wrathfull fyre,
Upon his brothers shield, which hong thereby:
Therewith redoubled was his raging yre,
And said; "Ah! wretched sonne of wofull syre,
Doest thou sit wayling by blacke Stygian lake,
Whylest here thy shield is hangd for victors hyre?
And, sluggish german, doest thy forces slake
To after-send his foe, that him may overtake?

XI. "Goe, caytive Elfe, him quickly overtake,
And soone redeeme from his long-wandring woe:
Goe, guiltie ghost, to him my message make,
That I his shield have quit from dying foe."
Therewith upon his crest he stroke him so,
That twise he reeled, readie twise to fall:
End of the doubtfull battaile deemed tho
The lookers on; and lowd to him gan call
The false Duessa, "Thine the shield, and I, and all!"

XII. Soone as the Faerie heard his Ladie speake,
Out of his swowning dreame he gan awake;
And quickning faith, that earst was woxen weake,
The creeping deadly cold away did shake:
Tho mov'd with wrath, and shame, and Ladies sake,
Of all attonce he cast avengd to be,
And with so' exceeding furie at him strake,
That forced him to stoupe upon his knee:
Had he not stouped so, he should have cloven bee.

xiii. And to him said; " Goe now, proud Miscreant,
Thyselfe thy message do to german deare;
Alone he, wandring, thee too long doth want:
Goe say, his foe thy shield with his doth beare."
Therewith his heavie hand he high gan reare,
Him to have slaine; when lo! a darkesome clowd
Upon him fell: he no where doth appeare,
But vanisht is.   The Elfe him calls alowd,
But answer none receives; the darknes him does shrowd.

xiv. In haste Duessa from her place arose,
And to him running said; " O! prowest knight,
That ever Ladie to her love did chose,
Let now abate the terrour of your might,
And quench the flame of furious despight,
And bloodie vengeance: lo! th' infernall powres,
Covering your foe with cloud of deadly night,
Have borne him hence to Plutoes balefull bowres:
The conquest yours; I yours; the shield, and glory yours."

xv. Not all so satisfide, with greedy eye
He sought all round about, his thristy blade
To bathe in blood of faithlesse enimy;
Who all that while lay hid in secret shade.
He standes amazed how he thence should fade:
At last the trumpets Triumph sound on hie;
And running Heralds humble homage made,
Greeting him goodly with new victorie,
And to him brought the shield, the cause of enmitie.

xvi. Wherewith he goeth to that soveraine Queene;
And falling her before on lowly knee,
To her makes present of his service seene:
Which she accepts with thankes and goodly gree,
Greatly advauncing his gay chevalree:
So marcheth home, and by her takes the knight,
Whom all the people followe with great glee,
Shouting, and clapping all their hands on hight,
That all the ayre it fills, and flyes to heaven bright.

xvii. Home is he brought, and layd in sumptous bed,
Where many skilfull leaches him abide
To salve his hurts, that yet still freshly bled.

In wine and oyle they wash his woundes wide,
And softly gan embalme on everie side:
And all the while most heavenly melody
About the bed sweet musicke did divide,
Him to beguile of griefe and agony;
And all the while Duessa wept full bitterly.

XVIII. As when a wearie traveiler, that strayes
By muddy shore of broad seven-mouthed Nile,
Unweeting of the perillous wandring wayes,
Doth meete a cruell craftie Crocodile,
Which, in false griefe hyding his harmefull guile,
Doth weepe full sore, and sheddeth tender teares;
The foolish man, that pities all this while
His mournefull plight, is swallowed up unwares,
Forgetfull of his owne that mindes an others cares.

XIX. So wept Duessa untill eventyde,
That shyning lampes in Joves high house were light;
Then forth she rose, ne lenger would abide,
But comes unto the place where th' Hethen knight,
In slombring swownd, nigh voyd of vitall spright,
Lay cover'd with inchaunted cloud all day:
Whom when she found, as she him left in plight,
To wayle his wofull case she would not stay,
But to the Easterne coast of heaven makes speedy way:

XX. Where griesly Night, with visage deadly sad,
That Phœbus chearefull face durst never vew,
And in a foule blacke pitchy mantle clad,
She findes forth comming from her darksome mew,
Where she all day did hide her hated hew.
Before the dore her yron charet stood,
Already harnessed for journey new,
And cole blacke steedes yborne of hellish brood,
That on their rusty bits did champ as they were wood.

XXI. Who when she saw Duessa, sunny bright,
Adornd with gold and jewels shining cleare,
She greatly grew amazed at the sight,
And th' unacquainted light began to feare,
For never did such brightnes there appeare;
And would have backe retyred to her cave,

Untill the witches speach she gan to heare,
Saying; " Yet, O thou dreaded Dame! I crave
Abyde, till I have told the message which I have."

XXII. She stayd; and foorth Duessa gan proceede:
" O! thou most auncient Grandmother of all,
More old then Jove, whom thou at first didst breede,
Or that great house of Gods cælestiall,
Which wast begot in Dæmogorgons hall,
And sawst the secrets of the world unmade,
Why suffredst thou thy Nephewes deare to fall,
With Elfin sword most shamefully betrade?
Lo! where the stout Sansjoy doth sleepe in deadly shade.

XXIII. " And him before, I saw with bitter eyes
The bold Sansfoy shrinck underneath his speare:
And now the pray of fowles in field he lyes,
Nor wayld of friends, nor layd on groning beare,
That whylome was to me too dearely deare.
O! what of gods then boots it to be borne,
If old Aveugles sonnes so evill heare?
Or who shall not great Nightes children scorne,
When two of three her Nephewes are so fowle forlorne?

XXIV. " Up, then! up, dreary Dame, of darknes Queene!
Go, gather up the reliques of thy race;
Or else goe them avenge, and let be seene
That dreaded Night in brightest day hath place,
And can the children of fayre light deface."
Her feeling speaches some compassion mov'd
In hart, and chaunge in that great mothers face:
Yet pitty in her heart was never prov'd
Till then, for evermore she hated, never lov'd:

XXV. And said, " Deare daughter, rightly may I rew
The fall of famous children borne of mee,
And good successes which their foes ensew:
But who can turne the stream of destinee,
Or breake the chayne of strong necessitee,
Which fast is tyde to Joves eternall seat?
The sonnes of Day he favoureth, I see,
And by my ruines thinkes to make them great:
To make one great by others losse is bad excheat.

XXVI. " Yet shall they not escape so freely all,
For some shall pay the price of others guilt;
And he the man that made Sansfoy to fall,
Shall with his owne blood price that he hath spilt.
But what art thou, that telst of Nephews kilt? "
" I, that do seeme not I, Duessa ame,"
Quoth she, " how ever now, in garments gilt
And gorgeous gold arrayd, I to thee came,
Duessa I, the daughter of Deceipt and Shame."

XXVII. Then, bowing downe her aged backe, she kist
The wicked witch, saying, " In that fayre face
The false resemblaunce of Deceipt, I wist,
Did closely lurke; yet so true-seeming grace
It carried, that I scarse in darksome place
Could it discerne, though I the mother bee
Of falsehood, and roote of Duessaes race.
O welcome, child! whom I have longd to see,
And now have seene unwares. Lo! now I goe with thee."

XXVIII. Then to her yron wagon she betakes,
And with her beares the fowle welfavourd witch.
Through mirkesome aire her ready way she makes:
Her twyfold Teme, of which two blacke as pitch,
And two were browne, yet each to each unlich,
Did softly swim away, ne ever stamp
Unlesse she chaunst their stubborne mouths to twitch;
Then, foming tarre, their bridles they would champ,
And trampling the fine element would fiercely ramp.

XXIX. So well they sped, that they be come at length
Unto the place whereas the Paynim lay,
Devoid of outward sence and native strength,
Coverd with charmed cloud from vew of day,
And sight of men, since his late luckelesse fray.
His cruell wounds, with cruddy bloud congeald,
They binden up so wisely as they may,
And handle softly, till they can be heald:
So lay him in her charett, close in night conceald.

XXX. And, all the while she stood upon the ground,
The wakefull dogs did never cease to bay,
As giving warning of th' unwonted sound,

With which her yron wheeles did them affray,
And her darke griesly looke them much dismay:
The messenger of death, the ghastly owle,
With drery shriekes did also her bewray;
And hungry wolves continually did howle
At her abhorred face, so filthy and so fowle.

XXXI. Thence turning backe in silence softe they stole,
And brought the heavy corse with easy pace
To yawning gulfe of deepe Avernus hole.
By that same hole an entraunce, darke and bace,
With smoake and sulphur hiding all the place,
Descends to hell: there creature never past,
That backe retourned without heavenly grace;
But dreadfull Furies, which their chaines have brast,
And damned sprights sent forth to make ill men aghast.

XXXII. By that same way the direfull dames doe drive
Their mournefull charett, fild with rusty blood,
And downe to Plutoes house are come bilive:
Which passing through, on every side them stood
The trembling ghosts with sad amazed mood,
Chattring their iron teeth, and staring wide
With stony eies; and all the hellish brood
Of feends infernall flockt on every side,
To gaze on erthly wight that with the Night durst ride.

XXXIII. They pas the bitter waves of Acheron,
Where many soules sit wailing woefully,
And come to fiery flood of Phlegeton,
Whereas the damned ghosts in torments fry,
And with sharp shrilling shriekes doe bootlesse cry,
Cursing high Jove, the which them thither sent.
The house of endlesse paine is built thereby,
In which ten thousand sorts of punishment
The cursed creatures doe eternally torment.

XXXIV. Before the threshold dreadfull Cerberus
His three deformed heads did lay along,
Curled with thousand adders venemous,
And lilled forth his bloody flaming tong:
At them he gan to reare his bristles strong,
And felly gnarre, untill Dayes enemy

Did him appease; then downe his taile he hong,
And suffered them to passen quietly;
For she in hell and heaven had power equally.

xxxv. There was Ixion turned on a wheele,
For daring tempt the Queene of heaven to sin;
And Sisyphus an huge round stone did reele
Against an hill, ne might from labour lin;
There thristy Tantalus hong by the chin;
And Tityus fed a vulture on his maw;
Typhœus joynts were stretched on a gin;
Theseus condemned to endlesse slouth by law;
And fifty sisters water in leke vessels draw.

xxxvi. They all, beholding worldly wights in place,
Leave off their worke, unmindfull of their smart,
To gaze on them; who forth by them doe pace,
Till they be come unto the furthest part;
Where was a Cave ywrought by wondrous art.
Deepe, darke, uneasy, dolefull, comfortlesse.
In which sad Aesculapius far apart
Emprisond was in chaines remedilesse;
For that Hippolytus rent corse he did redresse.

xxxvii. Hippolytus a jolly huntsman was,
That wont in charett chace the foming bore:
He all his Peeres in beauty did surpas,
But Ladies love as losse of time forbore:
His wanton stepdame loved him the more;
But, when she saw her offred sweets refusd,
Her love she turnd to hate, and him before
His father fierce of treason false accusd,
And with her gealous termes his open eares abusd:

xxxviii. Who, all in rage, his Sea-god syre besought
Some cursed vengeaunce on his sonne to cast.
From surging gulf two Monsters streight were brought,
With dread whereof his chacing steedes aghast
Both charett swifte and huntsman overcast:
His goodly corps, on ragged cliffs yrent,
Was quite dismembered, and his members chast
Scattered on every mountaine as he went,
That of Hippolytus was lefte no moniment.

xxxix. His cruell step-dame, seeing what was donne,
        Her wicked daies with wretched knife did end,
        In death avowing th' innocence of her sonne.
        Which hearing, his rash syre began to rend
        His heare, and hasty tong that did offend:
        Tho, gathering up the reliques of his smart,
        By Dianes meanes, who was Hippolyts frend,
        Them brought to Aesculape, that by his art
        Did heale them all againe, and joyned every part.

   xl. Such wondrous science in mans witt to rain
        When Jove avizd, that could the dead revive,
        And fates expired could renew again,
        Of endlesse life he might him not deprive,
        But unto hell did thrust him downe alive,
        With flashing thunderbolt ywounded sore:
        Where, long remaining, he did alwaies strive
        Himselfe with salves to health for to restore,
        And slake the heavenly fire that raged evermore.

  xli. There auncient Night arriving did alight
        From her high weary wayne, and in her armes
        To Aesculapius brought the wounded knight:
        Whome having softly disaraid of armes,
        Tho gan to him discover all his harmes,
        Beseeching him with prayer and with praise,
        If either salves, or oyles, or herbes, or charmes,
        A fordonne wight from dore of death mote raise,
        He would at her request prolong her nephews daies.

 xlii. "Ah Dame," (quoth he) "thou temptest me in vaine,
        To dare the thing, which daily yet I rew,
        And the old cause of my continued paine
        With like attempt to like end to renew.
        Is not enough, that, thrust from heaven dew,
        Here endlesse penaunce for one fault I pay,
        But that redoubled crime with vengeaunce new
        Thou biddest me to eeke?   Can Night defray
        The wrath of thundring Jove, that rules both night and
               day?"

xliii. "Not so," (quoth she) "but, sith that heavens king
        From hope of heaven hath thee excluded quight,

Why fearest thou, that canst not hope for thing;
And fearest not that more thee hurten might,
Now in the powre of everlasting Night?
Goe to then, O thou far renowmed sonne
Of great Apollo! shew thy famous might
In medicine, that els hath to thee wonne
Great pains, and greater praise, both never to be donne."

XLIV. Her words prevaild: And then the learned leach
His cunning hand gan to his wounds to lay,
And all things els the which his art did teach:
Which having seene, from thence arose away
The mother of dredd darkenesse, and let stay
Aveugles sonne there in the leaches cure;
And, backe retourning, took her wonted way
To ronne her timely race, whilst Phœbus pure
In westerne waves his weary wagon did recure.

XLV. The false Duessa, leaving noyous Night,
Returned to stately pallace of Dame Pryde:
Where when she came, she found the Faery knight
Departed thence; albee his woundes wyde
Not throughly heald unready were to ryde.
Good cause he had to hasten thence away;
For on a day his wary Dwarfe had spyde
Where in a dungeon deepe huge nombers lay
Of caytive wretched thralls, that wayled night and day:

XLVI. A ruefull sight as could be seene with eie;
Of whom he learned had in secret wise
The hidden cause of their captivitie;
How mortgaging their lives to Covetise,
Through wastfull Pride and wanton Riotise,
They were by law of that proud Tyrannesse,
Provokt with Wrath and Envyes false surmise,
Condemned to that Dongeon mercilesse,
Where they should live in wo, and dye in wretchednesse.

XLVII. There was that great proud king of Babylon,
That would compell all nations to adore,
And him as onely God to call upon;
Till, through celestiall doome thrown out of dore,
Into an Oxe he was transformd of yore.

There also was king Crœsus, that enhaunst
His hart too high through his great richesse store;
And proud Antiochus, the which advaunst
His cursed hand gainst God, and on his altares daunst.

XLVIII. And them long time before, great Nimrod was,
That first the world with sword and fire warrayd;
And after him old Ninus far did pas
In princely pomp, of all the world obayd.
There also was that mightie Monarch layd
Low under all, yet above all in pride,
That name of native syre did fowle upbrayd,
And would as Ammons sonne be magnified,
Till, scornd of God and man, a shamefull death he dide.

XLIX. All these together in one heape were throwne,
Like carkases of beastes in butchers stall.
And in another corner wide were strowne
The Antique ruins of the Romanes fall:
Great Romulus, the Grandsyre of them all;
Proud Tarquin, and too lordly Lentulus;
Stout Scipio, and stubborne Hanniball;
Ambitious Sylla, and sterne Marius;
High Cæsar, great Pompey, and fiers Antonius.

L. Amongst these mightie men were wemen mixt,
Proud wemen, vaine, forgetfull of their yoke;
The bold Semiramis, whose sides transfixt
With sonnes own blade her fowle reproches spoke:
Fayre Sthenobœa, that her selfe did choke
With wilfull chord for wanting of her will;
High minded Cleopatra, that with stroke
Of Aspes sting her selfe did stoutly kill;
And thousands moe the like that did that dongeon fill.

LI. Besides the endlesse routes of wretched thralles,
Which thither were assembled day by day
From all the world, after their wofull falles,
Through wicked pride and wasted welthes decay.
But most of all, which in that dongeon lay,
Fell from high Princes courtes, or Ladies bowres,
Where they in ydle pomp, or wanton play,
Consumed had their goods and thriftlesse howres,
And lastly thrown themselves into these heavy stowres.

LII. Whose case whenas the careful Dwarfe had tould,
And made ensample of their mournfull sight
Unto his Maister, he no lenger would
There dwell in perill of like painefull plight,
But earely rose; and, ere that dawning light
Discovered had the world to heaven wyde,
He by a privy Posterne tooke his flight,
That of no envious eyes he mote be spyde;
For, doubtlesse, death ensewd if any him descryde.

LIII. Scarse could he footing find in that fowle way,
For many corses, like a great Lay-stall,
Of murdred men, which therein strowed lay
Without remorse or decent funerall;
Which al through that great Princesse pride did fall,
And came to shamefull end. And them besyde,
Forth ryding underneath the castell wall,
A Donghill of dead carcases he spyde;
The dreadfull spectacle of that sad house of Pryde.

CANTO VI

From lawlesse lust by wondrous grace
Fayre Una is releast:
Whom salvage nation does adore,
And learnes her wise beheast.

1. As when a ship, that flyes fayre under sayle,
An hidden rocke escaped hath unwares,
That lay in waite her wrack for to bewaile,
The Marriner yet halfe amazed stares
At perill past, and yet in doubt ne dares
To joy at his foolhappie oversight:
So doubly is distrest twixt joy and cares
The dreadlesse corage of this Elfin knight,
Having escapt so sad ensamples in his sight.

2. Yet sad he was, that his too hastie speed
The fayre Duess' had forst him leave behind;
And yet more sad, that Una, his deare dreed,
Her truth hath staynd with treason so unkind:
Yet cryme in her could never creature find;
But for his love, and for her own selfe sake,
She wandred had from one to other Ynd,
Him for to seeke, ne ever would forsake,
Till her unwares the fiers Sansloy did overtake:

3. Who, after Archimagoes fowle defeat,
Led her away into a forest wilde;
And, turning wrathfull fyre to lustfull heat,
With beastly sin thought her to have defilde,
And made the vassall of his pleasures vilde.
Yet first he cast by treatie, and by traynes
Her to persuade that stubborne fort to yilde:
For greater conquest of hard love he gaynes,
That workes it to his will, then he that it constraines.

4. With fawning wordes he courted her a while;
And, looking lovely and oft sighing sore,
Her constant hart did tempt with diverse guile:

But wordes, and lookes, and sighes she did abhore;
As rock of Diamond stedfast evermore.
Yet for to feed his fyrie lustfull eye,
He snatcht the vele that hong her face before:
Then gan her beautie shyne as brightest skye,
And burnt his beastly hart t'efforce her chastitye.

v. So when he saw his flatt'ring artes to fayle,
And subtile engines bett from batteree;
With greedy force he gan the fort assayle,
Whereof he weend possessed soone to bee,
And win rich spoile of ransackt chastitee.
Ah heavens! that doe this hideous act behold,
And heavenly virgin thus outraged see,
How can ye vengeance just so long withhold,
And hurle not flashing flames upon that Paynim bold?

vi. The pitteous mayden, carefull, comfortlesse,
Does throw out thrilling shriekes, and shrieking cryes,
The last vaine helpe of wemens great distresse,
And with loud plaintes importuneth the skyes,
That molten starres doe drop like weeping eyes;
And Phœbus, flying so most shamefull sight,
His blushing face in foggy cloud implyes,
And hydes for shame.   What witt of mortal wight
Can now devise to quitt a thrall from such a plight?

vii. Eternall providence, exceeding thought,
Where none appeares can make her selfe a way.
A wondrous way it for this Lady wrought,
From Lyons clawes to pluck the gryped pray.
Her shrill outcryes and shrieks so loud did bray,
That all the woodes and forestes did resownd:
A troupe of Faunes and Satyres far away
Within the wood were dauncing in a rownd,
Whiles old Sylvanus slept in shady arber sownd:

viii. Who, when they heard that pitteous strained voice,
In haste forsooke their rurall meriment,
And ran towardes the far rebownded noyce,
To weet what wight so loudly did lament.
Unto the place they come incontinent:
Whom when the raging Sarazin espyde,

A rude, mishapen, monstrous rablement,
Whose like he never saw, he durst not byde,
But got his ready steed, and fast away gan ryde.

IX. The wyld woodgods, arrived in the place,
There find the virgin, doolfull, desolate,
With ruffled rayments, and fayre blubbred face,
As her outrageous foe had left her late;
And trembling yet through feare of former hate.
All stand amazed at so uncouth sight,
And gin to pittie her unhappie state:
All stand astonied at her beautie bright,
In their rude eyes unworthie of so wofull plight.

X. She, more amazd, in double dread doth dwell;
And every tender part for feare does shake.
As when a greedy Wolfe, through honger fell,
A seely Lamb far from the flock does take,
Of whom he meanes his bloody feast to make,
A Lyon spyes fast running towards him,
The innocent pray in hast he does forsake;
Which, quitt from death, yet quakes in every lim
With chaunge of feare, to see the Lyon looke so grim.

XI. Such fearefull fitt assaid her trembling hart,
Ne word to speake, ne joynt to move, she had;
The salvage nation feele her secret smart,
And read her sorrow in her count'nance sad;
Their frowning forheades, with rough hornes yclad,
And rustick horror, all asyde doe lay;
And, gently grenning, shew a semblance glad
To comfort her; and, feare to put away,
Their backward bent knees teach her humbly to obay.

XII. The doubtfull Damzell dare not yet committ
Her single person to their barbarous truth;
But still twixt feare and hope amazd does sitt,
Late learnd what harme to hasty trust ensu'th.
They, in compassion of her tender youth,
And wonder of her beautie soverayne,
Are wonne with pitty and unwonted ruth;
And, all prostrate upon the lowly playne,
Doe kisse her feete, and fawne on her with count'nance
fayne.

XIII. Their harts she ghesseth by their humble guise,
And yieldes her to extremitie of time:
So from the ground she fearelesse doth arise,
And walketh forth without suspect of crime.
They, all as glad as birdes of joyous Pryme,
Thence lead her forth, about her dauncing round,
Shouting, and singing all a shepheards ryme;
And with greene braunches strowing all the ground,
Do worship her as Queene with olive girlond cround.

XIV. And all the way their merry pipes they sound,
That all the woods with doubled Eccho ring;
And with their horned feet doe weare the ground,
Leaping like wanton kids in pleasant Spring.
So towards old Sylvanus they her bring;
Who, with the noyse awaked, commeth out
To weet the cause, his weake steps governing
And aged limbs on cypresse stadle stout;
And with an yvie twyne his waste is girt about.

XV. Far off he wonders what them makes so glad;
Or Bacchus merry fruit they did invent,
Or Cybeles franticke rites have made them mad:
They, drawing nigh, unto their God present
That flowre of fayth and beautie excellent.
The God himselfe, vewing that mirrhour rare,
Stood long amazd, and burnt in his intent:
His owne fayre Dryope now he thinkes not faire,
And Pholoe fowle, when her to this he doth compaire.

XVI. The woodborne people fall before her flat,
And worship her as Goddesse of the wood;
And old Sylvanus selfe bethinkes not what
To thinke of wight so fayre, but gazing stood
In doubt to deeme her borne of earthly brood:
Sometimes dame Venus selfe he seemes to see;
But Venus never had so sober mood:
Sometimes Diana he her takes to be,
But misseth bow and shaftes, and buskins to her knee.

XVII. By vew of her he ginneth to revive
His ancient love, and dearest Cyparisse;
And calles to mind his pourtraiture alive,

XXVI. And for to make his powre approved more,
     Wyld beastes in yron yokes he would compell;
     The spotted Panther, and the tusked Bore,
     The Pardale swift, and the Tigre cruell,
     The Antelope, and Wolfe both fiers and fell;
     And them constraine in equall teme to draw.
     Such joy he had their stubborne harts to quell,
     And sturdie courage tame with dreadfull aw,
     That his beheast they feared as a tyrans law.

XXVII. His loving mother came upon a day
     Unto the woodes, to see her little sonne;
     And chaunst unwares to meet him in the way,
     After his sportes and cruell pastime donne;
     When after him a Lyonesse did runne,
     That roaring all with rage did lowd requere
     Her children deare, whom he away had wonne:
     The Lyon whelpes she saw how he did beare,
     And lull in rugged armes withouten childish feare.

XXVIII. The fearefull Dame all quaked at the sight,
     And turning backe gan fast to fly away;
     Untill, with love revokt from vaine affright,
     She hardly yet perswaded was to stay,
     And then to him these womanish words gan say:
     " Ah Satyrane, my dearling and my joy,
     For love of me leave off this dreadfull play;
     To dally thus with death is no fit toy:
     Go, find some other play-fellowes, mine own sweet boy."

XXIX. In these and like delightes of bloody game
     He trayned was, till ryper years he raught;
     And there abode, whylst any beast of name
     Walkt in that forrest, whom he had not taught
     To feare his force: and then his courage haught
     Desyrd of forreine foemen to be knowne,
     And far abroad for strange adventures sought;
     In which his might was never overthrowne;
     But through al Faery lond his famous worth was blown.

XXX. Yet evermore it was his maner faire,
     After long labours and adventures spent,
     Unto those native woods for to repaire,

To see his syre and ofspring auncient.
And now he thither came for like intent;
Where he unwares the fairest Una found,
Straunge Lady in so straunge habiliment,
Teaching the Satyres, which her sat around,
Trew sacred lore, which from her sweet lips did redound.

XXXI. He wondred at her wisedome hevenly rare,
Whose like in womens witt he never knew;
And, when her curteous deeds he did compare,
Gan her admire, and her sad sorrowes rew,
Blaming of Fortune, which such troubles threw,
And joyd to make proofe of her cruelty
On gentle Dame, so hurtlesse and so trew:
Thenceforth he kept her goodly company,
And learnd her discipline of faith and verity.

XXXII. But she, all vowd unto the Redcrosse Knight,
His wandring perill closely did lament,
Ne in this new acquaintaunce could delight;
But her deare heart with anguish did torment,
And all her witt in secret counsels spent,
How to escape.   At last in privy wise
To Satyrane she shewed her intent;
Who, glad to gain such favour, gan devise,
How with that pensive Maid he best might thence arise.

XXXIII. So on a day, when Satyres all were gone
To do their service to Sylvanus old,
The gentle virgin, left behinde alone,
He led away with corage stout and bold.
Too late it was to Satyres to be told,
Or ever hope recover her againe:
In vaine he seekes that having cannot hold.
So fast he carried her with carefull paine,
That they the woods are past, and come now to the
      plaine.

XXXIV. The better part now of the lingring day
They traveild had, whenas they far espide
A weary wight forwandring by the way;
And towards him they gan in haste to ride,
To weete of newes that did abroad betide,
Or tidings of her knight of the Redcrosse;

But he them spying gan to turne aside
For feare, as seemd, or for some feigned losse:
More greedy they of newes fast towards him do crosse.

xxxv. A silly man, in simple weeds forworne,
And soild with dust of the long dried way;
His sandales were with toilsome travell torne,
And face all tand with scorching sunny ray,
As he had traveild many a sommers day
Through boyling sands of Arabie and Ynde,
And in his hand a Jacobs staffe, to stay
His weary limbs upon; and eke behind
His scrip did hang, in which his needments he did bind.

xxxvi. The knight, approching nigh, of him inquerd
Tidings of warre, and of adventures new;
But warres, nor new adventures, none he herd.
Then Una gan to aske, if ought he knew,
Or heard abroad of that her champion trew,
That in his armour bare a croslet red?
"Ay me! Deare dame," (quoth he) "well may I rew
To tell the sad sight which mine eies have red;
These eies did see that knight both living and eke ded."

xxxvii. That cruell word her tender hart so thrild,
That suddein cold did ronne through every vaine,
And stony horrour all her sences fild
With dying fitt, that downe she fell for paine.
The knight her lightly reared up againe,
And comforted with curteous kind reliefe:
Then, wonne from death, she bad him tellen plaine
The further processe of her hidden griefe:
The lesser pangs can beare who had endur'd the chief.

xxxviii. Then gan the Pilgrim thus: "I chaunst this day,
This fatall day that shall I ever rew,
To see two knights, in travell on my way,
(A sory sight) arraung'd in batteill new,
Both breathing vengeaunce, both of wrathfull hew.
My feareful flesh did tremble at their strife,
To see their blades so greedily imbrew,
That, dronke with blood, yet thristed after life:
What more? the Redcrosse knight was slain with
    Paynim knife."

XXXIX. "Ah! dearest Lord," (quoth she) "how might that bee,
And he the stoutest knight that ever wonne?"
"Ah! dearest dame," (quoth hee) "how might I see
The thing that might not be, and yet was donne?"
"Where is," (said Satyrane) "that Paynims sonne,
That him of life, and us of joy, hath refte?"
"Not far away," (quoth he) "he hence doth wonne,
Foreby a fountaine, where I late him lefte
Washing his bloody wounds, that through the steel
    were cleft."

XL. Therewith the knight thence marched forth in hast,
Whiles Una, with huge heavinesse opprest,
Could not for sorrow follow him so fast;
And soone he came, as he the place had ghest,
Whereas that Pagan proud him selfe did rest
In secret shadow by a fountaine side:
Even he it was, that earst would have supprest
Faire Una; whom when Satyrane espide,
With foule reprochfull words he boldly him defide.

XLI. And said; "Arise, thou cursed Miscreaunt,
That hast with knightlesse guile, and trecherous train,
Faire knighthood fowly shamed, and doest vaunt
That good knight of the Redcrosse to have slain:
Arise, and with like treason now maintain
The guilty wrong, or els thee guilty yield."
The Sarazin, this hearing, rose amain,
And, catching up in hast his three-square shield
And shining helmet, soone him buckled to the field.

XLII. And, drawing nigh him, said; "Ah! misborn Elfe,
In evill houre thy foes thee hither sent
Anothers wrongs to wreak upon thy selfe:
Yet ill thou blamest me for having blent
My name with guile and traiterous intent:
That Redcrosse knight, perdie, I never slew;
But had he beene where earst his armes were lent,
Th' enchaunter vaine his errour should not rew:
But thou his errour shalt, I hope, now proven trew."

XLIII. Therewith they gan, both furious and fell,
To thunder blowes, and fiersly to assaile

Each other, bent his enimy to quell,
That with their force they perst both plate and maile,
And made wide furrowes in their fleshes fraile,
That it would pitty any living eie.
Large floods of blood adowne their sides did raile,
But floods of blood could not them satisfie:
Both hongred after death; both chose to win, or die.

XLIV. So long they fight, and full revenge pursue,
That, fainting, each themselves to breathen lett,
And, ofte refreshed, battell oft renue.
As when two Bores, with rancling malice mett,
Their gory sides fresh bleeding fiercely frett;
Til breathlesse both themselves aside retire,
Where foming wrath their cruell tuskes they whett,
And trample th' earth, the whiles they may respire,
Then backe to fight againe, new breathed and entire.

XLV. So fiersly, when these knights had breathed once,
They gan to fight retourne, increasing more
Their puissant force, and cruell rage attonce,
With heaped strokes more hugely then before;
That with their drery wounds, and bloody gore,
They both, deformed, scarsely could bee known.
By this, sad Una fraught with anguish sore,
Led with their noise which through the aire was thrown,
Arriv'd wher they in erth their fruitles blood had sown.

XLVI. Whom all so soone as that proud Sarazin
Espide, he gan revive the memory
Of his leud lusts, and late attempted sin,
And lefte the doubtfull battell hastily,
To catch her, newly offred to his eie;
But Satyrane, with strokes him turning, staid,
And sternely bad him other businesse plie
Then hunt the steps of pure unspotted Maid:
Wherewith he al enrag'd these bitter speaches said.

XLVII. " O foolish faeries sonne! what fury mad
Hath thee incenst to hast thy dolefull fate?
Were it not better I that Lady had
Then that thou hadst repented it too late?
Most sencelesse man he, that himselfe doth hate,

To love another: Lo! then, for thine ayd,
Here take thy lovers token on thy pate."
So they to fight; the whiles the royall Mayd
Fledd farre away, of that proud Paynim sore afrayd.

XLVIII. But that false Pilgrim, which that leasing told
Being in deed old Archimage, did stay
In secret shadow all this to behold;
And much rejoyced in their bloody fray:
But, when he saw the Damsell passe away,
He left his stond, and her pursewd apace,
In hope to bring her to her last decay.
But for to tell her lamentable cace,
And eke this battels end, will need another place.

CANTO VII

The Redcrosse knight is captive made
By Tyaunt proud opprest:
Prince Arthure meets with Una great-
ly with those newes distrest.

I. WHAT man so wise, what earthly witt so ware,
   As to discry the crafty cunning traine,
   By which deceipt doth maske in visour faire,
   And cast her coulours, died deepe in graine,
   To seeme like truth, whose shape she well can faine,
   And fitting gestures to her purpose frame,
   The guiltlesse man with guile to entertaine?
   Great maistresse of her art was that false Dame,
   The false Duessa, cloked with Fidessaes name.

II. Who when, returning from the drery Night,
    She fownd not in that perilous hous of Pryde,
    Where she had left the noble Redcrosse knight,
    Her hoped pray, she would no lenger byde,
    But forth she went to seeke him far and wide.
    Ere long she fownd, whereas he wearie sate
    To reste him selfe foreby a fountaine syde,
    Disarmed all of yron-coted Plate;
    And by his side his steed the grassy forage ate.

III. Hee feedes upon the cooling shade, and bayes
     His sweatie forehead in the breathing wynd,
     Which through the trembling leaves full gently playes,
     Wherein the chearefull birds of sundry kynd
     Doe chaunt sweet musick to delight his mynd.
     The witch approching gan him fayrely greet,
     And with reproch of carelesnes unkynd
     Upbrayd, for leaving her in place unmeet,
     With fowle words tempring faire, soure gall with hony
        sweet.

IV. Unkindnesse past, they gan of solace treat,
    And bathe in pleasaunce of the joyous shade,

Which shielded them against the boyling heat,
And with greene boughes decking a gloomy glade,
About the fountaine like a girlond made;
Whose bubbling wave did ever freshly well,
Ne ever would through fervent sommer fade:
The sacred Nymph, which therein wont to dwell,
Was out of Dianes favor, as it then befell.

v. The cause was this: one day, when Phœbe fayre
With all her band was following the chace,
This nymph, quite tyr'd with heat of scorching ayre,
Satt downe to rest in middest of the race:
The goddesse wroth gan fowly her disgrace,
And badd the waters, which from her did flow,
Be such as she her selfe was then in place.
Thenceforth her waters wexed dull and slow,
And all that drinke thereof do faint and feeble grow.

vi. Hereof this gentle knight unweeting was;
And lying downe upon the sandie graile,
Dronke of the streame, as cleare as christall glas:
Eftsoones his manly forces gan to fayle,
And mightie strong was turnd to feeble frayle.
His chaunged powres at first them selves not felt;
Till crudled cold his corage gan assayle,
And chearefull blood in fayntnes chill did melt,
Which like a fever fit through all his bodie swelt.

vii. Yet goodly court he made still to his Dame,
Pourd out in loosnesse on the grassy grownd,
Both careless of his health, and of his fame;
Till at the last he heard a dreadfull sownd,
Which through the wood loud bellowing did rebownd,
That all the earth for terror seemd to shake,
And trees did tremble.   Th' Elfe, therewith astownd,
Upstarted lightly from his looser make,
And his unready weapons gan in hand to take.

viii. But ere he could his armour on him dight,
Or gett his shield, his monstrous enimy
With sturdie steps came stalking in his sight,
An hideous Geaunt, horrible and hye,
That with his tallnesse seemd to threat the skye;

The ground eke groned under him for dreed:
His living like saw never living eye,
Ne durst behold: his stature did exceed
The hight of three the tallest sonnes of mortall seed.

IX. The greatest Earth his uncouth mother was,
And blustring Æolus his boasted syre;
Who with his breath, which through the world doth pas,
Her hollow womb did secretly inspyre,
And fild her hidden caves with stormie yre,
That she conceiv'd; and trebling the dew time
In which the wombes of wemen doe expyre,
Brought forth this monstrous masse of earthly slyme,
Puft up with emptie wynd, and fild with sinfull cryme.

X. So growen great, through arrogant delight
Of th' high descent whereof he was yborne,
And through presumption of his matchlesse might,
All other powres and knighthood he did scorne.
Such now he marcheth to this man forlorne,
And left to losse; his stalking steps are stayde
Upon a snaggy Oke, which he had torne
Out of his mothers bowelles, and it made
His mortall mace, wherewith his foemen he dismayde.

XI. That, when the knight he spyde, he gan advaunce
With huge force and insupportable mayne,
And towardes him with dreadfull fury praunce;
Who haplesse, and eke hopelesse, all in vaine
Did to him pace sad battaile to darrayne,
Disarmd, disgraste, and inwardly dismayde;
And eke so faint in every joynt and vayne,
Through that fraile fountaine which him feeble made,
That scarsely could he weeld his bootlesse single blade.

XII. The Geaunt strooke so maynly mercilesse,
That could have overthrowne a stony towre;
And, were not hevenly grace that did him blesse,
He had beene pouldred all as thin as flowre:
But he was wary of that deadly stowre,
And lightly lept from underneath the blow:
Yet so exceeding was the villeins powre,
That with the winde it did him overthrow,
And all his sences stound that still he lay full low.

XIII. As when that divelish yron Engin, wrought
　　In deepest Hell, and framd by Furies skill,
　　With windy Nitre and quick Sulphur fraught,
　　And ramd with bollet rownd, ordaind to kill,
　　Conceiveth fyre, the heavens it doth fill
　　With thundring noyse, and all the ayre doth choke,
　　That none can breath, nor see, nor heare at will,
　　Through smouldry cloud of duskish stincking smoke;
　　That th' only breath him daunts, who hath escapt the
　　　　stroke.

XIV. So daunted when the Geaunt saw the knight,
　　His heavie hand he heaved up on hye,
　　And him to dust thought to have battred quight,
　　Untill Duessa loud to him gan crye,
　　" O great Orgoglio! greatest under skye,
　　O! hold thy mortall hand for Ladies sake;
　　Hold for my sake, and doe him not to dye,
　　But vanquisht thine eternall bondslave make,
　　And me, thy worthy meed, unto thy Leman take."

XV. He hearkned, and did stay from further harmes,
　　To gayne so goodly guerdon as she spake:
　　So willingly she came into his armes,
　　Who her as willingly to grace did take,
　　And was possessed of his newfound make,
　　Then up he tooke the slombred sencelesse corse,
　　And, ere he could out of his swowne awake,
　　Him to his castle brought with hastie forse,
　　And in a Dongeon deepe him threw without remorse.

XVI. From that day forth Duessa was his deare,
　　And highly honoured in his haughtie eye:
　　He gave her gold and purple pall to weare,
　　And triple crowne set on her head full hye,
　　And her endowd with royall majestye.
　　Then, for to make her dreaded more of men,
　　And peoples hartes with awfull terror tye,
　　A monstrous beast ybredd in filthy fen
　　He chose, which he had kept long time in darksom den.

XVII. Such one it was, as that renowmed Snake
　　Which great Alcides in Stremona slew,
　　Long fostred in the filth of Lerna lake:

Whose many heades, out budding ever new,
Did breed him endlesse labor to subdew.
But this same Monster much more ugly was,
For seven great heads out of his body grew,
An yron brest, and back of scaly bras,
And all embrewd in blood his eyes did shine as glas.

xviii. His tayle was stretched out in wondrous length,
That to the hous of hevenly gods it raught:
And with extorted powre, and borrow'd strength,
The everburning lamps from thence it braught,
And prowdly threw to ground, as things of naught;
And underneath his filthy feet did tread
The sacred thinges, and holy heastes foretaught.
Upon this dreadfull Beast with sevenfold head
He sett the false Duessa, for more aw and dread.

xix. The wofull Dwarfe, which saw his maisters fall
Whiles he had keeping of his grasing steed,
And valiant knight become a caytive thrall,
When all was past, tooke up his forlorne weed;
His mightie Armour, missing most at need;
His silver shield, now idle, maisterlesse;
His poynant speare that many made to bleed,
The rueful moniments of heavinesse;
And with them all departes to tell his great distresse.

xx. He had not travaild long, when on the way
He wofull Lady, wofull Una, met,
Fast flying from that Paynims greedy pray,
Whilest Satyrane him from pursuit did let:
Who when her eyes she on the Dwarf had set,
And saw the signes that deadly tydings spake,
She fell to ground for sorrowfull regret,
And lively breath her sad brest did forsake;
Yet might her pitteous hart be seene to pant and quake.

xxi. The messenger of so unhappie newes
Would faine have dyde: dead was his hart within,
Yet outwardly some little comfort shewes.
At last, recovering hart, he does begin
To rubb her temples, and to chaufe her chin,
And everie tender part does tosse and turne:

So hardly he the flitted life does win
Unto her native prison to retourne;
Then gins her grieved ghost thus to lament and mourne:

XXII. " Ye dreary instruments of dolefull sight,
That doe this deadly spectacle behold,
Why doe ye lenger feed on loathed light,
Or liking find to gaze on earthly mould,
Sith cruell fates the carefull threds unfould,
The which my life and love together tyde?
Now let the stony dart of sencelesse cold
Perce to my hart, and pas through everie side,
And let eternall night so sad sight fro me hyde.

XXIII. " O lightsome day! the lampe of highest Jove,
First made by him mens wandring wayes to guyde,
When darknesse he in deepest dongeon drove,
Henceforth thy hated face for ever hyde,
And shut up heavens windowes shyning wyde;
For earthly sight can nought but sorrow breed,
And late repentance which shall long abyde:
Mine eyes no more on vanitie shall feed,
But seeled up with death shall have their deadly meed."

XXIV. Then downe againe she fell unto the ground,
But he her quickly reared up againe:
Thrise did she sinke adowne in deadly swownd,
And thrise he her reviv'd with busie paine.
At last when life recover'd had the raine,
And over-wrestled his strong enimy,
With foltring tong, and trembling everie vaine,
" Tell on," (quoth she) " the wofull Tragedy,
The which these reliques sad present unto mine eye.

XXV. " Tempestuous fortune hath spent all her spight,
And thrilling sorrow throwne his utmost dart:
Thy sad tong cannot tell more heavy plight
Then that I feele, and harbour in mine hart:
Who hath endur'd the whole can beare ech part.
If death it be, it is not the first wound
That launched hath my brest with bleeding smart.
Begin, and end the bitter balefull stound;
If lesse then that I feare, more favour I have found."

XXVI. Then gan the Dwarfe the whole discourse declare;
The subtile traines of Archimago old;
The wanton loves of false Fidessa fayre,
Bought with the blood of vanquisht Paynim bold;
The wretched payre transformd to treën mould;
The house of Pryde, and perilles round about;
The combat which he with Sansjoy did hould;
The lucklesse conflict with the Gyaunt stout,
Wherein captiv'd, of life or death he stood in doubt.

XXVII. She heard with patience all unto the end,
And strove to maister sorrowfull assay,
Which greater grew the more she did contend,
And almost rent her tender hart in tway;
And love fresh coles unto her fire did lay;
For greater love, the greater is the losse.
Was never Lady loved dearer day
Then she did love the knight of the Redcrosse,
For whose deare sake so many troubles her did tosse.

XXVIII. At last when fervent sorrow slaked was,
She up arose, resolving him to find
Alive or dead; and forward forth doth pas,
All as the Dwarfe the way to her assynd;
And evermore, in constant carefull mind,
She fedd her wound with fresh renewed bale.
Long tost with stormes, and bet with bitter wind,
High over hills, and lowe adowne the dale,
She wandred many a wood, and measurd many a vale.

XXIX. At last she chaunced by good hap to meet
A goodly knight, faire marching by the way,
Together with his Squyre, arayed meet:
His glitterand armour shined far away,
Like glaunging light of Phœbus brightest ray;
From top to toe no place appeared bare,
That deadly dint of steele endanger may.
Athwart his brest a bauldrick brave he ware,
That shind, like twinkling stars, with stones most
    pretious rare.

XXX. And in the midst thereof one pretious stone
Of wondrous worth, and eke of wondrous mights,
Shapt like a Ladies head, exceeding shone,

I   D

Like Hesperus emongst the lesser lights,
And strove for to amaze the weaker sights:
Thereby his mortall blade full comely hong
In yvory sheath, ycarv'd with curious slights,
Whose hilts were burnisht gold, and handle strong
Of mother perle; and buckled with a golden tong.

XXXI. His haughtie Helmet, horrid all with gold,
Both glorious brightnesse and great terrour bredd:
For all the crest a Dragon did enfold
With greedie pawes, and over all did spredd
His golden winges: his dreadfull hideous hedd,
Close couched on the bever, seemd to throw
From flaming mouth bright sparckles fiery redd,
That suddeine horrour to faint hartes did show;
And scaly tayle was stretcht adowne his back full low.

XXXII. Upon the top of all his loftie crest,
A bounch of heares discoloured diversly,
With sprincled pearle and gold full richly drest,
Did shake, and seemd to daunce for jollity,
Like to an almond tree ymounted hye
On top of greene Selinis all alone,
With blossoms brave bedecked daintily;
Whose tender locks do tremble every one
At everie little breath that under heaven is blowne.

XXXIII. His warlike shield all closely cover'd was,
Ne might of mortall eye be ever seene;
Not made of steele, nor of enduring bras,
Such earthly mettals soon consumed beene,
But all of Diamond perfect pure and cleene
It framed was, one massy entire mould,
Hewen out of Adamant rocke with engines keene,
That point of speare it never percen could,
Ne dint of direfull sword divide the substance would.

XXXIV. The same to wight he never wont disclose,
But whenas monsters huge he would dismay,
Or daunt unequall armies of his foes,
Or when the flying heavens he would affray;
For so exceeding shone his glistring ray,
That Phœbus golden face it did attaint,

As when a cloud his beames doth over-lay;
And silver Cynthia wexed pale and faynt,
As when her face is staynd with magicke arts constraint.

xxxv. No magicke arts hereof had any might,
Nor bloody wordes of bold Enchaunters call;
But all that was not such as seemd in sight
Before that shield did fade, and suddeine fall:
And when him list the raskall routes appall,
Men into stones therewith he could transmew,
And stones to dust, and dust to nought at all;
And, when him list the prouder lookes subdew,
He would them gazing blind, or turne to other hew.

xxxvi. Ne let it seeme that credence this exceedes;
For he that made the same was knowne right well
To have done much more admirable deedes.
It Merlin was, which whylome did excell
All living wightes in might of magicke spell:
Both shield and sword, and armour all he wrought
For this young Prince, when first to armes he fell;
But, when he dyde, the Faery Queene it brought
To Faerie lond, where yet it may be seene, if sought:

xxxvii. A gentle youth, his dearely loved Squire,
His speare of heben wood behind him bare,
Whose harmefull head, thrise heated in the fire,
Had riven many a brest with pikehead square:
A goodly person, and could menage faire
His stubborne steed with curbed canon bitt,
Who under him did trample as the aire,
And chauft that any on his backe should sitt:
The yron rowels into frothy fome he bitt.

xxxviii. Whenas this knight nigh to the Lady drew,
With lovely court he gan her entertaine;
But, when he heard her answers loth, he knew
Some secret sorrow did her heart distraine;
Which to allay, and calme her storming paine,
Faire feeling words he wisely gan display,
And for her humor fitting purpose faine,
To tempt the cause it selfe for to bewray,
Wherewith enmovd, these bleeding words she gan to say.

XXXIX. "What worlds delight, or joy of living speach,
    Can hart, so plungd in sea of sorrowes deep,
    And heaped with so huge misfortunes, reach?
    The carefull cold beginneth for to creep,
    And in my heart his yron arrow steep,
    Soone as I thinke upon my bitter bale.
    Such helplesse harmes yts better hidden keep,
    Then rip up griefe where it may not availe:
    My last left comfort is my woes to weepe and waile."

XL. "Ah Lady deare," quoth then the gentle knight,
    "Well may I ween your griefe is wondrous great;
    For wondrous great griefe groneth in my spright,
    Whiles thus I heare you of your sorrowes treat.
    But, woefull Lady, let me you intrete,
    For to unfold the anguish of your hart:
    Mishaps are maistred by advice discrete,
    And counsell mitigates the greatest smart:
    Found never help who never would his hurts impart."

XLI. "O but," (quoth she) "great greife will not be tould,
    And can more easily be thought then said."
    "Right so," (quoth he) "but he that never would
    Could never: will to might gives greatest aid."
    "But griefe," (quoth she) "does greater grow displaid,
    If then it find not helpe, and breeds despaire."
    "Despaire breeds not," (quoth he) "where faith is staid."
    "No faith so fast," (quoth she) "but flesh does paire."
    "Flesh may empaire," (quoth he) "but reason can repaire."

XLII. His goodly reason, and well guided speach,
    So deepe did settle in her gracious thought,
    That her perswaded to disclose the breach
    Which love and fortune in her heart had wrought;
    And said; "Faire Sir, I hope good hap hath brought
    You to inquere the secrets of my griefe,
    Or that your wisedome will direct my thought,
    Or that your prowesse can me yield reliefe:
    Then, heare the story sad, which I shall tell you briefe.

XLIII. "The forlorne Maiden, whom your eies have seene
    The laughing stocke of fortunes mockeries,
    Am th' onely daughter of a King and Queene,

Whose parents deare, whiles equal destinies
Did ronne about, and their felicities
The favourable heavens did not envy,
Did spred their rule through all the territories,
Which Phison and Euphrates floweth by,
And Gehons golden waves doe wash continually:

XLIV. " Till that their cruell cursed enemy,
An huge great Dragon, horrible in sight,
Bred in the loathly lakes of Tartary,
With murdrous ravine, and devouring might,
Their kingdome spoild, and countrey wasted quight:
Themselves, for feare into his jawes to fall,
He forst to castle strong to take their flight;
Where, fast embard in mighty brasen wall,
He has them now fowr yeares besieged to make them thrall.

XLV. " Full many knights, adventurous and stout,
Have enterpriz'd that Monster to subdew:
From every coast that heaven walks about
Have thither come the noble Martial crew.
That famous harde atchievements still pursew;
Yet never any could that girlond win,
But all still shronke, and still he greater grew:
All they, for want of faith, or guilt of sin,
The pitteous pray of his fiers cruelty have bin.

XLVI. " At last, yled with far reported praise,
Which flying fame throughout the world had spred,
Of doughty knights, whom Faery land did raise,
That noble order hight of maidenhed,
Forthwith to court of Gloriane I sped,
Of Gloriane, great Queene of glory bright,
Whose kingdomes seat Cleopolis is red;
There to obtaine some such redoubted knight,
That Parents deare from tyrants powre deliver might.

XLVII. " Yt was my chaunce (my chaunce was faire and good)
There for to find a fresh unproved knight;
Whose manly hands imbrewd in guilty blood
Had never beene, ne ever by his might
Had throwne to ground the unregarded right:
Yet of his prowesse proofe he since hath made

(I witnes am) in many a cruell fight;
The groning ghosts of many one dismaide
Have felt the bitter dint of his avenging blade.

XLVIII. "An ye, the forlorne reliques of his powre,
His biting sword, and his devouring speare,
Which have endured many a dreadfull stowre,
Can speake his prowesse that did earst you beare,
And well could rule; now he hath left you heare
To be the record of his ruefull losse,
And of my dolefull disaventurous deare.
O! heavie record of the good Redcrosse,
Where have yee left your lord that could so well you
        tosse?

XLIX. "Well hoped I, and faire beginnings had,
That he my captive langour should redeeme:
Till, all unweeting, an Enchaunter bad
His sence abused, and made him to misdeeme
My loyalty, not such as it did seeme,
That rather death desire then such despight.
Be judge, ye heavens, that all things right esteeme,
How I him lov'd, and love with all my might.
So thought I eke of him, and think I thought aright.

L. "Thenceforth me desolate he quite forsooke,
To wander where wilde fortune would me lead,
And other bywaies he himselfe betooke,
Where never foote of living wight did tread,
That brought not backe the balefull body dead:
In which him chaunced false Duessa meete,
Mine onely foe, mine onely deadly dread;
Who with her witchcraft, and misseeming sweete,
Inveigled him to follow her desires unmeete.

LI. "At last, by subtile sleights she him betraid
Unto his foe, a Gyaunt huge and tall;
Who him disarmed, dissolute, dismaid,
Unwares surprised, and with mighty mall
The monster mercilesse him made to fall,
Whose fall did never foe before behold:
And now in darkesome dungeon, wretched thrall,
Remedilesse for aie he doth him hold.
This is my cause of griefe, more great then may be told."

LII. Ere she had ended all she gan to faint:
But he her comforted, and faire bespake:
" Certes, Madame, ye have great cause of plaint;
That stoutest heart, I weene, could cause to quake:
But be of cheare, and comfort to you take;
For till I have acquitt your captive knight,
Assure your selfe I will you not forsake."
His chearefull words reviv'd her chearelesse spright,
So forth they went, the Dwarfe them guiding ever right.

CANTO VIII

Faire virgin, to redeeme her deare,
Brings Arthure to the fight:
Who slayes the Gyaunt, wounds the beast,
And strips Duessa quight.

I. Ay me! how many perils doe enfold
The righteous man, to make him daily fall,
Were not that heavenly grace doth him uphold,
And stedfast truth acquite him out of all.
Her love is firme, her care continuall,
So oft as he, through his own foolish pride
Or weakness, is to sinfull bands made thrall:
Els should this Redcrosse knight in bands have dyde,
For whose deliverance she this Prince doth thither guyd.

II. They sadly traveild thus, untill they came
Nigh to a castle builded strong and hye:
Then cryde the Dwarfe, " Lo! yonder is the same,
In which my Lord, my liege, doth lucklesse ly
Thrall to that Gyaunts hatefull tyranny:
Therefore, deare Sir, your mightie powres assay."
The noble knight alighted by and by
From loftie steed, and badd the Ladie stay,
To see what end of fight should him befall that day.

III. So with his Squire, th' admirer of his might,
He marched forth towardes that castle wall,
Whose gates he fownd fast shutt, ne living wight
To warde the same, nor answere commers call.
Then tooke that Squire an horne of bugle small,
Which hong adowne his side in twisted gold
And tasselles gay.   Wyde wonders over all
Of that same hornes great virtues weren told,
Which had approved bene in uses manifold.

IV. Was never wight that heard that shrilling sownd,
But trembling feare did feel in every vaine:
Three miles it might be easy heard arownd,

And Ecchoes three aunswer'd it selfe againe:
No false enchauntment, nor deceiptfull traine,
Might once abide the terror of that blast,
But presently was void and wholly vaine:
No gate so strong, no locke so firme and fast,
But with that percing noise flew open quite, or brast.

v. The same before the Geaunts gate he blew,
That all the castle quaked from the grownd,
And every dore of freewill open flew.
The Gyaunt selfe, dismaied with that sownd,
Where he with his Duessa dalliaunce fownd,
In hast came rushing forth from inner bowre,
With staring countenance sterne, as one astownd,
And staggering steps, to weet what suddein stowre
Had wrought that horror strange, and dar'd his dreaded
        powre.

vi. And after him the proud Duessa came,
High mounted on her many headed beast,
And every head with fyrie tongue did flame,
And every head was crowned on his creast,
And bloody mouthed with late cruell feast.
That when the knight beheld, his mightie shild
Upon his manly arme he soone addrest,
And at him fiersly flew, with corage fild,
And eger greedinesse through every member thrild.

vii. Therewith the Gyant buckled him to fight,
Inflamd with scornefull wrath and high disdaine,
And lifting up his dreadfull club on hight,
All armd with ragged snubbes and knottie graine,
Him thought at first encounter to have slaine.
But wise and wary was that noble Pere;
And, lightly leaping from so monstrous maine,
Did fayre avoide the violence him nere:
It booted nought to thinke such thunderbolts to beare.

viii. Ne shame he thought to shonne so hideous might:
The ydle stroke, enforcing furious way,
Missing the marke of his misaymed sight,
Did fall to ground, and with his heavy sway
So deepely dinted in the driven clay,
That three yardes deepe a furrow up did throw.

The sad earth, wounded with so sore assay,
Did grone full grievous underneath the blow,
And trembling with strange feare did like an erthquake
    show.

IX. As when almightie Jove, in wrathfull mood,
To wreake the guilt of mortall sins is bent,
Hurles forth his thundring dart with deadly food
Enrold in flames, and smouldring dreriment,
Through riven cloudes and molten firmament;
The fiers threeforked engin, making way,
Both loftie towres and highest trees hath rent,
And all that might his angry passage stay;
And, shooting in the earth, castes up a mount of clay.

X. His boystrous club, so buried in the grownd,
He could not rearen up againe so light,
But that the Knight him at advantage fownd;
And, whiles he strove his combred clubbe to quight
Out of the earth, with blade all burning bright
He smott off his left arme, which like a block
Did fall to ground, depriv'd of native might:
Large streames of blood out of the truncked stock
Forth gushed, like fresh water streame from riven rocke.

XI. Dismayed with so desperate deadly wound,
And eke impatient of unwonted payne,
He loudly brayd with beastly yelling sownd,
That all the fieldes rebellowed againe.
As great a noyse, as when in Cymbrian plaine
An heard of Bulles, whom kindly rage doth sting,
Doe for the milky mothers want complaine,
And fill the fieldes with troublous bellowing:
The neighbor woods arownd with hollow murmur ring.

XII. That when his deare Duessa heard, and saw
The evil stownd that daungerd her estate,
Unto his aide she hastily did draw
Her dreadfull beast; who, swolne with blood of late,
Came ramping forth with proud presumpteous gate,
And threatned all his heades like flaming brandes.
But him the Squire made quickly to retrate,
Encountring fiers with single sword in hand;
And twixt him and his Lord did like a bulwarke stand.

XIII. The proud Duessa, full of wrathfull spight,
And fiers disdaine to be affronted so,
Enforst her purple beast with all her might,
That stop out of the way to overthroe,
Scorning the let of so unequall foe:
But nathemore would that corageous swayne
To her yeeld passage gainst his Lord to goe,
But with outrageous strokes did him restraine,
And with his body bard the way atwixt them twaine.

XIV. Then tooke the angrie witch her golden cup,
Which still she bore, replete with magick artes;
Death and despeyre did many thereof sup,
And secret poyson through their inner partes,
Th' eternall bale of heavie wounded harts:
Which, after charmes and some enchauntments said,
She lightly sprinkled on his weaker partes:
Therewith his sturdie corage soon was quayd,
And all his sences were with suddein dread dismayd.

XV. So downe he fell before the cruell beast,
Who on his neck his bloody clawes did seize,
That life nigh crusht out of his panting brest:
No powre he had to stirre, nor will to rize.
That when the carefull knight gan well avise,
He lightly left the foe with whom he fought,
And to the beast gan turne his enterprise;
For wondrous anguish in his hart it wrought,
To see his loved Squyre into such thraldom brought:

XVI. And, high advauncing his blood-thirstie blade,
Stroke one of those deformed heades so sore,
That of his puissaunce proud ensample made:
His monstrous scalpe downe to his teeth it tore,
And that misformed shape misshaped more.
A sea of blood gusht from the gaping wownd,
That her gay garments staynd with filthy gore,
And overflowed all the field arownd,
That over shoes in blood he waded on the grownd.

XVII. Thereat he rored for exceeding paine,
That to have heard great horror would have bred;
And scourging th' emptie ayre with his long trayne,

Through great impatience of his grieved hed,
His gorgeous ryder from her loftie sted
Would have cast downe, and trodd in durty myre,
Had not the Gyaunt soone her succoured;
Who, all enrag'd with smart and frantick yre,
Came hurtling in full fiers, and forst the knight retyre.

XVIII. The force, which wont in two to be disperst,
In one alone left hand he now unites,
Which is through rage more strong then both were erst;
With which his hideous club aloft he dites,
And at his foe with furious rigor smites,
That strongest Oake might seeme to overthrow.
The stroke upon his shield so heavie lites,
That to the ground it doubleth him full low:
What mortall wight could ever beare so monstrous blow?

XIX. And in his fall his shield, that covered was,
Did loose his vele by chaunce, and open flew;
The light whereof, that hevens light did pas,
Such blazing brightnesse through the ayer threw,
That eye mote not the same endure to vew.
Which when the Gyaunt spyde with staring eye,
He downe let fall his arme, and soft withdrew
His weapon huge, that heaved was on hye
For to have slaine the man, that on the ground did lye.

XX. And eke the fruitfull-headed beast, amazd
At flashing beames of that sunshiny shield,
Became stark blind, and all his sences dazd,
That downe he tumbled on the durtie field,
And seemd himselfe as conquered to yield.
Whom when his maistresse proud perceiv'd to fall,
Whiles yet his feeble feet for faintnesse reeld,
Unto the Gyaunt lowdly she gan call;
" O! helpe, Orgoglio; helpe! or els we perish all."

XXI. At her so pitteous cry was much amoov'd
Her champion stout; and for to ayde his frend,
Againe his wonted angry weapon proov'd,
But all in vaine, for he has redd his end
In that bright shield, and all their forces spend
Them selves in vaine: for, since that glauncing sight,

He hath no powre to hurt, nor to defend.
As where th' Almighties lightning brond does light,
It dimmes the dazed eyen, and daunts the sences quight.

XXII. Whom when the Prince, to batteill new addrest
And threatning high his dreadfull stroke, did see,
His sparkling blade about his head he blest,
And smote off quite his right leg by the knee,
That downe he tombled; as an aged tree,
High growing on the top of rocky clift,
Whose hartstrings with keene steele nigh hewen be;
The mightie trunck, halfe rent with ragged rift,
Doth roll adowne the rocks, and fall with fearefull drift.

XXIII. Or as a Castle, reared high and round,
By subtile engins and malitious slight
Is undermined from the lowest ground,
And her foundation forst, and feebled quight,
At last downe falles; and with her heaped hight
Her hastie ruine does more heavie make,
And yields it selfe unto the victours might:
Such was this Gyaunts fall, that seemd to shake
The stedfast globe of earth, as it for feare did quake.

XXIV. The knight, then lightly leaping to the pray,
With mortall steele him smot againe so sore,
That headlesse his unweldy bodie lay,
All wallowd in his owne fowle bloody gore,
Which flowed from his wounds in wondrous store.
But, soone as breath out of his brest did pas,
That huge great body, which the Gyaunt bore,
Was vanisht quite; and of that monstrous mas
Was nothing left, but like an emptie blader was.

XXV. Whose grievous fall when false Duessa spyde,
Her golden cup she cast unto the ground,
And crowned mitre rudely threw asyde:
Such percing griefe her stubborne hart did wound,
That she could not endure that dolefull stound
But leaving all behind her fled away:
The light-foot Squyre her quickly turnd around,
And, by hard meanes enforcing her to stay,
So brought unto his Lord as his deserved pray.

XXVI.   The roiall Virgin which beheld from farre,
    In pensive plight and sad perplexitie,
    The whole atchievement of this doubtfull warre,
    Came running fast to greet his victorie,
    With sober gladnesse and myld modestie;
    And with sweet joyous cheare him thus bespake:
    " Fayre braunch of noblesse, flowre of chevalrie,
    That with your worth the world amazed make,
    How shall I quite the paynes ye suffer for my sake?

XXVII.   " And you, fresh budd of vertue springing fast,
    Whom these sad eyes saw nigh unto deaths dore,
    What hath poore Virgin for such perill past
    Wherewith you to reward?   Accept therefore
    My simple selfe, and service evermore:
    And he that high does sit, and all things see
    With equall eye, their merites to restore,
    Behold what ye this day have done for mee,
    And what I cannot quite requite with usuree.

XXVIII.   " But sith the heavens, and your faire handeling,
    Have made you master of the field this day,
    Your fortune maister eke with governing,
    And, well begonne, end all so well, I pray!
    Ne let that wicked woman scape away;
    For she it is, that did my Lord bethrall,
    My dearest Lord, and deepe in dongeon lay,
    Where he his better dayes hath wasted all:
    O heare, how piteous he to you for ayd does call! "

XXIX.   Forthwith he gave in charge unto his Squyre,
    That scarlot whore to keepen carefully;
    Whyles he himselfe with greedie great desyre
    Into the Castle entred forcibly,
    Where living creature none he did espye.
    Then gan he lowdly through the house to call,
    But no man car'd to answere to his crye:
    There raignd a solemne silence over all:
    Nor voice was heard, nor wight was seene in bowre or hall.

XXX.   At last, with creeping crooked pace forth came
    An old old man, with beard as white as snow,
    That on a staffe his feeble steps did frame,

And guyde his wearie gate both too and fro,
For his eye sight him fayled long ygo;
And on his arme a bounch of keyes he bore,
The which unused rust did overgrow:
Those were the keyes of every inner dore;
But he could not them use, but kept them still in store.

XXXI. But very uncouth sight was to behold,
How he did fashion his untoward pace;
For as he forward moovd his footing old,
So backward still was turnd his wrincled face:
Unlike to men, who ever, as they trace,
Both feet and face one way are wont to lead.
This was the auncient keeper of that place,
And foster father of the Gyaunt dead;
His name Ignaro did his nature right aread.

XXXII. His reverend heares and holy gravitee
The knight much honord, as beseemed well;
And gently askt, where all the people bee,
Which in that stately building wont to dwell:
Who answerd him full soft, *he could not tell.*
Again he askt, where that same knight was layd,
Whom great Orgoglio with his puissaunce fell
Had made his caytive thrall: againe he sayde,
He could not tell ; ne ever other answere made.

XXXIII. Then asked he, which way he in might pas?
He could not tell, againe he answered.
Thereat the courteous knight displeased was,
And said; " Old syre, it seemes thou hast not red
How ill it sits with that same silver hed,
In vaine to mocke, or mockt in vaine to bee:
But if thou be, as thou art pourtrahed
With natures pen, in ages grave degree,
Aread in graver wise what I demaund of thee."

XXXIV. His answere likewise was, *he could not tell :*
Whose sencelesse speach, and doted ignorance,
Whenas the noble Prince had marked well,
He ghest his nature by his countenance,
And calmd his wrath with goodly temperance.
Then, to him stepping, from his arme did reach
Those keyes, and made himselfe free enterance.

Each dore he opened without any breach,
There was no barre to stop, nor foe him to empeach.

XXXV. There all within full rich arayd he found,
With royall arras, and resplendent gold,
And did with store of every thing abound,
That greatest Princes presence might behold.
But all the floore (too filthy to be told)
With blood of guiltlesse babes, and innocents trew,
Which there were slaine as sheepe out of the fold,
Defiled was, that dreadfull was to vew;
And sacred ashes over it was strowed new.

XXXVI. And there beside of marble stone was built
An Altare, carv'd with cunning ymagery,
On which trew Christians blood was often spilt,
And holy Martyres often doen to dye
With cruell malice and strong tyranny:
Whose blessed sprites, from underneath the stone,
To God for vengeance cryde continually;
And with great griefe were often heard to grone,
That hardest heart would bleede to hear their piteous
mone.

XXXVII. Through every rowme he sought, and everie bowr,
But no where could he find that wofull thrall:
At last he came unto an yron doore,
That fast was lockt, but key found not at all
Emongst that bounch to open it withall;
But in the same a little grate was pight,
Through which he sent his voyce, and lowd did call
With all his powre, to weet if living wight
Were housed therewithin, whom he enlargen might.

XXXVIII. Therewith an hollow, dreary, murmuring voyce
These pitteous plaintes and dolours did resound:
" O! who is that, which bringes me happy choyce
Of death, that here lye dying every stound,
Yet live perforce in balefull darkenesse bound?
For now three Moones have changed thrice their hew,
And have been thrice hid underneath the ground,
Since I the heavens chearefull face did vew.
O! welcome thou, that doest of death bring tydings
trew."

XXXIX. Which when that Champion heard, with percing point
Of pitty deare his hart was thrilled sore;
And trembling horrour ran through every joynt,
For ruth of gentle knight so fowle forlore;
Which shaking off, he rent that yron dore
With furious force and indignation fell;
Where entred in, his foot could find no flore,
But all a deepe descent, as darke as hell,
That breathed ever forth a filthie banefull smell.

XL. But nether darkenesse fowle, nor filthy bands,
Nor noyous smell, his purpose could withhold,
(Entire affection hateth nicer hands)
But that with constant zele and corage bold,
After long paines and labors manifold,
He found the meanes that Prisoner up to reare;
Whose feeble thighes, unable to uphold
His pined corse, him scarse to light could beare;
A ruefull spectacle of death and ghastly drere.

XLI. His sad dull eies, deepe sunck in hollow pits,
Could not endure th' unwonted sunne to view;
His bare thin cheekes for want of better bits,
And empty sides deceived of their dew,
Could make a stony hart his hap to rew;
His rawbone armes, whose mighty brawned bowrs
Were wont to rive steele plates, and helmets hew,
Were clene consum'd; and all his vitall powres
Decayd, and all his flesh shronk up like withered flowers.

XLII. Whome when his Lady saw, to him she ran
With hasty joy: to see him made her glad,
And sad to view his visage pale and wan,
Who earst in flowres of freshest youth was clad.
Tho, when her well of teares she wasted had,
She said; " Ah dearest Lord! what evill starre
On you hath frownd, and pourd his influence bad,
That of your selfe ye thus berobbed arre,
And this misseeming hew your manly looks doth marre?

XLIII. " But welcome now, my Lord in wele or woe,
Whose presence I have lackt too long a day:
And fie on Fortune, mine avowed foe,

Whose wrathful wreakes them selves doe now alay;
And for these wronges shall treble penaunce pay
Of treble good: good growes of evils priefe."
The chearelesse man, whom sorrow did dismay,
Had no delight to treaten of his griefe;
His long endured famine needed more reliefe.

XLIV. "Faire Lady," then said that victorious knight,
"The things, that grievous were to doe, or beare,
Them to renew, I wote, breeds no delight;
Best musicke breeds delight in loathing eare:
But th' only good that growes of passed feare
Is to be wise, and ware of like agein.
This daies ensample hath this lesson deare
Deepe written in my heart with yron pen,
That blisse may not abide in state of mortall men.

XLV. "Henceforth, Sir knight, take to you wonted strength,
And maister these mishaps with patient might.
Loe! where your foe lies stretcht in monstrous length;
And loe! that wicked woman in your sight,
The roote of all your care and wretched plight,
Now in your powre, to let her live, or die."
"To doe her die," (quoth Una) "were despight,
And shame t'avenge so weake an enimy;
But spoile her of her scarlot robe, and let her fly."

XLVI. So, as she bad, that witch they disaraid,
And robd of roiall robes, and purple pall,
And ornaments that richly were displaid;
Ne spared they to strip her naked all.
Then, when they had despoyld her tire and call,
Such as she was their eies might her behold,
That her misshaped parts did them appall:
A loathly, wrinckled hag, ill favoured, old,
Whose secret filth good manners biddeth not be told.

XLVII. Her crafty head was altogether bald,
And, as in hate of honorable eld,
Was overgrowne with scurfe and filthy scald;
Her teeth out of her rotten gummes were feld,
And her sowre breath abhominably smeld;
Her dried dugs, lyke bladders lacking wind,

Hong downe, and filthy matter from them weld;
Her wrizled skin, as rough as maple rind,
So scabby was that would have loathd all womankind.

XLVIII. Her neather parts, the shame of all her kind,
My chaster Muse for shame doth blush to write;
But at her rompe she growing had behind
A foxes taile, with dong all fowly dight;
And eke her feete most monstrous were in sight;
For one of them was like an Eagles claw,
With griping talaunts armd to greedy fight;
The other like a beares uneven paw,
More ugly shape yet never living creature saw.

XLIX. Which when the knights beheld amazd they were,
And wondred at so fowle deformed wight.
" Such then," (said Una,) " as she seemeth here,
Such is the face of falshood: such the sight
Of fowle Duessa, when her borrowed light
Is laid away, and counterfesaunce knowne."
Thus when they had the witch disrobed quight,
And all her filthy feature open showne,
They let her goe at will, and wander waies unknowne.

L. Shee, flying fast from heavens hated face,
And from the world that her discovered wide,
Fled to the wastfull wildernesse apace,
From living eies her open shame to hide,
And lurkt in rocks and caves, long unespide.
But that faire crew of knights, and Una faire,
Did in that castle afterwards abide,
To rest them selves, and weary powres repaire;
Where store they fownd of al that dainty was and rare.

CANTO IX

His loves and lignage Arthure tells:
The knights knitt friendly hands:
Sir Trevisan flies from Despeyre,
Whom Redcros knight withstands.

I. O GOODLY golden chayne, wherewith yfere
   The vertues linked are in lovely wize;
   And noble mindes of yore allyed were,
   In brave poursuitt of chevalrous emprize,
   That none did others safety despize,
   Nor aid envy to him in need that stands;
   But friendly each did others praise devize,
   How to advaunce with favourable hands,
   As this good Prince redeemd the Redcrosse knight from
      bands.

II. Who when their powres, empayrd through labor long,
    With dew repast they had recured well,
    And that weake captive wight now wexed strong,
    Them list no lenger there at leasure dwell,
    But forward fare as their adventures fell:
    But, ere they parted, Una faire besought
    That straunger knight his name and nation tell;
    Least so great good, as he for her had wrought,
    Should die unknown, and buried be in thankles thought.

III. " Faire virgin," (said the Prince,) " yee me require
     A thing without the compas of my witt;
     For both the lignage, and the certein Sire,
     From which I sprong, from mee are hidden yitt;
     For all so soone as life did me admitt
     Into this world, and shewed hevens light,
     From mothers pap I taken was unfitt,
     And streight deliver'd to a Fary knight,
     To be upbrought in gentle thewes and martiall might.

IV. " Unto Old Timon he me brought bylive;
    Old Timon, who in youthly yeares hath beene
    In warlike feates th' expertest man alive,

And is the wisest now on earth I weene:
His dwelling is low in a valley greene,
Under the foot of Rauran mossy hore,
From whence the river Dee, as silver cleene,
His tombling billowes rolls with gentle rore;
There all my daies he traind mee up in vertuous lore.

v. " Thither the great magicien Merlin came,
As was his use, ofttimes to visitt me;
For he had charge my discipline to frame,
And Tutors nouriture to oversee.
Him oft and oft I askt in privity,
Of what loines and what lignage I did spring;
Whose aunswere bad me still assured bee,
That I was sonne and heire unto a king,
As time in her just term the truth to light should bring."

vi. " Well worthy impe," said then the Lady gent,
" And Pupill fitt for such a Tutors hand!
But what adventure, or what high intent,
Hath brought you hither into Faery land,
Aread, Prince Arthure, crowne of Martiall band? "
" Full hard it is," (quoth he) " to read aright
The course of heavenly cause, or understand
The secret meaning of th' eternall might,
That rules mens waies, and rules the thoughts of living
wight.

vii. " For whether he, through fatal deepe foresight,
Me hither sent for cause to me unghest;
Or that fresh bleeding wound, which day and night
Whilome doth rancle in my riven brest,
With forced fury following his behest,
Me hither brought by wayes yet never found,
You to have helpt I hold my selfe yet blest."
" Ah! courteous Knight," (quoth she) " what secret wound
Could ever find to grieve the gentlest hart on ground? "

viii. " Dear Dame," (quoth he) " you sleeping sparkes awake,
Which, troubled once, into huge flames will grow;
Ne ever will their fervent fury slake,
Till living moysture into smoke do flow,
And wasted life doe lye in ashes low:
Yet sithens silence lesseneth not my fire,

But, told, it flames; and, hidden, it does glow,
I will revele what ye so much desire.
Ah, Love! lay down thy bow, the whiles I may respyre.

IX. " It was in freshest flowre of youthly yeares,
    When corage first does creepe in manly chest,
    Then first the cole of kindly heat appeares
    To kindle love in every living brest:
    But me had warnd old Timons wise behest,
    Those creeping flames by reason to subdew,
    Before their rage grew to so great unrest,
    As miserable lovers use to rew,
    Which still wex old in woe, whiles wo stil wexeth new.

X. " That ydle name of love, and lovers life,
    As losse of time, and vertues enimy,
    I ever scornd, and joyd to stirre up strife,
    In middest of their mournfull Tragedy;
    Ay wont to laugh when them I heard to cry,
    And blow the fire which them to ashes brent:
    Their God himselfe, grieved at my libertie,
    Shott many a dart at me with fiers intent;
    But I them warded all with wary government.

XI. " But all in vaine: no fort can be so strong,
    Ne fleshly brest can armed be so sownd,
    But will at last be wonne with battrie long,
    Or unawares at disavantage fownd.
    Nothing is sure that growes on earthly grownd;
    And who most trustes in arme of fleshly might,
    And boastes in beauties chaine not to be bownd,
    Doth soonest fall in disaventrous fight,
    And yeeldes his caytive neck to victours most despight.

XII. " Ensample make of him your haplesse joy,
     And of my selfe now mated, as ye see;
     Whose prouder vaunt that proud avenging boy
     Did soone pluck downe, and curbd my libertee.
     For on a day, prickt forth with jollitee
     Of looser life and heat of hardiment,
     Raunging the forest wide on courser free,
     The fields, the floods, the heavens, with one consent,
     Did seeme to laugh on me, and favour mine intent.

XIII. " Forwearied with my sportes, I did alight
    From loftie steed, and downe to sleepe me layd;
    The verdant gras my couch did goodly dight,
    And pillow was my helmett fayre displayd;
    Whiles every sence the humour sweet embayd,
    And slombring soft my hart did steale away,
    Me seemed, by my side a royall Mayd
    Her daintie limbes full softly down did lay:
    So fayre a creature yet saw never sunny day.

XIV. " Most goodly glee and lovely blandishment
    She to me made, and badd me love her deare;
    For dearely sure her love was to me bent,
    As, when just time expired, should appeare.
    But whether dreames delude, or true it were,
    Was never hart so ravisht with delight,
    Ne living man like wordes did ever heare,
    As she to me delivered all that night;
    And at her parting said, She Queene of Faeries hight.

XV. " When I awoke, and found her place devoyd,
    And nought but pressed gras where she had lyen,
    I sorrowed all so much as earst I joyd,
    And washed all her place with watry eyen.
    From that day forth I lov'd that face divyne;
    From that day forth I cast in carefull mynd,
    To seek her out with labor and long tyne,
    And never vowd to rest till her I fynd:
    Nyne monethes I seek in vain, yet ni'll that vow unbynd."

XVI. Thus as he spake, his visage wexed pale,
    And chaunge of hew great passion did bewray;
    Yett still he strove to cloke his inward bale,
    And hide the smoke that did his fire display,
    Till gentle Una thus to him gan say:
    " O happy Queene of Faeries! that hast fownd,
    Mongst many, one that with his prowesse may
    Defend thine honour, and thy foes confownd.
    True loves are often sown, but seldom grow on grownd."

XVII. " Thine, O! then," said the gentle Redcrosse knight,
    " Next to that Ladies love, shalbe the place,
    O fayrest virgin! full of heavenly light,

XXVI. " And am I now in safetie sure," (quoth he)
      " From him that would have forced me to dye?
      And is the point of death now turnd fro mee,
      That I may tell this haplesse history? "
      " Fear nought," (quoth he) " no daunger now is nye."
      " Then shall I you recount a ruefull cace,"
      (Said he) " the which with this unlucky eye
      I late beheld; and, had not greater grace
      Me reft from it, had bene partaker of the place.

XXVII. " I lately chaunst (Would I had never chaunst!)
       With a fayre knight to keepen companee,
       Sir Terwin hight, that well himselfe advaunst
       In all affayres, and was both bold and free;
       But not so happy as mote happy bee:
       He lov'd, as was his lot, a Lady gent
       That him againe lov'd in the least degree;
       For she was proud, and of too high intent,
       And joyd to see her lover languish and lament:

XXVIII. " From whom retourning sad and comfortlesse,
        As on the way together we did fare,
        We met that villen, (God from him me blesse!)
        That cursed wight, from whom I scapt whyleare,
        A man of hell that calls himselfe Despayre:
        Who first us greets, and after fayre areedes
        Of tydinges straunge, and of adventures rare:
        So creeping close, as Snake in hidden weedes,
        Inquireth of our states, and of our knightly deedes.

XXIX. " Which when he knew, and felt our feeble harts
       Embost with bale, and bitter byting griefe,
       Which love had launched with his deadly darts,
       With wounding words, and termes of foule repriefe,
       He pluckt from us all hope of dew reliefe,
       That earst us held in love of lingring life;
       Then hopelesse, hartlesse, gan the cunning thiefe
       Perswade us dye, to stint all further strife:
       To me he lent this rope, to him a rusty knife.

XXX. " With which sad instrument of hasty death,
      That wofull lover, loathing lenger light,
      A wyde way made to let forth living breath:

But I, more fearefull or more lucky wight,
Dismayd with that deformed dismall sight,
Fledd fast away, halfe dead with dying feare;
Ne yet assur'd of life by you, Sir knight,
Whose like infirmity like chaunce may beare;
But God you never let his charmed speaches heare!"

XXXI. " How may a man," (said he) " with idle speach
Be wonne to spoyle the Castle of his health?"
" I wote," (quoth he) " whom tryall late did teach,
That like would not for all this worldes wealth.
His subtile tong like dropping honny mealt'h
Into the heart, and searcheth every vaine;
That, ere one be aware, by secret stealth
His powre is reft, and weaknes doth remaine.
O! never, Sir, desire to try his guilefull traine."

XXXII. " Certes," (sayd he) " hence shall I never rest,
Till I that treachours art have heard and tryde;
And you, Sir knight, whose name mote I request,
Of grace do me unto his cabin guyde."
" I, that hight Trevisan," (quoth he) " will ryde
Against my liking backe to doe you grace:
But nor for gold nor glee will I abyde
By you, when ye arrive in that same place;
For lever had I die then see his deadly face."

XXXIII. Ere long they come where that same wicked wight
His dwelling has, low in an hollow cave,
For underneath a craggy cliff ypight,
Darke, dolefull, dreary, like a greedy grave,
That still for carrion carcases doth crave:
On top whereof ay dwelt the ghastly Owle,
Shrieking his balefull note, which ever drave
Far from that haunt all other chearefull fowle;
And all about it wandring ghostes did wayle and howle.

XXXIV. And all about old stockes and stubs of trees,
Whereon nor fruit nor leafe was ever seene,
Did hang upon the ragged rocky knees;
On which had many wretches hanged beene,
Whose carcases were scattred on the greene,
And throwne about the cliffs. Arrived there,

That bare-head knight, for dread and dolefull teene,
Would faine have fled, ne durst approchen neare;
But th' other forst him staye, and comforted in feare.

xxxv. That darkesome cave they enter, where they find
That cursed man, low sitting on the ground,
Musing full sadly in his sullein mind:
His griesie lockes, long growen and unbound,
Disordred hong about his shoulders round,
And hid his face, through which his hollow eyne
Lookt deadly dull, and stared as astound;
His raw-bone cheekes, through penurie and pine,
Were shronke into his jawes, as he did never dyne.

xxxvi. His garment, nought but many ragged clouts,
With thornes together pind and patched was,
The which his naked sides he wrapt abouts;
And him beside there lay upon the gras
A dreary corse, whose life away did pas,
All wallowd in his own yet luke-warme blood,
That from his wound yet welled fresh, alas!
In which a rusty knife fast fixed stood,
And made an open passage for the gushing flood.

xxxvii. Which piteous spectacle, approving trew
The wofull tale that Trevisan had told,
Whenas the gentle Redcrosse knight did vew,
With firie zeale he burnt in courage bold
Him to avenge before his blood were cold,
And to the villein sayd; "Thou damned wight,
The authour of this fact we here behold,
What justice can but judge against thee right,
With thine owne blood to price his blood, here shed in
    sight?"

xxxviii. "What franticke fit," (quoth he) "hath thus distraught
Thee, foolish man, so rash a doome to give?
What justice ever other judgement taught,
But he should dye who merites not to live?
None els to death this man despayring drive
But his owne guiltie mind, deserving death.
Is then unjust to each his dew to give?
Or let him dye, that loatheth living breath,
Or let him die at ease, that liveth here uneath?

XXXIX. " Who travailes by the wearie wandring way,
　　　　　To come unto his wished home in haste,
　　　　　And meetes a flood that doth his passage stay,
　　　　　Is not great grace to helpe him over past,
　　　　　Or free his feet that in the myre sticke fast?
　　　　　Most envious man, that grieves at neighbours good;
　　　　　And fond, that joyest in the woe thou hast!
　　　　　Why wilt not let him passe, that long hath stood
　　　　　Upon the bancke, yet wilt thy selfe not pas the flood?

XL. " He there does now enjoy eternall rest
　　　　　And happy ease, which thou doest want and crave,
　　　　　And further from it daily wanderest:
　　　　　What if some little payne the passage have,
　　　　　That makes frayle flesh to feare the bitter wave,
　　　　　Is not short payne well borne, that bringes long ease,
　　　　　And layes the soule to sleepe in quiet grave?
　　　　　Sleepe after toyle, port after stormie seas,
　　　　　Ease after warre, death after life, does greatly please."

XLI. The knight much wondred at his suddeine wit,
　　　　　And sayd; " The terme of life is limited,
　　　　　Ne may a man prolong, nor shorten, it:
　　　　　The souldier may not move from watchfull sted,
　　　　　Nor leave his stand untill his Captaine bed."
　　　　　" Who life did limit by almightie doome,"
　　　　　(Quoth he) " knowes best the termes established;
　　　　　And he, that points the Centonell his roome,
　　　　　Doth license him depart at sound of morning droome."

XLII. " Is not his deed, what ever thing is donne
　　　　　In heaven and earth? Did not he all create
　　　　　To die againe? All ends that was begonne:
　　　　　Their times in his eternall booke of fate
　　　　　Are written sure, and have their certein date.
　　　　　Who then can strive with strong necessitie,
　　　　　That holds the world in his still chaunging state,
　　　　　Or shunne the death ordaynd by destinie?
　　　　　When houre of death is come, let none aske whence, nor
　　　　　　　why.

XLIII. " The lenger life, I wote, the greater sin;
　　　　　The greater sin, the greater punishment:
　　　　　All those great battels, which thou boasts to win

Through strife, and blood-shed, and avengement,
Now praysd, hereafter deare thou shalt repent;
For life must life, and blood must blood, repay.
Is not enough thy evill life forespent?
For he that once hath missed the right way,
The further he doth goe, the further he doth stray.

XLIV. " Then doe no further goe, no further stray,
But here ly downe, and to thy rest betake,
Th' ill to prevent, that life ensewen may;
For what hath life that may it loved make,
And gives not rather cause it to forsake?
Feare, sicknesse, age, losse, labour, sorrow, strife,
Payne, hunger, cold that makes the hart to quake,
And ever fickle fortune rageth rife;
All which, and thousands mo, do make a loathsome life.

XLV. " Thou, wretched man, of death hast greatest need,
If in true ballaunce thou wilt weigh thy state;
For never knight, that dared warlike deed,
More luckless dissaventures did amate:
Witnes the dungeon deepe, wherein of late
Thy life shutt up for death so oft did call;
And though good lucke prolonged hath thy date,
Yet death then would the like mishaps forestall,
Into the which hereafter thou maist happen fall.

XLVI. " Why then doest thou, O man of sin! desire
To draw thy dayes forth to their last degree?
Is not the measure of thy sinfull hire
High heaped up with huge iniquitee,
Against the day of wrath to burden thee?
Is not enough, that to this Lady mild
Thou falsed hast thy faith with perjuree,
And sold thy selfe to serve Duessa vild,
With whom in al abuse thou hast thy selfe defild?

XLVII. " Is not he just, that all this doth behold
From highest heven, and beares an equall eie?
Shall he thy sins up in his knowledge fold,
And guilty be of thine impietie?
Is not his lawe, Let every sinner die;
Die shall all flesh? What then must needs be donne,

Is it not better to doe willinglie,
Then linger till the glas be all out ronne?
Death is the end of woes: die soone, O faeries sonne!"

XLVIII. The knight was much enmoved with his speach,
That as a swords poynt through his hart did perse,
And in his conscience made a secrete breach,
Well knowing trew all that he did reherse,
And to his fresh remembraunce did reverse
The ugly vew of his deformed crimes;
That all his manly powres it did disperse,
As he were charmed with inchaunted rimes;
That oftentimes he quakt, and fainted oftentimes.

XLIX. In which amazement when the Miscreaunt
Perceived him to waver, weake and fraile,
Whiles trembling horror did his conscience daunt,
And hellish anguish did his soule assaile;
To drive him to despaire, and quite to quaile,
Hee shewd him, painted in a table plaine,
The damned ghosts that doe in torments waile,
And thousand feends that doe them endlesse paine
With fire and brimstone, which for ever shall remaine.

L. The sight whereof so throughly him dismaid,
That nought but death before his eies he saw,
And ever burning wrath before him laid,
By righteous sentence of th' Almighties law.
Then gan the villein him to overcraw,
And brought unto him swords, ropes, poison, fire,
And all that might him to perdition draw;
And bad him choose what death he would desire;
For death was dew to him that had provokt Gods ire.

LI. But, whenas none of them he saw him take,
He to him raught a dagger sharpe and keene,
And gave it him in hand: his hand did quake
And tremble like a leafe of Aspin greene,
And troubled blood through his pale face was seene
To come and goe with tidings from the heart,
As it a ronning messenger had beene.
At last, resolv'd to work his finall smart,
He lifted up his hand, that backe againe did start.

LII. Which whenas Una saw, through every vaine
The crudled cold ran to her well of life,
As in a swowne: but, soone reliv'd againe,
Out of his hand she snatcht the cursed knife,
And threw it to the ground, enraged rife,
And to him said; " Fie, fie, faint hearted Knight!
What meanest thou by this reprochfull strife?
Is this the battaile which thou vauntst to fight
With that fire-mouthed Dragon, horrible and bright?

LIII. " Come; come away, fraile, feeble, fleshly wight,
Ne let vaine words bewitch thy manly hart,
Ne divelish thoughts dismay thy constant spright:
In heavenly mercies hast thou not a part?
Why shouldst thou then despeire, that chosen art?
Where justice growes, there grows eke greater grace,
The which doth quench the brond of hellish smart,
And that accurst hand-writing doth deface.
Arise, sir Knight; arise, and leave this cursed place."

LIV. So up he rose, and thence amounted streight.
Which when the carle beheld, and saw his guest
Would safe depart, for all his subtile sleight,
He chose an halter from among the rest,
And with it hong him selfe, unbid, unblest.
But death he could not worke himselfe thereby;
For thousand times he so him selfe had drest,
Yet nathelesse it could not doe him die,
Till he should die his last, that is, eternally.

CANTO X

Her faithfull knight faire Una brings
To house of Holinesse;
Where he is taught repentaunce, and
The way to hevenly blesse.

I. WHAT man is he, that boasts of fleshly might
And vaine assuraunce of mortality,
Which, all so soone as it doth come to fight
Against spirituall foes, yields by and by,
Or from the fielde most cowardly doth fly!
Ne let the man ascribe it to his skill,
That thorough grace hath gained victory:
If any strength we have, it is to ill,
But all the good is Gods, both power and eke will.

II. By that which lately hapned Una saw
That this her knight was feeble, and too faint;
And all his sinewes woxen weake and raw,
Through long enprisonment, and hard constraint,
Which he endured in his late restraint,
That yet he was unfitt for bloody fight.
Therefore, to cherish him with diets daint,
She cast to bring him where he chearen might,
Till he recovered had his late decayed plight.

III. There was an auncient house nor far away,
Renowmd throughout the world for sacred lore
And pure unspotted life: so well, they say,
It governd was, and guided evermore,
Through wisedome of a matrone grave and hore;
Whose onely joy was to relieve the needes
Of wretched soules, and helpe the helpelesse pore:
All night she spent in bidding of her bedes,
And all the day in doing good and godly deedes.

IV. Dame Cælia men did her call, as thought
From heaven to come, or thither to arise;
The mother of three daughters, well upbrought

I   E

In goodly thewes, and godly exercise:
The eldest two, most sober, chast, and wise,
Fidelia and Speranza, virgins were;
Though spousd, yet wanting wedlocks solemnize;
But faire Charissa to a lovely fere
Was lincked, and by him had many pledges dere.

v. Arrived there, the dore they find fast lockt,
For it was warely watched night and day,
For feare of many foes; but, when they knockt,
The Porter opened unto them streight way.
He was an aged syre, all hory gray,
With lookes full lowly cast, and gate full slow,
Wont on a staffe his feeble steps to stay,
Hight Humiltá.   They passe in, stouping low;
For streight and narrow was the way which he did show.

vi. Each goodly thing is hardest to begin;
But, entred in, a spatious court they see,
Both plaine and pleasaunt to be walked in;
Where them does meete a francklin faire and free,
And entertaines with comely courteous glee;
His name was Zele, that him right well became:
For in his speaches and behaviour hee
Did labour lively to expresse the same,
And gladly did them guide, till to the Hall they came.

vii. There fayrely them receives a gentle Squyre,
Of myld demeanure and rare courtesee,
Right cleanly clad in comely sad attyre,
In word and deede that shewd great modestee,
And knew his good to all of each degree,
Hight Reverence.   He them with speaches meet
Does faire entreat; no courting nicetee,
But simple, trew, and eke unfained sweet,
As might become a Squyre so great persons to greet.

viii. And afterwardes them to his Dame he leades,
That aged Dame, the Lady of the place,
Who all this while was busy at her beades;
Which doen, she up arose with seemely grace,
And toward them full matronely did pace.
Where, when that fairest Una she beheld,

Whom well she knew to spring from hevenly race,
Her heart with joy unwonted inly sweld,
As feeling wondrous comfort in her weaker eld:

IX. And, her embracing, said; "O happy earth,
Whereon thy innocent feet doe ever tread!
Most vertuous virgin, borne of hevenly berth,
That, to redeeme thy woefull parents head
From tyrans rage and ever-dying dread,
Hast wandred through the world now long a day,
Yett ceassest not thy weary soles to lead;
What grace hath thee now hither brought this way?
Or doen thy feeble feet unweeting hither stray?

X. "Straunge thing it is an errant knight to see
Here in this place; or any other wight,
That hither turnes his steps.   So few there bee,
That chose the narrow path, or seeke the right:
All keepe the broad high way, and take delight
With many rather for to goe astray,
And be partakers of their evill plight,
Then with a few to walke the rightest way.
O foolish men! why hast ye to your own decay?"

XI. "Thy selfe to see, and tyred limbes to rest,
O matrone sage," (quoth she) "I hither came;
And this good knight his way with me addrest,
Ledd with thy prayses, and broad-blazed fame,
That up to heven is blowne."   The auncient Dame
Him goodly greeted in her modest guyse,
And enterteynd them both, as best became,
With all the court'sies that she could devyse,
Ne wanted ought to shew her bounteous or wise.

XII. Thus as they gan of sondrie thinges devise,
Loe! two most goodly virgins came in place,
Ylinked arme in arme in lovely wise:
With countenance demure, and modest grace,
They numbred even steps and equall pace;
Of which the eldest, that Fidelia hight,
Like sunny beames threw from her Christall face
That could have dazd the rash beholders sight,
And round about her head did shine like hevens light.

XIII. She was araied all in lilly white,
      And in her right hand bore a cup of gold,
      With wine and water fild up to the hight,
      In which a Serpent did himselfe enfold,
      That horrour made to all that did behold;
      But she no whitt did chaunge her constant mood:
      And in her other hand she fast did hold
      A booke, that was both signd and seald with blood;
      Wherein darke things were writt, hard to be understood.

XIV. Her younger sister, that Speranza hight,
     Was clad in blew, that her beseemed well;
     Not all so chearefull seemed she of sight,
     As was her sister: whether dread did dwell
     Or anguish in her hart, is hard to tell.
     Upon her arme a silver anchor lay,
     Whereon she leaned ever, as befell;
     And ever up to heven, as she did pray,
     Her stedfast eyes were bent, ne swarved other way.

XV. They, seeing Una, towards her gan wend,
    Who them encounters with like courtesee;
    Many kind speeches they betweene them spend,
    And greatly joy each other for to see:
    Then to the knight with shamefast modestie
    They turne themselves, at Unaes meeke request,
    And him salute with well beseeming glee;
    Who faire them quites, as him beseemed best,
    And goodly gan discourse of many a noble gest.

XVI. Then Una thus: " But she, your sister deare,
     The deare Charissa, where is she become?
     Or wants she health, or busie is elsewhere?"
     " Ah! no," said they, " but forth she may not come;
     For she of late is lightned of her wombe,
     And hath encreast the world with one sonne more,
     That her to see should be but troublesome."
     " Indeed," (quoth she) " that should her trouble sore;
     But thankt be God, and her encrease so evermore!"

XVII. Then said the aged Cælia, " Deare dame,
      And you, good Sir, I wote that of youre toyle
      And labors long, through which ye hither came,

Ye both forwearied be: therefore, a whyle
I read you rest, and to your bowres recoyle."
Then called she a Groome, that forth him ledd
Into a goodly lodge, and gan despoile
Of puissant armes, and laid in easie bedd.
His name was meeke Obedience, rightfully aredd.

XVIII. Now when their wearie limbes with kindly rest,
And bodies were refresht with dew repast,
Fayre Una gan Fidelia fayre request,
To have her knight into her schoolehous plaste,
That of her heavenly learning he might taste,
And heare the wisdom of her wordes divine.
She graunted; and that knight so much agraste,
That she him taught celestiall discipline,
And opened his dull eyes, that light mote in them shine.

XIX. And that her sacred Booke, with blood ywritt,
That none could reade except she did them teach,
She unto him disclosed every whitt;
And heavenly documents thereout did preach,
That weaker witt of man could never reach;
Of God; of grace; of justice; of free-will;
That wonder was to heare her goodly speach:
For she was hable with her wordes to kill,
And rayse againe to life the hart that she did thrill.

XX. And, when she list poure out her larger spright,
She would commaund the hasty Sunne to stay,
Or backward turne his course from hevens hight:
Sometimes great hostes of men she could dismay;
Dry-shod to passe she parts the flouds in tway;
And eke huge mountaines from their native seat
She would commaund themselves to beare away,
And throw in raging sea with roaring threat.
Almightie God her gave such powre and puissaunce great.

XXI. The faithfull knight now grew in little space,
By hearing her, and by her sisters lore,
To such perfection of all hevenly grace,
That wretched world he gan for to abhore,
And mortall life gan loath as thing forlore,
Greevd with remembrance of his wicked wayes,

And prickt with anguish of his sinnes so sore,
That he desirde to end his wretched dayes:
So much the dart of sinfull guilt the soule dismayes.

XXII. But wise Speranza gave him comfort sweet,
And taught him how to take assured hold
Upon her silver anchor, as was meet;
Els had his sinnes, so great and manifold,
Made him forget all that Fidelia told.
In this distressed doubtfull agony,
When him his dearest Una did behold
Disdeining life, desiring leave to dye,
She found her selfe assayld with great perplexity;

XXIII. And came to Cælia to declare her smart;
Who, well acquainted with that commune plight,
Which sinfull horror workes in wounded hart,
Her wisely comforted all that she might,
With goodly counsell and advisement right;
And streightway sent with carefull diligence,
To fetch a Leach, the which had great insight
In that disease of grieved conscience,
And well could cure the same: His name was Patience.

XXIV. Who, comming to that sowle-diseased knight,
Could hardly him intreat to tell his grief:
Which knowne, and all that noyd his heavie spright
Well searcht, eftsoones he gan apply relief
Of salves and med'cines, which had passing prief;
And thereto added wordes of wondrous might.
By which to ease he him recured brief,
And much aswag'd the passion of his plight,
That he his paine endur'd, as seeming now more light.

XXV. But yet the cause and root of all his ill,
Inward corruption and infected sin,
Not purg'd nor heald, behind remained still,
And festring sore did ranckle yett within,
Close creeping twixt the marow and the skin:
Which to extirpe, he laid him privily
Downe in a darksome lowly place far in,
Whereas he meant his corrosives to apply,
And with streight diet tame his stubborne malady.

XXVI. In ashes and sackcloth he did array
His daintie corse, proud humors to abate;
And dieted with fasting every day,
The swelling of his woundes to mitigate;
And made him pray both earely and eke late:
And ever, as superfluous flesh did rott,
Amendment readie still at hand did wayt,
To pluck it out with pincers fyrie whott,
That soone in him was lefte no one corrupted jott.

XXVII. And bitter Penaunce, with an yron whip,
Was wont him once to disple every day:
And sharp Remorse his hart did prick and nip,
That drops of blood thence like a well did play:
And sad Repentance used to embay
His blamefull body in salt water sore,
The filthy blottes of sin to wash away.
So in short space they did to health restore
The man that would not live, but erst lay at deathes dore.

XXVIII. In which his torment often was so great,
That like a Lyon he would cry and rore,
And rend his flesh, and his owne synewes eat.
His owne deare Una, hearing evermore
His ruefull shriekes and gronings, often tore
Her guiltlesse garments and her golden heare,
For pitty of his payne and anguish sore:
Yet all with patience wisely she did beare,
For well she wist his cryme could els be never cleare.

XXIX. Whom, thus recover'd by wise Patience
And trew Repentaunce, they to Una brought;
Who, joyous of his cured conscience,
Him dearely kist, and fayrely eke besought
Himselfe to chearish, and consuming thought
To put away out of his carefull brest.
By this Charissa, late in child-bed brought,
Was woxen strong, and left her fruitfull nest:
To her fayre Una brought this unacquainted guest.

XXX. She was a woman in her freshest age,
Of wondrous beauty, and of bounty rare,
With goodly grace and comely personage,

That was on earth not easie to compare;
Full of great love, but Cupids wanton snare
As hell she hated; chaste in worke and will:
Her necke and brests were ever open bare,
That ay thereof her babes might sucke their fill;
The rest was all in yellow robes arayed still.

XXXI. A multitude of babes about her hong,
Playing their sportes, that joyd her to behold;
Whom still she fed whiles they were weake and young,
But thrust them forth still as they wexed old:
And on her head she wore a tyre of gold,
Adornd with gemmes and owches wondrous fayre,
Whose passing price uneath was to be told:
And by her syde there sate a gentle payre,
Of turtle doves, she sitting in an yvory chayre.

XXXII. The knight and Una entring fayre her greet,
And bid her joy of that her happy brood;
Who them requites with court'sies seeming meet,
And entertaynes with friendly chearefull mood.
Then Una her besought, to be so good
As in her vertuous rules to schoole her knight,
Now after all his torment well withstood
In that sad house of Penaunce, where his spright
Had past the paines of hell and long-enduring night.

XXXIII. She was right joyous of her just request;
And taking by the hand that Faeries sonne,
Gan him instruct in everie good behest,
Of love, and righteousness, and well to donne;
And wrath and hatred warely to shonne,
That drew on men Gods hatred and his wrath,
And many soules in dolours had fordonne:
In which when him she well instructed hath,
From thence to heaven she teacheth him the ready path.

XXXIV. Wherein his weaker wandring steps to guyde,
An aunciant matrone she to her does call,
Whose sober lookes her wisedome well descryde:
Her name was Mercy; well knowne over-all
To be both gratious and eke liberall:
To whom the carefull charge of him she gave,

To leade aright, that he should never fall
In all his waies through this wide worldes wave;
That Mercy in the end his righteous soule might save.

XXXV. The godly Matrone by the hand him beares
Forth from her presence, by a narrow way,
Scattred with bushy thornes and ragged breares,
Which still before him she remov'd away,
That nothing might his ready passage stay:
And ever, when his feet encombred were,
Or gan to shrinke, or from the right to stray,
She held him fast, and firmely did upbeare,
As carefull Nourse her child from falling oft does reare.

XXXVI. Eftsoones unto an holy Hospitall,
That was foreby the way, she did him bring;
In which seven Bead-men, that had vowed all
Their life to service of high heavens King,
Did spend their daies in doing godly thing.
Their gates to all were open evermore,
That by the wearie way were travelling;
And one sate wayting ever them before,
To call in commers-by that needy were and pore.

XXXVII. The first of them, that eldest was and best,
Of all the house had charge and government,
As Guardian and Steward of the rest.
His office was to give entertainement
And lodging unto all that came and went;
Not unto such as could him feast againe,
And double quite for that he on them spent;
But such as want of harbour did constraine:
Those for Gods sake his dewty was to entertaine.

XXXVIII. The second was as Almner of the place:
His office was the hungry for to feed,
And thristy give to drinke; a worke of grace.
He feard not once himselfe to be in need,
Ne car'd to hoord for those whom he did breede:
The grace of God he layd up still in store,
Which as a stocke he left unto his seede.
He had enough; what need him care for more?
And had he lesse, yet some he would give to the pore.

XXXIX. The third had of their wardrobe custody,
In which were not rich tyres, nor garments gay,
The plumes of pride, and winges of vanity,
But clothes meet to keepe keene cold away,
And naked nature seemely to aray;
With which bare wretched wights he dayly clad,
The images of God in earthly clay;
And, if that no spare clothes to give he had,
His owne cote he would cut, and it distribute glad.

XL. The fourth appointed by his office was
Poore prisoners to relieve with gratious ayd,
And captives to redeeme with price of bras
From Turkes and Sarazins, which them had stayd:
And though they faulty were, yet well he wayd,
That God to us forgiveth every howre
Much more then that why they in bands were layd;
And he, that harrowd hell with heavie stowre,
The faulty soules from thence brought to his heavenly
bowre.

XLI. The fift had charge sick persons to attend,
And comfort those in point of death which lay;
For them most needeth comfort in the end,
When sin, and hell, and death, doe most dismay
The feeble soule departing hence away.
All is but lost, that living we bestow,
If not well ended at our dying day.
O man! have mind of that last bitter throw;
For as the tree does fall, so lyes it ever low.

XLII. The sixt had charge of them now being dead,
In seemely sort their corses to engrave,
And deck with dainty flowres their brydall bed,
That to their heavenly spouse both sweet and brave
They might appeare, when he their soules shall save.
The wondrous workmanship of Gods owne mould,
Whose face he made all beastes to feare, and gave
All in his hand, even dead we honour should.
Ah, dearest God, me graunt, I dead be not defould!

XLIII. The seventh, now after death and buriall done,
Had charge the tender Orphans of the dead
And wydowes ayd, least they should be undone:

In face of judgement he their right would plead,
Ne ought the powre of mighty men did dread
In their defence; nor would for gold or fee
Be wonne their rightfull causes downe to tread;
And, when they stood in most necessitee,
He did supply their want, and gave them ever free.

XLIV. There when the Elfin knight arrived was,
The first and chiefest of the seven, whose care
Was guests to welcome, towardes him did pas;
Where seeing Mercie, that his steps upbare
And alwaies led, to her with reverence rare
He humbly louted in meeke lowlinesse,
And seemely welcome for her did prepare:
For of their order she was Patronesse,
Albe Charissa were their chiefest founderesse.

XLV. There she awhile him stayes, himselfe to rest,
That to the rest more hable he might bee;
During which time, in every good behest,
And godly worke of Almes and charitee,
Shee him instructed with great industree.
Shortly therein so perfect he became,
That, from the first unto the last degree,
His mortall life he learned had to frame
In holy righteousnesse, without rebuke or blame.

XLVI. Thence forward by that painfull way they pas
Forth to an hill that was both steepe and hy,
On top whereof a sacred chappell was,
And eke a litle Hermitage thereby,
Wherein an aged holy man did lie,
That day and night said his devotion,
Ne other worldly business did apply:
His name was hevenly Contemplation;
Of God and goodnes was his meditation.

XLVII. Great grace that old man to him given had;
For God he often saw from heavens hight:
All were his earthly eien both blunt and bad,
And through great age had lost their kindly sight,
Yet wondrous quick and persaunt was his spright,
As Eagles eie that can behold the Sunne.

That hill they scale with all their powre and might,
That his fraile thighes, nigh weary and fordonne,
Gan faile; but by her helpe the top at last he wonne.

XLVIII. There they doe finde that godly aged Sire,
With snowy lockes adowne his shoulders shed;
As hoary frost with spangles doth attire
The mossy braunches of an Oke halfe ded.
Each bone might through his body well be red
And every sinew seene, through his long fast:
For nought he car'd his carcas long unfed;
His mind was full of spiritual repast,
And pyn'd his flesh to keepe his body low and chast.

XLIX. Who, when these two approching he aspide,
At their first presence grew agrieved sore,
That forst him lay his hevenly thoughts aside;
And had he not that Dame respected more,
Whom highly he did reverence and adore,
He would not once have moved for the knight.
They him saluted, standing far afore,
Who, well them greeting, humbly did requight,
And asked to what end they clomb that tedious hight?

L. "What end," (quoth she) "should cause us take such paine,
But that same end, which every living wight
Should make his marke high heaven to attaine?
Is not from hence the way, that leadeth right
To that most glorious house, that glistreth bright
With burning starres and everliving fire,
Whereof the keies are to thy hand behight
By wise Fidelia? Shee doth thee require,
To shew it to this knight, according his desire."

LI. "Thrise happy man," said then the father grave,
"Whose staggering steps thy steady hand doth lead,
And shewes the way his sinfull soule to save!
Who better can the way to heaven aread
Then thou thyselfe, that was both borne and bred
In hevenly throne, where thousand Angels shine?
Thou doest the praiers of the righteous sead
Present before the majesty divine,
And his avenging wrath to clemency incline.

LII. " Yet, since thou bidst, thy pleasure shalbe donne.
Then come, thou man of earth, and see the way,
That never yet was seene of Faeries sonne;
That never leads the traveiler astray,
But after labors long and sad delay,
Brings them to joyous rest and endlesse blis.
But first thou must a season fast and pray,
Till from her hands the spright assoiled is,
And have her strength recur'd from fraile infirmitis.

LIII. " That done, he leads him to the highest Mount,
Such one as that same mighty man of God,
That blood-red billowes, like a walled front,
On either side disparted with his rod,
Till that his army dry-foot through them yod,
Dwelt forty daies upon; where, writt in stone
With bloody letters by the hand of God,
The bitter doome of death and balefull mone
He did receive, whiles flashing fire about him shone:

LIV. Or like that sacred hill, whose head full hie,
Adornd with fruitfull Olives all arownd,
Is, as it were for endlesse memory
Of that deare Lord who oft thereon was fownd,
For ever with a flowring girlond crownd:
Or like that pleasaunt Mount, that is for ay
Through famous Poets verse each where renownd,
On which the thrise three learned Ladies play
Their hevenly notes, and make full many a lovely lay.

LV. From thence, far off he unto him did shew
A little path that was both steepe and long,
Which to a goodly Citty led his vew,
Whose wals and towres were builded high and strong
Of perle and precious stone, that earthly tong
Cannot describe, nor wit of man can tell;
Too high a ditty for my simple song.
The City of the greate king hight it well,
Wherein eternall peace and happinesse doth dwell.

LVI. As he thereon stood gazing, he might see
The blessed Angels to and fro descend
From highest heven in gladsome companee,

And with great joy into that Citty wend,
As commonly as frend does with his friend.
Whereat he wondred much, and gan enquere,
What stately building durst so high extend
Her lofty towres unto the starry sphere,
And what unknowen nation there empeopled were

LVII. "Faire Knight," (quoth he) "Hierusalem that is,
The new Hierusalem, that God has built
For those to dwell in that are chosen his,
His chosen people, purg'd from sinful guilt
With pretious blood, which cruelly was spilt
On cursed tree, of that unspotted lam,
That for the sinnes of al the world was kilt:
Now are they Saints all in that Citty sam,
More dear unto their God then younglings to their dam."

LVIII. "Till now," said then the knight, "I weened well,
That great Cleopolis, where I have beene,
In which that fairest Faery Queene doth dwell,
The fairest citty that might be seene;
And that bright towre, all built of christall clene,
Panthea, seemd the brightest thing that was;
But now by proofe all otherwise I weene,
For this great Citty that does far surpas,
And this bright Angels towre quite dims that towre of glas."

LIX. "Most trew," then said the holy aged man;
"Yet is Cleopolis, for earthly frame,
The fairest peece that eie beholden can;
And well beseemes all knights of noble name,
That covett in th' immortall booke of fame
To be eternized, that same to haunt,
And doen their service to that soveraigne Dame,
That glory does to them for guerdon graunt:
For she is hevenly borne, and heaven may justly vaunt.

LX. "And thou, faire ymp, sprong out from English race,
How ever now accompted Elfins sonne,
Well worthy doest thy service for her grace,
To aide a virgin desolate, foredonne;
But when thou famous victory hast wonne,
And high emongst all knights hast hong thy shield,

Thenceforth the suitt of earthly conquest shonne,
And wash thy hands from guilt of bloody field:
For blood can nought but sin, and wars but sorrows yield.

LXI. " Then seek this path that I to thee presage,
Which after all to heaven shall thee send;
Then peaceably thy painefull pilgrimage
To yonder same Hierusalem doe bend,
Where is for thee ordaind a blessed end:
For thou, emongst those Saints whom thou doest see,
Shalt be a Saint, and thine owne nations frend
And Patrone: thou *Saint George* shalt called bee,
Saint George of mery *England*, the signe of victoree."

LXII. " Unworthy wretch," (quoth he) " of so great grace,
How dare I thinke such glory to attaine?"
" These, that have it attaynd, were in like cace,
As wretched men, and lived in like paine."
" But deeds of armes must I at last be faine
And Ladies love to leave, so dearely bought?"
" What need of armes, where peace doth ay remaine,"
(Said he) " and bitter battailes all are fought?
As for loose loves, they'are vaine, and vanish into nought."

LXIII. " O! let me not," (quoth he) " then turne againe
Backe to the world, whose joyes so fruitlesse are;
But let me heare for aie in peace remaine,
Or streightway on that last long voiage fare,
That nothing may my present hope empare."
" That may not be," (said he) " ne maist thou yitt
Forgoe that royal maides bequeathed care,
Who did her cause into thy hand committ,
Till from her cursed foe thou have her freely quitt."

LXIV. " Then shall I soone," (quoth he) " so God me grace,
Abett that virgins cause disconsolate,
And shortly back returne unto this place,
To walke this way in Pilgrims poore estate.
But now aread, old father, why of late
Didst thou behight me borne of English blood,
Whom all a Faeries sonne doen nominate?"
" That word shall I," (said he) " avouchen good,
Sith to thee is unknowne the cradle of thy brood.

LXV. " For, well I wote, thou springst from ancient race
Of Saxon kinges, that have with mightie hand,
And many bloody battailes fought in face,
High reard their royall throne in Britans land,
And vanquisht them, unable to withstand:
From thence a Faery thee unweeting reft,
There as thou slepst in tender swadling band,
And her base Elfin brood there for thee left:
Such, men do Chaungelings call, so chaung'd by Faeries
     theft.

LXVI. " Thence she thee brought into this Faery lond,
And in an heaped furrow did thee hyde;
Where thee a Ploughman all unweeting fond,
As he his toylesome teme that way did guyde,
And brought thee up in ploughmans state to byde,
Whereof Georgos he thee gave to name;
Till prickt with courage, and thy forces pryde,
To Faery court thou cam'st to seek for fame,
And prove thy puissant armes, as seemes thee best became."

LXVII. " O holy Sire! " (quoth he) " how shall I quight
The many favours I with thee have fownd,
That hast my name and nation redd aright,
And taught the way that does to heaven bownd! "
This saide, adowne he looked to the grownd
To have returnd; but dazed were his eyne
Through passing brightnes, which did quite confound
His feeble sence, and too exceeding shyne.
So darke are earthly thinges compard to things divine.

LXVIII. At last, whenas himselfe he gan to fynd,
To Una back he cast him to retyre,
Who him awaited still with pensive mynd.
Great thankes, and goodly meed, to that good syre
He thens departing gave for his paynes hyre
So came to Una, who him joyd to see;
And, after litle rest, gan him desyre
Of her adventure myndfull for to bee.
So leave they take of Cælia and her daughters three.

CANTO XI

The knight with that old Dragon fights
Two days incessantly:
The third him overthrowes, and gayns
Most glorious victory.

I. HIGH time now gan it wex for Una fayre
To thinke of those her captive Parents deare,
And their forwasted kingdom to repayre:
Whereto whenas they now approched neare,
With hartie wordes her knight she gan to cheare,
And in her modest maner thus bespake:
" Deare knight, as deare as ever knight was deare,
That all these sorrowes suffer for my sake,
High heven behold the tedious toyle ye for me take!

II. " Now are we come unto my native soyle,
And to the place where all our perilles dwell;
Here hauntes that feend, and does his dayly spoyle;
Therefore, henceforth, bee at your keeping well,
And ever ready for your foeman fell:
The sparke of noble corage now awake,
And strive your excellent selfe to excell:
That shall ye evermore renowmed make
Above all knights on earth, that batteill undertake."

III. And pointing forth, " Lo! yonder is," (said she)
" The brasen towre, in which my parents deare
For dread of that huge feend emprisond be;
Whom I from far see on the walles appeare,
Whose sight my feeble soule doth greatly cheare:
And on the top of all I do espye
The watchman wayting tydings glad to heare;
That, (O my Parents!) might I happily
Unto you bring, to ease you of your misery!"

IV. With that they heard a roaring hideous sownd,
That all the ayre with terror filled wyde,
And seemd uneath to shake the stedfast ground.

Eftsoones that dreadful Dragon they espyde,
Where stretcht he lay upon the sunny side
Of a great hill, himselfe like a great hill:
But, all so soone as he from far descryde
Those glistring armes that heven with light did fill,
He rousd himselfe full blyth, and hastned them untill.

v. Then badd the knight his Lady yede aloof,
And to an hill herselfe withdraw asyde;
From whence she might behold that battailles proof,
And eke be safe from daunger far descryde.
She him obayd, and turned a little wyde.—
Now, O thou sacred Muse! most learned Dame,
Fayre ympe of Phœbus and his aged bryde,
The Nourse of time and everlasting fame,
That warlike handes ennoblest with immortall name;

vi. O! gently come into my feeble brest;
Come gently, but not with that mightie rage,
Wherewith the martiall troupes thou doest infest,
And hartes of great Heroës doest enrage,
That nought their kindled corage may aswage:
Soone as thy dreadfull trompe begins to sownd,
The God of warre with his fiers equipage
Thou doest awake, sleepe never he so sownd;
And scared nations doest with horror sterne astownd.

vii. Fayre Goddesse, lay that furious fitt asyde,
Till I of warres and bloody Mars doe sing,
And Bryton fieldes with Sarazin blood bedyde,
Twixt that great faery Queene and Paynim king,
That with their horror heven and earth did ring;
A worke of labour long, and endlesse prayse:
But now a while lett downe that haughtie string,
And to my tunes thy second tenor rayse,
That I this man of God his godly armes may blaze.

viii. By this, the dreadful Beast drew nigh to hand,
Halfe flying and halfe footing in his haste,
That with his largenesse measured much land,
And made wide shadow under his huge waste,
As mountaine doth the valley overcaste.
Approching nigh, he reared high afore

His body monstrous, horrible, and vaste;
Which, to increase his wondrous greatnes more,
Was swoln with wrath and poyson, and with bloody gore;

IX. And over all with brasen scales was armd,
Like plated cote of steele, so couched neare
That nought mote perce; ne might his corse bee harmd
With dint of swerd, nor push of pointed speare:
Which as an Eagle, seeing pray appeare,
His aery plumes doth rouze, full rudely dight;
So shaked he, that horror was to heare:
For as the clashing of an Armor bright,
Such noyse his rouzed scales did send unto the knight.

X. His flaggy winges, when forth he did display,
Were like two sayles, in which the hollow wynd
Is gathered full, and worketh speedy way:
And eke the pennes, that did his pineons bynd,
Were like mayne-yardes with flying canvas lynd;
With which whenas him list the ayre to beat,
And there by force unwonted passage fynd,
The cloudes before him fledd for terror great,
And all the hevens stood still amazed with his threat.

XI. His huge long tayle, wownd up in hundred foldes,
Does overspred his long bras-scaly back,
Whose wreathed boughtes when ever he unfoldes,
And thick entangled knots adown does slack,
Bespotted as with shieldes of red and blacke,
It sweepeth all the land behind him farre,
And of three furlongs does but litle lacke;
And at the point two stinges in fixed arre,
Both deadly sharp, that sharpest steele exceeden farre.

XII. But stinges and sharpest steele did far exceed
The sharpnesse of his cruel rending clawes:
Dead was it sure, as sure as death in deed,
What ever thing does touch his ravenous pawes,
Or what within his reach he ever drawes.
But his most hideous head my tongue to tell
Does tremble; for his deepe devouring jawes
Wyde gaped, like the griesly mouth of hell,
Through which into his darke abysse all ravin fell.

XIII. And, that more wondrous was, in either jaw
    Three ranckes of yron teeth enraunged were,
    In which yett trickling blood, and gobbets raw,
    Of late devoured bodies did appeare,
    That sight thereof bredd cold congealed feare;
    Which to increase, and all atonce to kill,
    A cloud of smoothering smoke, and sulphure seare,
    Out of his stinking gorge forth steemed still,
    That all the ayre about with smoke and stench did fill.

XIV. His blazing eyes, like two bright shining shieldes,
    Did burne with wrath, and sparkled living fyre:
    As two broad Beacons, sett in open fieldes,
    Send forth their flames far off to every shyre,
    And warning give that enimies conspyre
    With fire and sword the region to invade:
    So flam'd his eyne with rage and rancorous yre;
    But far within, as in a hollow glade,
    Those glaring lampes were sett that made a dreadfull shade.

XV. So dreadfully he towardes him did pas,
    Forelifting up a-loft his speckled brest,
    And often bounding on the brused gras,
    As for great joyance of his newcome guest.
    Eftsoones he gan advance his haughty crest,
    As chauffed Bore his bristles doth upreare;
    And shoke his scales to battaile ready drest,
    That made the Redcrosse knight nigh quake for feare,
    As bidding bold defyaunce to his foeman neare.

XVI. The knight gan fayrely couch his steady speare,
    And fiersely ran at him with rigorous might:
    The pointed steele, arriving rudely theare,
    His harder hyde would nether perce nor bight,
    But, glauncing by, foorth passed forward right.
    Yet sore amoved with so puissaunt push,
    The wrathfull beast about him turned light,
    And him so rudely, passing by, did brush
    With his long tayle, that horse and man to ground did rush.

XVII. Both horse and man up lightly rose againe,
    And fresh encounter towardes him addrest;
    But th' ydle stroke yet backe recoyld in vaine,

And found no place his deadly point to rest.
Exceeding rage enflam'd the furious Beast,
To be avenged of so great despight;
For never felt his imperceable brest
So wondrous force from hand of living wight;
Yet had he prov'd the powre of many a puissant knight.

XVIII. Then, with his waving wings displayed wyde,
Himselfe up high he lifted from the ground,
And with strong flight did forcibly divyde
The yielding ayre, which nigh too feeble found
Her flitting parts, and element unsound,
To beare so great a weight: he, cutting way
With his broad sayles, about him soared round;
At last, low stouping with unweldy sway,
Snatcht up both horse and man, to beare them quite away.

XIX. Long he them bore above the subject plaine,
So far as Ewghen bow a shaft may send,
Till struggling strong did him at last constraine
To let them downe before his flightes end:
As hagard hauke, presuming to contend
With hardy fowle above his hable might,
His wearie pounces all in vaine doth spend
To trusse the pray too heavy for his flight;
Which, comming down to ground, does free it selfe by fight.

XX. He so disseized of his gryping grosse,
The knight his thrillant speare againe assayd
In his bras-plated body to embosse,
And three mens strength unto the stroake he layd;
Wherewith the stiffe beame quaked as affrayd,
And glauncing from his scaly necke did glyde
Close under his left wing, then broad displayd:
The percing steele there wrought a wound full wyde,
That with the uncouth smart the Monster lowdly cryde.

XXI. He cryde, as raging seas are wont to rore
When wintry storme his wrathful wreck does threat;
The rolling billowes beate the ragged shore,
As they the earth would shoulder from her seat;
And greedy gulfe does gape, as he would eat
His neighbour element in his revenge:

Then gin the blustring brethren boldly threat
To move the world from off his stedfast henge,
And boystrous battaile make, each other to avenge.

XXII. The steely head stuck fast still in his flesh,
Till with his cruell clawes he snatcht the wood,
And quite a sunder broke.   Forth flowed fresh
A gushing river of blacke gory blood,
That drowned all the land whereon he stood;
The streame thereof would drive a water-mill:
Trebly augmented was his furious mood
With bitter sence of his deepe rooted ill,
That flames of fire he threw forth from his large nosethril.

XXIII. His hideous tayle then hurled he about,
And therewith all enwrapt the nimble thyes
Of his froth-fomy steed, whose courage stout
Striving to loose the knott that fast him tyes,
Himselfe in streighter bandes too rash implyes,
That to the ground he is perforce constraynd
To throw his ryder; who can quickly ryse
From off the earth, with durty blood distaynd,
For that reprochfull fall right fowly he disdaynd;

XXIV. And fercely tooke his trenchand blade in hand,
With which he stroke so furious and so fell,
That nothing seemd the puissaunce could withstand:
Upon his crest the hardned yron fell,
But his more hardned crest was armd so well,
That deeper dint therein it would not make;
Yet so extremely did the buffe him quell,
That from thenceforth he shund the like to take,
But when he saw them come he did them still forsake.

XXV. The knight was wroth to see his stroke beguyld,
And smot againe with more outrageous might;
But backe againe the sparcling steele recoyld,
And left not any marke where it did light,
As if in Adamant rocke it had beene pight.
The beast, impatient of his smarting wound
And of so fierce and forcible despight,
Thought with his winges to stye above the ground;
But his late wounded wing unserviceable found.

XXVI. Then full of griefe and anguish vehement,
He lowdly brayd, that like was never heard;
And from his wide devouring oven sent
A flake of fire, that flashing in his beard
Him all amazd, and almost made afeard:
The scorching flame sore swinged all his face,
And through his armour all his body seard,
That he could not endure so cruell cace,
But thought his armes to leave, and helmet to unlace.

XXVII. Not that great Champion of the antique world,
Whom famous Poetes verse so much doth vaunt,
And hath for twelve huge labours high extold,
So many furies and sharpe fits did haunt,
When him the poysoned garment did enchaunt,
When Centaures blood and bloody verses charmd;
As did this knight twelve thousand dolours daunt,
Whom fyrie steele now burnt, that erst him armd;
That erst him goodly armd, now most of all him harmd.

XXVIII. Faynt, wearie, sore, emboyled, grieved, brent,
With heat, toyle, wounds, armes, smart, and inward fire,
That never man such mischiefes did torment:
Death better were; death did he oft desire,
But death will never come when needes require.
Whom so dismayd when that his foe beheld,
He cast to suffer him no more respire,
But gan his sturdy sterne about to weld,
And him so strongly stroke, that to the ground him feld.

XXIX. It fortuned, (as fayre it then befell)
Behynd his backe, unweeting, where he stood,
Of auncient time there was a springing well,
From which fast trickled forth a silver flood,
Full of great vertues, and for med'cine good:
Whylome, before that cursed Dragon got
That happy land, and all with innocent blood
Defyld those sacred waves, it rightly hot
The well of life, ne yet his vertues had forgot:

XXX. For unto life the dead it could restore,
And guilt of sinfull crimes cleane wash away;
Those that with sicknesse were infected sore

It could recure; and aged long decay
Renew, as one were borne that very day.
Both Silo this, and Jordan, did excell,
And th' English Bath, and eke the German Spau;
Ne can Cephise, nor Hebrus, match this well:
Into the same the knight back overthrowen fell.

XXXI. Now gan the golden Phœbus for to steepe
His fierie face in billowes of the west,
And his faint steedes watred in Ocean deepe,
Whiles from their journall labours they did rest;
When that infernall Monster, having kest
His wearie foe into that living well,
Gan high advaunce his broad discoloured brest
Above his wonted pitch, with countenance fell,
And clapt his yron wings as victor he did dwell.

XXXII. Which when his pensive Lady saw from farre,
Great woe and sorrow did her soule assay,
As weening that the sad end of the warre;
And gan to highest God entirely pray
That feared chaunce from her to turne away:
With folded hands, and knees full lowly bent,
All night shee watcht, ne once adowne would lay
Her dainty limbs in her sad dreriment,
But praying still did wake, and waking did lament.

XXXIII. The morrow next gan earely to appeare,
That Titan rose to runne his daily race;
But earely, ere the morrow next gan reare
Out of the sea faire Titans deawy face,
Up rose the gentle virgin from her place,
And looked all about, if she might spy
Her loved knight to move his manly pace:
For she had great doubt of his safety,
Since late she saw him fall before his enimy.

XXXIV. At last she saw where he upstarted brave
Out of the well, wherein he drenched lay:
As Eagle, fresh out of the ocean wave,
Where he hath lefte his plumes all hory gray,
And deckt himselfe with fethers youthly gay,
Like Eyas hauke up mounts unto the skies,

His newly-budded pineons to assay,
And marveiles at himselfe stil as he flies:
So new this new-borne knight to battell new did rise.

xxxv. Whom when the damned feend so fresh did spy
No wonder if he wondred at the sight,
And doubted whether his late enimy
It were, or other new supplied knight.
He now, to prove his late-renewed might,
High brandishing his bright deaw-burning blade,
Upon his crested scalp so sore did smite,
That to the scull a yawning wound it made:
The deadly dint his dulled sences all dismaid.

xxxvi. I wote not whether the revenging steele
Were hardned with that holy water dew
Wherein he fell, or sharper edge did feele,
Or his baptized hands now greater grew,
Or other secret vertue did ensew;
Els never could the force of fleshly arme,
Ne molten mettall, in his blood embrew;
For till that stownd could never wight him harme
By subtilty, nor slight, nor might, nor mighty charme.

xxxvii. The cruell wound enraged him so sore,
That loud he yelled for exceeding paine;
As hundred ramping Lions seemd to rore,
Whom ravenous hunger did thereto constraine:
Then gan he tosse aloft his stretched traine,
And therewith scourge the buxome aire so sore,
That to his force to yielden it was faine;
Ne ought his sturdy strokes might stand afore,
That high trees overthrew, and rocks in peeces tore.

xxxviii. The same advauncing high above his head,
With sharpe intended sting so rude him smott,
That to the earth him drove, as stricken dead;
Ne living wight would have him life behott:
The mortall sting his angry needle shott
Quite through his shield, and in his shoulder seasd,
Where fast it stucke, ne would thereout be gott:
The griefe thereof him wondrous sore diseasd,
Ne might his rancling paine with patience be appeasd.

XXXIX. But yet, more mindfull of his honour deare
       Then of the grievous smart which him did wring,
       From loathed soile he can him lightly reare,
       And strove to loose the far infixed sting:
       Which when in vaine he tryde with struggeling,
       Inflam'd with wrath, his raging blade he hefte,
       And strooke so strongly, that the knotty string
       Of his huge taile he quite a sonder clefte;
       Five joints thereof he hewd, and but the stump him lefte.

XL.   Hart cannot thinke what outrage and what cries,
       With fowle enfouldred smoake and flashing fire,
       The hell-bred beast threw forth unto the skies,
       That all was covered with darknesse dire:
       Then, fraught with rancour and engorged yre,
       He cast at once him to avenge for all,
       And, gathering up himselfe out of the mire
       With his uneven wings, did fiercely fall
       Upon his sunne-bright shield, and grypt it fast withall.

XLI.   Much was the man encombred with his hold,
       In feare to lose his weapon in his paw,
       Ne wist yett how his talaunts to unfold;
       Nor harder was from Cerberus greedy jaw
       To plucke a bone, then from his cruell claw
       To reave by strength the griped gage away:
       Thrise he assayd it from his foote to draw,
       And thrise in vaine to draw it did assay;
       It booted nought to thinke to robbe him of his pray.

XLII. Tho, when he saw no power might prevaile,
       His trusty sword he cald to his last aid,
       Wherewith he fiersly did his foe assaile,
       And double blowes about him stoutly laid,
       That glauncing fire out of the yron plaid,
       As sparkles from the Andvile use to fly,
       When heavy hammers on the wedge are swaid:
       Therewith at last he forst him to unty
       One of his grasping feete, him to defend thereby.

XLIII. The other foote, fast fixed on his shield,
       Whenas no strength nor stroks mote him constraine
       To loose, ne yet the warlike pledge to yield,

He smott thereat with all his might and maine,
That nought so wondrous puissaunce might sustaine:
Upon the joint the lucky steele did light,
And made such way that hewd it quite in twaine;
The paw yett missed not his minisht might,
But hong still on the shield, as it at first was pight.

XLIV. For griefe thereof and divelish despight,
From his infernall fournace forth he threw
Huge flames that dimmed all the hevens light,
Enrold in duskish smoke and brimstone blew:
As burning Aetna from his boyling stew
Doth belch out flames, and rockes in peeces broke,
And ragged ribs of mountaines molten new,
Enwrapt in coleblacke clowds and filthy smoke,
That al the land with stench and heven with horror choke.

XLV. The heate whereof, and harmefull pestilence,
So sore him noyd, that forst him to retire
A little backeward for his best defence,
To save his body from the scorching fire,
Which he from hellish entrailes did expire.
It chaunst, (eternall God that chaunce did guide)
As he recoiled backeward, in the mire
His nigh foreweried feeble feet did slide,
And downe he fell, with dread of shame sore terrifide.

XLVI. There grew a goodly tree him faire beside,
Loaden with fruit and apples rosy redd,
As they in pure vermilion had been dide,
Whereof great vertues over-all were redd;
For happy life to all which thereon fedd,
And life eke everlasting did befall:
Great God it planted in that blessed stedd
With his Almighty hand, and did it call
The tree of life, the crime of our first fathers fall.

XLVII. In all the world like was not to be fownd,
Save in that soile, where all good things did grow,
And freely sprong out of the fruitfull grownd,
As incorrupted Nature did them sow,
Till that dredd Dragon all did overthrow.
Another like faire tree eke grew thereby,

Whereof whoso did eat, eftsoones did know
Both good and ill.   O mournfull memory!
That tree through one mans fault hath doen us all to dy.

XLVIII. From that first tree forth flowd, as from a well,
A trickling streame of Balme, most soveraine
And dainty deare, which on the ground still fell,
And overflowed all the fertile plaine,
As it had deawed bene with timely raine:
Life and long health that gracious ointment gave,
And deadly wounds could heale, and reare againe
The sencelesse corse appointed for the grave:
Into that same he fell, which did from death him save.

XLIX. For nigh thereto the ever damned Beast
Durst not approch, for he was deadly made,
And al that life preserved did detest;
Yet he it oft adventur'd to invade.
By this the drouping day-light gan to fade,
And yield his rowme to sad succeeding night,
Who with her sable mantle gan to shade
The face of earth and wayes of living wight,
And high her burning torch set up in heaven bright.

L. When gentle Una saw the second fall
Of her deare knight, who, weary of long fight
And faint through losse of blood, moov'd not at all,
But lay, as in a dreame of deepe delight,
Besmeard with pretious Balme, whose vertuous might
Did heale his woundes, and scorching heat alay;
Againe she stricken was with sore affright,
And for his safetie gan devoutly pray,
And watch the noyous night, and wait for joyous day.

LI. The joyous day gan early to appeare;
And fayre Aurora from the deawy bed
Of aged Tithone gan herselfe to reare
With rosy cheekes, for shame as blushing red:
Her golden locks for hast were loosely shed
About her eares, when Una her did marke
Clymbe to her charet, all with flowers spred,
From heven high to chace the chearelesse darke;
With mery note her lowd salutes the mounting larke.

LII. Then freshly up arose the doughty knight,
    All healed of his hurts and woundes wide,
    And did himselfe to battaile ready dight;
    Whose early foe awaiting him beside
    To have devourd, so soone as day he spyde,
    When now he saw himselfe so freshly reare,
    As if late fight had nought him damnifyde,
    He woxe dismaid, and gan his fate to feare:
    Nathlesse with wonted rage he him advaunced neare.

LIII. And in his first encounter, gaping wyde,
    He thought attonce him to have swallowd quight,
    And rusht upon him with outragious pryde;
    Who him rencountring fierce, as hauke in flight,
    Perforce rebutted backe.   The weapon bright,
    Taking advantage of his open jaw,
    Ran through his mouth with so importune might,
    That deepe emperst his darksom hollow maw,
    And, back retyrd, his life blood forth with all did draw.

LIV. So downe he fell, and forth his life did breath,
    That vanisht into smoke and cloudes swift;
    So downe he fell, that th' earth him underneath
    Did grone, as feeble so great load to lift;
    So downe he fell, as an huge rocky clift,
    Whose false foundacion waves have washt away,
    With dreadfull poyse is from the mayneland rift,
    And rolling downe great Neptune doth dismay:
    So downe he fell, and like an heaped mountaine lay.

LV. The knight him selfe even trembled at his fall,
    So huge and horrible a masse it seemd;
    And his deare Lady, that beheld it all,
    Durst not approch for dread which she misdeemd;
    But yet at last, whenas the direfull feend
    She saw not stirre, off-shaking vaine affright
    She nigher drew, and saw that joyous end:
    Then God she praysd, and thankt her faithfull knight,
    That had atchievde so great a conquest by his might.

CANTO XII

Fayre Una to the Redcrosse Knight
Betrouthed is with joy:
Though false Duessa, it to barre,
Her false sleightes doe imploy.

I. BEHOLD! I see the haven nigh at hand
   To which I meane my wearie course to bend;
   Vere the maine shete, and beare up with the land,
   To which afore is fayrly to be kend,
   And seemeth safe from storms that may offend;
   There this fayre virgin wearie of her way
   Must landed bee, now at her journeyes end;
   There eke my feeble barke a while may stay,
   Till mery wynd and weather call her thence away.

II. Scarsely had Phœbus in the glooming East
    Yett harnessed his fyrie-footed teeme,
    Ne reard above the earth his flaming creast,
    When the last deadly smoke aloft did steeme,
    That signe of last outbreathed life did seeme
    Unto the watchman on the castle-wall;
    Who thereby dead that balefull Beast did deeme,
    And to his Lord and Lady lowd gan call,
    To tell how he had seene the Dragons fatall fall.

III. Uprose with hasty joy, and feeble speed,
     That aged Syre, the Lord of all that land,
     And looked forth, to weet if trew indeed
     Those tydinges were, as he did understand:
     Which whenas trew by tryall he out fond,
     He badd to open wyde his brasen gate,
     Which long time had beene shut, and out of hond
     Proclaymed joy and peace through all his state;
     For dead now was their foe, which them forrayed late.

IV. Then gan triumphant Trompets sownd on hye,
    That sent to heven the ecchoed report
    Of their new joy, and happie victory

Gainst him, that had them long opprest with tort,
And fast imprisoned in sieged fort.
Then all the people, as in solemne feast,
To him assembled with one full consort,
Rejoycing at the fall of that great beast,
From whose eternall bondage now thy were releast.

v. Forth came that auncient Lord, and aged Queene,
Arayd in antique robes downe to the grownd,
And sad habiliments right well beseene:
A noble crew about them waited rownd
Of sage and sober peres, all gravely gownd;
Whom far before did march a goodly band
Of tall young men, all hable armes to sownd;
But now they laurell braunches bore in hand,
Glad signe of victory and peace in all their land.

vi. Unto that doughtie Conquerour they came,
And him before themselves prostrating low,
Their Lord and Patrone loud did him proclame,
And at his feet their lawrell boughes did throw.
Soone after them, all dauncing on a row,
The comely virgins came, with girlands dight,
As fresh as flowres in medow greene doe grow
When morning deaw upon their leaves doth light;
And in their handes sweet Timbrels all upheld on hight.

vii. And them before the fry of children yong
Their wanton sportes and childish mirth did play,
And to the Maydens sownding tymbrels song
In well attuned notes a joyous lay,
And made delightfull musick all the way,
Untill they came where that faire virgin stood:
As fayre Diana in fresh sommers day
Beholdes her nymphes enraung'd in shady wood,
Some wrestle, some do run, some bathe in christall flood.

viii. So she beheld those maydens meriment
With chearefull vew; who, when to her they came,
Themselves to ground with gracious humblesse bent,
And her ador'd by honorable name,
Lifting to heven her everlasting fame:
Then on her head they sett a girlond greene,

And crowned her twixt earnest and twixt game:
Who, in her self-resemblance well beseene,
Did seeme, such as she was, a goodly maiden Queene.

IX. And after all the raskall many ran,
Heaped together in rude rablement,
To see the face of that victorious man,
Whom all admired as from heaven sent,
And gazd upon with gaping wonderment;
But when they came where that dead Dragon lay,
Stretcht on the ground in monstrous large extent,
The sight with ydle feare did them dismay,
Ne durst approch him nigh to touch, or once assay.

X. Some feard, and fledd; some feard, and well it faynd;
One, that would wiser seeme then all the rest,
Warnd him not touch, for yet perhaps remaynd
Some lingring life within his hollow brest,
Or in his wombe might lurke some hidden nest
Of many Dragonettes, his fruitfull seede:
Another saide, that in his eyes did rest
Yet sparckling fyre, and badd thereof take heed;
Another said, he saw him move his eyes indeed.

XI. One mother, whenas her foolehardy chyld
Did come too neare, and with his talants play,
Halfe dead through feare, her litle babe revyld,
And to her gossibs gan in counsell say;
" How can I tell, but that his talants may
Yet scratch my sonne, or rend his tender hand? "
So diversly them selves in vaine they fray;
Whiles some more bold to measure him nigh stand,
To prove how many acres he did spred of land.

XII. Thus flocked all the folke him rownd about;
The whiles that hoarie king, with all his traine,
Being arrived where that champion stout
After his foes defeasaunce did remaine,
Him goodly greetes, and fayre does entertayne
With princely gifts of yvory and gold,
And thousand thankes him yeeldes for all his paine.
Then when his daughter deare he does behold,
Her dearely doth imbrace, and kisseth manifold.

XIII. And after to his Pallace he them bringes,
    With shaumes, and trompets, and with Clarions sweet;
    And all the way the joyous people singes,
    And with their garments strowes the paved street;
    Whence mounting up, they fynd purveyaunce meet
    Of all, that royall Princes court became;
    And all the floore was underneath their feet
    Bespredd with costly scarlott of great name,
    On which they lowly sitt, and fitting purpose frame.

XIV. What needes me tell their feast and goodly guize,
    In which was nothing riotous nor vaine?
    What needes of dainty dishes to devize,
    Of comely services, or courtly trayne?
    My narrow leaves cannot in them contayne
    The large discourse of roiall Princes state.
    Yet was their manner then but bare and playne;
    For th' antique world excesse and pryde did hate:
    Such proud luxurious pompe is swollen up but late.

XV. Then, when with meates and drinkes of every kinde
    Their fervent appetites they quenched had,
    That auncient Lord gan fit occasion finde,
    Of straunge adventures, and of perils sad
    Which in his travell him befallen had,
    For to demaund of his renowmed guest:
    Who then with utt'rance grave, and count'nance sad,
    From poynt to poynt, as is before exprest,
    Discourst his voyage long, according his request.

XVI. Great pleasure, mixt with pittiful regard,
    That godly King and Queene did passionate,
    Whyles they his pittifull adventures heard;
    That oft they did lament his lucklesse state,
    And often blame the too importune fate
    That heapd on him so many wrathfull wreakes;
    For never gentle knight, as he of late,
    So tossed was in fortunes cruell freakes:
    And all the while salt teares bedeawd the hearers cheaks.

XVII. Then sayd that royall Pere in sober wise;
    " Deare Sonne, great beene the evils which ye bore
    From first to last in your late enterprise,

That I note whether praise or pitty more;
For never living man, I weene, so sore
In sea of deadly daungers was distrest:
But since now safe ye seised have the shore,
And well arrived are, (high God be blest!)
Let us devize of ease and everlasting rest."

XVIII. "Ah dearest Lord!" said then that doughty knight,
"Of ease or rest I may not yet devize;
For by the faith which I to armes have plight,
I bownden am streight after this emprize,
As that your daughter can ye well advize,
Backe to retourne to that great Faery Queene,
And her to serve sixe yeares in warlike wize,
Gainst that proud Paynim king that works her teene:
Therefore I ought crave pardon, till I there have beene."

XIX. "Unhappy falls that hard necessity,"
(Quoth he) "the troubler of my happy peace,
And vowed foe of my felicity;
Ne I against the same can justly preace:
But since that band ye cannot now release,
Nor doen undo, (for vowes may not be vayne)
Soone as the terme of those six yeares shall cease,
Ye then shall hither backe retourne agayne,
The marriage to accomplish vowd betwixt you twayn.

XX. "Which, for my part, I covet to performe
In sort as through the world I did proclame,
That who-so kild that monster most deforme,
And him in hardy battyle overcame,
Should have mine onely daughter to his Dame,
And of my kingdome heyre apparaunt bee:
Therefore, since now to thee perteynes the same
By dew desert of noble chevalree,
Both daughter and eke kingdome lo! I yield to thee."

XXI. Then forth he called that his daughter fayre,
The fairest Un', his onely daughter deare,
His onely daughter and his only hayre;
Who forth proceeding with sad sober cheare,
As bright as doth the morning starre appeare
Out of the East, with flaming lockes bedight,

To tell that dawning day is drawing neare,
And to the world does bring long-wished light:
So faire and fresh that Lady shewd herselfe in sight.

XXII. So faire and fresh, as freshest flowre in May;
For she had layd her mournefull stole aside,
And widow-like sad wimple throwne away,
Wherewith her heavenly beautie she did hide,
Whiles on her wearie journey she did ride;
And on her now a garment she did weare
All lilly white, withoutten spot or pride,
That seemd like silke and silver woven neare:
But neither silke nor silver therein did appeare.

XXIII. The blazing brightnesse of her beauties beame,
And glorious light of her sunshyny face,
To tell were as to strive against the streame:
My ragged rimes are all too rude and bace
Her heavenly lineaments for to enchace.
Ne wonder; for her own deare loved knight,
All were she daily with himselfe in place,
Did wonder much at her celestiall sight:
Oft had he seene her faire, but never so faire dight.

XXIV. So fairely dight when she in presence came,
She to her Syre made humble reverence,
And bowed low, that her right well became,
And added grace unto her excellence:
Who with great wisedome and grave eloquence
Thus gan to say—But, eare he thus had sayd,
With flying speede, and seeming great pretence,
Came running in, much like a man dismayd,
A Messenger with letters, which his message sayd.

XXV. All in the open hall amazed stood
At suddeinnesse of that unwary sight,
And wondred at his breathlesse hasty mood:
But he for nought would stay his passage right,
Till fast before the king he did alight;
Where falling flat great humblesse he did make,
And kist the ground whereon his foot was pight;
Then to his handes that writt he did betake,
Which he disclosing read thus, as the paper spake:

XXVI. " To thee, most mighty king of Eden fayre,
Her greeting sends in these sad lines addrest
The wofull daughter and forsaken heyre
Of that great Emperour of all the West;
And bids thee be advized for the best,
Ere thou thy daughter linck, in holy band
Of wedlocke, to that new unknowen guest:
For he already plighted his right hand
Unto another love, and to another land.

XXVII. " To me, sad mayd, or rather widow sad,
He was affyaunced long time before,
And sacred pledges he both gave, and had,
False erraunt knight, infamous, and forswore!
Witnesse the burning Altars, which he swore,
And guilty heavens of his bold perjury;
Which though he hath polluted oft of yore,
Yet I to them for judgement just doe fly,
And them conjure t'avenge this shamefull injury.

XXVIII. " Therefore, since mine he is, or free or bond,
Or false, or trew, or living or else dead,
Withhold, O soverayne Prince! your hasty hond
From knitting league with him, I you aread;
Ne weene my right with strength adowne to tread,
Through weaknesse of my widowhed or woe;
For truth is strong her rightfull cause to plead,
And shall finde friends, if need requireth soe.
So bids thee well to fare, Thy neither friend nor foe,
            Fidessa."

XXIX. When he these bitter byting wordes had red,
The tydings straunge did him abashed make,
That still he sate long time astonished,
As in great muse, ne word to creature spake.
At last his solemn silence thus he brake,
With doubtfull eyes fast fixed on his guest:
" Redoubted knight, that for myne only sake
Thy life and honor late adventurest,
Let nought be hid from me that ought to be exprest.

XXX. " What meane these bloody vowes and idle threats,
Throwne out from womanish impatient mynd?
What hevens? what altars? what enraged heates,

Here heaped up with termes of love unkynd,
My conscience cleare with guilty bands would bynd?
High God be witnesse that I guiltlesse ame;
But if yourselfe, Sir knight, ye faulty fynd,
Or wrapped be in loves of former Dame,
With cryme doe not it cover, but disclose the same."

XXXI. To whom the Redcrosse knight this answere sent:
" My Lord, my king, be nought hereat dismayd,
Till well ye wote by grave intendiment,
What woman, and wherefore, doth me upbrayd
With breach of love and loialty betrayd.
It was in my mishaps, as hitherward
I lately traveild, that unwares I strayd
Out of my way, through perils straunge and hard,
That day should faile me ere I had them all declard.

XXXII. " There did I find, or rather I was fownd
Of this false woman that Fidessa hight,
Fidessa hight the falsest Dame on grownd,
Most false Duessa, royall richly dight,
That easy was t' inveigle weaker sight:
Who by her wicked arts and wylie skill,
Too false and strong for earthly skill or might,
Unwares me wrought unto her wicked will,
And to my foe betrayd when least I feared ill."

XXXIII. Then stepped forth the goodly royall Mayd,
And on the ground herselfe prostrating low,
With sober countenance thus to him sayd:
" O! pardon me, my soveraine Lord, to sheow
The secret treasons, which of late I know
To have bene wrought by that false sorceresse:
Shee, onely she, it is, that earst did throw
This gentle knight into so great distresse,
That death him did awaite in daily wretchednesse.

XXXIV. " And now it seemes, that she suborned hath
This crafty messenger with letters vaine,
To worke new woe and improvided scath,
By breaking of the band betwixt us twaine;
Wherein she used hath the practicke paine
Of this false footman, clokt with simplenesse,

Whome if ye please for to discover plaine,
Ye shall him Archimago find, I ghesse,
The falsest man alive: who tries, shall find no lesse."

xxxv. The king was greatly moved at her speach;
And, all with sudden indignation fraight,
Bad on that Messenger rude hands to reach.
Eftsoones the Gard, which on his state did wait,
Attacht that faytor false, and bound him strait,
Who seeming sorely chauffed at his band,
As chained beare whom cruell dogs doe bait,
With ydle force did faine them to withstand,
And often semblaunce made to scape out of their hand.

xxxvi. But they him layd low in dungeon deepe,
And bound him hand and foote with yron chaines;
And with continual watch did warely keepe.
Who then would thinke that by his subtile trains
He could escape fowle death or deadly pains?
Thus, when that Princes wrath was pacifide,
He gan renew the late forbidden bains,
And to the knight his daughter deare he tyde
With sacred rites and vowes for ever to abyde.

xxxvii. His owne two hands the holy knotts did knitt,
That none but death for ever can divide;
His owne two hands, for such a turne most fitt,
The housling fire did kindle and provide,
And holy water thereon sprinckled wide;
At which the bushy Teade a groome did light,
And sacred lamp in secret chamber hide,
Where it should not be quenched day nor night,
For feare of evil fates, but burnen ever bright.

xxxviii. Then gan they sprinckle all the posts with wine,
And made great feast to solemnize that day:
They all perfumde with frankincense divine,
And precious odours fetcht from far away,
That all the house did sweat with great aray:
And all the while sweete Musicke did apply
Her curious skill the warbling notes to play,
To drive away the dull Melancholy;
The whiles one sung a song of love and jollity.

XXXIX. During the which there was an heavenly noise
    Heard sownd through all the Pallace pleasantly,
    Like as it had bene many an Angels voice
    Singing before th' eternall majesty,
    In their trinall triplicities on hye:
    Yett wist no creature whence that hevenly sweet
    Proceeded, yet each one felt secretly
    Himselfe thereby refte of his sences meet,
    And ravished with rare impression in his sprite.

XL. Great joy was made that day of young and old,
    And solemne feast proclaymd throughout the land,
    That their exceeding merth may not be told:
    Suffice it heare by signes to understand
    The usuall joyes at knitting of loves band.
    Thrise happy man the knight himselfe did hold,
    Possessed of his Ladies hart and hand;
    And ever, when his eie did her behold,
    His heart did seeme to melt in pleasures manifold.

XLI. Her joyous presence, and sweet company,
    In full content he there did long enjoy;
    Ne wicked envy, ne vile gealosy,
    His deare delights were hable to annoy:
    Yet, swimming in that sea of blisfull joy,
    He nought forgott how he whilome had sworne,
    In case he could that monstrous beast destroy,
    Unto his Faery Queene backe to retourne;
    The which he shortly did, and Una left to mourn.

XLII. Now, strike your sailes, yee jolly Mariners,
    For we be come unto a quiet rode,
    Where we must land some of our passengers,
    And light this weary vessell of her lode:
    Here she a while may make her safe abode,
    Till she repaired have her tackles spent,
    And wants supplide; And then againe abroad
    On the long voiage whereto she is bent:
    Well may she speede, and fairely finish her intent!

THE SECOND BOOK

CONTAYNING THE LEGEND OF SIR GUYON, OR OF TEMPERAUNCE

I. RIGHT well I wote, most mighty Soveraine,
   That all this famous antique history
   Of some th' aboundance of an ydle braine
   Will judged be, and painted forgery,
   Rather then matter of just memory;
   Sith none that breatheth living aire does know
   Where is that happy land of Faery,
   Which I so much doe vaunt, yet no where show,
   But vouch antiquities, which no body can know.

II. But let that man with better sence advize,
    That of the world least part to us is red;
    And daily how through hardy enterprize
    Many great Regions are discovered,
    Which to late age were never mentioned.
    Who ever heard of th' Indian Peru?
    Or who in venturous vessell measured
    The Amazon huge river, now found trew?
    Or fruitfullest Virginia who did ever vew?

III. Yet all these were, when no man did them know,
     Yet have from wisest ages hidden beene;
     And later times thinges more unknowne shall show.
     Why then should witlesse man so much misweene,
     That nothing is but that which he hath seene?
     What if within the Moones fayre shining sphaere,
     What if in every other starre unseene
     Of other worldes he happily should heare,
     He wonder would much more; yet such to some appeare.

IV. Of faery lond yet if he more inquyre,
    By certain signes, here sett in sondrie place,
    He may it fynd; ne let him then admyre,

169

But yield his sence to bee too blunt and bace,
That no'te without an hound fine footing trace.
And thou, O fayrest Princesse under sky!
In this fayre mirrhour maist behold thy face,
And thine owne realmes in lond of Faery,
And in this antique ymage thy great auncestry.

v. The which O! pardon me thus to enfold
In covert vele, and wrap in shadowes light,
That feeble eyes your glory may behold,
Which ells could not endure those beames bright,
But would bee dazled with exceeding light.
O! pardon, and vouchsafe with patient eare
The brave adventures of this faery knight,
The good Sir Guyon, gratiously to heare;
In whom great rule of Temp'raunce goodly doth appeare.

CANTO I

Guyon, by Archimage abusd,
The Redcrosse knight awaytes;
Fyndes Mordant and Amavia slaine
With pleasures poisoned haytes.

1. THAT conning Architect of cancred guyle,
    Whom Princes late displeasure left in bands,
    For falsed letters and suborned wyle,
    Soone as the Redcrosse knight he understands
    To beene departed out of Eden landes,
    To serve againe his soveraine Elfin Queene,
    His artes he moves, and out of caytives handes
    Himselfe he frees by secret meanes unseene;
    His shackles emptie lefte, himselfe escaped cleene.

11. And forth he fares, full of malicious mynd,
    To worken mischiefe, and avenging woe,
    Where ever he that godly knight may fynd,
    His onely hart-sore, and his onely foe;
    Sith Una now he algates must forgoe,
    Whom his victorious handes did earst restore
    To native crowne and kingdom late ygoe;
    Where she enjoyes sure peace for evermore,
    As wetherbeaten ship arryv'd on happie shore.

111. Him therefore now the object of his spight
    And deadly food he makes: him to offend,
    By forged treason or by open fight,
    He seekes, of all his drifte the aymed end:
    Thereto his subtile engins he does bend,
    His practick witt and his fayre fyled tonge,
    With thousand other sleightes; for well he kend
    His credit now in doubtfull ballaunce hong:
    For hardly could bee hurt who was already stong.

iv. Still as he went he craftie stales did lay,
    With cunning traynes him to entrap unwares,
    And privy spyals plast in all his way,

To weete what course he takes, and how he fares,
To ketch him at a vauntage in his snares.
But now so wise and wary was the knight
By tryall of his former harmes and cares,
That he descryde and shonned still his slight:
The fish that once was caught new bait wil hardly byte.

v. Nath'lesse th' Enchaunter would not spare his payne,
In hope to win occasion to his will;
Which when he long awaited had in vayne,
He chaungd his mynd from one to other ill;
For to all good he enimy was still.
Upon the way him fortuned to meete,
Fayre marching underneath a shady hill,
A goodly knight, all armd in harnesse meete,
That from his head no place appeared to his feete.

vi. His carriage was full comely and upright;
His countenance demure and temperate;
But yett so sterne and terrible in sight,
That cheard his friendes, and did his foes amate:
He was an Elfin borne of noble state
And mickle worship in his native land;
Well could he tourney, and in lists debate,
And knighthood tooke of good Sir Huons hand,
When with king Oberon he came to Faery land.

vii. Him als accompanyd upon the way
A comely Palmer, clad in black attyre,
Of rypest yeares, and heares all hoarie gray,
That with a staffe his feeble steps did stire,
Least his long way his aged limbes should tire:
And, if by lookes one may the mind aread,
He seemd to be a sage and sober syre;
And ever with slow pace the knight did lead,
Who taught his trampling steed with equall steps to tread.

viii. Such whenas Archimago them did view,
He weened well to worke some uncouth wyle:
Eftsoones untwisting his deceiptfull clew,
He gan to weave a web of wicked guyle,
And, with faire countenance and flattering style
To them approaching, thus the knight bespake;

" Fayre sonne of Mars, that seeke with warlike spoyle,
And great atchiev'ments, great your selfe to make,
Vouchsafe to stay your steed for humble misers sake."

ix. He stayd his steed for humble misers sake,
And badd tell on the tenor of his playnt:
Who feigning then in every limb to quake
Through inward feare, and seeming pale and faynt,
With piteous mone his percing speach gan paynt:
" Deare Lady! how shall I declare thy cace,
Whom late I left in languorous constraynt?
Would God! thy selfe now present were in place
To tell this ruefull tale: thy sight could win thee grace.

x. " Or rather would, O! would it so had chaunst,
That you, most noble Sir, had present beene
When that lewd rybauld, with vyle lust advaunst,
Laid first his filthie hands on virgin cleene,
To spoyle her dainty corps, so faire and sheene
As on the earth, great mother of us all,
With living eye more fayre was never seene
Of chastity and honour virginall:
Witnes, ye heavens, whom she in vaine to help did call."

xi. " How may it be," sayd then the knight halfe wroth,
" That knight should knighthood ever so have shent?"
" None but that saw," (quoth he) " would weene for troth,
How shamefully that Mayd he did torment:
Her looser golden lockes he rudely rent,
And drew her on the ground; and his sharpe sword
Against her snowy brest he fiercely bent,
And threatned death with many a bloodie word:
Tounge hates to tell the rest that eye to see abhord."

xii. Therewith amoved from his sober mood,
" And lives he yet," (said he) " that wrought this act?
And doen the heavens afford him vitall food?"
" He lives," (quoth he) " and boasteth of the fact,
Ne yet hath any knight his courage crackt."
" Where may that treachour then," (sayd he) " be found,
Or by what meanes may I his footing tract?"
" That shall I shew," (sayd he) " as sure as hound
The stricken Deare doth chalenge by the bleeding wound."

XIII. He stayd not lenger talke, but with fierce yre
And zealous haste away is quickly gone
To seeke that knight, where him that crafty Squyre
Supposd to be.   They do arrive anone
Where sate a gentle Lady all alone,
With garments rent, and heare discheveled,
Wringing her handes, and making piteous mone:
Her swollen eyes were much disfigured,
And her faire face with teares was fowly blubbered.

XIV. The knight, approching nigh, thus to her said:
" Fayre Lady, through fowle sorrow ill bedight,
Great pitty is to see you thus dismayd,
And marre the blossom of your beauty bright:
For-thy appease your griefe and heavy plight,
And tell the cause of your conceived payne;
For, if he live that hath you doen despight,
He shall you doe dew recompence agayne,
Or els his wrong with greater puissance maintaine."

XV. Which when she heard, as in despightfull wise
She wilfully her sorrow did augment,
And offred hope of comfort did despise:
Her golden lockes most cruelly she rent,
And scratcht her face with ghastly dreriment;
Ne would she speake, ne see, ne yet be seene,
But hid her visage, and her head downe bent,
Either for grievous shame, or for great teene,
As if her hart with sorrow had transfixed beene:

XVI. Till her that Squyre bespake: " Madame, my liefe,
For Gods deare love be not so wilfull bent,
But doe vouchsafe now to receive reliefe,
The which good fortune doth to you present.
For what bootes it to weepe and to wayment
When ill is chaunst, but doth the ill increase,
And the weake minde with double woe torment? "
When she her Squyre heard speake, she gan appease
Her voluntarie paine, and feele some secret ease.

XVII. Eftsoone she said; " Ah! gentle trustie Squyre,
What comfort can I, wofull wretch, conceave?
Or why should ever I henceforth desyre

To see faire heavens face, and life not leave,
Sith that false Traytour did my honour reave?"
"False traytour certes," (saide the Faerie knight)
"I read the man, that ever would deceave
A gentle Lady, or her wrong through might:
Death were too litle paine for such a fowle despight.

XVIII. "But now, fayre Lady, comfort to you make,
And read who hath ye wrought this shamefull plight,
That short revenge the man may overtake,
Where-so he be, and soone upon him light."
"Certes," (saide she) "I wote not how he hight,
But under him a gray steede he did wield,
Whose sides with dapled circles weren dight;
Upright he rode, and in his silver shield
He bore a bloodie Crosse that quartred all the field."

XIX. "Now by my head," (saide Guyon) "much I muse,
How that same knight should doe so fowle amis,
Or ever gentle Damzell so abuse:
For, may I boldly say, he surely is
A right good knight, and trew of word ywis:
I present was, and can it witnesse well,
When armes he swore, and streight did enterpris
Th' adventure of the Errant damozell;
In which he hath great glory wonne, as I heare tell.

XX. "Nathlesse he shortly shall againe be tryde,
And fairely quit him of th' imputed blame;
Els, be ye sure, he dearely shall abyde,
Or make you good amendment for the same:
All wrongs have mendes, but no amendes of shame.
Now therefore, Lady, rise out of your paine,
And see the salving of your blotted name."
Full loth she seemd thereto, but yet did faine,
For she was inly glad her purpose so to gaine.

XXI. Her purpose was not such as she did faine,
Ne yet her person such as it was seene;
But under simple shew, and semblant plaine,
Lurkt false Duessa secretly unseene,
As a chaste Virgin that had wronged beene:
So had false Archimago her disguysd,

To lett a weary wretch from her dew rest,
And trouble dying soules tranquilitee;
Take not away, now got, which none would give to me."

XLVIII. " Ah! far be it," (said he) " Deare dame, fro mee,
To hinder soule from her desired rest,
Or hold sad life in long captivitee;
For all I seeke is but to have redrest
The bitter pangs that doth your heart infest.
Tell then, O Lady! tell what fatall priefe
Hath with so huge misfortune you opprest;
That I may cast to compas your reliefe,
Or die with you in sorrow, and partake your griefe."

XLIX. With feeble hands then stretched forth on hye,
As heven accusing guilty of her death,
And with dry drops congealed in her eye,
In these sad wordes she spent her utmost breath:
" Heare then, O man! the sorrowes that uneath
My tong can tell, so far all sence they pas.
Loe! this dead corpse, that lies here underneath,
The gentlest knight, that ever on greene gras
Gay steed with spurs did pricke, the good Sir Mortdant was:

L. " Was, (ay the while, that he is not so now!)
My Lord, my love, my deare Lord, my deare love!
So long as hevens just with equall brow
Vouchsafed to behold us from above.
One day, when him high corage did emmove,
As wont ye knightes to seeke adventures wilde,
He pricked forth his puissant force to prove.
Me then he left enwombed of this childe,
This luckles childe, whom thus ye see with blood defild.

LI. " Him fortuned (hard fortune ye may ghesse)
To come, where vile Acrasia does wonne;
Acrasia, a false enchaunteresse,
That many errant knightes hath fowle fordonne;
Within a wandring Island, that doth ronne
And stray in perilous gulfe, her dwelling is.
Fayre Sir, if ever there ye travell, shonne
The cursed land where many wend amis,
And know it by the name: it hight the *Bowre of blis.*

LII. " Her blis is all in pleasure, and delight,
    Wherewith she makes her lovers dronken mad;
    And then with words, and weedes, of wondrous might,
    On them she workes her will to uses bad:
    My liefest Lord she thus beguiled had;
    For he was flesh: (all flesh doth frayltie breed)
    Whom when I heard to beene so ill bestad,
    Weake wretch, I wrapt myselfe in Palmers weed,
    And cast to seek him forth through danger and great dreed.

LIII. " Now had fayre Cynthia by even tournes
    Full measured three quarters of her yeare,
    And thrise three tymes had fild her crooked hornes,
    Whenas my wombe her burdein would forbeare,
    And bade me call Lucina to me neare.
    Lucina came; a manchild forth I brought;
    The woods, the nymphes, my bowres, my midwives, weare:
    Hard help at need! So deare thee, babe, I bought;
    Yet nought too dear I deemd, while so my deare I sought.

LIV. " Him so I sought; and so at last I fownd,
    Where him that witch had thralled to her will.
    In chaines of lust and lewde desyres ybownd,
    And so transformed from his former skill,
    That me he knew not, nether his owne ill;
    Till, through wise handling and faire governaunce,
    I him recured to a better will,
    Purged from drugs of fowle intemperaunce:
    Then meanes I gan devise for his deliveraunce.

LV. " Which when the vile Enchaunteresse perceiv'd,
    How that my Lord from her I would reprive,
    With cup thus charmd him parting she deceivd;
    ' Sad verse, give death to him that death does give,
    And losse of love to her that loves to live,
    So soone as Bacchus with the Nymphe does lincke! '
    So parted we, and on our journey drive;
    Till, coming to this well, he stoupt to drincke:
    The charme fulfild, dead suddeinly he downe did sincke.

LVI. " Which when I, wretch "—Not one word more she sayd,
    But breaking off the end for want of breath,
    And slyding soft, as downe to sleepe her layd,

CANTO II

Babes bloody handes may not be clensd:
The face of golden Meane:
Her sisters, two Extremities,
Strive her to banish cleane.

I. Thus when Sir Guyon with his faithful guyde
Had with dew rites and dolorous lament
The end of their sad Tragedie uptyde,
The litle babe up in his armes he hent;
Who with sweet pleasaunce, and bold blandishment,
Gan smyle on them, that rather ought to weepe,
As carelesse of his woe, or innocent
Of that was doen; that ruth emperced deepe
In that knightes hart, and wordes with bitter teares
    did steepe:

II. " Ah! lucklesse babe, borne under cruell starre,
And in dead parents balefull ashes bred,
Full little weenest thou what sorrowes are
Left thee for porcion of thy livelyhed;
Poore Orphane! in the wild world scattered,
As budding braunch rent from the native tree,
And throwen forth, till it be withered.
Such is the state of men: Thus enter we
Into this life with woe, and end with miseree! "

III. Then, soft himselfe inclyning on his knee
Downe to that well, did in the water weene
(So love does loath disdainefull nicitee)
His guiltie handes from bloody gore to cleene.
He washt them oft and oft, yet nought they beene
For all his washing cleaner.   Still he strove;
Yet still the litle hands were bloody seene:
The which him into great amaz'ment drove,
And into diverse doubt his wavering wonder clove.

IV. He wist not whether blott of fowle offence
Might not be purgd with water nor with bath;
Or that high God, in lieu of innocence,

Imprinted had that token of his wrath,
To shew how sore bloodguiltinesse he hat'th;
Or that the charme and veneme which they dronck,
Their blood with secret filth infected hath,
Being diffused through the senceless tronck,
That through the great contagion direful deadly stonck.

v. Whom thus at gaze the Palmer gan to bord
With goodly reason, and thus fayre bespake;
"Ye bene right hard amated, gratious Lord,
And of your ignorance great merveill make,
Whiles cause not well conceived ye mistake:
But know, that secret vertues are infusd
In every fountaine, and in everie lake,
Which who hath skill them rightly to have chusd,
To proofe of passing wonders hath full often usd:

vi. "Of those, some were so from their sourse indewd
By great Dame Nature, from whose fruitfull pap
Their welheads spring, and are with moisture deawd;
Which feedes each living plant with liquid sap,
And filles with flowres fayre Floraes painted lap:
But other some, by guifte of later grace,
Or by good prayers, or by other hap,
Had vertue pourd into their waters bace,
And thenceforth were renowmd, and sought from place
    to place.

vii. "Such is this well, wrought by occasion straunge,
Which to her Nymph befell. Upon a day,
As she the woodes with bow and shaftes did raunge,
The hartlesse Hynd and Robucke to dismay,
Dan Faunus chaunst to meet her by the way,
And, kindling fire at her faire-burning eye,
Inflamed was to follow beauties pray,
And chaced her that fast from him did fly;
As hynd from her, so she fled from her enimy.

viii. "At last, when fayling breath began to faint,
And saw no meanes to scape, of shame affrayd,
She set her downe to weepe for sore constraint;
And to Diana calling lowd for ayde,
Her deare besought to let her die a mayd.
The goddesse heard; and suddeine, where she sate

Welling out streames of teares, and quite dismayd
With stony feare of that rude rustick mate,
Transformd her to a stone from stedfast virgins state.

IX. "Lo! now she is that stone; from whose two heads,
As from two weeping eyes, fresh streames do flow,
Yet colde through feare and old conceived dreads;
And yet the stone her semblance seemes to show,
Shapt like a maide, that such ye may her know:
And yet her vertues in her water byde,
For it is chaste and pure as purest snow,
Ne lets her waves with any filth be dyde;
But ever, like herselfe, unstayned hath beene tryde.

X. "From thence it comes, that this babes bloody hand
May not be clensd with water of this well:
Ne certes, Sir, strive you it to withstand,
But let them still be bloody, as befell,
That they his mothers innocence may tell,
As she bequeathd in her last testament;
That, as a sacred Symbole, it may dwell
In her sonnes flesh, to mind revengement,
And be for all chaste Dames an endlesse moniment."

XI. He hearkned to his reason, and the childe
Uptaking, to the Palmer gave to beare;
But his sad fathers armes with blood defilde,
An heavie load, himselfe did lightly reare;
And turning to that place, in which whyleare
He left his loftie steed with golden sell
And goodly gorgeous barbes, him found not theare:
By other accident, that earst befell,
He is convaide; but how, or where, here fits not tell.

XII. Which when Sir Guyon saw, all were he wroth,
Yet algates mote he softe himselfe appease,
And fairely fare on foot, how ever loth:
His double burden did him sore disease.
So long they traveiled with litle ease,
Till that at last they to a Castle came,
Built on a rocke adjoyning to the seas:
It was an auncient worke of antique fame,
And wondrous strong by nature, and by skilful frame.

XIII. Therein three sisters dwelt of sundry sort,
The children of one syre by mothers three;
Who dying whylome did divide this fort
To them by equall shares in equall fee:
But stryfull mind and diverse qualitee
Drew them in partes, and each made others foe:
Still did they strive and daily disagree;
The eldest did against the youngest goe,
And both against the middest meant to worken woe.

XIV. Where when the knight arriv'd, he was right well
Receiv'd, as knight of so much worth became,
Of second sister, who did far excell
The other two: Medina was her name,
A sober sad and comely courteous Dame;
Who rich arayd, and yet in modest guize,
In goodly garments that her well became,
Fayre marching forth in honorable wize,
Him at the threshold mett, and well did enterprize.

XV. She led him up into a goodly bowre,
And comely courted with meet modestie;
Ne in her speach, ne in her haviour,
Was lightnesse seene or looser vanitie,
But gratious womanhood, and gravitie,
Above the reason of her youthly yeares.
Her golden lockes she roundly did uptye
In breaded tramels, that no looser heares
Did out of order stray about her daintie eares.

XVI. Whilest she her selfe thus busily did frame
Seemely to entertaine her new-come guest,
Newes hereof to her other sisters came,
Who all this while were at their wanton rest,
Accourting each her frend with lavish fest:
They were two knights of perelesse puissaunce,
And famous far abroad for warlike gest,
Which to these Ladies love did countenaunce,
And to his mistresse each himselfe strove to advaunce.

XVII. He that made love unto the eldest Dame,
Was hight Sir Huddibras, an hardy man;
Yet not so good of deedes as great of name,

Which he by many rash adventures wan,
Since errant armes to sew he first began:
More huge in strength then wise in workes he was,
And reason with foole-hardize over ran;
Sterne melancholy did his courage pas,
And was, for terrour more, all armd in shyning bras.

XVIII. But he that lov'd the youngest was Sansloy;
He, that faire Una late fowle outraged,
The most unruly and the boldest boy
That ever warlike weapons menaged,
And all to lawlesse lust encouraged
Through strong opinion of his matchlesse might;
Ne ought he car'd whom he endamaged
By tortious wrong, or whom bereav'd of right:
He, now this Ladies Champion, chose for love to fight.

XIX. These two gay knights, vowd to so diverse loves,
Each other does envy with deadly hate,
And daily warre against his foeman moves,
In hope to win more favour with his mate,
And th' others pleasing service to abate,
To magnifie his owne.   But when they heard
How in that place straunge knight arrived late,
Both knightes and ladies forth right angry far'd,
And fercely unto battell sterne themselves prepar'd.

XX. But ere they could proceede unto the place
Where he abode, themselves at discord fell,
And cruell combat joynd in middle space:
With horrible assault, and fury fell,
They heapt huge strokes the scorned life to quell,
That all on uprore from her settled seat,
The house was raysd, and all that in did dwell.
Seemd that lowde thunder with amazement great
Did rend the ratling skyes with flames of fouldring heat.

XXI. The noyse thereof cald forth that straunger knight,
To weet what dreadfull thing was there in hond;
Where whenas two brave knightes in bloody fight
With deadly rancour he enraunged fond,
His sunbroad shield about his wrest he bond,
And shyning blade unsheathd, with which he ran

Unto that stead, their strife to understond;
And at his first arrivall them began
With goodly meanes to pacifie, well as he can.

XXII. But they, him spying, both with greedy forse
Attonce upon him ran, and him beset
With strokes of mortall steele without remorse,
And on his shield like yron sledges bet:
As when a Beare and Tygre, being met
In cruell fight on Lybicke Ocean wide,
Espye a traveiler with feet surbet,
Whom they in equall pray hope to divide,
They stint their strife and him assayle on everie side.

XXIII. But he, not like a weary traveilere,
Their sharp assault right boldly did rebut,
And suffred not their blowes to byte him nere,
But with redoubled buffes them backe did put:
Whose grieved mindes, which choler did englut,
Against themselves turning their wrathfull spight,
Gan with new rage their shieldes to hew and cut;
But still, when Guyon came to part their fight,
With heavie load on him they freshly gan to smight.

XXIV. As a tall ship tossed in troublous seas,
Whom raging windes, threatning to make the pray
Of the rough rockes, doe diversly disease,
Meetes two contrarie billowes by the way,
That her on either side doe sore assay,
And boast to swallow her in greedy grave;
Shee, scorning both their spights, does make wide way,
And with her brest breaking the fomy wave,
Does ride on both their backs, and faire her self doth save.

XXV. So boldly he him beares, and rusheth forth
Betweene them both by conduct of his blade.
Wondrous great prowesse and heroick worth
He shewd that day, and rare ensample made,
When two so mighty warriours he dismade.
Attonce he wards and strikes; he takes and paies;
Now forst to yield, now forcing to invade;
Before, behind, and round about him laies;
So double was his paines, so double be his praise.

XXVI. Straunge sort of fight, three valiaunt knights to see
        Three combates joine in one, and to darraine
        A triple warre with triple enmitee,
        All for their Ladies froward love to gaine,
        Which gotten was but hate.   So love does raine
        In stoutest minds, and maketh monstrous warre;
        He maketh warre, he maketh peace againe,
        And yett his peace is but continual jarre:
        O miserable men that to him subject arre!

XXVII. Whilst thus they mingled were in furious armes,
        The faire Medina, with her tresses torne
        And naked brest, in pitty of their harmes,
        Emongst them ran; and, falling them beforne,
        Besought them by the womb which them had born,
        And by the loves which were to them most deare,
        And by the knighthood which they sure had sworn,
        Their deadly cruell discord to forbeare,
        And to her just conditions of faire peace to heare.

XXVIII. But her two other sisters, standing by,
        Her lowd gainsaid, and both their champions bad
        Pursew the end of their strong enmity,
        As ever of their loves they would be glad:
        Yet she with pitthy words, and counsell sad,
        Still strove their stubborne rages to revoke;
        That at the last, suppressing fury mad,
        They gan abstaine from dint of direfull stroke,
        And hearken to the sober speaches which she spoke.

XXIX. " Ah, puissaunt Lords! what cursed evil Spright,
        Or fell Erinnys, in your noble harts
        Her hellish brond hath kindled with despight,
        And stird you up to worke your wilfull smarts?
        Is this the joy of armes? be these the parts
        Of glorious knighthood, after blood to thrust,
        And not regard dew right and just desarts?
        Vaine is the vaunt, and victory unjust,
        That more to mighty hands then rightfull cause doth trust.

XXX. " And were there rightfull cause of difference,
        Yet were not better fayre it to accord
        Then with bloodguiltinesse to heape offence,

And mortal vengeaunce joyne to crime abhord?
O! fly from wrath; fly, O my liefest Lord!
Sad be the sights, and bitter fruites of warre,
And thousand furies wait on wrathfull sword;
Ne ought the praise of prowesse more doth marre
Then fowle revenging rage, and base contentious jarre.

XXXI. " But lovely concord, and most sacred peace,
Doth nourish vertue, and fast friendship breeds,
Weake she makes strong, and strong thing does increace,
Till it the pitch of highest praise exceeds:
Brave be her warres, and honorable deeds,
By which she triumphes over yre and pride,
And winnes an Olive girlond for her meeds.
Be, therefore, O my deare Lords! pacifide,
And this misseeming discord meekely lay aside."

XXXII. Her gracious words their rancour did appall,
And suncke so deepe into their boyling brests,
That downe they lett their cruell weapons fall,
And lowly did abase their lofty crests
To her faire presence and discrete behests.
Then she began a treaty to procure,
And stablish terms betwixt both their requests,
That as a law forever should endure;
Which to observe in word of knights they did assure

XXXIII. Which to confirme, and fast to bind their league,
After their weary sweat and bloody toile,
She them besought, during their quiet treague,
Into her lodging to repaire awhile,
To rest themselves, and grace to reconcile.
They soone consent: so forth with her they fare;
Where they are well receivd, and made to spoile
Themselves of soiled armes, and to prepare
Their minds to pleasure, and their mouths to dainty fare.

XXXIV. And those two froward sisters, their faire loves,
Came with them eke, all were they wondrous loth,
And fained cheare, as for the time behoves,
But could not colour yet so well the troth,
But that their natures bad appeard in both;
For both did at their second sister grutch

I

And inly grieve, as doth an hidden moth
The inner garment frett, not th' utter touch:
One thought her cheare too litle, th' other thought too
   mutch.

XXXV. Elissa (so the eldest hight) did deeme
Such entertainment base, ne ought would eat,
Ne ought would speake, but evermore did seeme
As discontent for want of merth or meat:
No solace could her Paramour intreat
Her once to show, ne court, nor dalliaunce;
But with bent lowring browes, as she would threat,
She scould, and frownd with froward countenaunce;
Unworthy of faire Ladies comely governaunce.

XXXVI. But young Perissa was of other mynd,
Full of disport, still laughing, loosely light,
And quite contrary to her sisters kynd,
No measure in her mood, no rule of right,
But poured out in pleasure and delight:
In wine and meats she flowd above the banck,
And in excesse exceeded her owne might;
In sumptuous tire she joyd her selfe to pranck,
But of her love too lavish: (litle have she thanck!)

XXXVII. Fast by her side did sitt the bold Sansloy,
Fitt mate for such a mincing mineon,
Who in her loosenesse tooke exceeding joy;
Might not be found a francker franion,
Of her leawd parts to make companion:
But Huddibras, more like a Malecontent,
Did see and grieve at his bold fashion;
Hardly could he endure his hardiment,
Yett still he satt, and inly did him selfe torment.

XXXVIII. Betwixt them both the faire Medina sate
With sober grace and goodly carriage:
With equall measure she did moderate
The strong extremities of their outrage.
That forward paire she ever would asswage,
When they would strive dew reason to exceed,
But that same froward twaine would accorage,
And of her plenty adde unto their need:
So kept she them in order, and her selfe in heed.

xxxix. Thus fairely shee attempered her feast,
And pleasd them all with meete satiety.
At last, when lust of meat and drinke was ceast,
She Guyon deare besought of curtesie
To tell from whence he came through jeopardy,
And whither now on new adventure bownd:
Who with bold grace, and comely gravity,
Drawing to him the eies of all arownd,
From lofty siege began these words aloud to sownd.

xl. " This thy demaund, O Lady! doth revive
Fresh memory in me of that great Queene,
Great and most glorious virgin Queene alive,
That with her soveraine power, and scepter shene,
All Faery lond does peaceably sustene,
In widest Ocean she her throne does reare,
That over all the earth it may be seene;
As morning Sunne her beames dispredden cleare,
And in her face faire peace and mercy doth appeare.

xli. " In her the richesse of all heavenly grace
In chiefe degree are heaped up on hye:
And all, that els this worlds enclosure bace
Hath great or glorious in mortall eye,
Adornes the person of her Majestye;
That men, beholding so great excellence
And rare perfection in mortalitye,
Doe her adore with sacred reverence,
As th' Idole of her makers great magnificence.

xlii. " To her I homage and my service owe,
In number of the noblest knightes on ground;
Mongst whom on me she deigned to bestowe
Order of Maydenhead, the most renownd
That may this day in all the world be found.
An yearely solemne feast she wontes to hold,
The day that first doth lead the yeare around,
To which all knights of worth and courage bold
Resort, to heare of straunge adventures to be told.

xliii. " There this old Palmer shewd himselfe that day,
And to that mighty Princesse did complaine
Of grievous mischiefes which a wicked Fay

Had wrought, and many whelmd in deadly paine;
Whereof he crav'd redresse.   My Soveraine,
Whose glory is in gracious deeds, and joyes
Throughout the world her mercy to maintaine,
Eftsoones devised redresse for such annoyes:
Me, all unfitt for so great purpose, she employes.

XLIV. " Now hath faire Phebe with her silver face
Thrise seene the shadowes of the neather world,
Sith last I left that honorable place,
In which her roiall presence is enrold;
Ne ever shall I rest in house nor hold,
Till I that false Acrasia have wonne;
Of whose fowle deedes, too hideous to bee told,
I witnesse am, and this their wretched sonne,
Whose wofull parents she hath wickedly fordonne."

XLV. " Tell on, fayre Sir," said she, " that dolefull tale,
From which sad ruth does seeme you to restraine,
That we may pitty such unhappie bale,
And learne from pleasures poyson to abstaine:
Ill by ensample good doth often gayne."
Then forward he his purpose gan pursew,
And told the story of the mortall payne,
Which Mordant and Amavia did rew,
As with lamenting eyes him selfe did lately vew.

XLVI. Night was far spent; and now in Ocean deep
Orion, flying fast from hissing snake,
His flaming head did hasten for to steep,
When of his pitteous tale he end did make:
Whilst with delight of that he wisely spake
Those guestes, beguyled, did beguyle their eyes
Of kindly sleepe that did them overtake.
At last, when they had markt the chaunged skyes,
They wist their houre was spent; then each to rest him hyes.

CANTO III

Vaine Braggadocchio, getting Guy-
ons horse, is made the scorne
Of knighthood trew; and is of fayre
Belphœbe fowle forlorne.

I. Soone as the morrow fayre with purple beames
Disperst the shadowes of the misty night,
And Titan, playing on the eastern streames,
Gan cleare the deawy ayre with springing light,
Sir Guyon, mindfull of his vow yplight,
Uprose from drowsie couch, and him addrest
Unto the journey which he had behight:
His puissant armes about his noble brest,
And many-folded shield he bound about his wrest.

II. Then, taking Congé of that virgin pure,
The bloody-handed babe unto her truth
Did earnestly committ, and her conjure
In vertuous lore to traine his tender youth,
And all that gentle noriture ensu'th;
And that, so soone as ryper yeares he raught,
He might, for memory of that dayes ruth,
Be called Ruddymane; and thereby taught
T' avenge his Parents death on them that had it wrought.

III. So forth he far'd, as now befell, on foot,
Sith his good steed is lately from him gone;
Patience perforce: helplesse what may it boot
To frett for anger, or for griefe to mone?
His Palmer now shall foot no more alone.
So fortune wrought, as under greene woodes syde
He lately heard that dying Lady grone,
He left his steed without, and speare besyde,
And rushed in on foot to ayd her ere she dyde.

IV. The whyles a losell wandring by the way,
One that to bountie never cast his mynd,
Ne thought of honour ever did assay

His baser brest, but in his kestrell kynd
A pleasing vaine of glory he did fynd,
To which his flowing toung and troublous spright
Gave him great ayd, and made him more inclynd:
He, that brave steed there finding ready dight,
Purloynd both steed and speare, and ran away full light.

v. Now gan his hart all swell in jollity,
And of him selfe great hope and help conceiv'd,
That puffed up with smoke of vanity,
And with selfe-loved personage deceiv'd,
He gan to hope of men to be receiv'd
For such as he him thought, or faine would bee:
But for in court gay portaunce he perceiv'd,
And gallant shew to be in greatest gree,
Eftsoones to court he cast t' advaunce his first degree.

vi. And by the way he chaunced to espy
One sitting ydle on a sunny banck,
To him avaunting in great bravery,
As Peacocke that his painted plumes doth pranck,
He smote his courser in the trembling flanck,
And to him threatned his hart-thrilling speare:
The seely man, seeing him ryde so ranck,
And ayme at him, fell flatt to ground for feare,
And crying, "Mercy!" loud, his pitious handes gan reare.

vii. Thereat the Scarcrow wexed wondrous prowd,
Through fortune of his first adventure fayre,
And with big thundring voice revyld him lowd:
"Vile Caytive, vassall of dread and despayre,
Unworthie of the commune breathed ayre,
Why livest thou, dead dog, a lenger day,
And doest not unto death thyselfe prepayre?
Dy, or thyselfe my captive yield for ay.
Great favour I thee graunt for aunswere thus to stay."

viii. "Hold, O deare Lord! hold your dead-doing hand,"
Then loud he cryde; "I am your humble thrall."
"Ay wretch," (quoth he) "thy destinies withstand
My wrathfull will, and doe for mercy call.
I give thee life: therefore prostrated fall,
And kisse my stirrup; that thy homage bee."

The Miser threw him selfe, as an Offall,
Streight at his foot in base humilitee,
And cleeped him his liege, to hold of him in fee.

IX. So happy peace they made and faire accord.
Eftsoones this liegeman gan to wexe more bold,
And when he felt the folly of his Lord,
In his owne kind he gan him selfe unfold;
For he was wylie witted, and growne old
In cunning sleightes and practick knavery.
From that day forth he cast for to uphold
His ydle humour with fine flattery,
And blow the bellowes to his swelling vanity.

X. Trompart, fitt man for Braggadochio,
To serve at court in view of vaunting eye;
Vaine-glorious man, when fluttring wind does blow
In his light winges, is lifted up to skye;
The scorne of knighthood and trew chevalrye,
To thinke, without desert of gentle deed
And noble worth, to be advaunced hye:
Such prayse is shame; but honour, vertues meed,
Doth beare the fayrest flowre in honourable seed.

XI. So forth they pas, a well consorted payre,
Till that at length with Archimage they meet:
Who seeing one, that shone in armour fayre,
On goodly courser thondring with his feet,
Eftsoones supposed him a person meet
Of his revenge to make the instrument;
For since the Redcrosse knight he erst did weet
To been with Guyon knitt in one consent,
The ill, which earst to him, he now to Guyon ment.

XII. And coming close to Trompart gan inquere
Of him, what mightie warriour that mote bee,
That rode in golden sell with single spere,
But wanted sword to wreake his enmitee?
" He is a great adventurer," (said he)
" That hath his sword through hard assay forgone,
And now hath vowd, till he avenged bee
Of that despight, never to wearen none:
That speare is him enough to doen a thousand grone."

XIII. Th' enchaunter greatly joyed in the vaunt,
And weened well ere long his will to win,
And both his foen with equall foyle to daunt.
Tho to him louting lowly did begin
To plaine of wronges, which had committed bin
By Guyon, and by that false Redcrosse knight;
Which two, through treason and deceiptfull gin,
Had slayne Sir Mordant and his Lady bright:
That mote him honour win to wreak so foule despight.

XIV. Therewith all suddeinly he seemd enragd,
And threatned death with dreadfull countenaunce,
As if their lives had in his hand beene gagd;
And with stiffe force shaking his mortall launce,
To let him weet his doughtie valiaunce,
Thus said: "Old man, great sure shal be thy meed,
If, where those knights for feare of dew vengeaunce
Doe lurke, thou certeinly to mee areed,
That I may wreake on them their hainous hatefull deed."

XV. "Certes, my Lord," (said he) "that shall I soone,
And give you eke good helpe to their decay.
But mote I wisely you advise to doon,
Give no ods to your foes, but doe purvay
Your selfe of sword before that bloody day;
For they be two the prowest knights on grownd,
And oft approv'd in many hard assay;
And eke of surest steele that may be fownd,
Do arme your self against that day, them to confownd."

XVI. "Dotard," (said he) "let be thy deepe advise:
Seemes that through many yeares thy wits thee faile,
And that weake eld hath left thee nothing wise;
Els never should thy judgement be so frayle
To measure manhood by the sword or mayle.
Is not enough fowre quarters of a man,
Withouten sword or shield, an hoste to quayle?
Thou litle wotest what this right-hand can:
Speake they which have beheld the battailes which it wan."

XVII. The man was much abashed at his boast;
Yet well he wist that whoso would contend
With either of those knightes on even coast,

Should neede of all his armes him to defend,
Yet feared least his boldnesse should offend,
When Braggadocchio saide; " Once I did sweare,
When with one sword seven knightes I brought to end,
Thenceforth in battaile never sword to beare,
But it were that which noblest knight on earth doth weare."

XVIII. " Perdy, Sir knight," saide then th' enchaunter blive,
" That shall I shortly purchase to your hond;
For now the best and noblest knight alive
Prince Arthur is, that wonnes in Faerie lond:
He hath a sword that flames like burning brond.
The same by my device I undertake
Shall by to morrow by thy side be fond."
At which bold word that boaster gan to quake,
And wondred in his minde what mote that Monster make.

XIX. He stayd not for more bidding, but away
Was suddein vanished out of his sight:
The Northerne winde his wings did broad display
At his commaund, and reared him up light
From off the earth to take his aerie flight.
They lookt about, but nowhere could espye
Tract of his foot: then dead through great affright
They both nigh were, and each bad other flye:
Both fled attonce, ne ever backe retourned eye;

XX. Till that they come unto a forrest greene,
In which they shrowd themselves from causeles feare;
Yet feare them followes still where so they beene.
Each trembling leafe and whistling wind they heare,
As ghastly bug, does greatly them affeare:
Yet both doe strive their fearefulnesse to faine.
At last they heard a horne that thrilled cleare
Throughout the wood that ecchoed againe,
And made the forrest ring, as it would rive in twaine.

XXI. Eft through the thicke they heard one rudely rush,
With noyse whereof he from his loftie steed
Downe fell to ground, and crept into a bush,
To hide his coward head from dying dreed:
But Trompart stoutly stayd to taken heed
Of what might hap.   Eftsoone there stepped foorth

A goodly Ladie clad in hunters weed,
That seemd to be a woman of great worth,
And by her stately portance borne of heavenly **birth.**

XXII. Her face so faire as flesh it seemed not,
But hevenly pourtraict of bright Angels hew,
Cleare as the skye, withouten blame or blot,
Through goodly mixture of complexions dew;
And in her cheekes the vermeill red did shew
Like roses in a bed of lillies shed,
The which ambrosiall odours from them threw,
And gazers sence with double pleasure fed,
Hable to heale the sicke, and to revive the ded.

XXIII. In her faire eyes two living lamps did flame,
Kindled above at th' hevenly makers light,
And darted fyrie beames out of the same,
So passing persant, and so wondrous bright,
That quite bereav'd the rash beholders sight:
In them the blinded god his lustfull fyre
To kindle oft assayd, but had no might;
For, with dredd Majestie and awfull yre,
She broke his wanton darts, and quenched bace **desyre.**

XXIV. Her yvorie forhead, full of bountie brave,
Like a broad table did it selfe dispred,
For Love his loftie triumphes to engrave,
And write the battailes of his great godhed:
All good and honour might therein be red,
For there their dwelling was.   And, when she **spake,**
Sweete wordes like dropping honny she did shed;
And twixt the perles and rubins softly brake
A silver sound, that heavenly musicke seemd **to make.**

XXV. Upon her eyelids many Graces sate,
Under the shadow of her even browes,
Working belgardes and amorous retrate;
And everie one her with a grace endowes,
And everie one with meekenesse to her bowes.
So glorious mirrhour of celestiall grace,
And soveraine moniment of mortall vowes,
How shall frayle pen descrive her heavenly face,
For feare, through want of skill, her beauty to disgrace?

XXVI. So faire, and thousand thousand times more faire,
    She seemd, when she presented was to sight;
    And was yclad, for heat of scorching aire,
    All in a silken Camus lilly whight,
    Purfled upon with many a folded plight,
    Which all above besprinckled was throughout
    With golden aygulets, that glistred bright
    Like twinckling starres; and all the skirt about
    Was hemd with golden fringe.

XXVII. Below her ham her weed did somewhat trayne,
    And her streight legs most bravely were embayld
    In gilden buskins of costly Cordwayne,
    All bard with golden bendes, which were entayld
    With curious antickes, and full fayre aumayld:
    Before, they fastned were under her knee
    In a rich jewell, and therein entrayld
    The ends of all the knots, that none might see
    How they within their fouldings close enwrapped bee:

XXVIII. Like two faire marble pillours they were seene,
    Which doe the temple of the Gods support,
    Whom all the people decke with girlands greene,
    And honour in their festivall resort;
    Those same with stately grace and princely port
    She taught to tread, when she herselfe would grace;
    But with the woody Nymphes when she did play,
    Or when the flying Libbard she did chace,
    She could then nimbly move, and after fly apace.

XXIX. And in her hand a sharpe bore-speare she held,
    And at her backe a bow and quiver gay,
    Stuft with steele-headed dartes, wherewith she queld
    The salvage beastes in her victorious play,
    Knit with a golden bauldricke, which forelay
    Athwart her snowy brest, and did divide
    Her daintie paps; which, like young fruit in May,
    Now little gan to swell, and being tide
    Through her thin weed their places only signifide.

XXX. Her yellow lockes, crisped like golden wyre,
    About her shoulders weren loosely shed,
    And, when the winde emongst them did inspyre,

They waved like a penon wyde dispred,
And low behinde her backe were scattered:
And, whether art it were or heedlesse hap,
As through the flouring forrest rash she fled,
In her rude heares sweet flowres themselves did lap,
And flourishing fresh leaves and blossomes did enwrap.

XXXI. Such as Diana by the sandy shore
Of swift Eurotas, or on Cynthus greene,
Where all the Nymphes have her unwares forlore,
Wandreth alone with bow and arrowes keene,
To seeke her game: Or as that famous Queene
Of Amazons, whom Pyrrhus did destroy,
The day that first of Priame she was seene,
Did shew her selfe in great triumphant joy,
To succour the weake state of sad afflicted Troy.

XXXII. Such when as hartlesse Trompart her did vew,
He was dismayed in his coward minde,
And doubted whether he himselfe should shew,
Or fly away, or bide alone behinde;
Both feare and hope he in her face did finde:
When she at last him spying thus bespake:
" Hayle, Groome! didst not thou see a bleeding Hynde,
Whose right haunch earst my stedfast arrow strake?
If thou didst, tell me, that I may her overtake."

XXXIII. Wherewith reviv'd, this answere forth he threw:
" O Goddesse, (for such I thee take to bee)
For nether doth thy face terrestriall shew,
Nor voyce sound mortall; I avow to thee,
Such wounded beast as that I did not see,
Sith earst into this forrest wild I came.
But mote thy goodlyhed forgive it mee,
To weete which of the gods I shall thee name,
That unto thee dew worship I may rightly frame."

XXXIV. To whom she thus—but ere her words ensewd,
Unto the bush her eye did suddein glaunce,
In which vaine Braggadocchio was mewd,
And saw it stirre: she lefte her percing launce,
And towards gan a deadly shafte advaunce,
In mind to marke the beast.   At which sad stowre

Trompart forth stept to stay the mortall chaunce,
Out crying; "O! what ever hevenly powre,
Or earthly wight thou be, withhold this deadly howre.

XXXV. "O! stay thy hand; for yonder is no game
For thy fiers arrowes, them to exercize;
But loe! my Lord, my liege, whose warlike name
Is far renowmd through many bold emprize;
And now in shade he shrowded yonder lies."
She staid: with that he crauld out of his nest,
Forth creeping on his caitive hands and thies;
And, standing stoutly up, his lofty crest
Did fiercely shake, and rowze as comming late from rest.

XXXVI. As fearfull fowle, that long in secret cave
For dread of soring hauke her selfe hath hid,
Nor caring how, her silly life to save,
She her gay painted plumes disorderid;
Seeing at last her selfe from daunger rid,
Peepes forth, and soone renews her native pride:
She gins her feathers fowle disfigured
Prowdly to prune, and sett on every side;
She shakes off shame, ne thinks how erst she did her hide.

XXXVII. So when her goodly visage he beheld,
He gan himselfe to vaunt: but, when he vewd
Those deadly tooles which in her hand she held,
Soone into other fitts he was transmewd,
Till she to him her gracious speach renewd:
"All haile, Sir knight! and well may thee befall,
As all the like, which honor have pursewd
Through deeds of armes and prowesse martiall.
All vertue merits praise, but such the most of all."

XXXVIII. To whom he thus: "O fairest under skie!
Trew be thy words, and worthy of thy praise,
That warlike feats doest highest glorifie.
Therein I have spent all my youthly daies,
And many battailes fought and many fraies
Throughout the world, wher-so they might be found,
Endevoring my dreaded name to raise
Above the Moone, that fame may it resound
In her eternall tromp, with laurell girlond cround.

XXXIX. " But what art thou, O Lady! which doest raunge
In this wilde forest, where no pleasure is,
And doest not it for joyous court exchaunge,
Emongst thine equall peres, where happy blis
And all delight does raigne, much more then this?
There thou maist love, and dearly loved be,
And swim in pleasure, which thou here doest mis:
There maist thou best be seene, and best maist see:
The wood is fit for beasts, the court is fitt for thee."

XL. " Who-so in pompe of prowd estate " (quoth she)
" Does swim, and bathes him selfe in courtly blis,
Does waste his dayes in darke obscuritee,
And in oblivion ever buried is;
Where ease abownds yt's eath to doe amis:
But who his limbs with labours, and his mynd
Behaves with cares, cannot so easy mis.
Abroad in armes, at home in studious kynd,
Who seekes with painfull toile shall honor soonest fynd:

XLI. " In woods, in waves, in warres, she wonts to dwell,
And wil be found with perill and with paine;
Ne can the man that moulds in ydle cell
Unto her happy mansion attaine:
Before her gate high God did Sweate ordaine,
And wakefull watches ever to abide;
But easy is the way and passage plaine
To pleasures pallace: it may soone be spide,
And day and night her dores to all stand open wide.

XLII. " In Princes court "—The rest she would have sayd,
But that the foolish man, fild with delight
Of her sweete words that all his sence dismayd,
And with her wondrous beauty ravisht quight,
Gan burne in filthy lust; and, leaping light,
Thought in his bastard armes her to embrace.
With that she, swarving backe, her Javelin bright
Against him bent, and fiercely did menace:
So turned her about, and fled away apace.

XLIII. Which when the Pesaunt saw, amazd he stood,
And grieved at her flight; yet durst he nott
Pursew her steps through wild unknowen wood:

Besides he feard her wrath, and threatned shott,
Whiles in the bush he lay, not yett forgott:
Ne car'd he greatly for her presence vayne,
But turning said to Trompart; " What fowle blott
Is this to knight, that Lady should agayne
Depart to woods untoucht, and leave so proud disdayne."

XLIV. " Perdy," (said Trompart) " lett her pas at will,
Least by her presence daunger mote befall;
For who can tell (and sure I feare it ill)
But that shee is some powre celestiall?
For whiles she spake her great words did appall
My feeble corage, and my heart oppresse,
That yet I quake and tremble over-all."
" And I," (said Braggadocchio) " thought no lesse,
When first I heard her horn sound with such ghastlinesse.

XLV. " For from my mothers wombe this grace I have
Me given by eternall destiny,
That earthly thing may not my corage brave
Dismay with feare, or cause one foot to flye,
But either hellish feends, or powres on hye:
Which was the cause, when earst that horne I heard,
Weening it had beene thunder in the skye,
I hid my selfe from it, as one affeard;
But, when I other knew, my self I boldly reard.

XLVI. " But now, for feare of worse that may betide,
Let us soone hence depart."   They soone agree:
So to his steed he gott, and gan to ride
As one unfitt therefore, that all might see
He had not trayned bene in chevalree.
Which well that valiaunt courser did discerne;
For he despisd to tread in dew degree,
But chaufd and fom'd with corage fiers and sterne,
And to be easd of that base burden still did erne.

CANTO IV

Guyon does Furor bind in chaines,
And stops occasion:
Delivers Phaon, and therefore
By strife is rayld uppon.

I. In brave poursuitt of honorable deed,
   There is I know not (what) great difference
   Betweene the vulgar and the noble seed,
   Which unto things of valorous pretence
   Seemes to be borne by native influence;
   As feates of armes, and love to entertaine:
   But chiefly skill to ride seemes a science
   Proper to gentle blood: some others faine
   To menage steeds, as did this vaunter, but in vaine.

II. But he, the rightfull owner of that steede,
    Who well could menage and subdew his pride,
    The whiles on foot was forced for to yeed
    With that blacke Palmer, his most trusty guide,
    Who suffred not his wandring feete to slide;
    But when strong passion, or weake fleshlinesse,
    Would from the right way seeke to draw him wide,
    He would, through temperaunce and stedfastnesse,
    Teach him the weak to strengthen, and the strong suppresse.

III. It fortuned, forth faring on his way,
     He saw from far, or seemed for to see,
     Some troublous uprore or contentious fray,
     Whereto he drew in hast it to agree.
     A mad man, or that feigned mad to bee,
     Drew by the heare along upon the grownd
     A handsom stripling with great crueltee,
     Whom sore he bett, and gor'd with many a wownd,
     That cheekes with teares, and sydes with blood, did all
        abownd.

IV. And him behynd a wicked Hag did stalke,
    In ragged robes and filthy disaray;
    Her other leg was lame, that she no'te walke,

But on a staffe her feeble steps did stay:
Her lockes, that loathly were and hoarie gray,
Grew all afore, and loosely hong unrold;
But all behinde was bald, and worne away,
That none thereof could ever taken hold;
And eke her face ill-favourd, full of wrinckles old.

v. And ever as she went her toung did walke
In fowle reproch, and termes of vile despight,
Provoking him, by her outrageous talke,
To heape more vengeance on that wretched wight:
Sometimes she raught him stones, wherwith to smite,
Sometimes her staffe, though it her one leg were,
Withouten which she could not goe upright;
Ne any evill meanes she did forbeare,
That might him move to wrath, and indignation reare.

vi. The noble Guyon, mov'd with great remorse,
Approching, first the Hag did thrust away;
And after, adding more impetuous forse,
His mighty hands did on the madman lay,
And pluckt him backe; who, all on fire streight way,
Against him turning all his fell intent,
With beastly brutish rage gan him assay,
And smott, and bitt, and kickt, and scratcht, and rent,
And did he wist not what in his avengement.

vii. And sure he was a man of mickle might,
Had he had governaunce it well to guyde;
But, when the frantick fitt inflamd his spright,
His force was vaine, and strooke more often wyde,
Then at the aymed marke which he had eyde:
And oft himselfe he chaunst to hurt unwares,
Whylest reason, blent through passion, nought descryde;
But, as a blindfold Bull, at randon fares,
And where he hits nought knowes, and whom he hurts
    nought cares.

viii. His rude assault and rugged handeling
Straunge seemed to the knight, that aye with foe
In fayre defence and goodly menaging
Of armes was wont to fight; yet nathemoe
Was he abashed now, not fighting so;
But more enfierced through his currish play,

Him sternly grypt, and hailing to and fro,
To overthrow him strongly did assay,
But overthrew him selfe unwares, and lower lay:

IX. And being downe the villein sore did beate
And bruze with clownish fistes his manly face;
And eke the Hag, with many a bitter threat,
Still cald upon to kill him in the place.
With whose reproch, and odious menace,
The knight emboyling in his haughtie hart
Knitt all his forces, and gan soone unbrace
His grasping hold: so lightly did upstart,
And drew his deadly weapon to maintaine his part.

X. Which when the Palmer saw, he loudly cryde,
" Not so, O Guyon! never thinke that so
That Monster can be maistred or destroyd:
He is not, ah! he is not such a foe,
As steele can wound, or strength can overthroe.
That same is Furor, cursed cruel wight,
That unto knighthood workes much shame and woe;
And that same Hag, his aged mother, hight
Occasion; the roote of all wrath and despight.

XI. " With her, whoso will raging Furor tame,
Must first begin, and well her amenage:
First her restraine from her reprochfull blame
And evill meanes, with which she doth enrage
Her frantick sonne, and kindles his corage;
Then, when she is withdrawne or strong withstood,
It's eath his ydle fury to aswage,
And calme the tempest of his passion wood:
The bankes are overflowne when stopped is the flood."

XII. Therewith Sir Guyon left his first emprise,
And, turning to that woman, fast her hent
By the hoare lockes that hong before her eyes,
And to the ground her threw: yet n'ould she stent
Her bitter rayling and foule revilement,
But still provokt her sonne to wreake her wrong;
But nathelesse he did her still torment,
And, catching hold of her ungratious tonge
Thereon an yron lock did fasten firme and strong.

XIII. Then, whenas use of speach was from her reft,
With her two crooked handes she signes did make,
And beckned him, the last help she had left;
But he that last left helpe away did take,
And both her handes fast bound unto a stake,
That she note stirre. Then gan her sonne to flye
Full fast away, and did her quite forsake;
But Guyon after him in hast did hye,
And soone him overtooke in sad perplexitye.

XIV. In his strong armes he stifly him embraste,
Who him gainstriving nought at all prevaild;
For all his power was utterly defaste,
And furious fitts at earst quite weren quaild:
Oft he re'nforst, and oft his forces fayld,
Yet yield he would not, nor his rancor slack.
Then him to ground he cast, and rudely hayld,
And both his hands fast bound behind his backe,
And both his feet in fetters to an yron racke.

XV. With hundred yron chaines he did him bind,
And hundred knots, that did him sore constraine;
Yet his great yron teeth he still did grind
And grimly gnash, threatning revenge in vaine:
His burning eyen, whom bloody strakes did staine,
Stared full wide, and threw forth sparkes of fyre;
And more for ranck despight then for great paine,
Shakt his long locks colourd like copper-wyre,
And bitt his tawny beard to shew his raging yre.

XVI. Thus when as Guyon Furor had captivd,
Turning about he saw that wretched Squyre,
Whom that mad man of life nigh late deprivd,
Lying on ground, all soild with blood and myre:
Whom whenas he perceived to respyre,
He gan to comfort, and his woundes to dresse.
Being at last recured, he gan inquyre
What hard mishap him brought to such distresse,
And made that caytives thrall, the thrall of wretchednesse.

XVII. With hart then throbbing, and with watry eyes,
" Fayre Sir " (quoth he) " What man can shun the hap,
That hidden lyes unwares him to surpryse?

Misfortune waites advantage to entrap
The man most wary in her whelming lap:
So me weake wretch, of many weakest one,
Unweeting and unware of such mishap,
She brought to mischiefe through Occasion,
Where this same wicked villein did me light upon.

XVIII. " It was a faithlesse Squire, that was the sourse
Of all my sorrow and of these sad teares,
With whom from tender dug of commune nourse
Attonce I was upbrought; and eft, when yeares
More rype us reason lent to chose our Peares,
Our selves in league of vowed love wee knitt;
In which we long time, without gealous feares
Or faultie thoughts, contynewd as was fitt;
And for my part, I vow, dissembled not a whitt.

XIX. " It was my fortune, commune to that age,
To love a Lady fayre of great degree,
The which was borne of noble parentage,
And set in highest seat of dignitee,
Yet seemd no lesse to love then lov'd to bee:
Long I her serv'd, and found her faithful still,
Ne ever thing could cause us disagree.
Love, that two harts makes one, makes eke one will;
Each strove to please, and others pleasure to fulfill.

XX. " My friend, hight Philemon, I did partake
Of all my love and all my privitie;
Who greatly joyous seemed for my sake,
And gratious to that Lady as to mee;
Ne ever wight that mote so welcome bee
As he to her, withouten blott or blame;
He ever thing that she could think or see,
But unto him she would impart the same.
O wretched man, that would abuse so gentle Dame!

XXI. " At last such grace I found, and meanes I wrought,
That I that Lady to my spouse had wonne;
Accord of friendes, consent of Parents sought,
Affyaunce made, my happinesse begonne,
There wanted nought but few rites to be donne,
Which mariage make: that day too farre did seeme.

Most joyous man, on whom the shining Sunne
Did shew his face, my selfe I did esteeme,
And that my falser friend did no less joyous deeme.

XXII. " But ear that wished day his beame disclosd,
He, either envying my toward good,
Or of him selfe to treason ill disposed,
One day unto me came in friendly mood,
And told for secret, how he understood
That Lady, whom I had to me assynd,
Had both distaind her honorable blood,
And eke the faith which she to me did bynd;
And therefore wisht me stay till I more truth should fynd.

XXIII. " The gnawing anguish, and sharp gelosy,
Which his sad speach infixed in my brest,
Ranckled so sore, and festred inwardly,
That my engreeved mind could find no rest,
Till that the truth thereof I did out wrest;
And him besought, by that same sacred band
Betwixt us both, to counsell me the best:
He then with solemne oath and plighted hand
Assurd, ere long the truth to let me understand.

XXIV. " Ere long with like againe he boorded mee,
Saying, he now had boulted all the floure,
And that it was a groome of base degree,
Which of my love was partener Paramoure:
Who used in a darkesome inner bowre
Her oft to meete: which better to approve,
He promised to bring me at that howre,
When I should see that would me nearer move,
And drive me to withdraw my blind abused love.

XXV. " This gracelesse man, for furtherance of his guile,
Did court the handmayd of my Lady deare,
Who, glad t' embosome his affection vile,
Did all she might more pleasing to appeare.
One day, to worke her to his will more neare,
He woo'd her thus: Pryene, (so she hight,)
What great despight doth fortune to thee beare,
Thus lowly to abase thy beautie bright,
That it should not deface all others lesser light?

XXVI. " But if she had her least helpe to thee lent,
  T'adorne thy forme according thy desart,
  Their blazing pride thou wouldest soone have blent,
  And staynd their prayses with thy least good part;
  Ne should faire Claribell with all her art,
  Tho' she thy Lady be, approch thee neare:
  For proofe thereof, this evening, as thou art,
  Aray thyselfe in her most gorgeous geare,
  That I may more delight in thy embracement deare.

XXVII. " The Mayden, proud through praise and mad through
   love,
  Him hearkned to, and soone her selfe arrayd,
  The whiles to me the treachour did remove
  His craftie engin; and, as he had sayd,
  Me leading, in a secret corner layd,
  The sad spectatour of my Tragedie:
  Where left, he went, and his owne false part playd,
  Disguised like that groome of base degree,
  Whom he had feignd th' abuser of my love to bee.

XXVIII. " Eftsoones he came unto th' appointed place,
  And with him brought Pryene, rich arayd,
  In Claribellaes clothes. Her proper face
  I not descerned in that darkesome shade,
  But weend it was my love with whom he playd.
  Ah God! what horrour and tormenting griefe
  My hart, my handes, mine eies, and all assayd!
  Me liefer were ten thousand deathes priefe
  Then wounde of gealous worme, and shame of such
   repriefe.

XXIX. " I home retourning, fraught with fowle despight,
  And chawing vengeaunce all the way I went,
  Soone as my loathed love appeard in sight,
  With wrathfull hand I slew her innocent,
  That after soone I dearely did lament;
  For, when the cause of that outrageous deede
  Demaunded, I made plaine and evident,
  Her faultie Handmayd, which that bale did breede,
  Confest how Philemon her wrought to chaunge her
   weede.

XXX. "Which when I heard, with horrible affright
And hellish fury all enragd, I sought
Upon myselfe that vengeable despight
To punish: yet it better first I thought
To wreake my wrath on him that first it wrought:
To Philemon, false faytour Philemon,
I cast to pay that I so dearely bought.
Of deadly drugs I gave him drinke anon,
And washt away his guilt with guilty potion.

XXXI. "Thus heaping crime on crime, and griefe on griefe,
To losse of love adjoyning losse of frend,
I meant to purge both with a third mischiefe,
And in my woes beginner it to end:
That was Pryene; she did first offend,
She last should smart: with which cruell intent,
When I at her my murdrous blade did bend,
She fled away with ghastly dreriment,
And I, poursewing my fell purpose, after went.

XXXII. "Feare gave her winges, and rage enforst my flight
Through woods and plaines so long I did her chace,
Till this mad man, whom your victorious might
Hath now fast bound, me met in middle space.
As I her, so he me poursewd apace,
And shortly overtooke: I, breathing yre,
Sore chauffed at my stay in such a cace,
And with my heat kindled his cruell fyre;
Which kindled once, his mother did more rage inspyre.

XXXIII. "Betwixt them both they have me doen to dye,
Through wounds, and strokes, and stubborne handeling,
That death were better then such agony
As griefe and fury unto me did bring;
Of which in me yet stickes the mortall sting,
That during life will never be appeased!"
When he thus ended had his sorrowing,
Said Guyon; "Squyre, sore have ye beene diseasd,
But all your hurts may soone through temperance be
    easd."

XXXIV. Then gan the Palmer thus; "Most wretched man,
That to affections does the bridle lend!
In their beginning they are weake and wan,

But soone through suff'rance growe to fearefull end:
Whiles they are weake, betimes with them contend;
For, when they once to perfect strength do grow,
Strong warres they make, and cruell battry bend
Gainst fort of Reason, it to overthrow:
Wrath, gelosy, griefe, love, this Squyre have laide thus
low.

XXXV. " Wrath, gealosie, griefe, love, do thus expell:
Wrath is a fire; and gealosie a weede;
Griefe is a flood; and love a monster fell;
The fire of sparkes, the weede of little seede,
The flood of drops, the Monster filth did breede:
But sparks, seed, drops, and filth, do thus delay;
The sparks soone quench, the springing seed outweed,
The drops dry up, and filth wipe cleane away:
So shall wrath, gealosy, griefe, love, die and decay."

XXXVI. " Unlucky Squire," (saide Guyon) " sith thou hast
Falne into mischiefe through intemperaunce,
Henceforth take heede of that thou now hast past.
And guyde thy waies with warie governaunce,
Least worse betide thee by some later chaunce,
But read how art thou nam'd, and of what kin? "
" Phaon I hight," (quoth he) " and do advaunce
Mine auncestry from famous Coradin,
Who first to rayse our house to honour did begin."

XXXVII. Thus as he spake, lo! far away they spyde
A varlet ronning towardes hastily,
Whose flying feet so fast their way applyde,
That round about a cloud of dust did fly,
Which, mingled all with sweate, did dim his eye.
He soone approched, panting, breathlesse, whot,
And all so soyld that none could him descry:
His countenance was bold, and bashed not
For Guyons lookes, but scornefull eyeglaunce at him shot.

XXXVIII. Behind his backe he bore a brasen shield,
On which was drawen faire, in colours fit,
A flaming fire in midst of bloody field,
And round about the wreath this word was writ,
Burnt I doe burne. Right well beseemed it
To be the shield of some redoubted knight;

And in his hand two dartes, exceeding flit
And deadly sharpe, he held, whose heads were dight
In poyson and in blood of malice and despight.

XXXIX. When he in presence came, to Guyon first
He boldly spake; " Sir knight, if knight thou bee,
Abandon this forestalled place at erst,
For feare of further harme, I counsell thee;
Or bide the chaunce at thine owne jeopardee."
The knight at his great boldnesse wondered;
And, though he scornd his ydle vanitee,
Yet mildly him to purpose answered;
For not to grow of nought he it conjectured.

XL. " Varlet, this place most dew to me I deeme,
Yielded by him that held it forcibly:
But whence should come that harme, which thou dost
seeme
To threat to him that mindes his chaunce t' abye? "
" Perdy," (sayd he) " here comes, and is hard by,
A knight of wondrous powre and great assay,
That never yet encountred enemy
But did him deadly daunt, or fowle dismay;
Ne thou for better hope, if thou his presence stay."

XLI. " How hight he then," (said Guyon) " and from
whence? "
" Pyrochles is his name, renowmed farre
For his bold feates and hardy confidence,
Full oft approvd in many a cruell warre;
The brother of Cymochles, both which arre
The sonnes of old Acrates and Despight;
Acrates, sonne of Phlegeton and Jarre;
But Phlegeton is sonne of Herebus and Night;
But Herebus sonne of Aeternitie is hight.

XLII. " So from immortall race he does proceede,
That mortall hands may not withstand his might,
Drad for his derring doe and bloody deed;
For all in blood and spoile is his delight.
His am I Atin, his in wrong and right,
That matter make for him to worke upon,
And stirre him up to strife and cruell fight.

Fly therefore, fly this fearefull stead anon,
Least thy foolhardize worke thy sad confusion."

XLIII. " His be that care, whom most it doth concerne,"
(Sayd he) " but whither with such hasty flight
Art thou now bownd? for well mote I discerne
Great cause, that carries thee so swifte and light."
" My Lord," (quoth he) " me sent, and streight behight
To seeke Occasion, where so she bee:
For he is all disposd to bloody fight,
And breathes out wrath and hainous crueltee:
Hard is his hap that first fals in his jeopardee."

XLIV. " Mad man," (said then the Palmer) " that does seeke
Occasion to wrath, and cause of strife:
Shee comes unsought, and shonned followes eke.
Happy! who can abstaine, when Rancor rife
Kindles Revenge, and threats his rusty knife.
Woe never wants where every cause is caught;
And rash Occasion makes unquiet life!"
" Then loe! wher bound she sits, whom thou hast
    sought,"
Said Guyon: " let that message to thy Lord be
    brought."

XLV. That when the varlett heard and saw, streight way
He wexed wondrous wroth, and said; " Vile knight,
That knights and knighthood doest with shame upbray,
And shewst th' ensample of thy childishe might,
With silly weake old woman that did fight!
Great glory and gay spoile, sure hast thou gott,
And stoutly prov'd thy puissance here in sight.
That shall Pyrochles well requite, I wott,
And with thy blood abolish so reprochfull blott."

XLVI. With that one of his thrillant darts he threw,
Headed with yre and vengeable despight.
The quivering steele his aymed end wel knew,
And to his brest it selfe intended right:
But he was wary, and, ere it empight
In the meant marke, advaunst his shield atweene,
On which it seizing no way enter might,
But backe rebownding left the forckhead keene:
Eftsoones he fled away, and might no where be seene.

CANTO V

Pyrochles does with Guyon fight,
And Furors chayne untyes,
Who him sore wounds: whiles Atin to
Cymochles for ayd flyes.

I. Who ever doth to temperaunce apply
His stedfast life, and all his actions frame,
Trust me, shal find no greater enimy
Then stubborne perturbation to the same;
To which right wel the wise doe give that name,
For it the goodly peace of staied mindes
Does overthrow, and troublous warre proclame:
His owne woes author, who so bound it findes,
As did Pyrochles, and it wilfully unbindes.

II. After that varlets flight, it was not long
Ere on the plaine fast pricking Guyon spide
One in bright armes embatteiled full strong,
That, as the Sunny beames do glaunce and glide
Upon the trembling wave, so shined bright,
And round about him threw forth sparkling fire,
That seemd him to enflame on every side:
His steed was bloody red, and fomed yre,
When with the maistring spur he did him roughly stire.

III. Approching nigh, he never staid to greete,
Ne chaffar words, prowd corage to provoke,
But prickt so fiers, that underneath his feete
The smouldring dust did rownd about him smoke,
Both horse and man nigh able for to choke;
And fayrly couching his steeleheaded speare,
Him first saluted with a sturdy stroke:
It booted nought Sir Guyon, comming neare,
To thincke such hideous puissaunce on foot to beare;

IV. But lightly shunned it; and, passing by,
With his bright blade did smite at him so fell,
That the sharpe steele, arriving forcibly

On his broad shield, bitt not, but glauncing fell
On his horse necke before the quilted sell,
And from the head the body sundred quight.
So him dismounted low he did compell
On foot with him to matchen equall fight:
The truncked beast fast bleeding did him fowly dight.

v. Sore bruzed with the fall he slow uprose,
And all enraged thus him loudly shent;
"Disleall Knight, whose coward corage chose
To wreake it selfe on beast all innocent,
And shund the marke at which it should be ment;
Therby thine armes seem strong, but manhood frayl:
So hast thou oft with guile thine honor blent;
But litle may such guile thee now avayl,
If wonted force and fortune doe me not much fayl."

vi. With that he drew his flaming sword, and strooke
At him so fiercely, that the upper marge
Of his sevenfolded shield away it tooke,
And, glauncing on his helmet, made a large
And open gash therein: were not his targe
That broke the violence of his intent,
The weary sowle from thence it would discharge;
Nathelesse so sore a buff to him it lent,
That made him reele, and to his brest his bever bent.

vii. Exceeding wroth was Guyon at that blow,
And much ashamd that stroke of living arme
Should him dismay, and make him stoup so low,
Though otherwise it did him litle harme:
Tho, hurling high his yron braced arme,
He smote so manly on his shoulder plate,
That all his left side it did quite disarme;
Yet there the steel stayd not, but inly bate
Deepe in his flesh, and opened wide a red floodgate.

viii. Deadly dismayd with horror of that dint
Pyrochles was, and grieved eke entyre;
Yet nathemore did it his fury stint,
But added flame unto his former fire,
That wel nigh molt his hart in raging yre:
Ne thenceforth his approved skill, to ward,

Or strike, or hurtle rownd in warlike gyre,
Remembred he, ne car'd for his saufgard,
But rudely rag'd, and like a cruell tygre far'd.

IX. He hewd, and lasht, and foynd, and thondred blowes,
And every way did seeke into his life;
Ne plate, ne male, could ward so mighty throwes,
But yielded passage to his cruell knife.
But Guyon, in the heat of all his strife,
Was wary wise, and closely did awayt
Avauntage, whilest his foe did rage most rife:
Sometimes athwart, sometimes he strook him strayt,
And falsed oft his blowes t' illude him with such bayt.

X. Like as a Lyon, whose imperiall powre
A prowd rebellious Unicorn defyes,
T' avoide the rash assault and wrathful stowre
Of his fiers foe, him to a tree applyes,
And when him ronning in full course he spyes,
He slips aside; the whiles that furious beast
His precious horne, sought of his enimyes,
Strikes in the stocke, ne thence can be releast,
But to the mighty victor yields a bounteous feast.

XI. With such faire sleight him Guyon often fayld,
Till at the last all breathlesse, weary, faint,
Him spying, with fresh onsett he assayld,
And kindling new his corage seeming queint,
Strooke him so hugely, that through great constraint
He made him stoup perforce unto his knee,
And doe unwilling worship to the Saint,
That on his shield depainted he did see:
Such homage till that instant never learned hee.

XII. Whom Guyon seeing stoup, poursewed fast
The present offer of faire victory,
And soone his dreadfull blade about he cast,
Wherewith he smote his haughty crest so hye,
That streight on grownd made him full low to lye;
Then on his brest his victor foote he thrust:
With that he cryde, " Mercy! doe me not dye,
Ne deeme thy force by fortunes doome unjust,
That hath (maugre her spight) thus low me laid in dust."

XIII. Eftsoones his cruel hand Sir Guyon stayd,
Tempring the passion with advizement slow,
And maistring might on enimy dismayd;
For th' equall die of warre he well did know:
Then to him said, " Live, and alleagaunce owe
To him that gives thee life and liberty;
And henceforth by this daies ensample trow,
That hasty wroth, and heedlesse hazardry,
Doe breede repentaunce late, and lasting infamy."

XIV. So up he let him rise; who, with grim looke
And count'naunce sterne, upstanding, gan to grind
His grated teeth for great disdeigne, and shooke
His sandy lockes, long hanging downe behind,
Knotted in blood and dust, for grief of mind
That he in ods of armes was conquered:
Yet in himselfe some comfort he did find,
That him so noble knight had maystered;
Whose bounty more then might, yet both, he wondered.

XV. Which Guyon marking said, " Be nought agriev'd,
Sir knight, that thus ye now subdewed arre:
Was never man, who most conquestes atchiev'd,
But sometimes had the worse, and lost by warre,
Yet shortly gaynd that losse exceeded farre.
Losse is no shame, nor to bee lesse then foe;
But to bee lesser than himselfe doth marre
Both loosers lott, and victours prayse alsoe:
Vaine others overthrowes who selfe doth overthrow.

XVI. " Fly, O Pyrochles! fly the dreadfull warre
That in thy selfe thy lesser partes do move;
Outrageous anger, and woe-working jarre,
Direfull impatience, and hart-murdring love:
Those, those thy foes, those warriours far remove,
Which thee to endlesse bale captived lead,
But sith in might thou didst my mercy prove,
Of courtesie to mee the cause aread
That thee against me drew with so impetuous dread."

XVII. " Dreadlesse," (said he) " that shall I soone declare.
It was complaind that thou hadst done great tort
Unto an aged woman, poore and bare,

And thralled her in chaines with strong effort,
Voide of all succour and needfull comfort;
That ill beseemes thee, such as I thee see,
To worke such shame.   Therefore, I thee exhort
To chaunce thy will, and set Occasion free,
And to her captive sonne yield his first libertee."

XVIII. Thereat Sir Guyon smylde, " And is that all,
(Said he) " that thee so sore displeased hath?
Great mercy, sure, for to enlarge a thrall,
Whose freedom shall thee turne to greatest scath!
Nath'lesse now quench thy whott emboyling wrath:
Loe! there they bee; to thee I yield them free."
Thereat he, wondrous glad, out of the path
Did lightly leape, where he them bound did see,
And gan to breake the bands of their captivitee.

XIX. Soone as Occasion felt her selfe untyde,
Before her sonne could well assoyled bee,
She to her use returnd, and streight defyde
Both Guyon and Pyrochles; th' one (said shee)
Bycause he wonne; the other, because hee
Was wonne.   So matter did she make of nought,
To stirre up strife, and garre them disagree:
But, soone as Furor was enlargd, she sought
To kindle his quencht fyre, and thousand causes wrought.

XX. It was not long ere she inflam'd him so,
That he would algates with Pyrochles fight,
And his redeemer chalengd for his foe,
Because he had not well mainteind his right,
But yielded had to that same straunger knight.
Now gan Pyrochles wex as wood as hee,
And him affronted with impatient might:
So both together fiers engrasped bee,
Whyles Guyon standing by their uncouth strife does see.

XXI. Him all that while Occasion did provoke
Against Pyrochles, and new matter fram'd
Upon the old, him stirring to bee wroke
Of his late wronges, in which she oft him blam'd
For suffering such abuse as knighthood sham'd,
And him dishabled quyte.   But he was wise,

Ne would with vaine occasions be inflam'd;
Yet others she more urgent did devise;
Yet nothing could him to impatience entise.

XXII. Their fell contention still increased more,
And more thereby increased Furors might,
That he his foe has hurt and wounded sore,
And him in blood and durt deformed quight.
His mother eke, more to augment his spight,
Now brought to him a flaming fyer brond,
Which she in Stygian lake, ay burning bright,
Had kindled: that she gave into his hond,
That armd with fire more hardly he mote him withstond

XXIII. Tho gan that villein wex so fiers and strong,
That nothing might sustaine his furious forse.
He cast him downe to ground, and all along
Drew him through durt and myre without remorse,
And fowly battered his comely corse,
That Guyon much disdeigned so loathly sight.
At last he was compeld to cry perforse,
"Help, O Sir Guyon! helpe, most noble knight,
To ridd a wretched man from handes of hellish wight!"

XXIV. The knight was greatly moved at his playnt,
And gan him dight to succour his distresse,
Till that the Palmer, by his grave restraynt,
Him stayd from yielding pitifull redresse,
And said; "Deare sonne, thy causelesse ruth represse,
Ne let thy stout hart melt in pitty vayne:
He that his sorrow sought through wilfulnesse,
And his foe fettred would release agayne,
Deserves to taste his follies fruit, repented payne."

XXV. Guyon obayd: So him away he drew
From needlesse trouble of renewing fight
Already fought, his voyage to poursew.
But rash Pyrochles varlett, Atin hight,
When late he saw his Lord in heavie plight
Under Sir Guyons puissaunt stroke to fall,
Him deeming dead, as then he seemd in sight,
Fledd fast away to tell his funerall
Unto his brother, whom Cymochles men did call.

XXVI. He was a man of rare redoubted might,
Famous throughout the world for warlike prayse,
And glorious spoiles, purchast in perilous fight:
Full many doughtie knightes he in his dayes
Had doen to death, subdewde in equall frayes
Whose carkases, for terrour of his name,
Of fowles and beastes he made the piteous prayes,
And hong their conquered armes, for more defame,
On gallow trees, in honour of his dearest Dame.

XXVII. His dearest Dame is that Enchaunteresse,
The vyle Acrasia, that with vaine delightes,
And ydle pleasures in her Bowre of Blisse,
Does charme her lovers, and the feeble sprightes
Can call out of the bodies of fraile wightes:
Whom then she does transforme to monstrous hewes,
And horribly misshapes with ugly sightes,
Captiv'd eternally in yron mewes
And darksom dens, where Titan his face never shewes.

XXVIII. There Atin fownd Cymochles sojourning,
To serve his Lemans love: for he by kynd
Was given all to lust and loose living,
When ever his fiers handes he free mote fynd:
And now he has pourd out his ydle mynd
In daintie delices, and lavish joyes,
Having his warlike weapons cast behynd,
And flowes in pleasures and vaine pleasing toyes,
Mingled emongst loose Ladies and lascivious boyes.

XXIX. And over him art, stryving to compayre
With nature, did an Arber greene dispred,
Framed of wanton Yvie, flouring fayre,
Through which the fragrant Eglantine did spred
His prickling armes, entrayld with roses red,
Which daintie odours round about them threw:
And all within with flowres was garnished,
That, when myld Zephyrus emongst them blew,
Did breath out bounteous smels, and painted colors shew.

XXX. And fast beside there trickled softly downe
A gentle streame, whose murmuring wave did play
Emongst the pumy stones, and made a sowne,

I   H

To lull him soft asleepe that by it lay:
The wearie Traveiler, wandring that way,
Therein did often quench his thristy heat,
And then by it his wearie limbes display,
Whiles creeping slomber made him to forget
His former payne, and wypt away his toilsom sweat.

XXXI. And on the other syde a pleasaunt grove
Was shott up high, full of the stately tree
That dedicated is t' Olympick Jove,
And to his sonne Alcides, whenas hee
In Nemus gayned goodly victoree:
Therein the mery birdes of every sorte
Chaunted alowd their chearefull harmonee,
And made emongst them selves a sweete consort,
That quickned the dull spright with musicall comfort.

XXXII. There he him found all carelessly displaid,
In secrete shadow from the sunny ray,
On a sweet bed of lillies softly laid,
Amidst a flock of Damzelles fresh and gay,
That rownd about him dissolute did play
Their wanton follies and light meriments:
Every of which did loosely disaray
Her upper partes of meet habiliments,
And shewd them naked, deckt with many ornaments.

XXXIII. And every of them strove with most delights
Him to aggrate, and greatest pleasures shew:
Some framd faire lookes, glancing like evening lights;
Others sweet wordes, dropping like honny dew;
Some bathed kisses, and did soft embrew
The sugred licour through his melting lips:
One boastes her beautie, and does yield to vew
Her dainty limbes above her tender hips;
Another her out boastes, and all for tryall strips.

XXXIV. He, like an Adder lurking in the weedes,
His wandring thought in deepe desire does steepe,
And his frayle eye with spoyle of beauty feedes:
Sometimes he falsely faines himselfe to sleepe,
Whiles through their lids his wanton eies do peepe
To steale a snatch of amorous conceipt,

Whereby close fire into his heart does creepe:
So he them deceives, deceivd in his deceipt,
Made dronke with drugs of deare voluptuous receipt.

XXXV. Atin, arriving there, when him he spyde
Thus in still waves of deepe delight to wade
Fiercely approaching to him lowdly cryde,
" Cymochles; oh! no, but Cymochles shade,
In which that manly person late did fade.
What is become of great Acrates sonne?
Or where hath he hong up his mortall blade,
That hath so many haughty conquests wonne?
Is all his force forlorne, and all his glory donne?

XXXVI. Then, pricking him with his sharp-pointed dart,
He saide; " Up, up! thou womanish weake knight,
That here in Ladies lap entombed art,
Unmindfull of thy praise and prowest might,
And weetlesse eke of lately wrought despight,
Whiles sad Pyrochles lies on sencelesse ground,
And groneth out his utmost grudging spright
Through many a stroke and many a streaming wound,
Calling thy helpe in vaine that here in joyes art dround."

XXXVII. Suddeinly out of his delightfull dreame
The man awoke, and would have questiond more;
But he would not endure that wofull theame
For to dilate at large, but urged sore,
With percing wordes and pittifull implore,
Him hasty to arise. As one affright
With hellish feends, or Furies made uprore,
He then uprose, inflamd with fell despight,
And called for his armes, for he would algates fight:

XXXVIII. They bene ybrought; he quickly does him dight,
And lightly mounted passeth on his way;
Ne Ladies loves, ne sweete entreaties, might
Appease his heat, or hastie passage stay;
For he has vowd to beene avengd that day
(That day it selfe him seemed all too long)
On him, that did Pyrochles deare dismay:
So proudly pricketh on his courser strong,
And Atin ay him pricks with spurs of shame and wrong.

CANTO VI

Guyon is of immodest Merth
Led into loose desyre;
Fights with Cymochles, whiles his bro-
ther burns in furious fyre.

I. A HARDER lesson to learne Continence
    In joyous pleasure then in grievous paine;
    For sweetnesse doth allure the weaker sence
    So strongly, that uneathes it can refraine
    From that which feeble nature covets faine:
    But griefe and wrath, that be her enemies
    And foes of life, she better can abstaine:
    Yet vertue vauntes in both her victories,
    And Guyon in them all shewes goodly maysteries.

II. Whom bold Cymochles traveiling to finde,
    With cruell purpose bent to wreake on him
    The wrath which Atin kindled in his mind,
    Came to a river, by whose utmost brim
    Wayting to passe, he saw whereas did swim
    Along the shore, as swift as glaunce of eye,
    A litle Gondelay, bedecked trim
    With boughes and arbours woven cunningly,
    That like a litle forrest seemed outwardly.

III. And therein sate a Lady fresh and fayre,
    Making sweet solace to herselfe alone:
    Sometimes she song as lowd as larke in ayre,
    Sometimes she laught, as merry as Pope Jone;
    Yet was there not with her else any one,
    That to her might move cause of meriment:
    Matter of merth enough, though there were none,
    She could devise; and thousand waies invent
    To feede her foolish humour and vaine jolliment.

IV. Which when far off Cymochles heard and saw,
    He lowdly cald to such as were abord
    The little barke unto the shore to draw,

And him to ferry over that deepe ford.
The merry mariner unto his word
Soone hearkned, and her painted bote streightway
Turnd to the shore, where that same warlike Lord
She in receiv'd; but Atin by no way
She would admit, albe the knight her much did pray.

v. Eftsoones her shallow ship away did slide,
More swift then swallow sheres the liquid skye,
Withouten oare or Pilot it to guide,
Or winged canvas with the wind to fly:
Onely she turnd a pin, and by and by
It cut away upon the yielding wave,
Ne cared she her course for to apply;
For it was taught the way which she would have,
And both from rocks and flats it selfe could wisely save.

vi. And all the way the wanton Damsell found
New merth her passenger to entertaine;
For she in pleasaunt purpose did abound,
And greatly joyed merry tales to faine,
Of which a store-house did with her remaine:
Yet seemed, nothing well they her became;
For all her wordes she drownd with laughter vaine,
And wanted grace in utt'ring of the same,
That turnd all her pleasaunce to a scoffing game.

vii. And other whiles vaine toyes she would devize,
As her fantasticke wit did most delight:
Sometimes her head she fondly would aguize
With gaudy girlonds, or fresh flowrets dight
About her necke, or rings of rushes plight:
Sometimes, to do him laugh, she would assay
To laugh at shaking of the leaves light
Or to behold the water worke and play
About her little frigot, therein making way.

viii. Her light behaviour and loose dalliaunce
Gave wondrous great contentment to the knight,
That of his way he had no sovenaunce,
Nor care of vow'd revenge and cruell fight,
But to weake wench did yield his martiall might:
So easie was to quench his flamed minde

With one sweete drop of sensuall delight.
So easie is t' appease the stormy winde
Of malice in the calme of pleasaunt womankind.

IX. Diverse discourses in their way they spent;
Mongst which Cymochles of her questioned
Both what she was, and what that usage ment,
Which in her cott she daily practized?
" Vaine man," (saide she) " that wouldest be reckoned
A straunger in thy home, and ignoraunt
Of Phædria, (for so my name is red)
Of Phædria, thine owne fellow servaunt;
For thou to serve Acrasia thy selfe doest vaunt.

X. " In this wide Inland sea, that hight by name
The Idle lake, my wandring ship I row,
That knowes her port, and thither sayles by ayme,
Ne care, ne feare I how the wind do blow,
Or whether swift I wend, or whether slow:
Both slow and swift alike do serve my tourne;
Ne swelling Neptune ne lowd thundring Jove
Can chaunge my cheare, or make me ever mourne:
My little boat can safely passe this perilous bourne."

XI. Whiles thus she talked, and whiles thus she toyd,
They were far past the passage which he spake,
And come unto an Island waste and voyd,
That floted in the midst of that great lake;
There her small Gondelay her port did make,
And that gay payre, issewing on the shore,
Disburdned her. Their way they forward take
Into the land that lay them faire before,
Whose pleasaunce she him shewd, and plentifull great store.

XII. It was a chosen plott of fertile land,
Emongst wide waves sett, like a litle nest,
As if it had by Natures cunning hand
Bene choycely picked out from all the rest,
And laid forth for ensample of the best:
No daintie flowre or herbe that growes on grownd,
No arborett with painted blossomes drest
And smelling sweete, but there it might be fownd
To bud out faire, and throwe her sweete smels al arownd.

XIII. No tree whose braunches did not bravely spring;
No braunch whereon a fine bird did not sitt;
No bird but did her shrill notes sweetely sing;
No song but did containe a lovely ditt.
Trees, braunches, birds, and songs, were framed fitt
For to allure fraile mind to carelesse ease:
Carelesse the man soone woxe, and his weake witt
Was overcome of thing that did him please;
So pleased did his wrathfull purpose faire appease.

XIV. Thus when shee had his eyes and sences fed
With false delights, and fild with pleasures vayn,
Into a shady dale she soft him led,
And layd him downe upon a grassy playn;
And her sweete selfe without dread or disdayn
She sett beside, laying his head disarmd
In her loose lap, it softly to sustayn,
Where soone he slumbred fearing not be harmd:
The whiles with a love lay she thus him sweetly charmd.

XV. " Behold, O man! that toilesome paines doest take,
The flowrs, the fields, and all that pleasaunt growes,
How they them selves doe thine ensample make,
Whiles nothing envious nature them forth throwes
Out of her fruitfull lap; how no man knowes,
They spring, they bud, they blossome fresh and faire,
And decke the world with their rich pompous showes;
Yet no man for them taketh paines or care,
Yet no man to them can his carefull paines compare.

XVI. " The lilly, Lady of the flowring field,
The flowre-deluce, her lovely Paramoure,
Bid thee to them thy fruitlesse labors yield,
And soone leave off this toylsome weary stoure:
Loe, loe! how brave she decks her bounteous boure,
With silkin curtens and gold coverletts,
Therein to shrowd her sumptuous Belamoure;
Yet nether spinnes nor cardes, ne cares nor fretts,
But to her mother Nature all her care she letts.

XVII. " Why then doest thou, O man! that of them all
Art Lord, and eke of nature Soveraine,
Wilfully make thyselfe a wretched thrall,

And waste thy joyous howres in needlesse paine,
Seeking for daunger and adventures vaine?
What bootes it al to have, and nothing use?
Who shall him rew that swimming in the maine
Will die for thrist, and water doth refuse?
Refuse such fruitlesse toile, and present pleasures chuse."

XVIII. By this she had him lulled fast asleepe,
That of no worldly thing he care did take:
Then she with liquors strong his eies did steepe,
That nothing should him hastily awake.
So she him lefte, and did her selfe betake
Unto her boat again, with which she clefte
The slothfull wave of that great griesy lake:
Soone shee that Island far behind her lefte,
And now is come to that same place where first she wefte.

XIX. By this time was the worthy Guyon brought
Unto the other side of that wide strond
Where she was rowing, and for passage sought.
Him needed not long call; shee soone to hond
Her ferry brought, where him she byding fond
With his sad guide: him selfe she tooke aboord,
But the Blacke Palmer suffred still to stond,
Ne would for price or prayers once affoord
To ferry that old man over the perlous foord.

XX. Guyon was loath to leave his guide behind,
Yet being entred might not backe retyre;
For the flitt barke, obaying to her mind,
Forth launched quickly as she did desire,
Ne gave him leave to bid that aged sire
Adieu; but nimbly ran her wonted course
Through the dull billowes thicke as troubled mire,
Whom nether wind out of their seat could forse
Nor timely tides did drive out of their sluggish sourse.

XXI. And by the way, as was her wonted guize,
Her mery fitt shee freshly gan to reare,
And did of joy and jollity devize,
Her selfe to cherish, and her guest to cheare.
The knight was courteous, and did not forbeare
Her honest merth and pleasaunce to partake;

But when he saw her toy, and gibe, and geare,
And passe the bonds of modest merimake,
Her dalliaunce he despis'd, and follies did forsake.

XXII. Yet she still followed her former style,
And said and did all that mote him delight,
Till they arrived in that pleasaunt Ile,
Where sleeping late she lefte her other knight.
But whenas Guyon of that land had sight,
He wist him selfe amisse, and angry said;
" Ah, Dame! perdy ye have not doen me right,
Thus to mislead mee, whiles I you obaid:
Me litle needed from my right way to have straid."

XXIII. " Faire Sir," (quoth she) " be not displeased at all.
Who fares on sea may not commaund his way,
Ne wind and weather at his pleasure call:
The sea is wide, and easy for to stray;
The wind unstable, and doth never stay.
But here a while ye may in safety rest,
Till season serve new passage to assay:
Better safe port then be in seas distrest."
Therewith she laught, and did her earnest end in jest.

XXIV. But he, halfe discontent, mote nathelesse
Himselfe appease, and issewd forth on shore;
The joyes whereof and happy fruitfulnesse,
Such as he saw she gan him lay before,
And all, though pleasaunt, yet she made much more:
The fields did laugh, the flowres did freshly spring,
The trees did bud, and early blossomes bore;
And all the quire of birds did sweetly sing,
And told that gardins pleasures in their caroling.

XXV. And she, more sweete then any bird on bough,
Would oftentimes emongst them beare a part,
And strive to passe (as she could well enough)
Their native musicke by her skilful art:
So did she all that might his constant hart
Withdraw from thought of warlike enterprize,
And drowne in dissolute delights apart,
Where noise of armes, or vew of martiall guize,
Might not revive desire of knightly exercize.

XXVI. But he was wise, and wary of her will,
　　　　And ever held his hand upon his hart;
　　　　Yet would not seeme so rude, and thewed ill,
　　　　As to despise so curteous seeming part
　　　　That gentle Lady did to him impart:
　　　　But, fairly tempring, fond desire subdewd,
　　　　And ever her desired to depart.
　　　　She list not heare, but her disports poursewd,
　　　　And ever bad him stay till time the tide renewd.

XXVII. And now by this Cymochles howre was spent,
　　　　That he awoke out of his ydle dreme;
　　　　And, shaking off his drowsy dreriment,
　　　　Gan him avize, howe ill did him beseme
　　　　In slouthfull sleepe his molten hart to steme,
　　　　And quench the brond of his conceived yre:
　　　　Tho up he started, stird with shame extreme,
　　　　Ne staied for his Damsell to inquire,
　　　　But marched to the Strond there passage to require.

XXVIII. And in the way he with Sir Guyon mett,
　　　　Accompanyde with Phædria the faire:
　　　　Eftsoones he gan to rage, and inly frett,
　　　　Crying; " Let be that Lady debonaire,
　　　　Thou recreaunt knight, and soone thyselfe prepaire
　　　　To batteile, if thou meane her love to gayn.
　　　　Loe, loe! already how the fowles in aire
　　　　Doe flocke, awaiting shortly to obtayn
　　　　Thy carcas for their pray, the guerdon of thy payn."

XXIX. And therewithall he fiersly at him flew,
　　　　And with importune outrage him assayld;
　　　　Who, soone prepard to field, his sword forth drew,
　　　　And him with equall valew countervayld:
　　　　Their mightie strokes their haberjeons dismayld,
　　　　And naked made each others manly spalles;
　　　　The mortall steele despiteously entayld
　　　　Deepe in their flesh, quite through the yron walles,
　　　　That a large purple streame adowne their giambeux
　　　　　　falles.

XXX. Cymochles, that had never mett before
　　　　So puissant foe, with envious despight
　　　　His prowd presumed force increased more,

price ...

...ents' Shirts,

...l Offer—300 Men's ...
...RTS, in various smal...
... white grounds, soft ...
...le cuffs; neck sizes, 1...
...ual value 8/11, Sale pri...

...en Men's heavy WORK S...
...ey colour, were 8/6, Sale p...

...AT B...

IN

...y

...ure

...rimmings

...V CROSS

d
ly
ed
om
lter
eld'
hich

Runciman s
and buys the
He's not a
State-owned s
Sir John Bair
ciation, is of
makes for "su

ion in

y Webb
were a
estitution
reign than
it, and Sir
asserted,
e were twelve
try who lived
unger.

like Sir John
ntry ascribing
rsailles Peace,
nk enough to
hat we shall
the whole em-
at the very top

Major Lionel
been orating at
ing to the *Bucks*
News (3/2/23)
are very funny—
very funny."
came to the concl

' *These Lab*
capable of look
needs of their
he would far
Party back in

Sure thing!
the Rothschilds
the money bags o

But it is abou
may even need t

Disdeigning to bee held so long in fight.
Sir Guyon, grudging not so much his might
As those unknightly raylinges which he spoke,
With wrathfull fire his corage kindled bright,
Thereof devising shortly to be wroke,
And doubling all his powers redoubled every stroke.

XXXI. Both of them high attonce their handes enhaunst,
And both attonce their huge blowes down did sway.
Cymochles sword on Guyons shield yglaunst,
And thereof nigh one quarter sheard away;
But Guyons angry blade so fiers did play
On th' others helmett, which as T⟨. .⟩n shone,
That quite it clove his plumed cre⟨. .⟩ in tway,
And bared all his head unto the bone;
Wherewith astonisht, still he stood as sencelesse stone.

XXXII. Still as he stood, fayre Phædria, that beheld
That deadly daunger, soone atweene them ran;
And at their feet her selfe most humbly feld,
Crying with pitteous voyce, and count'nance wan,
" Ah, well away! most noble Lords, how can
Your cruell eyes endure so pitteous sight,
To shed your lives on ground?   Wo worth the man,
That first did teach the cursed steele to bight
In his owne flesh, and make way to the living spright!

XXXIII. " If ever love of Lady did empierce
Your yron brestes, or pittie could find place,
Withhold your bloody handes from battaill fierce;
And, sith for me ye fight, to me this grace
Both yield, to stay your deadly stryfe a space."
They stayd a while, and forth she gan proceede:
" Most wretched woman and of wicked race,
That am the authour of this hainous deed,
And cause of death betweene two doughtie knights ⟨o⟩
    breed!

XXXIV. " But, if for me ye fight, or me will serve,
Not this rude kynd of battaill, nor these armes
Are meet, the which doe men in bale to sterve,
And doolefull sorrow heape with deadly harmes:
Such cruell game my scarmoges disarmes.
Another warre, and other weapons, I

Doe love, where love does give his sweet Alarmes
Without bloodshed, and where the enimy
Does yield unto his foe a pleasaunt victory.

xxxv. " Debatefull strife, and cruell enmity,
The famous name of knighthood fowly shend;
But lovely peace, and gentle amity,
And in Amours the passing howres to spend,
The mightie martiall handes doe most commend:
Of love they ever greater glory bore
Then of their armes; Mars is Cupidoes frend,
And is for Venus loves renowmed more
Then all his wars and spoiles, the which he did of yore."

xxxvi. Therewith she sweetly smyld.   They, though full bent
To prove extremities of bloody fight,
Yet at her speach their rages gan relent,
And calme the sea of their tempestuous spight.
Such powre have pleasing wordes: such is the might
Of courteous clemency in gentle hart.
Now after all was ceast, the Faery knight
Besought that Damzell suffer him depart,
And yield him ready passage to that other part.

xvii. She no lesse glad then he desirous was
Of his departure thence; for of her joy
And vaine delight she saw he light did pas,
A foe of folly and immodest toy,
Still solemne sad, or still disdainfull coy;
Delighting all in armes and cruell warre,
That her sweet peace and pleasures did annoy,
Troubled with terrour and unquiet jarre,
That she well pleased was thence to amove him farre

o   him she brought abord, and her swift bote
       hwith directed to that further strand;
       which on the dull waves did lightly flote,
       one arrived on the shallow sand,
       gladsome Guyon salied forth to land,
       hat Damsell thankes gave for reward.
       t shore he spyed Atin stand,
       his maister left, when late he far'd
       s flitt barck over that perlous shard.

XXXIX. Well could he him remember, sith of late
He with Pyrochles sharp debatement made:
Streight gan he him revyle, and bitter rate,
As Shepheardes curre, that in darke eveninges shade
Hath tracted forth some salvage beastes trade:
"Vile Miscreaunt," (said he) "whither dost thou flye
The shame and death, which will thee soone invade?
What coward hand shall doe thee next to dye,
That art thus fowly fledd from famous enimy?"

XL. With that he stifly shooke his steelhead dart:
But sober Guyon, hearing him so rayle,
Though somewhat moved in his mightie hart,
Yet with strong reason maistred passion fraile,
And passed fayrely forth.   He, turning taile,
Back to the strond retyrd, and there still stayd,
Awaiting passage which him late did faile;
The whiles Cymochles with that wanton mayd
The hasty heat of his avowd revenge delayd.

XLI. Whylest there the varlet stood, he saw from farre
An armed knight that towardes him fast ran;
He ran on foot, as if in lucklesse warre
His forlorne steed from him the victour wan:
He seemed breathlesse, hartlesse, faint, and wan;
And all his armour sprinckled was with blood,
And soyld with durtie gore, that no man can
Discerne the hew thereof.   He never stood,
But bent his hastie course towardes the ydle flood.

XLII. The varlett saw, when to the flood he came,
How without stop or stay he fiersly lept,
And deepe him selfe beducked in the same,
That in the lake his loftie crest was stept,
Ne of his safetie seemed care he kept;
But with his raging armes he rudely flasht
The waves about, and all his armour swept,
That all the blood and filth away was washt;
Yet still he bet the water, and the billowes dasht.

XLIII. Atin drew nigh to weet what it mote bee,
For much he wondred at that uncouth sight:
Whom should he but his owne deare Lord there see,

His owne deare Lord Pyrochles in sad plight,
Ready to drowne him selfe for fell despight:
" Harrow now out, and well away! " he cryde,
" What dismall day hath lent this cursed light,
To see my Lord so deadly damnifyde?
Pyrochles, O Pyrochles! what is thee betyde? "

XLIV. " I burne, I burne, I burne! " then lowd he cryde,
" O! how I burne with implacable fyre;
Yet nought can quench mine inly flaming syde,
Nor sea of licour cold, nor lake of myre:
Nothing but death can doe me to respyre."
" Ah! be it," (said he) " from Pyrochles farre
After pursewing death once to requyre,
Or think, that ought those puissant hands may marre:
Death is for wretches borne under unhappy starre."

XLV. " Perdye, then is it fitt for me," (said he)
" That am, I weene, most wretched man alive;
Burning in flames, yet no flames can I see,
And dying dayly, dayly yet revive.
O Atin! helpe to me last death to give."
The varlet at his plaint was grieved so sore,
That his deepe wounded hart in two did rive;
And, his owne health remembring now no more,
Did follow that ensample which he blam'd afore.

XLVI. Into the lake he lept his Lord to ayd,
(So Love the dread of daunger doth despise)
And of him catching hold him strongly stayd
From drowning. But more happy he then wise,
Of that seas nature did him not avise:
The waves thereof so slow and sluggish were,
Engrost with mud which did them fowle agrise,
That every weighty thing they did upbeare,
Ne ought mote ever sinck downe to the bottom there.

XLVII. Whiles thus they strugled in that ydle wave,
And strove in vaine, the one him selfe to drowne,
The other both from drowning for to save,
Lo! to that shore one in an auncient gowne,
Whose hoary locks great gravitie did crowne,
Holding in hand a goodly arming sword,

By fortune came, ledd with the troublous sowne:
Where drenched deepe he fownd in that dull ford
The carefull servaunt stryving with his raging Lord.

XLVIII. Him Atin spying knew right well of yore,
And lowdly cald; "Helpe, helpe! O Archimage!
To save my Lord in wretched plight forlore;
Helpe with thy hand, or with thy counsell sage:
Weake handes, but counsell is most strong in age."
Him when the old man saw, he wondred sore
To see Pyrochles there so rudely rage;
Yet sithens helpe, he saw, he needed more
Then pitty, he in hast approched to the shore,

XLIX. And cald; "Pyrochles! what is this I see?
What hellish fury hath at earst thee hent?
Furious ever I thee knew to bee,
Yet never in this straunge astonishment."
"These flames, these flames" (he cryde) "doe me
torment."
"Wha flames," (quoth he), when I thee present see
In daunger rather to be drent then brent?"
"Harrow! the flames which me consume," (said hee)
"Ne can be quencht, within my secret bowelles bee.

L. "That cursed man, that cruel feend of hell,
Furor, oh! Furor hath me thus bedight:
His deadly woundes within my liver swell,
And his whott fyre burnes in mine entralles bright,
Kindled through his infernall brond of spight,
Sith late with him I batteill vaine would boste;
That now, I weene, Joves dreaded thunder light
Does scorch not halfe so sore, nor damned ghoste
In flaming Phlegeton does not so felly roste."

LI. Which when as Archimago heard, his griefe
He knew right well, and him attonce disarm'd;
Then searcht his secret woundes, and made a priefe
Of every place that was with bruzing harmd,
Or with the hidden fire too inly warmd.
Which doen, he balmes and herbes thereto applyde,
And evermore with mightie spels them charmd;
That in short space he has them qualifyde,
And him restor'd to helth that would have algates dyde.

CANTO VII

Guyon findes Mamon in a delve
Sunning his threasure hore;
Is by him tempted, and led downe
To see his secrete store.

I. As Pilot well expert in perilous wave,
That to a stedfast starre his course hath bent,
When foggy mistes or cloudy tempests have
The faithful light of that faire lampe yblent,
And cover'd heaven with hideous dreriment,
Upon his card and compas firmes his eye,
The maysters of his long experiment,
And to them does the steddy helme apply,
Bidding his winged vessell fairely forward fly:

II. So Guyon having lost his trustie guyde,
Late left beyond that Ydle lake, proceedes
Yet on his way, of none accompanyde;
And evermore himselfe with comfort feedes
Of his own vertues and praise-worthie deedes.
So, long he yode, yet no adventure found,
Which fame of her shrill trompet worthy reedes;
For still he traveild through wide wastfull ground,
That nought but desert wildernesse shewed all around.

III. At last he came unto a gloomy glade,
Cover'd with boughes and shrubs from heavens light,
Whereas he sitting found in secret shade
An uncouth, salvage, and uncivile wight,
Of griesly hew and fowle ill favour'd sight;
His face with smoke was tand, and eies were bleard,
His head and beard with sout were ill bedight,
His cole-blacke hands did seeme to have ben seard
In smythes fire-spitting forge, and nayles like clawes
   appeard.

IV. His yron cote, all overgrowne with rust,
Was underneath enveloped with gold;
Whose glistring glosse, darkned with filthy dust,

Well yet appeared to have beene of old
A worke of rich entayle and curious mould,
Woven with antickes and wyld ymagery;
And in his lap a masse of coyne he told,
And turned upside downe, to feede his eye
And covetous desire with his huge threasury.

v. And round about him lay on every side
Great heapes of gold that never could be spent;
Of which some were rude owre, not purifide
Of Mulcibers devouring element;
Some others were new driven, and distent
Into great Ingowes and to wedges square;
Some in round plates withouten moniment;
But most were stampt, and in their metal bare
The antique shapes of kinges and kesars straunge and rare.

vi. Soone as he Guyon saw, in great affright
And haste he rose for to remove aside
Those pretious hils from straungers envious sight,
And downe them poured through an hole full wide
Into the hollow earth, them there to hide.
But Guyon, lightly to him leaping, stayd
His hand that trembled as one terrifyde;
And though himselfe were at the sight dismayd,
Yet him perforce restraynd, and to him doubtfull sayd:

vii. " What art thou, man, (if man at all thou art)
That here in desert hast thine habitaunce,
And these rich hils of welth doest hide apart
From the worldes eye, and from her right usaunce? "
Thereat, with staring eyes fixed askaunce,
In great disdaine he answerd: " Hardy Elfe,
That darest view my direfull countenaunce,
I read thee rash and heedelesse of thy selfe,
To trouble my still seate, and heapes of pretious pelfe.

viii. " God of the world and worldlings I me call,
Great Mammon, greatest god below the skye,
That of my plenty poure out unto all,
And unto none my graces do envye:
Riches, renowme, and principality,
Honour, estate, and all this worldes good,

For which men swinck and sweat incessantly,
Fro me do flow into an ample flood,
And in the hollow earth have their eternal brood.

IX. " Wherefore, if me thou deigne to serve and sew,
At thy commaund lo! all these mountaines bee:
Or if to thy great mind, or greedy vew,
All these may not suffise, there shall to thee
Ten times so much be nombred francke and free."
" Mammon," (said he) " thy godheads vaunt is vaine,
And idle offers of thy golden fee;
To them that covet such eye-glutting gaine
Proffer thy giftes, and fitter servaunts entertaine.

X. " Me ill besits, that in der-doing armes
And honours suit my vowed daies do spend,
Unto thy bounteous baytes and pleasing charmes,
With which weake men thou witchest, to attend;
Regard of worldly mucke doth fowly blend,
And low abase the high heroicke spright,
That joyes for crownes and kingdomes to contend:
Faire shields, gay steedes, bright armes be my delight;
Those be the riches fit for an advent'rous knight."

XI. " Vaine glorious Elfe," (saide he) " doest not thou weet,
That money can thy wantes at will supply?
Sheilds, steeds, and armes, and all things for thee meet,
It can purvay in twinckling of an eye;
And crownes and kingdomes to thee multiply.
Do not I kings create, and throw the crowne
Sometimes to him that low in dust doth ly,
And him that raignd into his rowme thrust downe,
And whom I lust do heape with glory and renowne? "

XII. " All otherwise " (saide he) " I riches read,
And deeme them roote of all disquietnesse;
First got with guile, and then preserv'd with dread,
And after spent with pride and lavishnesse,
Leaving behind them griefe and heavinesse:
Infinite mischiefes of them doe arize,
Strife and debate, bloodshed and bitternesse,
Outrageous wrong, and hellish covetize,
That noble heart as great dishonour doth despize.

xiii. " Ne thine be kingdomes, ne the scepters thine;
But realmes and rulers thou doest both confound,
And loyall truth to treason doest incline:
Witnesse the guiltlesse blood pourd oft on ground,
The crowned often slaine, the slayer crownd;
The sacred Diademe in peeces rent,
And purple robe gored with many a wound,
Castles surprizd, great cities sackt and brent:
So mak'st thou kings, and gaynest wrongfull government.

xiv. " Long were to tell the troublous stormes that tosse
The private state, and make the life unsweet:
Who swelling sayles in Caspian sea doth crosse,
And in frayle wood on Adrian gulf doth fleet,
Doth not, I weene, so many evils meet."
Then Mammon wexing wroth; " And why then," sayd,
" Are mortall men so fond and undiscreet
So evill thing to seeke unto their ayd,
And having not complaine, and having it upbrayd? "

xv. " Indeede," (quoth he) " through fowle intemperaunce,
Frayle men are oft captiv'd to covetise;
But would they thinke with how small allowaunce
Untroubled Nature doth her selfe suffise,
Such superfluities they would despise,
Which with sad cares empeach our native joyes.
At the well-head the purest streames arise;
But mucky filth his braunching armes annoyes,
And with uncomely weedes the gentle wave accloyes.

xvi. " The antique world, in his first flowring youth,
Fownd no defect in his Creators grace;
But with glad thankes, and unreproved truth,
The guifts of soveraine bounty did embrace:
Like Angels life was then mens happy cace;
But later ages pride, like corn-fed steed,
Abusd her plenty and fat swolne encreace
To all licentious lust, and gan exceed
The measure of her meane and naturall first need.

xvii. " Then gan a cursed hand the quiet wombe
Of his great Grandmother with steele to wound,
And the hid treasures in her sacred tombe

With Sacriledge to dig.   Therein he fownd
Fountaines of gold and silver to abownd,
Of which the matter of his huge desire
And pompous pride eftsoones he did compownd;
Then avarice gan through his veines inspire
His greedy flames, and kindled life-devouring fire."

XVIII. " Sonne," (said he then) " lett be thy bitter scorne,
And leave the rudenesse of that antique age
To them that liv'd therein in state forlorne:
Thou, that doest live in later times, must wage
Thy workes for wealth, and life for gold engage.
If then thee list my offred grace to use,
Take what thou please of all this surplusage;
If thee list not, leave have thou to refuse:
But thing refused doe not afterward accuse."

XIX. " Me list not " (said the Elfin knight) " receave
Thing offred, till I know it well be gott;
Ne wote I but thou didst these goods bereave
From rightfull owner by unrighteous lott,
Or that bloodguiltinesse or guile them blott."
" Perdy," (quoth he) " yet never eie did vew,
Ne tong did tell, ne hand these handled not;
But safe I have them kept in secret mew
From hevens sight, and powre of al which them poursew."

XX. " What secret place " (quoth he) " can safely hold
So huge a masse, and hide from heavens eie?
Or where hast thou thy wonne, that so much gold
Thou canst preserve from wrong and robbery? "
" Come thou," (quoth he) " and see."   So by and by
Through that thick covert he him led, and fownd
A darkesome way, which no man could descry,
That deep descended through the hollow grownd,
And was with dread and horror compassed arownd.

XXI. At length they came into a larger space,
That stretcht itselfe into an ample playne;
Through which a beaten broad high way did trace,
That streight did lead to Plutoes griesly rayne.
By that wayes side there sate internall Payne,
And fast beside him sat tumultuous Strife:

The one in hand an yron whip did strayne,
The other brandished a bloody knife;
And both did gnash their teeth, and both did threten life.

XXII. On thother side in one consort there sate
Cruell Revenge, and rancorous Despight,
Disloyall Treason, and hart-burning Hate;
But gnawing Gealousy, out of their sight
Sitting alone, his bitter lips did bight;
And trembling Feare still to and fro did fly,
And found no place wher safe he shroud him might:
Lamenting Sorrow did in darknes lye,
And shame his ugly face did hide from living eye.

XXIII. And over them sad horror with grim hew
Did alwaies sore, beating his yron wings;
And after him Owles and Night-ravens flew,
The hatefull messengers of heavy things,
Of death and dolor telling sad tidings;
Whiles sad Celeno, sitting on a clifte,
A song of bale and bitter sorrow sings,
That hart of flint asonder could have rifte;
Which having ended after him she flyeth swifte.

XXIV. All these before the gates of Pluto lay,
By whom they passing spake unto them nought;
But th' Elfin knight with wonder all the way
Did feed his eyes, and fild his inner thought.
At last him to a litle dore he brought,
That to the gate of Hell, which gaped wide,
Was next adjoyning, ne them parted ought:
Betwixt them both was but a litle stride,
That did the house of Richesse from hell-mouth divide.

XXV. Before the dore sat selfe-consuming Care,
Day and night keeping wary watch and ward,
For feare least Force or Fraud should unaware
Breake in, and spoile the treasure there in gard:
Ne would he suffer Sleepe once thither-ward
Approch, albe his drowsy den were next;
For next to death is Sleepe to be compard;
Therefore his house is unto his annext:
Here Sleep, ther Richesse, and Hel-gate them both betwext.

XXVI. So soon as Mammon there arrivd, the dore
To him did open and affoorded way:
Him followed eke Sir Guyon evermore,
Ne darkenesse him, ne daunger might dismay.
Soone as he entred was, the dore streight way
Did shutt, and from behind it forth there lept
An ugly feend, more fowle then dismall day,
The which with monstrous stalke behind him stept,
And ever as he went dew watch upon him kept.

XXVII. Well hoped hee, ere long that hardy guest,
If ever covetous hand, or lustfull eye,
Or lips he layd on thing that likte him best,
Or ever sleepe his eie-strings did untye,
Should be his pray. And therefore still on hye
He over him did hold his cruell clawes,
Threatning with greedy gripe to doe him dye,
And rend in peeces with his ravenous pawes,
If ever he transgrest the fatall Stygian lawes.

XXVIII. That houses forme within was rude and strong,
Lyke an huge cave hewne out of rocky clifte,
From whose rough vaut the ragged breaches hong
Embost with massy gold of glorious guifte,
And with rich metall loaded every rifte,
That heavy ruine they did seeme to threatt;
And over them Arachne did lifte
Her cunning web, and spred her subtile nett,
Enwrapped in fowle smoke and clouds more black
than Jett.

XXIX. Both roofe, and floore, and walls, were all of gold,
But overgrowne with dust and old decay,
And hid in darkenes, that none could behold
The hew thereof; for vew of cherefull day
Did never in that house it selfe display,
But a faint shadow of uncertein light:
Such as a lamp, whose life does fade away,
Or as the Moone, cloathed with clowdy night,
Does show to him that walkes in feare and sad affright.

XXX. In all that rowme was nothing to be seene
But huge great yron chests, and coffers strong,
All bard with double bends, that none could weene

Them to efforce by violence or wrong:
On every side they placed were along;
But all the grownd with sculs was scattered,
And dead mens bones, which round about were flong;
Whose lives, it seemed, whilome there were shed,
And their vile carcases now left unburied.

XXXI. They forward passe; ne Guyon yet spoke word,
Till that they came unto an yron dore,
Which to them opened of his owne accord,
And shewd of richesse such exceeding store,
As eie of man did never see before,
Ne ever could within one place be fownd,
Though all the wealth which is, or was of yore,
Could gathered be through all the world arownd,
And that above were added to that under grownd.

XXXII. The charge thereof unto a covetous Spright
Commaunded was, who thereby did attend,
And warily awaited day and night,
From other covetous feends it to defend,
Who it to rob and ransacke did intend.
Then Mammon, turning to that warriour, said;
" Loe! here the worldes blis: loe! here the end,
To which al men doe ayme, rich to be made:
Such grace now to be happy is before thee laid."

XXXIII. " Certes," (sayd he) " I n'ill thine offred grace,
Ne to be made so happy doe intend:
Another blis before mine eyes I place,
Another happines, another end.
To them that list these base regardes I lend;
But I in armes, and in atchievements brave,
Do rather choose my flitting houres to spend,
And to be Lord of those that riches have,
Then them to have my selfe, and be their servile sclave."

XXXIV. Thereat the feend his gnashing teeth did grate,
And griev'd so long to lacke his greedie pray;
For well he weened that so glorious bayte
Would tempt his guest to take thereof assay;
Had he so doen, he had him snatcht away,
More light then Culver in the Faulcons fist.

Eternall God thee save from such decay!
But, whenas Mammon saw his purpose mist,
Him to entrap unwares another way he wist.

XXXV. Thence forward he him ledd, and shortly brought
Unto another rowme, whose dore forthright
To him did open, as it had been taught.
Therein an hundred raunges weren pight,
And hundred fournaces all burning bright:
By every fournace many feendes did byde,
Deformed creatures, horrible in sight;
And every feend his busie paines applyde
To melt the golden metall, ready to be tryde.

XXXVI. One with great bellowes gathered filling ayre,
And with forst wind the fewell did inflame;
Another did the dying bronds repayre
With yron tongs, and sprinckled ofte the same
With liquid waves, fiers Vulcans rage to tame,
Who, maystring them, renewd his former heat:
Some scumd the drosse that from the metall came;
Some stird the molten owre with ladles great;
And every one did swincke, and every one did sweat.

XXXVII. But, when an earthly wight they present saw
Glistring in armes and battailous aray,
From their whot work they did themselves withdraw
To wonder at the sight; for till that day
They never creature saw that cam that way:
Their staring eyes sparckling with fervent fyre
And ugly shapes did nigh the man dismay,
That, were it not for shame, he would retyre;
Till that him thus bespake their soveraine Lord and
syre;

XXXVIII. "Behold, thou Faeries sonne, with mortall eye,
That living eye before did never see.
The thing, that thou didst crave so earnestly,
To weet whence all the wealth late shewd by mee
Proceeded, lo! now is reveald to thee.
Here is the fountaine of the worldes good:
Now, therefore, if thou wilt enriched bee,
Avise thee well, and chaunge thy wilfull mood,
Least thou perhaps hereafter wish, and be withstood."

XXXIX. "Suffise it then, thou Money God," (quoth hee)
      " That all thine ydle offers I refuse.
      All that I need I have: what needeth mee
      To covet more then I have cause to use?
      With such vaine shewes thy worldlinges vyle abuse;
      But give me leave to follow mine emprise."
      Mammon was much displeasd, yet no'te he chuse
      But beare the rigour of his bold mesprise;
      And thence him forward ledd him further to entise.

XL. He brought him, through a darksom narrow strayt,
      To a broad gate all built of beaten gold:
      The gate was open; but therein did wayt
      A sturdie villein, stryding stiffe and bold,
      As if the highest God defy he would:
      In his right hand an yron club he held,
      But he himselfe was all of golden mould,
      Yet had both life and sence, and well could weld
      That cursed weapon, when his cruell foes he queld.

XLI. Disdayne he called was, and did disdayne
      To be so cald, and who so did him call:
      Sterne was his looke, and full of stomacke vayne;
      His portaunce terrible, and stature tall,
      Far passing th' hight of men terrestriall,
      Like an huge Gyant of the Titans race;
      That made him scorne all creatures great and small.
      And with his pride all others powre deface:
      More fitt emongst black fiendes then men to have his
          place.

XLII. Soone as those glitterand armes he did espye,
      That with their brightnesse made that darknes light,
      His harmefull club he gan to hurtle hye,
      And threaten batteill to the Faery knight;
      Who likewise gan himselfe to batteill dight,
      Till Mammon did his hasty hand withhold,
      And counseld him abstaine from perilous fight;
      For nothing might abash the villein bold,
      Ne mortall steele emperce his miscreated mould.

XLIII. So having him with reason pacifyde,
      And that fiers Carle commaunding to forbeare,

He brought him in.   The rowme was large and wyde,
As it some Gyeld or solemne Temple weare.
Many great golden pillours did upbeare
The massy roofe, and riches huge sustayne;
And every pillour decked was full deare
With crownes, and Diademes, and titles vaine,
Which mortall Princes wore whiles they on earth did
        rayne.

XLIV. A route of people there assembled were,
Of every sort and nation under skye,
Which with great uprore preaced to draw nere
To th' upper part, where was advaunced hye
A stately siege of soveraine majestye;
And thereon satt a woman, gorgeous gay
And richly cladd in robes of royaltye,
That never earthly Prince in such array
His glory did enhaunce, and pompous pryde display.

XLV. Her face right wondrous faire did seeme to bee,
That her broad beauties beam great brightnes threw
Through the dim shade, that all men might it see:
Yet was not that same her owne native hew,
But wrought by art and counterfetted shew,
Thereby more lovers unto her to call:
Nath'lesse most hevenly faire in deed and vew
She by creation was, till she did fall;
Thenceforth she sought for helps to cloke her crime
        withall.

XLVI. There, as in glistring glory she did sitt,
She held a great gold chaine ylincked well,
Whose upper end to highest heven was knitt,
And lower part did reach to lowest Hell;
And all that preace did rownd about her swell
To catchen hold of that long chaine, thereby
To climbe aloft, and others to excell:
That was Ambition, rash desire to sty,
And every linck thereof a step of dignity.

XLVII. Some thought to raise themselves to high degree
By riches and unrighteous reward;
Some by close shouldring; some by flatteree;

Others through friendes; others for base regard,
And all by wrong waies for themselves prepard:
Those that were up themselves kept others low;
Those that were low themselves held others hard,
Ne suffred them to ryse or greater grow;
But every one did strive his fellow downe to throw.

XLVIII. Which whenas Guyon saw, he gan inquire,
What meant that preace about that Ladies throne,
And what she was that did so high aspyre?
Him Mammon answered; " That goodly one,
Whom all that folke with such contention
Doe flock about, my deare, my daughter is:
Honour and dignitie from her alone
Derived are, and all this worldes blis,
For which ye men doe strive; few gett, but many mis:

XLIX. " And fayre Philotime she rightly hight,
The fairest wight that wonneth under skie,
But that this darksom neather world her light
Doth dim with horror and deformity;
Worthie of heven and hye felicitie,
From whence the gods have her for envy thrust:
But, sith thou hast found favour in mine eye,
Thy spouse I will her make, if that thou lust,
That she may thee advance for works and merits just."

L. " Gramercy, Mammon," (said the gentle knight)
" For so great grace and offred high estate;
But I, that am fraile flesh and earthly wight,
Unworthy match for such immortall mate
My selfe well wote, and mine unequall fate:
And were I not, yet is my trouth yplight,
And love avowd to other Lady late,
That to remove the same I have no might:
To chaunge love causelesse is reproch to warlike knight."

LI. Mammon emmoved was with inward wrath;
Yet, forcing it to fayne, him forth thence ledd,
Through griesly shadowes by a beaten path,
Into a gardin goodly garnished
With hearbs and fruits, whose kinds mote not be redd:
Not such as earth out of her fruitfull woomb

Throwes forth to men, sweet and well savored,
But direfull deadly black, both leafe and bloom,
Fitt to adorne the dead, and deck the drery toombe.

LII. There mournfull Cypresse grew in greatest store,
And trees of bitter Gall, and Heben sad;
Dead sleeping Poppy, and black Hellebore;
Cold Coloquintida, and Tetra mad;
Mortall Samnitis, and Cicuta bad,
With which th' unjust Atheniens made to dy
Wise Socrates; who, thereof quaffing glad,
Pourd out his life and last Philosophy
To the fayre Critias, his dearest Belamy!

LIII. The Gardin of Proserpina this hight;
And in the midst thereof a silver seat,
With a thick Arber goodly over-dight,
In which she often usd from open heat
Her selfe to shroud, and pleasures to entreat:
Next thereunto did grow a goodly tree,
With braunches broad dispredd and body great,
Clothed with leaves, that non the wood mote see,
And loaden all with fruit as thick as it might bee.

LIV. Their fruit were golden apples glistring bright,
That goodly was their glory to behold;
On earth like never grew, ne living wight
Like ever saw, but they from hence were sold;
For those which Hercules, with conquest bold
Got from great Atlas daughters, hence began,
And planted there did bring forth fruit of gold;
And those with which th' Euboean young man wan
Swift Atalanta, when through craft he her out ran.

LV. Here also sprong that goodly golden fruit,
With which Acontius got his lover trew,
Whom he had long time sought with fruitlesse suit:
Here eke that famous golden Apple grew
The which emongst the gods false Ate threw;
For which th' Idaean Ladies disagreed,
Till partiall Paris dempt it Venus dew,
And had of her fayre Helen for his meed,
That many noble Greekes and Trojans made to bleed.

LVI. The warlike Elfe much wondred at this tree,
So fayre and great that shadowed all the ground,
And his broad braunches, laden with rich fee,
Did stretcht themselves without the utmost bound
Of this great gardin, compast with a mound;
Which over-hanging, they themselves did steepe
In a blacke flood, which flow'd about it round.
That is the river of Cocytus deepe,
In which full many soules do endlesse wayle and weepe.

LVII. Which to behold he clomb up to the bancke,
And looking downe saw many damned wightes
In those sad waves, which direfull deadly stancke,
Plonged continually of cruell Sprightes,
That with their piteous cryes, and yelling shrightes,
They made the further shore resounden wide.
Emongst the rest of those same ruefull sightes,
One cursed creature he by chaunce espide,
That drenched lay full deepe under the Garden side.

LVIII. Deepe was he drenched to the upmost chin,
Yet gaped still as coveting to drinke
Of the cold liquor which he waded in;
And stretching forth his hand did often thinke
To reach the fruit which grew upon the brincke;
But both the fruit from hand, and flood from mouth,
Did fly abacke, and made him vainely swincke;
The whiles he sterv'd with hunger, and with drouth,
He daily dyde, yet never throughly dyen couth.

LIX. The knight, him seeing labour so in vaine,
Askt who he was, and what he ment thereby?
Who, groning deepe, thus answerd him againe;
" Most cursed of all creatures under skye,
Lo! Tantalus, I here tormented lye:
Of whom high Jove wont whylome feasted bee;
Lo! here I now for want of food doe dye:
But, if that thou be such as I thee see,
Of grace I pray thee, give to eat and drinke to mee! "

LX. " Nay, nay, thou greedy Tantalus," (quoth he)
" Abide the fortune of thy present fate;
And unto all that live in high degree,

Ensample be of mind intemperate,
To teach them how to use their present state."
Then gan the cursed wretch alowd to cry,
Accusing highest Jove and gods ingrate;
And eke blaspheming heaven bitterly,
As author of unjustice, there to let him dye.

LXI. He lookt a litle further, and espyde
Another wretch, whose carcas deepe was drent
Within the river, which the same did hyde;
But both his handes, most filthy feculent,
Above the water were on high extent,
And faynd to wash themselves incessantly,
Yet nothing cleaner were for such intent,
But rather fowler seemed to the eye;
So lost his labour vaine and ydle industry.

LXII. The knight him calling asked who he was?
Who, lifting up his head, him answered thus;
" I Pilate am, the falsest Judge, alas!
And most unjust; that, by unrighteous
And wicked doome, to Jewes despiteous
Delivered up the Lord of life to dye,
And did acquite a murdrer felonous;
The whiles my handes I washt in purity,
The whiles my soule was soyld with fowle iniquity."

LXIII. Infinite moe tormented in like paine
He there beheld, too long here to be told:
Ne Mammon would there let him long remayne,
For terrour of the tortures manifold,
In which the damned soules he did behold,
But roughly him bespake: " Thou fearefull foole,
Why takest not of that same fruite of gold?
Ne sittest downe on that same silver stoole,
To rest thy weary person in the shadow coole? "

LXIV. All which he did to do him deadly fall
In frayle intemperaunce through sinfull bayt;
To which if he inclyned had at all,
That dreadfull feend, which did behinde him wayt,
Would him have rent in thousand peeces strayt:
But he was wary wise in all his way,

And well perceived his deceiptfull sleight,
Ne suffred lust his safety to betray.
So goodly did beguile the Guyler of his pray.

LXV. And now he has so long remained theare,
That vitall powres gan wexe both weake and wan
For want of food and sleepe, which two upbeare,
Like mightie pillours, this frayle life of man,
That none without the same enduren can:
For now three dayes of men were full out-wrought,
Since he this hardy enterprize began:
Forthy great Mammon fayrely he besought
Into the world to guyde him backe, as he him brought.

LXVI. The God, though loth, yet was constraynd t' obay;
For lenger time then that no living wight
Below the earth might suffred be to stay:
So backe againe him brought to living light.
But all so soone as his enfeebled spright
Gan sucke this vitall ayre into his brest,
As overcome with too exceeding might,
The life did flit away out of her nest,
And all his sences were with deadly fit opprest.

CANTO VIII

> Sir Guyon, layd in swowne, is by
> Acrates sonnes despoyld;
> Whom Arthure soone hath reskewed,
> And Paynim brethren foyld.

I. AND is there care in heaven?   And is there love
In heavenly spirits to these creatures bace,
That may compassion of their evilles move?
There is: else much more wretched were the cace
Of men then beasts.   But O! th' exceeding grace
Of highest God that loves his creatures so,
And all his workes with mercy doth embrace,
That blessed Angels he sends to and fro,
To serve to wicked man, to serve his wicked foe.

II. How oft do they their silver bowers leave,
To come to succour us that succour want!
How oft do they with golden pineons cleave
The flitting skyes, like flying Pursuivant,
Against fowle feendes to ayd us militant!
They for us fight, they watch and dewly ward,
And their bright Squadrons round about us plant;
And all for love, and nothing for reward.
O! why should hevenly God to men have such regard?

III. During the while that Guyon did abide
In Mamons house, the Palmer, whom whyleare
That wanton Mayd of passage had denide,
By further search had passage found elsewhere;
And, being on his way, approched neare
Where Guyon lay in traunce; when suddeinly
He heard a voyce that called lowd and cleare,
" Come hither! hither! O, come hastily! "
That all the fields resounded with the ruefull cry.

IV. The Palmer lent his eare unto the noyce,
To weet who called so importunely:
Againe he heard a more efforced voyce,

That bad him come in haste.   He by and by
His feeble feet directed to the cry;
Which to that shady delve him brought at last,
Where Mammon earst did sunne his threasury;
There the good Guyon he found slumbring fast
In senceles dreame; which sight at first him sore aghast.

v. Beside his head there sàtt a faire young man,
Of wondrous beauty and of freshest yeares,
Whose tender bud to blossome new began,
And florish faire above his equall peares:
His snowy front, curled with golden heares,
Like Phœbus face adornd with sunny rayes,
Divinely shone; and two sharpe winged sheares,
Decked with diverse plumes, like painted Jayes,
Were fixed at his backe to cut his ayery wayes.

vi. Like as Cupido on Idæan hill,
When having laid his cruell bow away
And mortall arrowes, wherewith he doth fill
The world with murdrous spoiles and bloody pray,
With his faire mother he him dights to play,
And with his goodly sisters, Graces three:
The Goddesse, pleased with his wanton play,
Suffers her selfe through sleepe beguild to bee,
The whiles the other Ladies mind theyr mery glee.

vii. Whom when the Palmer saw, abasht he was
Through fear and wonder that he nought could say,
Till him the childe bespoke; " Long lackt, alas!
Hath bene thy faithfull aide in hard assay,
Whiles deadly fitt thy pupill doth dismay.
Behold this heavy sight, thou reverend Sire!
But dread of death and dolor doe away;
For life ere long shall to her home retire,
And he that breathlesse seems shal corage both respire.

viii. " The charge, which God doth unto me arrett,
Of his deare safety, I to thee commend;
Yet will I not forgoe, ne yet forgett
The care thereof my selfe unto the end,
But evermore him succour, and defend
Against his foe and mine: watch thou, I pray,

For evill is at hand him to offend."
So having said, eftsoones he gan display
His painted nimble wings, and vanisht quite away.

IX. The Palmer seeing his lefte empty place,
And his slow eies beguiled of their sight,
Woxe sore affraid, and standing still a space
Gaz'd after him, as fowle escapt by flight.
At last, him turning to his charge behight,
With trembling hand his troubled pulse gan try;
Where finding life not yet dislodged quight,
He much rejoyst, and courd it tenderly,
As chicken newly hatcht, from dreaded destiny.

X. At last he spide where towards him did pace
Two Paynim knights al armd as bright as skie,
And them beside an aged Sire did trace,
And far before a light-foote Page did flie,
That breathed strife and troublous enmitie.
Those were the two sonnes of Acrates old,
Who, meeting earst with Archimago slie
Foreby that idle strond, of him were told
That he which earst them combatted was Guyon bold.

XI. Which to avenge on him they dearly vowd,
Where ever that on ground they mote him find:
False Archimage provokte their corage prowd,
And stryful Atin in their stubborne mind
Coles of contention and whot vengeaunce tind.
Now bene they come whereas the Palmer sate,
Keeping that slombred corse to him assind:
Well knew they both his person, sith of late
With him in bloody armes they rashly did debate.

XII. Whom when Pyrochles saw, inflam'd with rage
That sire he fowl bespake: Thou dotard vile,
That with thy brutenesse shendst thy comely age,
Abandon soone, I read, the caytive spoile
Of that same outcast carcas, that erewhile
Made it selfe famous through false trechery,
And crownd his coward crest with knightly stile;
Loe! where he now inglorious doth lye,
To proove he lived il that did thus fowly dye.

XIII. To whom the Palmer fearlesse answered:
 " Certes, Sir knight, ye bene too much to blame,
 Thus for to blott the honor of the dead,
 And with fowle cowardize his carcas shame,
 Whose living handes immortalizd his name.
 Vile is the vengeaunce on the ashes cold,
 And envy base to barke at sleeping fame.
 Was never wight that treason of him told:
 Your self his prowesse prov'd, and found him fiers and
 bold."

XIV. Then sayd Cymochles: " Palmer, thou doest dote,
 Ne canst of prowesse ne of knighthood deeme,
 Save as thou seest or hearst. But well I wote,
 That of his puissance tryall made extreeme:
 Yet gold al is not that doth golden seeme;
 Ne all good knights that shake well speare and shield.
 The worth of all men by their end esteeme,
 And then dew praise or dew reproch them yield;
 Bad therefore I him deeme that thus lies dead on field."

XV. " Good or bad," gan his brother fiers reply,
 " What doe I recke, sith that he dide entire?
 Or what doth his bad death now satisfy
 The greedy hunger of revenging yre,
 Sith wrathfull hand wrought not her owne desire?
 Yet since no way is lefte to wreake my spight,
 I will him reave of armes, the victors hire,
 And of that shield, more worthy of good knight;
 For why should a dead dog be deckt in armour bright? "

XVI. " Fayr Sir," said then the Palmer suppliaunt,
 " For knighthoods love doe not so fowle a deed,
 Ne blame your honor with so shamefull vaunt
 Of vile revenge. To spoile the dead of weed
 Is sacrilege, and doth all sinnes exceed:
 But leave these relicks of his living might
 To decke his herce, and trap his tomb-blacke steed."
 " What herce or steed " (said he) " should he have dight,
 But be entombed in the raven or the kight? "

XVII. With that, rude hand upon his shield he laid,
 And th' other brother gan his helme unlace,
 Both fiercely bent to have him disaraid;

Till that they spyde where towards them did pace
An armed knight, of bold and bounteous grace,
Whose squire bore after him an heben launce
And covered shield.   Well kend him so far space
Th' enchaunter by his armes and amenaunce,
When under him he saw his Lybian steed to praunce;

XVIII. And to those brethren sayd; "Rise, rise bylive,
And unto batteil doe your selves addresse;
For yonder comes the prowest knight alive,
Prince Arthur, flowre of grace and nobilesse,
That hath to Paynim knights wrought gret distresse,
And thousand Sar'zins fowly donne to dye."
That word so deepe did in their harts impresse,
That both eftsoones upstarted furiously,
And gan themselves prepare to batteill greedily.

XIX. But fiers Pyrochles, lacking his owne sword,
The want thereof now greatly gan to plaine,
And Archimage besought, him that afford
Which he had brought for Braggadochio vaine.
"So would I," (said th' enchaunter) "glad and faine
Beteeme to you this sword, you to defend,
Or ought that els your honour might maintaine;
But that this weapons powre I well have kend
To be contrary to the worke which ye intend:

XX. "For that same knights owne sword that is, of yore
Which Merlin made by his almightie art
For that his noursling, when he knighthood swore,
Therewith to doen his foes eternall smart.
The metall first he mext with Medæwart,
That no enchauntment from his dint might save;
Then it in flames of Aetna wrought apart,
And seven times dipped in the bitter wave
Of hellish Styx, which hidden vertue to it gave.

XXI. "The vertue is, that nether steele nor stone
The stroke thereof from entraunce may defend;
Ne ever may be used by his fone,
Ne forst his rightfull owner to offend;
Ne ever will it breake, ne ever bend:
Wherefore *Morddure* it rightfully is hight.

In vaine therefore, Pyrochles, should I lend
The same to thee, against his lord to fight;
For sure yt would deceive thy labor and thy might."

XXII. " Foolish old man," said then the Pagan wroth,
" That weenest words or charms may force withstond:
Soone shalt thou see, and then beleeve for troth,
That I can carve with this inchaunted brond
His Lords owne flesh."   Therewith out of his hond
That vertuous steele he rudely snatcht away,
And Guyons shield about his wrest he bond:
So ready dight fierce battaile to assay,
And match his brother proud in battailous aray.

XXIII. By this, that straunger knight in presence came,
And goodly salued them; who nought againe
Him answered, as courtesie became;
But with sterne lookes, and stomachous disdaine,
Gave signes of grudge and discontentment vaine.
Then, turning to the Palmer, he gan spy
Where at his feet, with sorrowfull demayne
And deadly hew, an armed corse did lye,
In whose dead face he redd great magnanimity.

XXIV. Sayd he then to the Palmer: " Reverend Syre,
What great misfortune hath betidd this knight?
Or did his life her fatall date expyre,
Or did he fall by treason, or by fight?
How ever, sure I rew his pitteous plight."
" Not one, nor other," sayd the Palmer grave,
" Hath him befalne; but cloudes of deadly night
A while his heavy eylids cover'd have,
And all his sences drowned in deep sencelesse wave:

XXV. " Which those his cruell foes, that stand hereby,
Making advauntage, to revenge their spight,
Would him disarme and treaten shamefully;
Unworthie usage of redoubted knight.
But you, faire Sir, whose honourable sight
Doth promise hope of helpe and timely grace,
Mote I beseech to succour his sad plight,
And by your powre protect his feeble cace?
First prayse of knighthood is fowle outrage to deface."

XXVI. " Palmer," (said he) " no knight so rude, I weene,
As to doen outrage to a sleeping ghost;
Ne was there ever noble corage seene,
That in advauntage would his puissaunce bost:
Honour is least where oddes appeareth most.
May bee, that better reason will aswage
The rash revengers heat.　Words, well dispost,
Have secrete powre t' appease inflamed rage:
If not, leave unto me thy knights last patronage."

XXVII. Tho, turning to those brethren, thus bespoke:
" Ye warlike payre, whose valorous great might,
It seemes, just wronges to vengeaunce doe provoke,
To wreake your wrath on this dead seeming knight,
Mote ought allay the storme of your despight,
And settle patience in so furious heat?
Not to debate the chalenge of your right,
But for his carkas pardon I entreat,
Whom fortune hath already laid in lowest seat."

XXVIII. To whom Cymochles said; " For what art thou,
That mak'st thy selfe his dayes-man, to prolong
The vengeaunce prest?　Or who shall let me now
On this vile body from to wreak my wrong,
And made his carkas as the outcast dong?
Why should not that dead carrion satisfye
The guilt which, if he lived had thus long,
His life for dew revenge should deare abye?
The trespass still doth live, albee the person dye."

XXIX. " Indeed," then said the Prince, " the evill donne
Dyes not, when breath the body first doth leave;
But from the grandsyre to the Nephewes sonne,
And all his seede the curse doth often cleave,
Till vengeaunce utterly the guilt bereave:
So streightly God doth judge.　But gentle Knight,
That doth against the dead his hand upheave,
His honour staines with rancour and despight,
And great disparagment makes to his former might."

XXX. Pyrochles gan reply the second tyme,
And to him said: " Now, felon, sure I read,
How that thou art partaker of his cryme:

Therefore, by Termagaunt thou shalt be dead."
With that his hand, more sad then lomp of lead,
Uplifting high, he weened with Morddure,
His owen good sword Morddure, to cleave his head.
The faithfull steele such treason no'uld endure,
But, swarving from the marke, his Lordes life did assure.

XXXI. Yet was the force so furious and so fell,
That horse and man it made to reele asyde:
Nath'lesse the Prince would not forsake his sell,
For well of yore he learned had to ryde,
But full of anger fiersly to him cryde;
"False traitour! miscreaunt! thou broken hast
The law of armes to strike foe undefide:
But thou thy treasons fruit, I hope, shalt taste
Right sowre, and feele the law the which thou hast
    defast."

XXXII. With that his balefull speare he fiercely bent
Against the Pagans brest, and therewith thought
His cursed life out of her lodge have rent;
But ere the point arrived where it ought,
That seven fold shield, which he from Guyon brought,
He cast between to ward the bitter stownd:
Through all those foldes the steelehead passage wrought,
And through his shoulder perst; wherwith to ground
He groveling fell, all gored in his gushing wound.

XXXIII. Which when his brother saw, fraught with great griefe
And wrath, he to him leaped furiously,
And fowly saide: "By Mahoune, cursed thiefe,
That direfull stroke thou dearely shalt aby:"
Then, hurling up his harmefull blade on hy,
Smote him so hugely on his haughtie crest,
That from his saddle forced him to fly;
Els mote it needes downe to his manly brest
Have cleft his head in twaine, and life thence dispossest.

XXXIV. Now was the Prince in daungerous distresse,
Wanting his sword when he on foot should fight:
His single speare could doe him small redresse
Against two foes of so exceeding might,
The least of which was match for any knight.
And now the other, whom he earst did daunt,

Had reard him selfe againe to cruel fight
Three times more furious and more puissaunt,
Unmindfull of his wound, of his fate ignoraunt.

xxxv. So both attonce him charge on either syde
With hideous strokes and importable powre,
That forced him his ground to traverse wyde,
And wisely watch to ward that deadly stowre;
For in his shield, as thicke as stormie showre,
Their strokes did raine: yet did he never quaile,
Ne backward shrinke, but as a stedfast towre,
Whom foe with double battry doth assaile,
Them on her bulwarke beares, and bids them nought
availe.

xxxvi. So stoutly he withstood their strong assay;
Till that at last, when he advantage spyde,
His poynant speare he thrust with puissant sway
At proud Cymochles, whiles his shield was wyde,
That through his thigh the mortall steele did gryde:
He, swarving with the force, within his flesh
Did breake the launce, and let the head abyde.
Out of the wound the red blood flowed fresh,
That underneath his feet soone made a purple plesh.

xxxvii. Horribly then he gan to rage and rayle,
Cursing his Gods, and him selfe damning deepe:
Als when his brother saw the red blood rayle
Adowne so fast, and all his armour steepe,
For very felnesse lowd he gan to weepe,
And said; "Caytive, curse on thy cruell hond,
That twise hath spedd; yet shall it not thee keepe
From the third brunt of this my fatall brond:
Lo! where the dreadfull Death behynd thy backe doth
stond."

xxxviii. With that he strooke, and thother strooke withall,
That nothing seemd mote beare so monstrous might:
The one upon his covered shield did fall,
And glauncing downe would not his owner byte;
But thother did upon his troncheon smyte,
Which hewing quite asunder, further way
It made, and on his hacqueton did lyte,

The which dividing with importune sway,
It seized in his right side, and there the dint did stay.

XXXIX. Wyde was the wound, and a large lukewarme flood,
Red as the Rose, thence gushed grievously;
That when the Paynym spyde the streaming blood,
Gave him great hart and hope of victory.
On th' other side, in huge perplexity
The Prince now stood, having his weapon broke;
Nought could he hurt, but still at warde did ly:
Yet with his troncheon he so rudely stroke
Cymochles twise, that twise him forst his foot revoke.

XL. Whom when the Palmer saw in such distresse,
Sir Guyon's sword he lightly to him raught,
And said; "Fayre Sonne, great God thy right hand
blesse,
To use that sword so well as he it ought!"
Glad was the knight, and with fresh courage fraught,
When as againe he armed felt his hond:
Then like a Lyon, which hath long time saught
His robbed whelpes, and at the last them fond
Emongst the shepeheard swaynes, then wexeth wood
and yond:

XLI. So fierce he laid about him, and dealt blowes
On either side, that neither mayle could hold,
Ne shield defend the thunder of his throwes:
Now to Pyrochles many strokes he told;
Eft to Cymochles twise so many fold;
Then, backe againe turning his busie hond,
Them both atonce compeld with courage bold
To yield wide way to his hart-thrilling brond;
And though they both stood stiffe, yet could not both
withstond.

XLII. As salvage Bull, whom two fierce mastives bayt,
When rancour doth with rage him once engore,
Forgets with wary warde them to awayt,
But with his dreadfull hornes them drives afore,
Or flings aloft, or treades downe in the flore,
Beathing out wrath, and bellowing disdaine,
That all the forest quakes to heare him rore:

So rag'd Prince Arthur twixt his foemen twaine,
That neither could his mightie puissaunce sustaine.

XLIII. But ever at Pyrochles when he smitt,
(Who Guyons shield cast ever him before,
Whereon the Faery Queenes pourtract was writt,)
His hand relented and the stroke forbore,
And his deare hart the picture gan adore;
Which oft the Paynim sav'd from deadly stowre:
But him henceforth the same can save no more:
For now arrived is his fatall howre,
That no'te avoyded be by earthly skill or powre.

XLIV. For when Cymochles saw the fowle reproch,
Which them appeached, prickt with guiltie shame
And inward griefe, he fiercely gan approch,
Resolv'd to put away that loathly blame,
Or dye with honour and desert of fame;
And on the haubergh stroke the Prince so sore,
That quite disparted all the linked frame,
And pierced to the skin, but bit no more;
Yet made him twise to reele, that never moov'd afore.

XLV. Whereat renfierst with wrath and sharp regret,
He stroke so hugely with his borrow blade,
That it empierst the Pagans burganet;
And, cleaving the hard steele, did deepe invade
Into his head, and cruell passage made
Quite through his brayne. He, tombling downe on
        ground,
Breathd out his ghost, which, to th' infernall shade
Fast flying, there eternall torment found
For all the sinnes wherewith his lewd life did abound.

XLVI. Which when his german saw, the stony feare
Ran to his hart, and all his sence dismayd,
Ne thenceforth life ne corage did appeare;
But as a man whom hellish feendes have frayd,
Long trembling still he stoode: at last thus sayd;
" Traytour, what hast thou doen?   How ever may
Thy cursed hand so cruelly have swayd
Against that knight!   Harrow and well away!
After so wicked deede why liv'st thou lenger day? "

XLVII. With that all desperate, as loathing light,
        And with revenge desyring soone to dye,
        Assembling all his force and utmost might,
        With his owne swerd he fierce at him did flye,
        And strooke, and foynd, and lasht outrageously,
        Withouten reason or regard.   Well knew
        The Prince, with pacience and sufferaunce sly
        So hasty heat soone cooled to subdew:
Tho, when this breathlesse woxe, that batteil gan renew.

XLVIII. As when a windy tempest bloweth hye,
        That nothing may withstand his stormy stowre,
        The clowdes, as thinges affrayd, before him flye;
        But all so soone as his outrageous powre
        Is layd, they fiercely then begin to showre;
        And, as in scorne of his spent stormy spight,
        Now all attonce their malice forth do poure:
        So did Prince Arthur beare himselfe in fight,
And suffred rash Pyrochles waste his ydle might.

XLIX. At last, when as the Sarazin perceiv'd
        How that straunge sword refusd to serve his neede,
        But when he stroke most strong the dint deceiv'd,
        He flong it from him; and, devoyd of dreed,
        Upon him lightly leaping without heed
        Twixt his two mighty armes engrasped fast,
        Thinking to overthrowe and downe him tred:
        But him in strength and skill the Prince surpast,
And through his nimble sleight did under him down cast.

L. Nought booted it the Paynim then to strive;
        For as a Bittur in the Eagles clawe,
        That may not hope by flight to scape alive,
        Still waytes for death with dread and trembling aw;
        So he, now subject to the victours law,
        Did not once move, nor upward cast his eye,
        For vile disdaine and rancour, which did gnaw
        His hart in twaine with sad melancholy;
As one that loathed life, and yet despysd to dye.

LI. But full of princely bounty and great mind,
        The Conquerour nought cared him to slay;
        But casting wronges and all revenge behind,

More glory thought to give life then decay,
And sayd; " Paynim, this is thy dismall day;
Yet if thou wilt renounce thy miscreaunce,
And my trew liegeman yield thy selfe for ay,
Life will I graunt thee for thy valiaunce,
And all thy wronges will wipe out of my sovenaunce."

LII. " Foole ! " (sayd the Pagan) " I thy gift defye,
But use thy fortune as it doth befall;
And say, that I not overcome doe dye,
But in despight of life for death doe call."
Wroth was the Prince, and sory yet withall,
That he so wilfully refused grace;
Yet sith his fate so cruelly did fall,
His shining Helmet he gan soone unlace,
And left his headlesse body bleeding all the place.

LIII. By this Sir Guyon from his traunce awakt,
Life having maystered her sencelesse foe,
And looking up, whenas his shield he lakt
And sword saw not, he wexed wondrous woe;
But when the Palmer, whom he long ygoe
Had lost, he by him spyde, right glad he grew,
And saide; " Deare sir, whom wandring to and fro
I long have lackt, I joy thy face to vew:
Firme is thy faith, whom daunger never fro me drew.

LIV. " But read, what wicked hand hath robbed mee
Of my good sword and shield? " The Palmer, glad
With so fresh hew uprysing him to see,
Him answered: " Fayre sonne, be no whit sad
For want of weapons; they shall soone be had."
So gan he to discourse the whole debate,
Which that straunge knight for him sustained had,
And those two Sarazins confounded late,
Whose carcases on ground were horribly prostrate.

LV. Which when he heard, and saw the tokens trew,
His hart with great affection was embayd,
And to the Prince, bowing with reverence dew
As to the patrone of his life, thus sayd;
" My Lord, my liege, by whose most gratious ayd
I live this day, and see my foes subdewd,

What may suffice to be for meede repayd
Of so great graces as ye have me shewd,
But to be ever bound "——
　　　　　　　　　　・

LVI. To whom the Infant thus; " Fayre Sir, what need
Good turnes be counted as a servile bond
To bind their doers to receive their meed?
Are not all knightes by oath bound to withstond
Oppressours powre by armes and puissant hond?
Suffise that I have done my dew in place."
So goodly purpose they together fond
Of kindnesse and of courteous aggrace;
The whiles false Archimage and Atin fled apace.

CANTO IX

The house of Temperance, in which
Doth sober Alma dwell,
Besiegd of many foes, whom straung-
er knightes to flight compell.

I. Of all Gods workes which doe this worlde adorne,
There is no one more faire and excellent
Then is mans body, both for powre and forme,
Whiles it is kept in sober government;
But none then it more fowle and indecent,
Distempred through misrule and passions bace;
It growes a Monster, and incontinent
Doth loose his dignity and native grace:
Behold, who list, both one and other in this place.

II. After the Paynim brethren conquer'd were,
The Briton Prince recov'ring his stolne sword,
And Guyon his lost shield, they both yfere
Forth passed on their way in fayre accord,
Till him the Prince with gentle court did bord:
" Sir knight, mote I of you this court'sy read,
To weet why on your shield, so goodly scord,
Beare ye the picture of that Ladies head?
Full lively is the semblaunt, though the substance dead."

III. " Fayre Sir," (sayd he) " if in that picture dead
Such life ye read, and vertue in vaine shew;
What mote ye weene, if the trew lively-head
Of that most glorious visage ye did vew:
But yf the beauty of her mind ye knew,
That is, her bounty, and imperiall powre,
Thousand times fairer than her mortall hew,
O! how great wonder would your thoughts devoure,
And infinite desire into your spirite poure.

IV. " Shee is the mighty Queene of Faery,
Whose faire retraitt I in my shield doe beare;
Shee is the flowre of grace and chastity

Throughout the world, renowmed far and neare,
My liefe, my liege, my Soveraine, my deare,
Whose glory shineth as the morning starre,
And with her light the earth enlumines cleare:
Far reach her mercies, and her praises farre,
As well in state of peace, as puissaunce in warre."

v. "Thrise happy man," (said then the Briton knight)
"Whom gracious lott and thy great valiaunce
Have made thee soldier of that Princesse bright,
Which with her bounty and glad countenaunce
Doth blesse her servaunts, and them high advaunce.
How may straunge knight hope ever to aspire,
By faithfull service and meete amenaunce,
Unto such blisse? sufficient were that hire
For losse of thousand lives, to die at her desire."

vi. Said Guyon, "Noble Lord, what meed so great,
Or grace of earthly Prince so soveraine,
But by your wondrous worth and warlike feat
Ye well may hope, and easely attaine?
But were your will her sold to entertaine,
And numbred be mongst knights of Maydenhed,
Great guerdon, well I wote, should you remaine,
And in her favor high bee reckoned,
As Arthegall and Sophy now beene honored."

vii. "Certes," (then said the Prince) "I God avow,
That sith I armes and knighthood first did plight,
My whole desire hath beene, and yet is now,
To serve that Queene with al my powre and might.
Seven times the Sunne, with his lamp-burning light,
Hath walkte about the world, and I no lesse,
Sith of that Goddesse I have sought the sight,
Yet no where can her find: such happinesse
Heven doth to me envy, and fortune favourlesse."

viii. "Fortune, the foe of famous chevisaunce,
"Seldom" (said Guyon) "yields to vertue aide,
But in her way throwes mischiefe and mischaunce,
Whereby her course is stopt and passage staid:
But you, faire Sir, be not herewith dismaid,
But constant keepe the way in which ye stand;

Which, were it not that I am els delaid
With hard adventure which I have in hand,
I labour would to guide you through al Faery land."

IX. "Gramercy Sir," said he; "but mote I weete
What straunge adventure doe ye now pursew?
Perhaps my succour or advizement meete
Mote stead you much your purpose to subdew."
Then gan Sir Guyon all the story shew
Of false Acrasia, and her wicked wiles;
Which to avenge the Palmer him forth drew
From Faery court.   So talked they, the whiles
They wasted had much way, and measurd many miles.

x. And now faire Phœbus gan decline in haste
His weary wagon to the Westerne vale,
Whenas they spide a goodly castle, plaste
Foreby a river in a pleasaunt dale;
Which choosing for that evenings hospitale,
They thither marcht: but when they came in sight,
And from their sweaty Coursers did avale,
They found the gates fast barred long ere night,
And every loup fast lockt, as fearing foes despight.

XI. Which when they saw, they weened fowle reproch
Was to them doen, their entraunce to forestall,
Till that the Squire gan nigher to approch,
And wind his horne under the castle wall,
That with the noise it shooke as it would fall.
Eftsoones forth looked from the highest spire
The watch, and lowd unto the knights did call,
To weete what they so rudely did require?
Who gently answered, They entraunce did desire.

XII. "Fly fly, good knights," (said he) "fly fast away,
If that your lives ye love, as meete ye should;
Fly fast, and save your selves from neare decay;
Here may ye not have entraunce, though we would:
We would, and would againe, if that we could;
But thousand enemies about us rave,
And with long siege us in the castle hould.
Seven yeares this wize they us besieged have,
And many good knights slaine that have us sought to save."

XIII. Thus as he spoke, loe! with outragious cry
        A thousand villeins rownd about them swarmd
        Out of the rockes and caves adjoyning nye;
        Vile caitive wretches, ragged, rude, deformd,
        All threatning death, all in straunge manner armd;
        Some with unweldy clubs, some with long speares,
        Some rusty knifes, some staves in fier warmd:
        Sterne was their looke; like wild amazed steares,
        Staring with hollow eies, and stiffe upstanding heares.

XIV. Fiersly at first those knights they did assayle,
        And drove them to recoile; but when againe
        They gave fresh charge, their forces gan to fayle,
        Unhable their encounter to sustaine;
        For with such puissaunce and impetuous maine
        Those Champions broke on them, that forst them fly,
        Like scattered Sheepe, whenas the Shepherds swaine
        A Lyon and a Tigre doth espye,
        With greedy pace forth rushing from the forest nye.

XV. A while they fled, but soone retournd againe
        With greater fury then before was fownd;
        And evermore their cruell Capitaine
        Sought with his raskall routs t' enclose them rownd,
        And, overronne, to tread them to the grownd:
        But soone the knights with their bright burning blades
        Broke their rude troupes, and orders did confownd,
        Hewing and slashing at their idle shades;
        For though they bodies seem, yet substaunce from
            them fades.

XVI. As when a swarme of Gnats at eventide
        Out of the fennes of Allan doe arise,
        Their murmuring small trompetts sownden wide,
        Whiles in the aire their clustring army flies,
        That as a cloud doth seeme to dim the skies;
        Ne man nor beast may rest, or take repast
        For their sharpe wounds and noyous injuries,
        Till the fierce Northerne wind with blustring blast
        Doth blow them quite away, and in the Ocean cast.

XVII. Thus when they had that troublous rout disperst,
        Unto the castle gate they come againe,
        And entraunce crav'd which was denied erst.

Now when report of that their perlous paine,
And combrous conflict which they did sustaine,
Came to the Ladies eare which there did dwell,
Shee forth issewed with a goodly traine
Of Squires and Ladies equipaged well,
And entertained them right fairely, as befell.

XVIII. Alma she called was; a virgin bright,
That had not yet felt Cupides wanton rage;
Yet was shee woo'd of many a gentle knight,
And many a Lord of noble parentage,
That sought with her to lincke in marriage:
For shee was faire as faire mote ever bee,
And in the flowre now of her freshest age;
Yet full of grace and goodly modestee,
That even heven rejoyced her sweete face to see.

XIX. In robe of lilly white she was arayd,
That from her shoulder to her heele downe raught;
The traine whereof loose far behind her strayd,
Braunched with gold and perle most richly wrought,
And borne of two faire Damsels which were taught
That service well. Her yellow golden heare
Was trimly woven and in tresses wrought,
Ne other tire she on her head did weare,
But crowned with a garland of sweete Rosiere.

XX. Goodly shee entertaind those noble knights,
And brought them up into her castle hall;
Where gentle court and gracious delight
Shee to them made, with mildnesse virginall,
Shewing her selfe both wise and liberall.
Then, when they rested had a season dew,
They her besought of favour speciall
Of that faire Castle to affoord them vew:
Shee graunted; and, them leading forth, the same did shew.

XXI. First she them lead up to the Castle wall,
That was so high as foe might not it clime,
And all so faire and fensible withall;
Not built of bricke, ne yet of stone and lime,
But of thing like to that Ægyptian slime,
Whereof king Nine whilome built Babell towre.

But O great pitty! that no lenger time
So goodly workemanship should not endure:
Soone it must turne to earth; no earthly thing is sure.

XXII. The frame thereof seemd partly circulare,
And part triangulare; O worke divine!
Those two the first and last proportions are;
The one imperfect, mortall, fœminine,
Th' other immortall, perfect, masculine;
And twixt them both a quadrate was the base
Proportiond equally by seven and nine;
Nine was the circle sett in heavens place:
All which compacted made a goodly Diapase.

XXIII. Therein two gates were placed seemly well:
The one before, by which all in did pas,
Did th' other far in workmanship excell;
For not of wood, nor of enduring bras,
But of more worthy substance fram'd it was:
Doubly disparted, it did locke and close,
That when it locked none might thorough pas,
And when it opened, no man might it close,
Still open to their friendes, and closed to their foes.

XXIV. Of hewen stone the porch was fayrely wrought,
Stone more of valew, and more smooth and fine,
Then Jett or Marble far from Ireland brought;
Over the which was cast a wandring vine,
Enchaced with a wanton yvie twine;
And over it a fayre Portcullis hong,
Which to the gate directly did incline
With comely compasse and compacture strong,
Nether unseemly short, nor yet exceeding long.

XXV. Within the Barbican a Porter sate,
Day and night duely keeping watch and ward;
Nor wight nor word mote passe out of the gate,
But in good order, and with dew regard;
Utterers of secrets he from thence debard,
Bablers of folly, and blazers of cryme:
His larumbell might lowd and wyde be hard
When cause requyrd, but never out of time;
Early and late it rong, at evening and at prime.

XXVI. And rownd about the porch on every syde
    Twise sixteene warders satt, all armed bright
    In glistring steele, and strongly fortifyde:
    Tall yeomen seemed they and of great might,
    And were enraunged ready still for fight.
    By them as Alma passed with her guestes,
    They did obeysaunce, as beseemed right,
    And then againe retourned to their restes:
    The Porter eke to her did lout with humble gestes.

XXVII. Thence she them brought into a stately Hall,
    Wherein were many tables fayre dispred,
    And ready dight with drapets festivall,
    Against the viaundes should be ministred.
    At th' upper end there sate, yclad in red
    Downe to the ground, a comely personage,
    That in his hand a white rod menaged:
    He Steward was, hight Diet; rype of age,
    And in demeanure sober, and in counsell sage.

XXVIII. And through the Hall there walked to and fro
    A jolly yeoman, Marshall of the same,
    Whose name was Appetite: he did bestow
    Both guestes and meate, when ever in they came,
    And knew them how to order without blame,
    As him the Steward badd.   They both attone
    Did dewty to their Lady, as became;
    Who, passing by, forth ledd her guestes anone
    Into the kitchen rowme, ne spard for nicenesse none.

XXIX. It was a vaut ybuilt for great dispence,
    With many raunges reard along the wall,
    And one great chimney, whose long tonnell thence
    The smoke forth threw.   And in the midst of all
    There placed was a caudron wide and tall
    Upon a mightie fornace, burning whott,
    More whott then Aetn', or flaming Mongiball
    For day and night it brent, ne ceased not,
    So long as any thing it in the caudron gott.

XXX. But to delay the heat, least by mischaunce
    It might breake out and sett the whole on fyre,
    There added was by goodly ordinaunce

An huge great payre of bellowes, which did styre
Continually, and cooling breath inspyre.
About the Caudron many Cookes accoyld
With hookes and ladles, as need did requyre;
The whyles the viaundes in the vessell boyld
They did about their businesse sweat, and sorely **toyld.**

XXXI. The maister Cooke was cald Concoction;
A carefull man, and full of comely guyse.
The kitchin clerke, that hight Digestion,
Did order all th' Achates in seemely wise,
And set them forth, as well he could devise.
The rest had severall offices assynd;
Some to remove the scum as it did rise;
Others to beare the same away did mynd;
And others it to use according to his kynd.

XXXII. But all the liquour, which was fowle and waste,
Not good nor serviceable elles for ought,
They in another great rownd vessell plaste,
Till by a conduit pipe it thence were brought:
And all the rest, that noyous was and nought,
By secret wayes, that none might it espy,
Was close convaid, and to the backgate brought,
That cleped was Port Esquiline, whereby
It was avoided quite, and throwne out privily.

XXXIII. Which goodly order and great workmans skill
Whenas those knightes beheld, with rare delight
And gazing wonder they their mindes did fill;
For never had they seene so straunge a sight.
Thence backe againe faire Alma led them right,
And soone into a goodly Parlour brought,
That was with royall arras richly dight,
In which was nothing pourtrahed nor wrought;
Not wrought nor pourtrahed, but easie to be **thought.**

XXXIV. And in the midst thereof upon the floure
A lovely bevy of faire Ladies sate,
Courted of many a jolly Paramoure,
The which them did in modest wise amate,
And each one sought his Lady to aggrate:
And eke emongst them litle Cupid playd

His wanton sportes, being retourned late
From his fierce warres, and having from him layd
His cruel bow, wherewith he thousands hath dismayd.

xxxv. Diverse delights they fownd them selves to please;
Some song in sweet consort; some laught for joy;
Some plaid with strawes; some ydly satt at ease;
But other some could not abide to toy;
All pleasaunce was to them griefe and annoy:
This frownd, that faund, the third for shame did blush,
Another seemd envious or coy,
Another in her teeth did gnaw a rush;
But at these straungers presence every one did hush.

xxxvi. Soone as the gracious Alma came in place,
They all attonce out of their seates arose,
And to her homage made with humble grace:
Whom when the knights beheld, they gan dispose
Themselves to court, and each a damzell chose.
The Prince by chaunce did on a Lady light,
That was right faire and fresh as morning rose,
But somwhat sad and solemne eke in sight,
As if some pensive thought constraind her gentle spright.

xxxvii. In a long purple pall, whose skirt with gold
Was fretted all about, she was arayd;
And in her hand a Poplar braunch did hold:
To whom the Prince in courteous maner sayd;
"Gentle Madame, why beene ye thus dismayd,
And your faire beautie doe with sadnes spill?
Lives any that you hath thus ill apayd?
Or doen you love? or doen you lack your will?
What ever bee the cause, it sure beseemes you ill."

xxxviii. "Fayre Sir," said she, halfe in disdaineful wise,
"How is it that this mood in me ye blame,
And in your selfe doe not the same advise?
Him ill beseemes anothers fault to name,
That may unwares bee blotted with the same:
Pensive I yeeld I am, and sad in mind,
Through great desire of glory and of fame;
Ne ought, I weene, are ye therein behynd,
That have three years sought one, yet no where can her
      find."

XXXIX. The Prince was inly moved at her speach,
Well weeting trew what she had rashly told;
Yet with faire semblaunt sought to hyde the breach,
Which chaunge of colour did perforce unfold,
Now seeming flaming whott, now stony cold:
Tho, turning soft aside, he did inquyre
What wight she was that Poplar braunch did hold?
It answered was, her name was Prays-desire,
That by well doing sought to honour to aspyre.

XL. The whyles the Faery knight did entertayne
Another Damsell of that gentle crew,
That was right fayre and modest of demayne,
But that too oft she chaung'd her native hew.
Straunge was her tyre, and all her garment blew,
Close rownd about her tuckt with many a plight:
Upon her fist the bird, which shonneth vew,
And keepes in coverts close from living wight,
Did sitt, as yet ashamed how rude Pan did her dight.

XLI. So long as Guyon with her commoned,
Unto the grownd she cast her modest eye,
And ever and anone with rosy red
The bashfull blood her snowy cheekes did dye,
That her became, as polisht yvory
Which cunning Craftesman hand hath overlayd
With fayre vermilion or pure Castory.
Great wonder had the knight to see the mayd
So straungely passioned, and to her gently said:

XLII. "Fayre Damzell, seemeth by your troubled cheare,
That either me too bold ye weene, this wise
You to molest, or other ill to feare
That in the secret of your hart close lyes,
From whence it doth, as cloud from sea, aryse.
If it be I, of pardon I you pray;
But if ought else that I mote not devyse,
I will, if please you it discure, assay
To ease you of that ill, so wisely as I may."

XLIII. She answerd nought, but more abasht for shame
Held downe her head, the whiles her lovely face
The flashing blood with blushing did inflame,

And the strong passion mard her modest grace,
That Guyon mervayld at her uncouth cace;
Till Alma him bespake: " Why wonder yee,
Faire Sir, at that which ye so much embrace?
She is the fountaine of your modestee:
You shamefast are, but Shamefastnes it selfe is shee."

XLIV. Thereat the Elfe did blush in privitee,
And turned his face away, but she the same
Dissembled faire, and faynd to oversee.
Thus they awhile with court and goodly game
Themselves did solace each one with his Dame,
Till that great Lady thence away them sought
To vew her Castles other wondrous frame:
Up to a stately Turret she them brought,
Ascending by ten steps of Alabaster wrought.

XLV. That Turrets frame most admirable was,
Like highest heaven compassed around,
And lifted high above this earthly masse,
Which it survewd as hils doen lower ground;
But not on ground mote like to this be found:
Not that, which antique Cadmus whylome built
In Thebes, which Alexander did confound;
Nor that proud towre of Troy, though richly guilt,
From which young Hectors blood by cruell Greekes was
    spilt.

XLVI. The roofe hereof was arched over head,
And deckt with flowers and herbars daintily:
Two goodly Beacons, set in watches stead,
Therein gave light, and flamd continually;
For they of living fire most subtilly
Were made, and set in silver sockets bright,
Cover'd with lids deviz'd of substance sly,
That readily they shut and open might.
O! who can tell the prayses of that makers might?

XLVII. Ne can I tell, ne can I stay to tell,
This parts great workemanship and wondrous powre,
That all this other worldes worke doth excell,
And likest is unto that heavenly towre
That God hath built for his owne blessed bowre.
Therein were divers rowmes, and divers stages;

But three the chiefest and of greatest powre,
In which there dwelt three honorable sages,
The wisest men, I weene, that lived in their ages.

XLVIII. Not he, whom Greece, the Nourse of all good arts,
By Phœbus doome the wisest thought alive,
Might be compar'd to these by many parts:
Nor that sage Pylian syre, which did survive
Three ages, such as mortall men contrive,
By whose advise old Priams citie fell,
With these in praise of pollicies mote strive.
These three in these three rowmes did sondry dwell,
And counselled faire Alma how to governe well.

XLIX. The first of them could things to come foresee;
The next could of thinges present best advize;
The third things past could keep in memoree:
So that no time nor reason could arize,
But that the same could one of these comprize.
For-thy the first did in the forepart sit,
That nought mote hinder his quicke prejudize:
He had a sharpe foresight and working wit
That never idle was, ne once would rest a whit.

L. His chamber was dispainted all within
With sondry colours, in the which were writ
Infinite shapes of thinges dispersed thin;
Some such as in the world were never yit,
Ne can devized be of mortall wit;
Some daily seene and knowen by their names,
Such as in idle fantasies do flit;
Infernall Hags, Centaurs, feendes, Hippodames,
Apes, Lyons, Aegles, Owles, fooles, lovers, children, Dames.

LI. And all the chamber filled was with flyes
Which buzzed all about, and made such sound
That they encombred all mens eares and eyes;
Like many swarmes of Bees assembled round,
After their hives with honny do abound.
All those were idle thoughtes and fantasies,
Devices, dreames, opinions unsound,
Shewes, visions, sooth-sayes, and prophesies;
And all that fained is, as leasings, tales, and lies.

LII. Emongst them all sate he which wonned there,
That hight Phantastes by his nature trew;
A man of yeares yet fresh, as mote appere,
Of swarth complexion, and of crabbed hew,
That him full of melancholy did shew;
Bent hollow beetle browes, sharpe staring eyes,
That mad or foolish seemd: one by his vew
Mote deeme him borne with ill-disposed skyes,
When oblique Saturne sate in th' house of agonyes.

LIII. Whom Alma having shewed to her guestes,
Thence brought them to the second rowme, whose wals
Were painted faire with memorable gestes
Of famous Wisards; and with picturals
Of Magistrates, of courts, of tribunals,
Of commen-wealthes, of states, of pollicy,
Of lawes, of judgementes, and of decretals,
All artes, all science, all Philosophy,
And all that in the world was ay thought wittily.

LIV. Of those that rowme was full; and them among
There sate a man of ripe and perfect age,
Who did them meditate all his life long,
That through continuall practise and usage
He now was growne right wise and wondrous sage:
Great pleasure had those straunger knightes to see
His goodly reason and grave personage,
That his disciples both desyrd to bee;
But Alma thence them led to th' hindmost rowme of three.

LV. That chamber seemed ruinous and old,
And therefore was removed far behind,
Yet were the wals, that did the same uphold,
Right firme and strong, though somewhat they declind;
And therein sat an old old man, halfe blind,
And all decrepit in his feeble corse,
Yet lively vigour rested in his mind,
And recompenst them with a bitter scorse:
Weake body wel is chang'd for minds redoubled forse.

LVI. This man of infinite remembraunce was,
And things foregone through many ages held,
Which he recorded still as they did pas,
Ne suffred them to perish through long eld,

As all things els the which this world doth weld;
But laid them up in his immortall scrine,
Where they for ever incorrupted dweld:
The warres he well remembred of king Nine,
Of old Assaracus, and Inachus divine.

LVII. The yeares of Nestor nothing were to his,
Ne yet Mathusalem, though longest liv'd;
For he remembred both their infancis:
Ne wonder then, if that he were depriv'd
Of native strength now that he them surviv'd.
His chamber all was hangd about with rolls
And old records from auncient times derivd,
Some made in books, some in long parchment scrolls,
That were all worm-eaten and full of canker holes.

LVIII. Amidst them all he in a chaire was sett,
Tossing and turning them withouten end;
But for he was unhable them to fett,
A litle boy did on him still attend
To reach, when ever he for ought did send;
And oft when thinges were lost, or laid amis,
That boy them sought and unto him did lend:
Therefore he Anamnestes cleped is;
And that old man Eumnestes, by their propertis.

LIX. The knightes there entring did him reverence dew,
And wondred at his endlesse exercise:
Then as they gan his Library to vew,
And antique Regesters for to avise,
There chaunced to the Princes hand to rize
An auncient booke, hight *Briton moniments*,
That of this lands first conquest did devize,
And old division into Regiments,
Till it reduced was to one mans governements.

LX. Sir Guyon chaunst eke on another booke,
That hight *Antiquitee of Faery lond* :
In which whenas he greedily did looke,
Th' ofspring of Elves and Faeryes there he fond,
As it delivered was from hond to hond:
Whereat they, burning both with fervent fire
Their countreys auncestry to understond,
Crav'd leave of Alma and that aged sire
To read those bookes; who glady graunted their desire.

CANTO X

A chronicle of Briton kings,
From Brute to Uthers rayne;
And rolls of Elfin Emperours,
Till time of Gloriane.

I. Who now shall give unto me words and sound
Equall unto this haughty enterprise?
Or who shall lend me wings, with which from ground
My lowly verse may loftily arise,
And lift it selfe unto the highest skyes?
More ample spirit than hitherto was wount
Here needes me, whiles the famous auncestryes
Of my most dreaded Soveraigne I recount,
By which all earthly Princes she doth far surmount.

II. Ne under Sunne that shines so wide and faire,
Whence all that lives does borrow life and light,
Lives ought that to her linage may compaire;
Which though from earth it be derived right
Yet doth it selfe stretch forth to hevens hight,
And all the world with wonder overspred;
A labor huge, exceeding far my might.
How shall fraile pen, with feare disparaged,
Conceive such soveraine glory and great bountyhed?

III. Argument worthy of Mæonian quill;
Or rather worthy of great Phœbus rote,
Whereon the ruines of great Ossa hill,
And triumphes of Phlegræan Jove, he wrote,
That all the Gods admird his lofty note.
But if some relish of that hevenly lay
His learned daughters would to me report
To decke my song withall, I would assay
Thy name, O soveraine Queene! to blazon far away.

IV. Thy name, O soveraine Queene! thy realme, and race,
From this renowmed Prince derived arre,
Who mightily upheld that royall mace

Which now thou bear'st, to thee descended farre
From mighty kings and conquerours in warre,
Thy fathers and great Grandfathers of old,
Whose noble deeds above the Northern starre
Immortall fame for ever hath enrold;
As in that old mans booke they were in order told.

v. The land which warlike Britons now possesse,
And therein have their mighty empire raysd,
In antique times was salvage wildernesse,
Unpeopled, unmannurd, unprovd, unpraysd;
Ne was it Island then, ne was it paysd
Amid the ocean waves, ne was it sought
Of merchants farre for profits therein praysd;
But was all desolate, and of some thought
By sea to have been from the Celticke maynland brought.

vi. Ne did it then deserve a name to have,
Till that the venturous Mariner that way
Learning his ship from those white rocks to save,
Which all along the Southerne sea-coast lay
Threatning unheedy wrecke and rash decay,
For safety that same his sea-marke made,
And named it ALBION: But later day,
Finding in it fit ports for fishers trade,
Gan more the same frequent, and further to invade.

vii. But far in land a salvage nation dwelt
Of hideous Giaunts, and halfe beastly men,
That never tasted grace, nor goodnes felt;
But wild like beastes lurking in loathsome den,
And flying fast as Roebucke through the fen,
All naked without shame or care of cold,
By hunting and by spoiling liveden;
Of stature huge, and eke of corage bold,
That sonnes of men amazd their sternnesse to behold.

viii. But whence they sprong, or how they were begott,
Uneath is to assure; uneath to wene
That monstrous error, which doth some assott,
That Dioclesians fifty daughters shene
Into this land by chaunce have driven bene;
Where, companing with feends and filthy Sprights

Through vaine illusion of their lust unclene,
They brought forth Geaunts, and such dreadful wights
As far exceeded men in their immeasurd mights.

IX. They held this land, and with their filthinesse
Polluted this same gentle soyle long time;
That their owne mother loathed their beastlinesse,
And gan abhorre her broods unkindly crime,
All were they borne of her owne native slime:
Until that Brutus, anciently deriv'd
From roiall stocke of old Assaracs line,
Driven by fatall error here arriv'd,
And them of their unjust possession depriv'd.

X. But ere he had established his throne,
And spred his empire to the utmost shore,
He fought great batteils with his salvage fone;
In which he them defeated evermore,
And many Giaunts left on groning flore:
That well can witness yet unto this day
The westerne Hogh, besprincled with the gore
Of mighty Goëmot, whome in stout fray
Corineus conquered, and cruelly did slay.

XI. And eke that ample Pitt, yet far renownd
For the large leape which Debon did compell
Coulin to make, being eight lugs of grownd,
Into the which retourning backe he fell:
But those three monstrous stones doe most excell,
Which that huge sonne of hideous Albion,
Whose father Hercules in Fraunce did quell,
Great Godmer threw, in fierce contention,
At bold Canutus; but of him was slaine anon.

XII. In meed of these great conquests by them gott,
Corineus had that Province utmost west
To him assigned for his worthy lott,
Which of his name and memorable gest
He called Cornwaile, yet so called best;
And Debons shayre was that is Devonshyre:
But Canute had his portion from the rest,
The which he cald Canutium, for his hyre;
Now Cantium, which Kent we comenly inquyre.

XIII. Thus Brute this Realme unto his rule subdewd,
And raigned long in great felicity,
Lov'd of his freends, and of his foes eschewd:
He left three sonnes, his famous progeny,
Borne of fayre Inogene of Italy;
Mongst whom he parted his imperiall state,
And Locrine left chiefe Lord of Britany.
At last ripe age bad him surrender late
His life, and long good fortune, unto finall fate.

XIV. Locrine was left the soveraine Lord of all:
But Albanact had all the Northerne part,
Which of himselfe Albania he did call;
And Camber did possesse the Westerne quart,
Which Severne now from Logris doth depart:
And each his portion peaceably enjoyed,
Ne was there outward breach, nor grudge in hart,
That once their quiet government annoyd;
But each his paynes to others profit still employd.

XV. Until a nation straunge, with visage swart,
And corage fierce that all men did affray,
Which through the world then swarmd in every part,
And overflowd all countries far away,
Like Noyes great flood, with their importune sway,
This land invaded with like violence,
And did themselves through all the North display:
Untill that Locrine for his Realmes defence,
Did head against them make and strong munificence.

XVI. He them encountred, a confused rout,
Foreby the River that whylome was hight
The ancient Abus, where with courage stout
He them defeated in victorious fight,
And chaste so fiercely after fearefull flight,
That forst their chiefetain, for his safeties sake,
(Their Chiefetain Humber named was aright,)
Unto the mighty streame him to betake,
Where he an end of batteill and of life did make.

XVII. The king retourned proud of victory,
And insolent wox through unwonted ease,
That shortly he forgot the jeopardy,

Which in his land he lately did appease,
And fell to vaine voluptuous disease:
He lov'd faire Ladie Estrild, leudly lov'd,
Whose wanton pleasures him too much did please,
That quite his hart from Guendolene remov'd,
From Guendolene his wife, though alwaies faithful prov'd.

xviii. The noble daughter of Corinëus
Would not endure to bee so vile disdaind,
But, gathering force and corage valorous,
Encountred him in batteill well ordaind,
In which him vanquisht she to fly constraind:
But she so fast pursewd, that him she tooke
And threw in bands, where he till death remaind;
Als his faire Leman flying through a brooke
She overhent, nought moved with her piteous looke;

xix. But both her selfe, and eke her daughter deare,
Begotten by her kingly Paramoure,
The faire Sabrina, almost dead with feare,
She there attached, far from all succoure;
The one she slew upon the present floure;
But the sad virgin, innocent of all,
Adowne the rolling river she did poure,
Which of her name now Severne men do call:
Such was the end that to disloyall love did fall.

xx. Then for her sonne, which she to Locrin bore,
Madan was young, unmeet the rule to sway,
In her owne hand the crowne she kept in store,
Till ryper years he raught and stronger stay;
During which time her powre she did display
Through all this Realme, the glory of her sex,
And first taught men a woman to obay:
But, when her sonne to mans estate did wex,
She it surrendred, ne her selfe would lenger vex.

xxi. Tho Madan raignd, unworthie of his race,
For with all shame that sacred throne he fild.
Next Memprise, as unworthy of that place;
In which being consorted with Manild,
For thrist of single kingdom him he kild.
But Ebranck salved both their infamies

With noble deedes, and warreyd on Brunchild
In Henault, where yet of his victories
Brave moniments remaine, which yet that land envies.

XXII. An happy man in his first dayes he was,
And happy father of faire progeny:
For all so many weekes as the yeare has,
So many children he did multiply:
Of which were twentie sonnes, which did apply
Their mindes to prayse and chevalrous desyre:
Those germans did subdew all Germany,
Of whom it hight; but in the end their Syre
With foule repulse from Fraunce was forced to retyre.

XXIII. Which blott his sonne succeeding in his seat,
The second Brute, the second both in name
And eke in semblaunce of his puissaunce great,
Right well recur'd, and did away that blame
With recompence of everlasting fame:
He with his victour sword first opened
The bowels of wide Fraunce, a forlorne Dame,
And taught her first how to be conquered;
Since which, with sondrie spoiles she hath been ransacked.

XXIV. Let Scaldis tell, and let tell Hania,
And let the marsh of Esthambruges tell,
What colour were their waters that same day,
And all the moore twixt Elversham and Dell,
With blood of Henalois which therein fell.
How oft that day did sad Brunchildis see
The greene shield dyde in dolorous vermell?
That not *Scuith guiridh* it mote seeme to bee,
But rather *y scuith gogh*, signe of sad crueltee.

XXV. His sonne, king Leill, by fathers labour long,
Enjoyd an heritage of lasting peace,
And built Cairleill, and built Cairleon strong.
Next Huddibras his realme did not encrease,
But taught the land from wearie wars to cease:
Whose footsteps Bladud following, in artes
Exceld at Athens all the learned preace,
From whence he brought them to these salvage parts,
And with sweet science mollifide their stubborne harts.

I   K

XXVI. Ensample of his wondrous faculty,
        Behold the boyling bathes at Cairbadon,
        Which seeth with secret fire eternally,
        And in their entrailles, full of quick Brimston,
        Nourish the flames which they are warmd upon,
        That to their people wealth they forth do well,
        And health to every forreyne nation:
        Yet he at last, contending to excell
        The reach of men, through flight into fond mischief fell.

XXVII. Next him king Leyr in happie peace long raynd,
        But had no issue male him to succeed,
        But three faire daughters, which were well uptraind
        In all that seemed fitt for kingly seed:
        Mongst whom his realme he equally decreed
        To have divided.   Tho, when feeble age
        Nigh to his utmost date he saw proceed,
        He cald his daughters, and with speeches sage
        Inquyrd, which of them most did love her parentage?

XXVIII. The eldest, Gonorill, gan to protest
        That she much more than her owne life him lov'd;
        And Regan greater love to him profest
        Then all the world, when ever it were proov'd;
        But Cordeill said she lov'd him as behoov'd:
        Whose simple answere, wanting colours fayre
        To paint it forth, him to displeasaunce moov'd,
        That in his crown he counted her no hayre,
        But twixt the other twain his kingdom whole did shayre.

XXIX.   So wedded th' one to Maglan king of Scottes,
        And thother to the king of Cambria,
        And twixt them shayrd his realme by equall lottes;
        But without dowre the wise Cordelia
        Was sent to Aggannip of Celtica.
        Their aged Syre, thus eased of his crowne,
        A private life ledd in Albania
        With Gonorill, long had in great renowne,
        That nought him griev'd to beene from rule deposed
            downe.

XXX.   But true it is that, when the oyle is spent,
        The light goes out, and weeke is throwne away:
        So, when he had resignd his regiment,

His daughter gan despise his drouping day,
And wearie wax of his continuall stay.
Tho to his daughter Regan he repayrd,
Who him at first well used every way;
But when of his departure she despayrd,
Her bountie she abated, and his cheare empayrd.

XXXI. The wretched man gan then avise too late,
That love is not where most it is profest;
Too truely tryde in his extremest state.
At last, resolv'd likewise to prove the rest,
He to Cordelia him selfe addrest,
Who with entyre affection him receav'd,
As for her Syre and king her seemed best;
And after all an army strong she leav'd,
To war on those which him had of his realme bereav'd.

XXXII. So to his crowne she him restord againe;
In which he dyde, made ripe for death by eld,
And after wild it should to her remaine,
Who peaceably the same long time did weld,
And all mens harts in dew obedience held;
Till that her sisters children, woxen strong,
Through proud ambition against her rebeld,
And overcommen kept in prison long,
Till weary of that wretched life her selfe she hong.

XXXIII. Then gan the bloody brethren both to raine;
But fierce Cundah gan shortly to envy
His brother Morgan, prickt with proud disdaine
To have a pere in part of soverainty;
And kindling coles of cruell enmity,
Raisd warre, and him in batteill overthrew.
Whence as he to those woody hilles did fly,
Which hight of him Glamorgan, there him slew:
Then did he raigne alone, when he none equall knew.

XXXIV. His sonne Rivall' his dead rowme did supply;
In whose sad time blood did from heaven rayne.
Next great Gurgustus, then faire Cæcily,
In constant peace their kingdomes did contayne.
After whom Lago, and Kinmarke did rayne,
And Gorbogud, till far in years he grew:

Then his ambitious sonnes unto them twayne
Arraught the rule, and from their father drew;
Stout Ferrex and sterne Porrex him in prison threw.

xxxv. But O! the greedy thirst of royall crowne,
That knowes no kinred, nor regardes no right,
Stird Porrex up to put his brother downe;
Who, unto him assembling forreigne might,
Made warre on him, and fell him selfe in fight:
Whose death t'avenge, his mother mercilesse,
Most mercilesse of women, Wyden hight,
Her other sonne fast sleeping did oppresse,
And with most cruell hand him murdred pittilesse.

xxxvi. Here ended Brutus sacred progeny,
Which had seven hundred yeares this scepter borne
With high renowme and great felicity:
The noble braunch from th' antique stocke was torne
Through discord, and the roiall throne forlorne.
Thenceforth this Realme was into factions rent,
Whilest each of Brutus boasted to be borne,
That in the end was left no moniment
Of Brutus, nor of Britons glorie auncient.

xxxvii. Then up arose a man of matchlesse might,
And wondrous wit to menage high affayres,
Who, stird with pitty of the stressed plight
Of this sad realme, cut into sondry shayres
By such as claymd themselves Brutes rightfull hayres,
Gathered the Princes of the people loose
To taken counsell of their common cares;
Who, with his wisedom won, him streight did choose
Their king, and swore him fealty to win or loose.

xxxviii. Then made he head against his enimies,
And Ymner slew of Logris miscreate;
Then Ruddoc and proud Stater, both allyes,
This of Albany newly nominate,
And that of Cambry king confirmed late,
He overthrew through his owne valiaunce;
Whose countries he redus'd to quiet state,
And shortly brought to civile governaunce,
Now one, which earst were many made through
        variaunce.

XXXIX. Then made he sacred lawes, which some men say
    Were unto him reveald in vision;
    By which he freed the Traveilers high-way,
    The Churches part, and Ploughmans portion,
    Restraining stealth and strong extortion,
    The gratious Numa of great Britany;
    For till his dayes, the chiefe dominion
    By strength was wielded without pollicy:
    Therefore he first wore crowne of gold for dignity.

XL. Donwallo dyde, (for what may live for ay?)
    And left two sonnes, of pearelesse prowesse both,
    That sacked Rome too dearely did assay,
    The recompence of their perjured oth;
    And ransackt Greece wel tryde, when they were wroth;
    Besides subjected France and Germany,
    Which yet their praises speake, all be they loth,
    And inly tremble at the memory
    Of Brennus and Belinus, kinges of Britany.

XLI. Next them did Gurgiunt, great Belinus sonne,
    In rule succeede, and eke in fathers praise;
    He Easterland subdewd, and Denmarke wonne,
    And of them both did foy and tribute raise,
    The which was dew in his dead fathers daies.
    He also gave to fugitives of Spayne,
    Whom he at sea found wandring from their waies,
    A seate in Ireland safely to remayne,
    Which they should hold of him, as subject to Britayne.

XLII. After him raigned Guitheline his hayre,
    The justest man and trewest in his daies,
    Who had to wife Dame Mertia the fayre,
    A woman worthy of immortall praise,
    Which for this Realme found many goodly layes,
    And wholesome Statutes to her husband brought.
    Her many deemd to have beene of the Fayes,
    As was Aegerie that Numa tought:
    Those yet of her be Mertian lawes both nam'd and thought.

XLIII. Her sonne Sisillus after her did rayne;
    And then Kimarus; and then Danius:
    Next whom Morindus did the crowne sustayne;

Who, had he not with wrath outrageous
And cruell rancour dim'd his valorous
And mightie deedes, should matched have the best:
As well in that same field victorious
Against the forreine Morands he exprest;
Yet lives his memorie, though carcas sleepe in rest.

XLIV. Five sonnes he left, begotten of one wife,
All which successively by turnes did rayne:
First Gorboman, a man of vertuous life;
Next Archigald, who for his proud disdayne
Deposed was from princedome soverayne,
And pitteous Elidure put in his sted;
Who shortly it to him restord agayne,
Till by his death he it recovered:
But Peridure and Vigent him disthronized.

XLV. In wretched prison long he did remaine,
Till they outraigned had their utmost date,
And then therein reseized was againe,
And ruled long with honorable state,
Till he surrendered Realme and life to fate.
Then all the sonnes of these five brethren raynd
By dew successe, and all their Nephewes late;
Even thrise eleven descents the crowne retaynd,
Till aged Hely by dew heritage it gaynd.

XLVI. He had two sonnes, whose eldest, called Lud,
Left of his life most famous memory,
And endlesse moniments of his great good:
The ruin'd wals he did reædifye
Of Troynovant, gainst force of enimy,
And built that gate which of his name is hight,
By which he lyes entombed solemnly.
He left two sonnes, too young to rule aright,
Androgeus and Tenantius, pictures of his might.

XLVII. Whilst they were young, Cassibalane, their Eme,
Was by the people chosen in their sted,
Who on him tooke the roiall Diademe,
And goodly well long time it governed;
Till the prowde Romanes him disquieted,
And warlike Cæsar, tempted with the name

Of this sweet Island never conquered,
And envying the Britons blazed fame,
(O hideous hunger of dominion!) hither came.

XLVIII. Yet twise they were repulsed backe againe,
And twise renforst backe to their ships to fly;
The whiles with blood they all the shore did staine,
And the gray Ocean into purple dy:
Ne had they footing found at last, perdie,
Had not Androgeus, false to native soyle,
And envious of Uncles soveraintie,
Betrayd his countrey unto forreine spoyle.
Nought els but treason from the first this land did foyle.

XLIX. So by him Cæsar got the victory,
Through great bloodshed and many a sad assay,
In which himselfe was charged heavily
Of hardy Nennius, whom he yet did slay,
But lost his sword, yet to be seene this day.
Thenceforth this land was tributarie made
T' ambitious Rome, and did their rule obay,
Till Arthur all that reckoning defrayd:
Yet oft the Briton kings against them strongly swayd.

L. Next him Tenantius raignd; then Kimbeline,
What time th' eternall Lord in fleshly slime
Enwombed was, from wretched Adams line
To purge away the guilt of sinfull crime.
O joyous memorie of happy time,
That heavenly grace so plenteously displayd!
(O too high ditty for my simple rime!)
Soone after this the Romanes him warrayd;
For that their tribute he refusd to let be payd.

LI. Good Claudius, that next was Emperour,
An army brought, and with him batteile fought,
In which the king was by a Treachetour
Disguised slaine, ere any thereof thought:
Yet ceased not the bloody fight for ought;
For Arvirage his brothers place supplyde
Both in his armes and crowne, and by that draught
Did drive the Romanes to the weaker syde,
That they to peace agreed.   So all was pacifyde.

LII. Was never king more highly magnifide,
    Nor dredd of Romanes, then was Arvirage;
    For which the Emperour to him allide
    His daughter Genuiss' in marriage:
    Yet shortly he renounst the vassallage
    Of Rome againe, who hither hastly sent
    Vespasian, that with great spoile and rage
    Forwasted all, till Genuissa gent
    Persuaded him to ceasse, and her lord to relent.

LIII. He dide, and him succeeded Marius,
    Who joyd his dayes in great tranquillity.
    Then Coyll; and after him good Lucius,
    That first received Christianity,
    The sacred pledge of Christes Evangely.
    Yet true it is, that long before that day
    Hither came Joseph of Arimathy,
    Who brought with him the holy grayle, they say,
    And preacht the truth; but since it greatly did decay.

LIV. This good king shortly without issew dide,
    Whereof great trouble in the kingdome grew,
    That did her selfe in sondry parts divide,
    And with her powre her owne selfe overthrew,
    Whilest Romanes daily did the weake subdew:
    Which seeing, stout Bunduca up arose,
    And taking armes the Britons to her drew;
    With whom she marched streight against her foes,
    And them unwares besides the Severne did enclose.

LV. There she with them a cruell batteill tryde,
    Not with so good successe as shee deserv'd;
    By reason that the Captaines on her syde,
    Corrupted by Paulinus, from her swerv'd:
    Yet, such as were through former flight preserv'd
    Gathering againe, her Host she did renew,
    And with fresh corage on the victor servd:
    But being all defeated, save a few,
    Rather then fly, or be captiv'd, her selfe she slew.

LVI. O famous moniment of womens prayse!
    Matchable either to Semiramis,
    Whom antique history so high doth rayse,

Or to Hypsiphil', or to Thomiris.
Her Host two hundred thousand numbred is;
Who, whiles good fortune favoured her might,
Triumphed oft against her enemis;
And yet, though overcome in haplesse fight,
Shee triumphed on death, in enemies despight.

LVII. Her reliques Fulgent having gathered,
Fought with Severus, and him overthrew;
Yet in the chace was slaine of them that fled,
So made them victors whome he did subdew.
Then gan Carausius tirannize anew,
And gainst the Romanes bent their proper powre;
But him Allectus treacherously slew,
And tooke on him the robe of Emperoure:
Nath'lesse the same enjoyed but short happy howre:

LVIII. For Asclepiodate him overcame,
And left inglorious on the vanquisht playne,
Without or robe or rag to hide his shame:
Then afterwards he in his stead did raigne,
But shortly was by Coyll in batteill slaine:
Who after long debate, since Lucies tyme,
Was of the Britons first crownd Soveraine.
Then gan this Realme renew her passed prime:
He of his name Coylchester built of stone and lime.

LIX. Which when the Romanes heard, they hither sent
Constantius, a man of mickle might,
With whome king Coyll made an agreëment,
And to him gave for wife his daughter bright,
Fayre Helena, the fairest living wight;
Who in all godly thewes and goodly praise
Did far excell, but was most famous hight
For skil in Musicke of all in her daies,
As well in curious instruments as cunning laies.

LX. Of whom he did great Constantine begett,
Who afterward was Emperour of Rome,
To which whiles absent he his mind did sett,
Octavius here lept into his roome,
And it usurped by unrighteous doome:
But he his title justifide by might,

Slaying Traherne, and having overcome
The Romane legion in dreadfull fight.
So settled he his kingdome, and confirmd his right:

LXI. But wanting yssew male, his daughter deare
He gave in wedlocke to Maximian,
And him with her made of his kingdome heyre,
Who soone by meanes thereof the Empire wan,
Till murdred by the freends of Gratian.
Then gan the Hunnes and Picts invade this land,
During the raigne of Maximinian;
Who dying left none heire them to withstand,
But that they overran all parts with easy hand.

LXII. The weary Britons, whose war-hable youth,
Was by Maximian lately ledd away,
With wretched miseryes and woefull ruth,
Were to those Pagans made an open pray,
And daily spectacle of sad decay:
Whome Romane warres, which now fowr hundred yeares
And more had wasted, could no whit dismay;
Til, by consent of Commons and of Peares,
Thy crowned the second Constantine with joyous teares.

LXIII. Who having oft in batteill vanquished
Those spoylefull Picts, and swarming Easterlings,
Long time in peace his realme established,
Yet oft annoyd with sondry bordragings,
Of neighbour Scots, and forrein Scatterlings
With which the world did in those dayes abound:
Which to outbarre, with painefull pyonings
From sea to sea he heapt a mighty mound,
Which from Alcluid to Panwelt did that border bownd.

LXIV. Three sones he dying left, all under age;
By meanes whereof their uncle Vortigere
Usurpt the crowne during their pupillage;
Which th' Infants tutors gathering to feare
Them closely into Armorick did beare:
For dread of whom, and for those Picts annoyes,
He sent to Germany straunge aid to reare;
From whence eftsoones arrived here three hoyes
Of Saxons, whom he for his safety imployes.

LXV. Two brethren were their Capitayns, which hight
Hengist and Horsus, well approv'd in warre,
And both of them men of renowmed might;
Who making vantage of their civile jarre,
And of those forreyners which came from farre,
Grew great, and got large portions of land,
That in the Realme ere long they stronger arre
Then they which sought at first their helping hand,
And Vortiger have forst the kingdome to aband.

LXVI. But by the helpe of Vortimere his sonne,
He is againe unto his rule restord;
And Hengist, seeming sad for that was donne,
Received is to grace and new accord,
Through his faire daughters face and flattring word.
Soone after which three hundred Lords he slew
Of British blood, all sitting at his bord;
Whose dolefull moniments who list to rew,
Th' eternall marks of treason may at Stonheng vew.

LXVII. By this the sonnes of Constantine, which fled,
Ambrose and Uther, did ripe yeares attayne,
And, here arriving, strongly challenged
The crowne which Vortiger did long detayne:
Who, flying from his guilt, by them was slayne;
And Hengist eke soon brought to shamefull death.
Thenceforth Aurelius peaceably did rayne,
Till that through poyson stopped was his breath;
So now entombed lies at Stoneheng by the heath.

LXVIII. After him Uther, which Pendragon hight,
Succeeding—There abruptly it did end,
Without full point, or other Cesure right;
As if the rest some wicked hand did rend,
Or th' Author selfe could not at least attend
To finish it: that so untimely breach
The Prince him selfe halfe seemed to offend;
Yet secret pleasure did offence empeach,
And wonder of antiquity long stopt his speach.

LXIX. At last, quite ravisht with delight to heare
The royall Ofspring of his native land,
Cryde out; "Deare countrey! O! how dearely deare

Ought thy remembraunce and perpetuall band
Be to thy foster Childe, that from thy hand
Did commun breath and nouriture receave.
How brutish is it not to understand
How much to her we owe, that all us gave;
That gave unto us all what ever good we have.

LXX. But Guyon all this while his booke did read,
Ne yet has ended; for it was a great
And ample volume, that doth far excead
My leasure so long leaves here to repeat:
It told how first Prometheus did create
A man, of many parts from beasts deryv'd,
And then stole fire from heven to animate
His worke, for which he was by Jove depryv'd
Of life him selfe, and hart-strings of an Aegle ryv'd.

LXXI. That man so made he called Elfe, to weet
Quick, the first author of all Elfin kynd;
Who, wandring through the world with wearie feet,
Did in the gardins of Adonis fynd
A goodly creature, whom he deemed in mynd
To be no earthly wight, but either Spright,
Or Angell, th' authour of all woman kynd;
Therefore a Fay he her according hight,
Of whom all Faeryes spring, and fetch their lignage right.

LXXII. Of these a mighty people shortly grew,
And puissant kinges which all the world warrayd,
And to them selves all Nations did subdew.
The first and eldest, which that scepter swayd,
Was Elfin; him all India obayd,
And all that now America men call:
Next him was noble Elfinan, who laid
Cleopolis foundation first of all:
But Elfiline enclosd it with a golden wall.

LXXIII. His sonne was Elfinell, who overcame
The wicked Gobbelines in bloody field;
But Elfant was of most renowmed fame,
Who all of Christall did Panthea build:
Then Elfar, who two brethren gyauntes kild,
The one of which had two heades, th' other three:

Then Elfinor, who was in magick skild;
He built by art upon the glassy See
A bridge of bras, whose sound hevens thunder seem'd
    to bee.

LXXIV. He left three sonnes, the which in order raynd,
And all their Ofspring, in their dew descents;
Even seven hundred Princes, which maintaynd
With mightie deedes their sondry governments;
That were too long their infinite contents
Here to record, ne much materiall:
Yet should they be most famous moniments,
And brave ensample, both of martiall
And civil rule, to kinges and states imperiall.

LXXV. After all these Elficleos did rayne,
The wise Elficleos, in great Majestie,
Who mightily that scepter did sustayne,
And with rich spoyles and famous victorie
Did high advaunce the crowne of Faery:
He left two sonnes, of which faire Elferon,
The eldest brother, did untimely dy;
Whose emptie place the mightie Oberon
Doubly supplide, in spousall and dominion.

LXXVI. Great was his power and glorie over all
Which, him before, that sacred seate did fill,
That yet remaines his wide memoriall.
He dying left the fairest Tanaquill,
Him to succeede therein, by his last will:
Fairer and nobler liveth none this howre,
Ne like in grace, ne like in learned skill;
Therefore they Glorian call that glorious flowre:
Long mayst thou, Glorian, live in glory and great powre!

LXXVII. Beguyld thus with delight of novelties,
And naturall desire of countryes state,
So long they redd in those antiquities,
That how the time was fled they quite forgate;
Till gentle Alma, seeing it so late,
Perforce their studies broke, and them besought
To thinke how supper did them long awaite:
So halfe unwilling from their bookes them brought,
And fayrely feasted as so noble knightes she ought.

CANTO XI

The enimies of Temperaunce
Besiege her dwelling place:
Prince Arthure them repelles, and fowle
Maleger doth deface.

I. WHAT warre so cruel, or what siege so sore,
   As that which strong affections doe apply
   Against the forte of reason evermore,
   To bring the sowle into captivity?
   Their force is fiercer through infirmity
   Of the fraile flesh, relenting to their rage,
   And exercise most bitter tyranny
   Upon the partes brought into their bondage:
   No wretchednesse is like to sinfull vellenage.

II. But in a body which doth freely yeeld
    His partes to reasons rule obedient,
    And letteth her that ought the scepter weeld,
    All happy peace and goodly government
    Is setled there in sure establishment.
    There Alma, like a virgin Queene most bright,
    Doth florish in all beautie excellent;
    And to her guestes doth bounteous banket dight,
    Attempred goodly well for health and for delight.

III. Early, before the Morne with cremosin ray
     The windowes of bright heaven opened had,
     Through which into the world the dawning day
     Might looke, that maketh every creature glad,
     Uprose Sir Guyon, in bright armour clad,
     And to his purposd journey him prepar'd:
     With him the Palmer eke in habit sad
     Him selfe addrest to that adventure hard:
     So to the rivers syde they both together far'd:

IV. Where them awaited ready at the ford
    The Ferriman, as Alma had behight,
    With his well-rigged bote: They goe abord,

And he eftsoones gan launch his barke forthright.
Ere long they rowed were quite out of sight,
And fast the land behynd them fled away.
But let them pas, whiles wind and wether right
Doe serve their turnes: here I a while must stay,
To see a cruell fight doen by the prince this day.

v. For all so soone as Guyon thence was gon
Upon his voyage with his trustie guyde,
That wicked band of villeins fresh begon
That castle to assaile on every side,
And lay strong siege about it far and wyde.
So huge and infinite their numbers were,
That all the land they under them did hyde;
So fowle and ugly, that exceeding feare
Their visages imprest when they approched neare.

vi. Them in twelve troupes their Captein did dispart,
And round about in fittest steades did place,
Where each might best offend his proper part,
And his contrary object most deface,
As every one seem'd meetest in that cace.
Seven of the same against the Castle gate
In strong entrenchments he did closely place,
Which with incessaunt force and endlesse hate
They battred day and night, and entraunce did awate.

vii. The other five five sondry wayes he sett
Against the five great Bulwarkes of that pyle,
And unto each a Bulwarke did arrett,
T' assayle with open force or hidden guyle,
In hope thereof to win victorious spoile.
They all that charge did fervently apply
With greedie malice and importune toyle,
And planted there their huge artillery,
With which they dayly made most dreadfull battery.

viii. The first troupe was a monstrous rablement
Of fowle misshapen wightes, of which some were
Headed like Owles, with beckes uncomely bent;
Others like Dogs; others like Gryphons dreare;
And some had wings, and some had clawes to teare:
And every one of them had Lynces eyes;

And every one did bow and arrowes beare.
All those were lawlesse lustes, currupt envyes,
And covetous aspects, all cruell enimyes.

ix. Those same against the bulwarke of the Sight
Did lay strong siege and battailous assault,
Ne once did yield it respitt day nor night;
But soone as Titan gan his head exault,
And soone againe as he his light withhault,
Their wicked engins they against it bent;
That is, each thing by which the eyes may fault
But two then all more huge and violent,
Beautie and Money, they that Bulwarke sorely rent.

x. The second Bulwarke was the Hearing sence,
Gainst which the second troupe assignment makes;
Deformed creatures, in straunge difference,
Some having heads like Harts, some like to Snakes,
Some like wilde Bores late rouzd out of the brakes:
Slaunderous reproches, and fowle infamies.
Leasinges, backbytinges, and vain-glorious crakes,
Bad counsels, prayses, and false flatteries:
All those against that fort did bend their batteries.

xi. Likewise that same third Fort, that is the Smell,
Of that third troupe was cruelly assayd;
Whose hideous shapes were like to feendes of hell,
Some like to houndes, some like to Apes, dismayd,
Some like to Puttockes, all in plumes arayd;
All shap't according their conditions:
For by those ugly formes weren pourtrayd
Foolish delights, and fond abusions,
Which doe that sence besiege with light illusions.

xii. And that fourth band which cruell battry bent
Against the fourth Bulwarke, that is the Taste,
Was, as the rest, a grysie rablement;
Some mouth'd like greedy Oystriges; some faste
Like loathly Toades; some fashioned in the waste
Like swine: for so deformd is luxury,
Surfeat, misdiet, and unthriftie waste,
Vaine feastes, and ydle superfluity:
All those this sences Fort assayle incessantly.

And bid them strike the marke which he had eyde;
Ne was there salve, ne was there medicine,
That mote recure their wounds; so inly they did tine.

XXII. As pale and wan as ashes was his looke,
His body leane and meagre as a rake,
And skin all withered like a dryed rooke;
Thereto as cold and drery as a snake,
That seemd to tremble evermore and quake;
All in a canvas thin he was bedight,
And girded with a belt of twisted brake:
Upon his head he wore an Helmet light,
Made of a dead mans skull, that seemd a ghastly sight.

XXIII. Maleger was his name; and after him
There follow'd fast at hand two wicked Hags,
With hoary lockes all loose, and visage grim;
Their feet unshod, their bodies wrapt in rags,
And both as swift on foot as chased Stags;
And yet the one her other legge had lame,
Which with a staffe, all full of litle snags,
She did support, and Impotence her name.
But th' other was Impatience, arm'd with raging flame.

XXIV. Soone as the Carle from far the Prince espyde
Glistring in armes and warlike ornament,
His Beast he felly prickt on either syde,
And his mischievous bow full readie bent,
With which at him a cruell shaft he sent:
But he was warie, and it warded well
Upon his shield, that it no further went,
But to the ground the idle quarrell fell:
Then he another and another did expell.

XXV. Which to prevent the Prince his mortall speare
Soone to him raught, and fierce at him did ride,
To be avenged of that shot whyleare;
But he was not so hardy to abide
That bitter stownd, but turning quicke aside
His light-foot beast, fled fast away for feare:
Whom to poursue the Infant after hide
So fast as his good Courser could him beare;
But labour lost it was to weene approch him neare.

XXVI. For as the winged wind his Tigre fled,
That vew of eye could scarse him overtake,
Ne scarse his feet on ground were seene to tred:
Through hils and dales he speedy way did make,
Ne hedge ne ditch his readie passage brake;
And in his flight the villein turn'd his face
(As wonts the Tartar by the Caspian lake,
Whenas the Russian him in fight does chace)
Unto his Tygres taile, and shot at him apace.

XXVII. Apace he shot, and yet he fled apace,
Still as the greedy knight nigh to him drew;
And oftentimes he would relent his pace,
That him his foe more fiercely should poursew:
But when his uncouth manner he did vew,
He gan avize to follow him no more,
But keepe his standing, and his shaftes eschew,
Untill he quite had spent his perlous store,
And then assayle him fresh, ere he could shift for more.

XXVIII. But that lame Hag, still as abroad he strew
His wicked arrowes, gathered them againe,
And to him brought, fresh batteill to renew;
Which he espying cast her to restraine
From yielding succour to that cursed Swaine,
And her attaching thought her hands to tye;
But soone as him dismounted on the plaine
That other Hag did far away espye
Binding her sister, she to him ran hastily;

XXIX. And catching hold of him, as downe he lent,
Him backeward overthrew, and downe him stayd
With their rude handes and gryesly graplement;
Till that the villein, comming to their ayd,
Upon him fell, and lode upon him layd:
Full litle wanted but he had him slaine,
And of the battell balefull end had made,
Had not his gentle Squire beheld his paine,
And commen to his reskew, ere his bitter bane.

XXX. So greatest and most glorious thing on ground
May often need the helpe of weaker hand;
So feeble is mans state, and life unsound,

That in assuraunce it may never stand,
Till it dissolved be from earthly band.
Proofe be thou, Prince, the prowest man alyve,
And noblest borne of all in Britayne land;
Yet thee fierce Fortune did so nearely drive,
That, had not grace thee blest, thou shouldest not
    survive.

XXXI. The Squyre arriving fiercely in his armes
Snatcht first the one, and then the other Jade,
His chiefest letts and authors of his harmes,
And them perforce withheld with threatned blade,
Least that his Lord they should behinde invade;
The whiles the Prince, prickt with reprochful shame,
As one awakte out of long slombring shade,
Revivyng thought of glory and of fame,
United all his powres to purge him selfe from blame.

XXXII. Like as a fire, the which in hollow cave
Hath long bene underkept and down supprest,
With murmurous disdayne doth inly rave,
And grudge in so streight prison to be prest,
At last breakes forth with furious unrest,
And strives to mount unto his native seat;
All that did earst it hinder and molest,
Yt now devoures with flames and scorching heat,
And carries into smoake with rage and horror great.

XXXIII. So mightely the Briton Prince him rouzd
Out of his holde, and broke his caytive bands;
And as a Beare, whom angry curres have touzd,
Having off-shakt them and escapt their hands,
Becomes more fell, and all that him withstands
Treads down and overthrowes. Now had the Carle
Alighted from his Tigre, and his hands
Discharged of his bow and deadly quar'le,
To seize upon his foe flatt lying on the marle.

XXXIV. Which now him turnd to disavantage deare;
For neither can he fly, nor other harme,
But trust unto his strength and manhood meare,
Sith now he is far from his monstrous swarme,
And of his weapons did himselfe disarme.
The knight, yet wrothfull for his late disgrace,

Fiercely advaunst his valorous right arme,
And him so sore smott with his yron mace,
That groveling to the ground he fell, and fild his place.

XXXV. Wel weened hee that field was then his owne,
And all his labor brought to happy end;
When suddein up the villeine overthrowne
Out of his swowne arose, fresh to contend,
And gan him selfe to second battaill bend,
As hurt he had not beene.   Thereby there lay
An huge great stone, which stood upon one end,
And had not bene removed many a day;
Some land-marke seemd to bee, or signe of sundry way:

XXXVI. The same he snatcht, and with exceeding sway
Threw at his foe, whe was right well aware
To shonne the engin of his meant decay;
It booted not to thinke that throw to beare,
But grownd he gave, and lightly lept areare:
Eft fierce retourning, as a faulcon fayre,
That once hath failed of her souse full neare,
Remounts againe into the open ayre,
And unto better fortune doth her selfe prepayre.

XXXVII. So brave retourning, with his brandisht blade
He to the Carle him selfe agayn addrest,
And strooke at him so sternely, that he made
An open passage through his riven brest,
That halfe the steele behind his backe did rest;
Which drawing backe, he looked evermore
When the hart blood should gush out of his chest,
Or his dead corse should fall upon the flore;
But his dead corse upon the flore fell nathemore.

XXXVIII. Ne drop of blood appeared shed to bee,
All were the wownd so wide and wonderous
That through his carcas one might playnly see.
Halfe in amaze with horror hideous,
And halfe in rage to be deluded thus,
Again through both the sides he strooke him quight,
That made his spright to grone full piteous;
Yet nathemore forth fled his groning spright,
But freshly, as at first, prepared himselfe to fight.

XXXIX. Thereat he smitten was with great affright,
And trembling terror did his hart apall;
Ne wist he what to thinke of that same sight,
Ne what to say, ne what to doe at all:
He doubted least it were some magicall
Illusion that did beguile his sense,
Or wandring ghost that wanted funerall,
Or aery spirite under false pretence,
Or hellish feend raysd up through divelish science.

XL. His wonder far exceeded reasons reach,
That he began to doubt his dazeled sight,
And oft of error did himselfe appeach:
Flesh without blood, a person without spright,
Wounds without hurt, a body without might,
That could doe harme, yet could not harmed bee,
That could not die, yet seemd a mortall wight,
That was most strong in most infirmitee;
Like did he never heare, like did he never see.

XLI. Awhile he stood in this astonishment,
Yet would he not for all his great dismay
Give over to effect his first intent,
And th' utmost meanes of victory assay,
Or th' utmost yssew of his owne decay.
His owne good sword Mordure, that never fayld
At need till now, he lightly threw away,
And his bright shield that nought him now avayld;
And with his naked hands him forcibly assayld.

XLII. Twixt his two mighty armes him up he snatcht,
And crusht his carcas so against his brest,
That the disdainfull sowle he thence dispatcht,
And th' ydle breath all utterly exprest.
Tho, when he felt him dead, adowne he kest
The lumpish corse unto the sencelesse grownd;
Adowne he kest it with so puissant wrest,
That backe againe it did alofte rebownd,
And gave against his mother earth a gronefull sownd.

XLIII. As when Joves harnesse-bearing Bird from hye
Stoupes at a flying heron with proud disdayne,
The stone-dead quarrey falls so forciblye,

That yt rebownds against the lowly playne,
A second fall redoubling backe agayne.
Then thought the Prince all peril sure was past,
And that he victor onely did remayne;
No sooner thought, then that the Carle as fast
Gan heap huge strokes on him, as ere he down was cast.

XLIV. Nigh his wits end then woxe th' amazed knight,
And thought his labour lost, and travell vayne,
Against this lifelesse shadow so to fight:
Yet life he saw, and felt his mighty mayne,
That, whiles he marveild still, did still him payne;
Forthy he gan some other wayes advize,
How to take life from that dead-living swayne,
Whom still he marked freshly to arize
From th' earth, and from her womb new spirits to reprize.

XLV. He then remembered well, that had bene sayd,
How th' Earth his mother was, and first him bore;
She eke, so often as his life decayd,
Did life with usury to him restore,
And reysd him up much stronger than before,
So soone as he unto her wombe did fall:
Therefore to grownd he would him cast no more,
Ne him committ to grave terrestriall,
But beare him farre from hope of succour usuall.

XLVI. Tho up he caught him twixt his puissant hands,
And having scruzd out of his carrion corse
The lothfull life, now loosd from sinfull bands,
Upon his shoulders carried him perforse
Above three furlongs, taking his full course
Until he came unto a standing lake;
Him thereinto he threw without remorse,
Ne stird, till hope of life did him forsake:
So end of that Carles dayes and his owne paynes did
make.

XLVII. Which when those wicked Hags from far did spye,
Like two mad dogs they ran about the lands,
And th' one of them with dreadfull yelling crye,
Throwing away her broken chaines and bands,
And having quencht her burning fier-brands,

Hedlong her selfe did cast into that lake;
But Impotence with her owne wilfull hands
One of Malegers cursed darts did take,
So ryv'd her trembling hart, and wicked end did make.

XLVIII. Thus now alone he conquerour remaines:
Tho, cumming to his Squyre that kept his steed,
Thought to have mounted; but his feeble vaines
Him faild thereto, and served not his need,
Through losse of blood which from his wounds did bleed,
That he began to faint, and life decay:
But his good Squyre, him helping up with speed,
With stedfast hand upon his horse did stay,
And led him to the Castle by the beaten way.

XLIX. Where many Groomes and Squyres ready were
To take him from his steed full tenderly;
And eke the fayrest Alma mett him there
With balme, and wine, and costly spicery,
To comfort him in his infirmity.
Eftesoones shee causd him up to be convayd,
And of his armes despoyled easily
In sumptuous bed shee made him to be layd;
And al the while his wounds were dressing by him stayd.

CANTO XII

Guyon, by Palmers governaunce,
Passing through perilles great,
Doth overthrow the Bowre of blis,
And Acrasy defeat.

1. Now ginnes that goodly frame of Temperaunce
   Fayrely to rise, and her adorned hed
   To pricke of highest prayse forth to advaunce,
   Formerly grounded and fast setteled
   On firme foundation of true bountyhed:
   And this brave knight, that for this vertue fightes,
   Now comes to point of that same perilous sted,
   Where Pleasure dwelles in sensuall delights,
   Mongst thousand dangers, and ten thousand Magick
       mights.

2. Two dayes now in that sea he sayled has,
   Ne ever land beheld, ne living wight,
   Ne ought save perill still as he did pas:
   Tho, when appeared the third Morrow bright
   Upon the waves to spred her trembling light,
   An hideous roring far away they heard,
   That all their sences filled with affright;
   And streight they saw the raging surges reard
   Up to the skyes, that them of drowning made affeard.

3. Said then the Boteman, " Palmer, stere aright.
   And keepe an even course; for yonder way
   We needes must pas (God doe us well acquight!)
   That is the Gulfe of Greedinesse, they say,
   That deepe engorgeth all this worldes pray;
   Which having swallowd up excessively,
   He soone in vomit up againe doth lay,
   And belcheth forth his superfluity,
   That all the seas for feare doe seeme away to fly.

4. " On thother syde an hideous Rocke is pight
   Of mightie Magnes stone, whose craggie clift
   Depending from on high, dreadfull to sight,

Over the waves his rugged armes doth lift,
And threatneth downe to throw his ragged rift
On whoso cometh nigh; yet nigh it drawes
All passengers, that none from it can shift:
For, whiles they fly that Gulfes devouring jawes,
They on this rock are rent, and sunck in helples wawes."

v. Forward they passe, and strongly he them rowes,
Untill they nigh unto that Gulfe arryve,
Where streame more violent and greedy growes:
Then he with all his puisaunce doth stryve
To strike his oares, and mightily doth drive
The hollow vessell through the threatfull wave;
Which, gaping wide to swallow them alyve
In th' huge abysse of his engulfing grave,
Doth rore at them in vaine, and with great terrour rave.

vi. They, passing by, that grisely mouth did see
Sucking the seas into his entralles deepe,
That seemd more horrible then hell to bee,
Or that darke dreadfull hole of Tartare steepe
Through which the damned ghosts doen often creepe
Backe to the world, bad livers to torment:
But nought that falles into this direfull deepe
Ne that approcheth nigh the wyde descent,
May backe retourne, but is condemned to be drent.

vii. On thother side they saw that perilous Rocke,
Threatning it selfe on them to ruinate,
On whose sharp cliftes the ribs of vessels broke;
And shivered ships, which had beene wrecked late,
Yet stuck with carkases exanimate
Of such, as having all their substance spent
In wanton joyes and lustes intemperate,
Did afterwards make shipwrack violent
Both of their life and fame, for ever fowly blent.

viii. Forthy this hight The Rocke of vile Reproch,
A daungerous and detestable place,
To which nor fish nor fowle did once approch,
But yelling Meawes, with Seagulles hoars and bace,
And Cormoyraunts, with birds of ravenous race,
Which still sat waiting on that wastfull clift

For spoile of wretches, whose unhappy cace,
After lost credit and consumed thrift,
At last them driven hath to this despairefull drift.

IX. The Palmer, seeing them in safetie past,
Thus saide; " Behold th' ensamples in our sights
Of lustfull luxurie and thriftlessse wast.
What now is left of miserable wightes,
Which spent their looser daies in leud delightes,
But shame and sad reproch, here to be red
By these rent reliques, speaking their ill plightes?
Let all that live hereby be counselled
To shunne Rocke of Reproch, and it as death to dred! "

X. So forth they rowed; and that Ferryman
With his stiffe oares did brush the sea so strong,
That the hoare waters from his frigot ran,
And the light bubles daunced all along,
Whiles the salt brine out of the billowes sprong.
At last far off they many Islandes spy
On every side floting the floodes emong:
Then said the knight; " Lo! I the land descry;
Therefore, old Syre, thy course doe thereunto apply."

XI. " That may not bee," said then the Ferryman,
" Least wee unweeting hap to be fordonne;
For those same Islands, seeming now and than,
Are not firme land, nor any certein wonne,
But stragling plots which to and fro doe ronne
In the wide waters: therefore are they hight
The Wandring Islands.   Therefore doe them shonne;
For they have ofte drawne many a wandring wight
Into most deadly daunger and distressed plight.

XII. " Yet well they seeme to him, that farre doth vew,
Both faire and fruitfull, and the grownd dispred
With grassy greene of delectable hew;
And the tall trees with leaves appareled
Are deckt with blossoms dyde in white and red,
That mote the passengers thereto allure;
But whosoever once hath fastened
His foot thereon, may never it recure,
But wandreth evermore uncertain and unsure.

XIII. " As th' Isle of Delos whylome, men report,
    Amid th' Aegæan sea long time did stray,
    Ne made for shipping any certeine port,
    Till that Latona traveiling that way,
    Flying from Junoes wrath and hard assay,
    Of her fayre twins was there delivered,
    Which afterwards did rule the night and day:
    Thenceforth it firmely was established,
    And for Apolloes temple highly herried."

XIV. They to him hearken, as beseemeth meete,
    And passe on forward: so their way does ly,
    That one of those same Islands, which doe fleet
    In the wide sea, they needes must passen by,
    Which seemd so sweet and pleasaunt to the eye,
    That it would tempt a man to touchen there:
    Upon the banck they sitting did espy
    A daintie damsell dressing of her heare,
    By whom a little skippet floting did appeare.

XV. She, them espying, loud to them can call,
    Bidding them nigher draw unto the shore,
    For she had cause to busie them withall;
    And therewith lowdly laught: But nathemore
    Would they once turne, but kept on as afore:
    Which when she saw, she left her lockes undight,
    And running to her boat withouten ore,
    From the departing land it launched light,
    And after them did drive with all her power and might.

XVI. Whom overtaking, she in merry sort
    Them gan to bord, and purpose diversly;
    Now faining dalliaunce and wanton sport,
    Now throwing forth lewd wordes immodestly;
    Till that the Palmer gan full bitterly
    Her to rebuke for being loose and light:
    Which not abiding, but more scornfully
    Scoffing at him that did her justly wite,
    She turnd her bote about, and from them rowed quite.

XVII. That was the wanton Phædria, which late
    Did ferry him over the Idle lake:
    Whom nought regarding they kept on their gate,

And all her vaine allurements did forsake;
When them the wary Boteman thus bespake:
" Here now behoveth us well to avyse,
And of our safety good heede to take;
For here before a perlous passage lyes,
Where many Mermayds haunt making false melodies:

XVIII. " But by the way there is a great Quicksand,
And a whirlpoole of hidden jeopardy;
Therefore, Sir Palmer, keepe an even hand.
For twixt them both the narrow way doth ly."
Scarse had he saide, when hard at hand they spy
That quicksand nigh with water covered;
But by the checked wave they did descry
It plaine, and by the sea discoloured:
It called was the quickesand of Unthriftyhed.

XIX. They, passing by, a goodly Ship did see
Laden from far with precious merchandize,
And bravely furnished as ship might bee,
Which through great disaventure, or mesprize,
Her selfe had ronne into that hazardize;
Whose mariners and merchants with much toyle
Labour'd in vaine to have recur'd their prize,
And the rich wares to save from pitteous spoyle;
But neither toyle nor traveill might her backe recoyle.

XX. On th' other side they see that perilous Poole,
That called was the Whirlepoole of decay;
In which full many had with haplesse doole
Beene suncke, of whom no memorie did stay:
Whose circled waters rapt with whirling sway,
Like to a restlesse wheele, still ronning round,
Did covet, as they passed by that way,
To draw their bote within the utmost bound
Of his wide Labyrinth, and then to have them dround.

XXI. But th' heedful Boteman strongly forth did stretch
His brawnie armes, and all his bodie straine,
That th' utmost sandy breach they shortly fetch,
Whiles the dredd daunger does behind remaine.
Suddeine they see from midst of all the Maine
The surging waters like a mountaine rise,

And the great sea, puft up with proud disdaine,
To swell above the measure of his guise,
As threatning to devoure all that his powre despise.

XXII. The waves come rolling, and the billowes rore
Outragiously, as they enraged were,
Or wrathfull Neptune did them drive before
His whirling charet for exceeding feare;
For not one puffe of winde there did appeare,
That all the three thereat woxe much afrayd,
Unweeting what such horrour straunge did reare.
Eftsoones they saw an hideous hoast arrayd
Of huge Sea monsters, such as living sence dismayd:

XXIII. Most ugly shapes and horrible aspects,
Such as Dame Nature selfe mote feare to see,
Or shame that ever should so fowle defects
From her most cunning hand escaped bee;
All dreadfull pourtraicts of deformitee:
Spring-headed Hydres; and sea-shouldring Whales;
Great whirlpooles which all fishes make to flee;
Bright Scolopendraes arm'd with silver scales;
Mighty Monoceroses with immeasured tayles.

XXIV. The dreadful Fish that hath deserv'd the name
Of Death, and like him lookes in dreadfull hew;
The griesly Wasserman, that makes his game
The flying ships with swiftnes to pursew:
The horrible Sea-satyre, that doth shew
His fearefull face in time of greatest storme;
Huge Ziffius, whom Mariners eschew
No lesse then rockes, (as travellers informe)
And greedy Rosmarines with visages deforme.

XXV. All these, and thousand thousands many more,
And more deformed Monsters thousand fold,
With dreadfull noise and hollow rombling rore
Came rushing, in the fomy waves enrold,
Which seem'd to fly for feare them to behold.
Ne wonder, if these did the knight appall;
For all that here on earth we dreadfull hold,
Be but as bugs to fearen babes withall,
Compared to the creatures in the seas entrall.

XXVI. " Feare nought," then saide the Palmer well aviz'd,
" For these same Monsters are not these in deed,
But are into these fearefull shapes disguiz'd
By that same witch, to worke us dreed,
And draw from on this journey to proceed."
Tho lifting up his vertuous staffe on hye,
He smote the sea, which calmed was with speed,
And all that dreadfull Armie fast gan flye
Into great Tethys bosome, where they hidden lye.

XXVII. Quit from that danger forth their course they kept;
And as they went they heard a ruefull cry
Of one that wayld and pittifully wept,
That through the sea resounding plaints did fly:
At last they in an Island did espy
A seemely Maiden sitting by the shore,
That with great sorrow and sad agony
Seemed some great misfortune to deplore,
And lowd to them for succour called evermore.

XXVIII. Which Guyon hearing streight his Palmer bad
To stere the bote towards that dolefull Mayd,
That he might know and ease her sorrow sad;
Who, him avizing better, to him sayd:
" Faire Sir, be not displeasd if disobayd:
For ill it were to hearken to her cry,
For she is inly nothing ill apayd;
But onely womanish fine forgery,
Your stubborne hart t'affect with fraile infirmity.

XXIX. " To which when she your courage hath inclind
Through foolish pitty, then her guilefull bayt
She will embosome deeper in your mind,
And for your ruine at the last awayt."
The Knight was ruled, and the Boteman strayt
Held on his course with stayed stedfastnesse,
Ne ever shroncke, ne ever sought to bayt
His tyred armes for toylesome wearinesse,
But with his oares did sweepe the watry wildernesse.

XXX. And now they nigh approched to the sted
Whereas those Mermayds dwelt: it was a still
And calmy bay, on th' one side sheltered

With the brode shadow of an hoarie hill;
On th'other side an high rocke toured still,
That twixt them both a pleasaunt port they made,
And did like an halfe Theatre fulfill:
There those five sisters had continuall trade,
And usd to bath themselves in that deceiptfull shade.

XXXI. They were faire Ladies, till they fondly striv'd
With th' Heliconian maides for maystery;
Of whom they, over-comen, were depriv'd
Of their proud beautie, and th' one moyity
Transformd to fish for their bold surquedry;
But th' upper halfe their hew retayned still,
And their sweet skill in wonted melody;
Which ever after they abusd to ill,
T' allure weake traveillers, whom gotten they did kill.

XXXII. So now to Guyon, as he passed by,
Their pleasaunt tunes they sweetly thus applyde:
" O thou fayre sonne of gentle Faery,
That art in mightie armes most magnifyde
Above all knights that ever batteill tryde,
O! turne thy rudder hitherward awhile
Here may thy storme-bett vessell safely ryde,
This is the Port of rest from troublous toyle,
The worldes sweet In from paine and wearisome
    turmoyle."

XXXIII. With that the rolling sea, resounding soft,
In his big base them fitly answered;
And on the rocke the waves breaking aloft
A solemne Meane unto them measured;
The whiles sweet Zephyrus lowd whisteled
His treble, a straunge kinde of harmony,
Which Guyons senses softly tickeled,
That he the boteman bad row easily,
And let him heare some part of their rare melody.

XXXIV. But him the Palmer from that vanity
With temperate advice discounselled,
That they it past, and shortly gan descry
The land to which their course they leveled;
When suddeinly a grosse fog over-spred
With his dull vapour all that desert has,

I   L

And heavens chearefull face enveloped,
That all things one, and one as nothing was,
And this great Universe seemd one confused mas.

XXXV. Thereat they greatly were dismayd, ne wist
How to direct theyr way in darkenes wide,
But feard to wander in that wastefull mist,
For tombling into mischiefe unespide:
Worse is the daunger hidden then descride.
Suddeinly an innumerable flight
Of harmefull fowles about them fluttering cride,
And with their wicked wings them ofte did smight,
And sore annoyed, groping in that griesly night.

XXXVI. Even all the nation of unfortunate
And fatall birds about them flocked were,
Such as by nature men abhorre and hate;
The ill-faste Owle, deaths dreadfull messengere;
The hoars Night-raven, trump of dolefull drere;
The lether-winged Batt, dayes enimy;
The ruefull Strich, still waiting on the bere;
The whistler shrill, that whoso heares doth dy;
The hellish Harpyes, prophets of sad destiny.

XXXVII. All those, and all that els does horror breed,
About them flew, and fild their sayles with feare:
Yet stayd they not, but forward did proceed,
Whiles th' one did row, and th' other stifly steare;
Till that at last the weather gan to cleare,
And the faire land it selfe did playnly sheow.
Said then the Palmer; "Lo! where does appeare
The sacred soile where all our perills grow.
Therfore, Sir knight, your ready arms about you throw."

XXXVIII. He hearkned, and his armes about him tooke,
The whiles the nimble bote so well her sped,
That with her crooked keele the land she strooke:
Then forth the noble Guyon sallied,
And his sage Palmer that him governed;
But th' other by his bote behind did stay.
They marched fayrly forth, of nought ydred.
Both firmely armd for every hard assay,
With constancy and care, gainst daunger and dismay.

XXXIX. Ere long they heard an hideous bellowing
    Of many beasts, that roard outrageously,
    As if that hungers poynt or Venus sting
    Had them enraged with fell surquedry:
    Yet nought they feard, but past on hardily,
    Untill they came in vew of those wilde beasts,
    Who all attonce, gaping full greedily,
    And rearing fercely their upstaring crests,
    Ran towards to devoure those unexpected guests.

XL. But soone as they approcht with deadly threat,
    The Palmer over them his staffe upheld,
    His mighty staffe, that could all charmes defeat.
    Eftesoones their stubborne corages were queld,
    And high advaunced crests downe meekely feld;
    Instead of fraying, they them selves did feare,
    And trembled as them passing they beheld:
    Such wondrous powre did in that staffe appeare,
    All monsters to subdew to him that did it beare.

XLI. Of that same wood it fram'd was cunningly,
    Of which Caduceus whilome was made,
    Caduceus, the rod of Mercury,
    With which he wonts the Stygian realmes invade
    Through ghastly horror and eternall shade:
    Th' infernall feends with it he can asswage,
    And Orcus tame, whome nothing can persuade,
    And rule the Furyes when they most doe rage.
    Such vertue in his staffe had eke this Palmer sage.

XLII. Thence passing forth, they shortly doe arryve
    Whereas the Bowre of Blisse was situate;
    A place pickt out by choyce of best alyve,
    That natures worke by art can imitate:
    In which whatever in this worldly state
    Is sweete and pleasing unto living sense,
    Or that may dayntest fantasy aggrate,
    Was poured forth with plentifull dispence,
    And made there to abound with lavish affluence.

XLIII. Goodly it was enclosed rownd about,
    As well their entred guestes to keep within,
    As those unruly beasts to hold without;

Yet was the fence thereof but weake and thin:
Nought feard theyr force that fortilage to win,
But wisedomes powre, and temperaunces might,
By which the mightiest things efforced bin:
And eke the gate was wrought of substaunce light,
Rather for pleasure then for battery or fight.

XLIV. Yt framed was of precious yvory,
That seemd a worke of admirable witt;
And therein all the famous history
Of Jason and Medæa was ywritt;
Her mighty charmes, her furious loving fitt;
His goodly conquest of the golden fleece,
His falsed fayth, and love too lightly flitt;
The wondred Argo, which in venturous peece
First through the Euxine seas bore all the flowr of Greece.

XLV. Ye might have seene the frothy billowes fry
Under the ship as thorough them she went,
That seemd the waves were into yvory,
Or yvory into the waves were sent;
And otherwhere the snowy substaunce sprent
With vermell, like the boyes blood therein shed,
A piteous spectacle did represent;
And otherwhiles, with gold besprinkeled,
Yt seemd thenchaunted flame which did Crëusa wed.

XLVI. All this and more might in that goodly gate
Be red, that ever open stood to all
Which thither came; but in the Porch there sate
A comely personage of stature tall,
And semblaunce pleasing, more then naturall,
That traveilers to him seemd to entize:
His looser garment to the ground did fall,
And flew about his heeles in wanton wize,
Not fitt for speedy pace, or manly exercize.

XLVII. They in that place him Genius did call:
Not that celestiall powre, to whom the care
Of life, and generation of all
That lives, perteines in charge particulare,
Who wondrous things concerning our welfare,
And straunge phantomes doth lett us ofte foresee,

And ofte of secret ill bids us beware:
That is our Selfe, whom though we do not see,
Yet each doth in him selfe it well perceive to bee.

XLVIII. Therefore a God him sage Antiquity
Did wisely make, and good Agdistes call;
But this same was to that quite contrary,
The foe of life, that good envyes to all,
That secretly doth us procure to fall
Through guilefull semblants which he makes us see:
He of this Gardin had the governall,
And Pleasures porter was devizd to bee,
Holding a staffe in hand for mere formalitee.

XLIX. With diverse flowres he daintily was deckt,
And strowed rownd about; and by his side
A mighty Mazer bowle of wine was sett,
As if it had to him bene sacrifide,
Wherewith all new-come guests he gratyfide:
So did he eke Sir Guyon passing by;
But he his ydle curtesie defide,
And overthrew his bowle disdainfully,
And broke his staffe with which he charmed semblants
sly.

L. Thus being entred, they behold arownd
A large and spacious plaine, on every side
Strowed with pleasauns; whose fayre grassy grownd
Mantled with greene, and goodly beautifide
With all the ornaments of Floraes pride,
Wherewith her mother Art, as halfe in scorne
Of niggard Nature, like a pompous bride
Did decke her, and too lavishly adorne,
When forth from virgin bowre she comes in th' early
morne.

LI. Therewith the Heavens alwayes joviall
Lookte on them lovely, still in stedfast state,
Ne suffred storme nor frost on them to fall,
Their tender buds or leaves to violate;
Nor scorching heat, nor cold intemperate,
T' afflict the creatures which therein did dwell;
But the milde ayre with season moderate

Gently attempred, and disposd so well,
That still it breathed forth sweet spirit and holesom
    smell:

LII. More sweet and holesome then the pleasaunt hill
Of Rhodope, on which the Nimphe that bore
A gyaunt babe herselfe for griefe did kill;
Or the Thessalian Tempe, where of yore
Fayre Daphne Phœbus hart with love did gore;
Or Ida, where the Gods lov'd to repayre,
When ever they their heavenly bowres forlore;
Or sweet Parnasse, the haunt of Muses fayre;
Or Eden selfe, if ought with Eden mote compayre.

LIII. Much wondred Guyon at the fayre aspect
Of that sweet place, yet suffred no delight
To sincke into his sence, nor mind affect,
But passed forth, and lookt still forward right,
Brydling his will and maystering his might,
Till that he came unto another gate;
No gate, but like one, being goodly dight
With bowes and braunches, which did broad dilate
Their clasping armes in wanton wreathings intricate:

LIV. So fashioned a Porch with rare device.
Archt over head with an embracing vine,
Whose bounches hanging downe seemd to entice
All passers by to taste their lushious wine,
And did them selves into their hands incline,
As freely offering to be gathered;
Some deepe empurpled as the Hyacine,
Some as the Rubine laughing sweetely red,
Some like faire Emeraudes, not yet well ripened.

LV. And them amongst some were of burnisht gold,
So made by art to beautify the rest,
Which did themselves emongst the leaves enfold,
As lurking from the vew of covetous guest,
That the weake boughes, with so rich load opprest
Did bow adowne as overburdened.
Under that Porch a comely dame did rest
Clad in fayre weedes but fowle disordered,
And garments loose that seemd unmeet for womanhed.

LVI. In her left hand a Cup of gold she held,
    And with her right the riper fruit did reach,
    Whose sappy liquor, that with fulnesse sweld,
    Into her cup she scruzd with daintie breach
    Of her fine fingers, without fowle empeach,
    That so faire winepresse made the wine more sweet:
    Thereof she usd to give to drinke to each,
    Whom passing by she happened to meet:
    It was her guise all Straungers goodly so to greet.

LVII. So she to Guyon offred it to tast,
    Who, taking it out of her tender hond,
    The cup to ground did violently cast,
    That all in peeces it was broken fond,
    And with the liquor stained all the lond:
    Whereat Excesse exceedingly was wroth,
    Yet no'te the same amend, ne yet withstond,
    But suffered him to passe, all were she loth;
    Who, nought regarding her displeasure, forward goth.

LVIII. There the most daintie Paradise on ground
    It selfe doth offer to his sober eye,
    In which all pleasures plenteously abownd,
    And none does others happinesse envye;
    The painted flowres, the trees upshooting hye,
    The dales for shade, the hilles for breathing space,
    The trembling groves, the christall running by,
    And, that which all faire workes doth most aggrace,
    The art which all that wrought appeared in no place.

LIX. One would have thought, (so cunningly the rude
    And scorned partes were mingled with the fine)
    That nature had for wantonesse ensude
    Art, and that Art at nature did repine;
    So striving each th' other to undermine,
    Each did the others worke more beautify;
    So diff'ring both in willes agreed in fine:
    So all agreed, through sweet diversity,
    This Gardin to adorne with all variety.

LX. And in the midst of all a fountaine stood,
    Of richest substance that on earth might bee,
    So pure and shiny that the silver flood

Through every channell running one might see;
Most goodly it with curious ymageree
Was overwrought, and shapes of naked boyes,
Of which some seemd with lively jollitee
To fly about, playing their wanton toyes,
Whylest others did them selves embay in liquid joyes.

LXI. And over all of purest gold was spred
A trayle of yvie in his native hew;
For the rich metall was so coloured,
That wight who did not well avis'd it vew
Would surely deeme it to bee yvie trew:
Low his lascivious armes adown did creepe,
That themselves dipping in the silver dew
Their fleecy flowres they fearefully did steepe,
Which drops of Christall seemd for wantones to weep.

LXII. Infinit streames continually did well
Out of this fountaine, sweet and faire to see,
The which into an ample laver fell,
And shortly grew into so great quantitie,
That like a litle lake it seemd to bee;
Whose depth exceeded not three cubits hight,
That through the waves one might the bottom see,
All pav'd beneath with Jaspar shining bright,
That seemd the fountaine in that sea did sayle upright.

LXIII. And all the margent round about was sett
With shady Laurell trees, thence to defend
The sunny beames which on the billowes bett,
And those which therein bathed mote offend.
As Guyon hapned by the same to wend,
Two naked Damzelles he therein espyde,
Which therein bathing seemed to contend
And wrestle wantonly, ne car'd to hyde
Their dainty partes from vew of any which them eyd.

LXIV. Sometimes the one would lift the other quight
Above the waters, and then downe againe
Her plong, as over-maystered by might,
Where both awhile would covered remaine,
And each the other from to rise restraine;
The whiles their snowy limbes, as through a vele,

So through the christall waves appeared plaine:
Then suddeinly both would themselves unhele,
And th' amarous sweet spoiles to greedy eyes revele.

LXV. As that faire Starre, the messenger of morne,
His deawy face out of the sea doth reare;
Or as the Cyprian goddesse, newly borne
Of th' Ocean's fruitfull froth, did first appeare:
Such seemed they, and so their yellow heare
Christalline humor dropped downe apace.
Whom such when Guyon saw, he drew him neare,
And somewhat gan relent his earnest pace;
His stubborne brest gan secret pleasaunce to embrace.

LXVI. The wanton Maidens, him espying, stood
Gazing awhile at his unwonted guise;
Then th' one her selfe low ducked in the flood,
Abasht that her a straunger did avise;
But thother rather higher did arise,
And her two lilly paps aloft displayd,
And all that might his melting hart entyse
To her delights she unto him bewrayd;
The rest hidd underneath him more desirous made.

LXVII. With that the other likewise up arose,
And her faire lockes, which formerly were bownd
Up in one knott, she low adowne did lose,
Which flowing low and thick her cloth'd arownd,
And th' yvorie in golden mantle gownd:
So that faire spectacle from him was reft,
Yet that which reft it no lesse faire was fownd.
So hidd in lockes and waves from lookers theft,
Nought but her lovely face she for his looking left.

LXVIII. Withall she laughed, and she blusht withall,
That blushing to her laughter gave more grace,
And laughter to her blushing, as did fall.
Now when they spyde the knight to slacke his pace
Them to behold, and in his sparkling face
The secrete signes of kindled lust appeare,
Their wanton meriments they did encreace,
And to him beckned to approch more neare,
And shewd him many sights that corage cold could
reare.

LXIX. On which when gazing him the Palmer saw,
He much rebukt those wandring eyes of his,
And counseld well him forward thence did draw.
Now are they come nigh to the Bowre of blis,
Of her fond favorites so nam'd amis,
When thus the Palmer: "Now, Sir, well avise;
For here the end of all our traveill is:
Here wonnes Acrasia, whom we must surprise,
Els she will slip away, and all our drift despise."

LXX. Eftsoones they heard a most melodious sound,
Of all that mote delight a daintie eare,
Such as attonce might not on living ground,
Save in this Paradise, be heard elsewhere:
Right hard it was for wight which did it heare,
To read what manner musicke that mote bee;
For all that pleasing is to living eare
Was there consorted in one harmonee;
Birdes, voices, instruments, windes, waters, all agree:

LXXI. The joyous birdes, shrouded in chearefull shade
Their notes unto the voice attempred sweet;
Th' Angelicall soft trembling voyces made
To th' instruments divine respondence meet;
The silver sounding instruments did meet
With the base murmure of the waters fall;
The waters fall with difference discreet,
Now soft, now loud, unto the wind did call;
The gentle warbling wind low answered to all.

LXXII. There, whence that Musick seemed heard to bee,
Was the faire Witch her selfe now solacing
With a new Lover, whom, through sorceree
And witchcraft, she from farre did thither bring:
There she had him now laid aslombering
In secret shade after long wanton joyes;
Whilst round about them pleasauntly did sing
Many faire Ladies and lascivious boyes,
That ever mixt their song with light licentious toyes.

LXXIII. And all that while right over him she hong
With her false eyes fast fixed in his sight,
As seeking medicine whence she was stong,

Or greedily depasturing delight;
And oft inclining downe, with kisses light
For feare of waking him, his lips bedewd,
And through his humid eyes did sucke his spright,
Quite molten into lust and pleasure lewd;
Wherewith she sighed soft, as if his case she rewd.

LXXIV. The whiles some one did chaunt this lovely lay:
Ah! see, whoso fayre thing doest faine to see,
In springing flowre the image of thy day.
Ah! see the Virgin Rose, how sweetly shee
Doth first peepe foorth with bashfull modestee,
That fairer seemes the lesse ye see her may.
Lo! see soone after how more bold and free
Her bared bosome she doth broad display;
Lo! see soone after how she fades and falls away.

LXXV. So passeth, in the passing of a day,
Of mortall life the leafe, the bud, the flowre;
Ne more doth florish after first decay,
That earst was sought to deck both bed and bowre
Of many a lady', and many a Paramowre.
Gather therefore the Rose whilest yet is prime,
For soone comes age that will her pride deflowre;
Gather the Rose of love whilest yet is time,
Whilest loving thou mayst loved be with equall crime.

LXXVI. He ceast; and then gan all the quire of birdes
Their diverse notes t'attune unto his lay,
As in approvaunce of his pleasing wordes,
The constant payre heard all that he did say,
Yet swarved not, but kept their forward way
Through many covert groves and thickets close,
In which they creeping did at last display
That wanton Lady with her lover lose,
Whose sleepie head she in her lap did soft dispose.

LXXVII. Upon a bed of Roses she was layd,
As faint through heat, or dight to pleasant sin;
And was arayd, or rather disarayd,
All in a vele of silke and silver thin,
That hid no whit her alablaster skin,
But rather shewd more white, if more might bee:
More subtile web Arachne cannot spin;

Nor the fine nets, which oft we woven see
Of scorched deaw, do not in th' ayre more lightly flee.

LXXVIII. Her snowy brest was bare to ready spoyle
Of hungry eies, which n'ote therewith be fild;
And yet, through languour of her late sweet toyle,
Few drops, more cleare then Nectar, forth distild,
That like pure Orient perles adowne it trild;
And her faire eyes, sweet smyling in delight,
Moystened their fierie beames, with which she thrild
Fraile harts, yet quenched not; like starry light,
Which, sparckling on the silent waves, does seeme more
    bright.

LXXIX. The young man, sleeping by her, seemd to be
Some goodly swayne of honorable place,
That certes it great pitty was to see
Him his nobility so fowle deface:
A sweet regard and amiable grace,
Mixed with manly sternesse, did appeare,
Yet sleeping, in his well proportiond face;
And on his tender lips the downy heare
Did now but freshly spring, and silken blossoms beare.

LXXX. His warlike Armes, the ydle instruments
Of sleeping praise, were hong upon a tree;
And his brave shield, full of old moniments,
Was fowly ras't, that none the signes might see:
Ne for them ne for honour cared hee,
Ne ought that did to his advauncement tend;
But in lewd loves, and wastfull luxuree,
His dayes, his goods, his bodie, he did spend:
O horrible enchantment, that him so did blend!

LXXXI. The noble Elfe and carefull Palmer drew
So nigh them, minding nought but lustfull game,
That suddein forth they on them rusht, and threw
A subtile net, which only for that same
The skilfull Palmer formally did frame:
So held them under fast; the whiles the rest
Fled all away for feare of fowler shame.
The faire Enchauntresse, so unwares opprest,
Tryde all her arts and all her sleights thence out to
    wrest.

LXXXII. And eke her lover strove, but all in vaine;
For that same net so cunningly was wound,
That neither guile nor force might it distraine.
They tooke them both, and both them strongly bound
In captives bandes, which there they readie found:
But her in chaines of adamant he tyde;
For nothing else might keepe her safe and sound:
But Verdant (so he hight) he soone untyde,
And counsell sage in steed thereof to him applyde.

LXXXIII. But all those pleasaunt bowres, and Pallace brave,
Guyon broke downe with rigour pittilesse;
Ne ought their goodly workmanship might save
Them from the tempest of his wrathfulnesse,
But that their blisse he turn'd to balefulnesse.
Their groves he feld; their gardins did deface;
Their arbers spoyle; their Cabinets suppresse;
Their banket houses burne; their buildings race;
And, of the fayrest late, now made the fowlest place.

LXXXIV. Then led they her away, and eke that knight
They with them led, both sorrowfull and sad.
The way they came, the same retourn'd they right,
Till they arrived where they lately had
Charm'd those wild-beasts that rag'd with furie mad;
Which, now awaking, fierce at them gan fly,
As in their mistresse reskew whom they lad;
But them the Palmer soone did pacify.
Then Guyon askt, what meant those beastes which
    there did ly?

LXXXV. Sayd he; "These seeming beasts are men indeed,
Whom this Enchauntress hath transformed thus;
Whylome her lovers, which her lustes did feed,
Now turned into figures hideous,
According to their mindes like monstruous."
"Sad end," (quoth he) "of life intemperate,
And mourneful meed of joyes delicious!
But, Palmer, if it mote thee so aggrate,
Let them returned be unto their former state."

LXXXVI. Streight way he with his vertuous staffe them strooke,
And streight of beastes they comely men became;

Yet being men they did unmanly looke,
And stared ghastly; some for inward shame,
And some for wrath to see their captive Dame:
But one above the rest in speciall
That had an hog beene late, hight Grylle by name,
Repyned greatly and did him miscall
That had from hoggish forme him brought to naturall.

LXXXVII. Saide Guyon; " See the mind of beastly man,
That hath so soone forgot the excellence
Of his creation, when he life began,
That now he chooseth with vile difference
To be a beast, and lacke intelligence! "
To whom the Palmer thus: " The donghill kinde
Delightes in filth and fowle incontinence:
Let Gryll be Gryll, and have his hoggish minde;
But let us hence depart whilest wether serves and
        winde."

THE THIRD BOOKE

CONTAYNING THE LEGEND OF BRITOMARTIS, OR OF CHASTITY.

I. IT falls me here to write of Chastity,
The fayrest vertue, far above the rest:
For which what needes me fetch from Faery
Forreine ensamples it to have exprest?
Sith it is shrined in my Soveraines brest,
And formd so lively in each perfect part,
That to all Ladies, which have it profest,
Need but behold the pourtraict of her hart;
If pourtrayd it might bee by any living art.

II. But living art may not least part expresse,
Nor life-resembling pencill it can paynt:
All were it Zeuxis or Praxiteles,
His dædale hand would faile and greatly faynt,
And her perfections with his error taynt:
Ne Poets witt, that passeth Painter farre
In picturing the parts of beauty daynt,
So hard a workemanship adventure darre,
For feare, through want of words, her excellence to
marre.

III. How then shall I, Apprentice to the skill
That whilome in divinest wits did rayne,
Presume so high to stretch mine humble quill?
Yet now my lucklesse lott doth me constrayne
Hereto perforce.   But, O dredd Soverayne!
Thus far-forth pardon, sith that choicest witt
Cannot your glorious pourtraict figure playne,
That I in colour showes may shadow itt,
And antique praises unto present persons fitt.

IV. But if in living colours, and right hew,
Thy selfe thou covet to see pictured,
Who can it doe more lively, or more trew,
Then that sweete verse, with Nectar sprinckeled,

In which a gracious servaunt pictured
His Cynthia, his heavens fayrest light?
That with his melting sweetnes ravished,
And with the wonder of her beames bright,
My sences lulled are in slomber of delight.

v. But let that same delitious Poet lend
A little leave unto a rusticke Muse
To sing his mistresse prayse; and let him mend.
If ought amis her liking may abuse:
Ne let his fayrest Cynthia refuse
In mirrours more then one her selfe to see;
But either Gloriana let her chuse,
Or in Belphœbe fashioned to bee;
In th' one her rule, in th' other her rare chastitee.

CANTO I

I. THE famous Briton Prince and Faery knight,
   After long wayes and perilous paines endur'd,
   Having their weary limbes to perfect plight
   Restord, and sory wounds right well recur'd,
   Of the faire Alma greatly were procur'd
   To make there lenger sojourne and abode;
   But when thereto they might not be allur'd,
   From seeking praise and deeds of armes abrode,
   They courteous congé tooke, and forth together yode.

II. But the captiv'd Acrasia he sent,
    Because of traveill long, a nigher way,
    With a strong gard, all reskew to prevent,
    And her to Faery court safe to convay;
    That her for witnes of his hard assay
    Unto his Faery Queene he might present:
    But he him selfe betooke another way,
    To make more triall of his hardiment,
    And seek adventures as he with Prince Arthure went.

III. Long so they traveiled through wastefull wayes,
     Where daungers dwelt, and perils most did wonne,
     To hunt for glory and renowmed prayse.
     Full many Countreyes they did overronne,
     From the uprising to the setting Sunne,
     And many hard adventures did atchieve;
     Of all the which they honour ever wonne,
     Seeking the weake oppressed to relieve,
     And to recover right for such as wrong did grieve.

IV. At last, as through an open plaine they yode,
    They spide a knight that towards pricked fayre;
    And him beside an aged Squire there rode,

That seemd to couch under his shield three-square,
As if that age badd him that burden spare,
And yield it those that stouter could it wield.
He them espying gan him selfe prepare,
And on his arme addresse his goodly shield
That bore a Lion passant in a golden field.

v. Which seeing, good Sir Guyon deare besought
The Prince of grace to let him ronne that turne.
He graunted: then the Faery quickly raught
His poynant speare, and sharply gan to spurne
His fomy steed, whose fiery feete did burne
The verdant gras as he thereon did tread;
Ne did the other backe his foote returne,
But fiercely forward came withouten dread,
And bent his dreadful speare against the others head.

vi. They beene ymett, and both theyr points arriv'd;
But Guyon drove so furious and fell,
That seemd both shield and plate it would have riv'd;
Nathelesse it bore his foe not from his sell,
But made him stagger, as he were not well:
But Guyon selfe, ere well he was aware,
Nigh a speares length behind his crouper fell;
Yet in his fall so well him selfe he bare,
That mischievous mischaunce his life and limbs did spare.

vii. Great shame and sorrow of that fall he tooke;
For never yet, sith warlike armes he bore
And shivering speare in bloody field first shooke,
He fownd him selfe dishonored so sore.
Ah! gentlest knight, that ever armor bore,
Let not thee grieve dismounted to have beene,
And brought to grownd that never wast before;
For not thy fault, but secret powre unseene:
That speare enchaunted was which layd thee on the greene.

viii. But weenedst thou what wight thee overthrew,
Much greater griefe and shamefuller regrett
For thy hard fortune then thou wouldst renew,
That of a single damzell thou wert mett
On equall plaine, and there so hard besett:
Even the famous Britomart it was,

Whom straunge adventure did from Britayne sett
To seeke her lover (love far sought alas!)
Whose image shee had seene in Venus looking glas.

IX. Full of disdainefull wrath he fierce uprose
For to revenge that fowle reprochefull shame,
And snatching his bright sword began to close
With her on foot, and stoutly forward came:
Dye rather would he then endure that same.
Which when his Palmer saw, he gan to feare
His toward perill, and untoward blame,
Which by that new rencounter he should reare;
For death sate on the point of that enchaunted speare:

X. And hasting towards him gan fayre perswade
Not to provoke misfortune, nor to weene
His speares default to mend with cruell blade;
For by his mightie Science he had seene
The secrete vertue of that weapon keene,
That mortall puissaunce mote not withstond.
Nothing on earth mote alwaies happy beene:
Great hazard were it, and adventure fond,
To loose long gotten honour with one evill hond.

XI. By such good meanes he him discounselled
From prosecuting his revenging rage:
And eke the Prince like treaty handeled,
His wrathfull will with reason to aswage;
And laid the blame, not to his carriage,
But to his starting steed that swarv'd asyde,
And to the ill purveyaunce of his page,
That had his furnitures not firmely tyde.
So is his angry corage fayrly pacifyde.

XII. Thus reconcilement was betweene them knitt,
Through goodly temperaunce and affection chaste;
And either vowd with all their power and witt
To let not others honour be defaste
Of friend or foe, who ever it embaste;
Ne armes to beare against the others syde:
In which accord the Prince was also plaste,
And with that golden chaine of concord tyde.
So goodly all agreed they forth yfere did ryde

XIII. O! goodly usage of those antique tymes,
 In which the sword was servaunt unto right;
 When not for malice and contentious crymes,
 But all for prayse, and proofe of manly might,
 The martiall brood accustomed to fight:
 Then honour was the meed of victory,
 And yet the vanquished had no despight.
 Let later age that noble use envy,
 Vyle rancor to avoid and cruel surquedry.

XIV. Long they thus traveiled in friendly wise,
 Through countreyes waste, and eke well edifyde,
 Seeking adventures hard, to exercise
 Their puissaunce, whylome full dernly tryde.
 At length they came into a forest wyde,
 Whose hideous horror and sad trembling sownd,
 Full griesly seemd: Therein they long did ryde,
 Yet tract of living creature none they fownd,
 Save Beares, Lyons, and Buls, which romed them arownd.

XV. All suddenly out of the thickest brush,
 Upon a milkwhite Palfrey all alone,
 A goodly Lady did foreby them rush,
 Whose face did seeme as cleare as Christall stone,
 And eke, through feare, as white as whales bone:
 Her garments all were wrought of beaten gold,
 And all her steed with tinsell trappings shone,
 Which fledd so fast that nothing mote him hold,
 And scarse them leasure gave her passing to behold.

XVI. Still as she fledd her eye she backward threw,
 As fearing evill that poursewd her fast;
 And her faire yellow locks behind her flew,
 Loosely disperst with puff of every blast:
 All as a blazing starre doth farre outcast
 His hearie beames, and flaming lockes dispredd,
 At sight whereof the people stand aghast;
 But the sage wisard telles, as he has redd,
 That it importunes death and dolefull dreryhedd.

XVII. So as they gazed after her a whyle,
 Lo! where a griesly foster forth did rush,
 eathing out beastly lust her to defyle:

His tyreling Jade he fiersly forth did push
Through thicke and thin, both over banck and bush,
In hope her to attaine by hooke or crooke,
That from his gory sydes the blood did gush.
Large were his limbes, and terrible his looke,
And in his clownish hand a sharp bore speare he shooke.

XVIII. Which outrage when those gentle knights did see,
Full of great envy and fell gealosy
They stayd not to avise who first should bee,
But all spurd after, fast as they mote fly,
To reskew her from shamefull villany.
The Prince and Guyon equally bylive
Her selfe pursewd, in hope to win thereby
Most goodly meede, the fairest Dame alive:
But after the foule foster Timias did strive.

XIX. The whiles faire Britomart, whose constant mind
Would not so lightly follow beauties chace,
Ne reckt of Ladies Love, did stay behynd,
And them awayted there a certaine space,
To weet if they would turne backe to that place;
But when she saw them gone she forward went,
As lay her journey, through that perlous Pace,
With stedfast corage and stout hardiment:
Ne evil thing she feard, ne evill thing she ment.

XX. At last, as nigh out of the wood she came,
A stately Castle far away she spyde,
To which her steps directly she did frame.
That Castle was most goodly edifyde,
And plaste for pleasure nigh that forrest syde:
But faire before the gate a spatious playne,
Mantled with greene, it selfe did spredden wyde,
On which she saw six knights, that did darrayne
Fiers battaill against one with cruell might and mayne.

XXI. Mainely they all attonce upon him laid,
And sore beset on every side arownd,
That nigh he breathlesse grew, yet nought dismaid,
Ne ever to them yielded foot of grownd,
All had he lost much blood through many a wownd,
But stoutly dealt his blowes, and every way,

To which he turned in his wrathfull stownd,
Made them recoile, and fly from dredd decay,
That none of all the six before him durst assay.

XXII. Like dastard Curres that, having at a bay
The salvage beast embost in wearie chace,
Dare not adventure on the stubborne pray,
Ne byte before, but rome from place to place
To get a snatch when turned is his face.
In such distresse and doubtfull jeopardy
When Britomart him saw, she ran apace
Unto his reskew, and with earnest cry
Badd those same six forbeare that single enimy.

XXIII. But to her cry they list not lenden eare,
Ne ought the more their mightie strokes surceasse.
But gathering him rownd about more neare,
Their direfull rancour rather did encreasse;
Till that she rushing through the thickest preasse
Perforce disparted their compacted gyre,
And soone compeld to hearken unto peace.
Tho gan she myldly of them to inquyre
The cause of their dissention and outrageous yre.

XXIV. Whereto that single knight did answere frame:
" These six would me enforce by oddes of might
To chaunge my liefe, and love another Dame;
That death me liefer were then such despight,
So unto wrong to yield my wrested right:
For I love one, the truest one on grownd,
Ne list me chaunge; she th' Errant Damzell hight;
For whose deare sake full many a bitter stownd
I have endurd, and tasted many a bloody wownd."

XXV. " Certes," (said she) " then beene ye sixe to blame,
To weene your wrong by force to justify;
For knight to leave his Lady were great shame
That faithfull is, and better were to dy.
All losse is lesse, and lesse the infamy,
Then losse of love to him that loves but one:
Ne may love be compeld by maistery;
For soone as maistery comes sweet Love anone
Taketh his nimble winges, and soone away is gone."

XXVI. Then spake one of those six; "There dwelleth here
Within this castle wall a Lady fayre,
Whose soveraine beautie hath no living pere;
Thereto so bounteous and so debonayre,
That never any mote with her compayre:
She hath ordaind this law, which we approve,
That every knight which doth this way repayre,
In case he have no Lady nor no love,
Shall doe unto her service, never to remove:

XXVII. "But if he have a Lady or a Love,
Then must he her forgoe with fowle defame,
Or els with us by dint of sword approve,
That she is fairer then our fairest Dame;
As did this knight, before ye hither came."
"Perdy," (said Britomart) "the choise is hard;
But what reward had he that overcame?"
"He should advaunced bee to high regard,"
(Said they) "and have our Ladies love for his reward.

XXVIII. "Therefore aread, Sir, if thou have a love."
"Love hath I sure," (quoth she) "but Lady none;
Yet will I not fro mine own love remove,
Ne to your Lady will I service done,
But wreake your wronges wrought to this knight alone,
And prove his cause." With that, her mortall speare
She mightily aventred towards one,
And downe him smot ere well aware he weare;
Then to the next she rode, and downe the next did beare.

XXIX. Ne did she stay till three on ground she layd
That none of them himselfe could reare againe:
The fourth was by that other knight dismayd,
All were he wearie of his former paine;
That now there do but two of six remaine,
Which two did yield before she did them smight.
"Ah!" (said she then) "now may ye all see plaine,
That truth is strong, and trew love most of might,
That for his trusty servaunts doth so strongly fight."

XXX. "Too well we see," (saide they) "and prove too well
Our faulty weakenes, and your matchlesse might:
Forthy, faire Sir, yours be the Damozell,

Which by her owne law to your lot doth light,
And we your liegemen faith unto you plight."
So underneath her feet their swords they mard,
And, after, her besought, well as they might,
To enter in and reape the dew reward.
She graunted; and then in they all together far'd.

XXXI. Long were it to describe the goodly frame,
And stately port of Castle Joyeous,
(For so that Castle hight by commun name)
Where they were entertaynd with courteous
And comely glee of many gratious
Faire Ladies, and of many a gentle knight,
Who, through a Chamber long and spacious,
Eftsoones them brought unto their Ladies sight,
That of them cleeped was the Lady of Delight.

XXXII. But for to tell the sumptuous aray
Of that great chamber should be labour lost;
For living wit, I weene, cannot display
The roiall riches and exceeding cost
Of every pillour and of every post,
Which all of purest bullion framed were,
And with great perles and pretious stones embost;
That the bright glister of their beames cleare
Did sparckle forth great light, and glorious did appeare.

XXXIII. These stranger knights, through passing, forth were led
Into an inner rowme, whose royaltee
And rich purveyance might uneath be red;
Mote Princes place be seeme so deckt to bee.
Which stately manner whenas they did see,
The image of superfluous riotize,
Exceeding much the state of meane degree,
They greatly wondred whence so sumptuous guize
Might be maintaynd, and each gan diversely devize.

XXXIV. The wals were round about appareiled
With costly clothes of Arras and of Toure;
In which with cunning hand was pourtrahed
The love of Venus and her Paramoure,
The fayre Adonis, turned to a flowre;
A worke of rare device and wondrous wit.

First did it shew the bitter balefull stowre,
Which her essayd with many a fervent fit,
When first her tender hart was with his beautie smit.

XXXV. Then with what sleights and sweet allurements she
Entyst the Boy, as well that art she knew,
And wooed him her Paramoure to bee;
Now making girlonds of each flowre that grew,
To crowne his golden lockes with honour dew;
Now leading him into a secret shade
From his Beauperes, and from bright heavens vew,
Where him to sleepe she gently would perswade,
Or bathe him in a fountaine by some covert glade:

XXXVI. And whilst he slept she over him would spred
Her mantle, colour'd like the starry skyes,
And her soft arme lay underneath his hed,
And with ambrosiall kisses bathe his eyes;
And whilst he bath'd with her two crafty spyes
She secretly would search each daintie lim,
And throw into the well sweet Rosemaryes,
And fragrant violets, and Paunces trim;
And ever with sweet Nectar she did sprinkle him.

XXXVII. So did she steale his heedelesse hart away,
And joyd his love in secret unespyde:
But for she saw him bent to cruell play,
To hunt the salvage beast in forrest wyde,
Dreadfull of daunger that mote him betyde,
She oft and oft adviz'd him to refraine
From chase of greater beastes, whose brutish pryde
Mote breede him scath unwares: but all in vaine;
For who can shun the chance that dest'ny doth
ordaine?

XXXVIII. Lo! where beyond he lyeth languishing,
Deadly engored of a great wilde Bore;
And by his side the Goddesse groveling
Makes for him endlesse mone, and evermore
With her soft garment wipes away the gore
Which staynes his snowy skin with hatefull hew:
But, when she saw no helpe might him restore,
Him to a dainty flowre she did transmew,
Which in that cloth was wrought as if it lively grew.

XXXIX. So was that chamber clad in goodly wize:
And rownd about it many beds were dight,
As whylome was the antique worldes guize,
Some for untimely ease, some for delight,
As pleased them to use that use it might;
And all was full of Damzels and of Squyres,
Dauncing and reveling both day and night,
And swimming deepe in sensuall desyres;
And Cupid still emongest them kindled lustfull fyres.

XL. And all the while sweet Musicke did divide
Her looser notes with Lydian harmony;
And all the while sweet birdes thereto applide
. Their daintie layes and dulcet melody,
Ay caroling of love and jollity,
That wonder was to heare their trim consort.
Which when those knights beheld, with scornefull eye
They sdeigned such lascivious disport,
And loath'd the loose demeanure of that wanton sort.

XLI. Thence they were brought to that great Ladies vew,
Whom they found sitting on a sumptuous bed
That glistred all with gold and glorious shew,
As the proud Persian Queenes accustomed.
She seemd a woman of great bountihed,
And of rare beautie, saving that askaunce
Her wanton eyes, ill signes of womanhed,
Did roll too lightly, and too often glaunce,
Without regard of grace or comely amenaunce.

XLII. Long worke it were, and needlesse, to devize
Their goodly entertainement and great glee.
She caused them be led in courteous wize
Into a bowre, disarmed for to be,
And cheared well with wine and spiceree:
The Redcrosse Knight was soon disarmed there;
But the brave Mayd would not disarmed bee,
But onely vented up her umbriere,
And so did let her goodly visage to appere.

XLIII. As when fayre Cynthia, in darkesome night
Is in a noyous cloud enveloped,
Where she may finde the substance thin and light,

Breakes forth her silver beames, and her bright hed
Discovers to the world discomfited:
Of the poore traveiler that went astray
With thousand blessings she is heried.
Such was the beautie and the shining ray,
With which fayre Britomart gave light unto the day.

XLIV. And eke those six, which lately with her fought,
Now were disarmd, and did them selves present
Unto her vew, and company unsought;
For they all seemed courteous and gent,
And all sixe brethren, borne of one parent,
Which had them traynd in all civilitee,
And goodly taught to tilt and turnament:
Now were they liegmen to this Ladie free,
And her knights service ought, to hold of her in fee.

XLV. The first of them by name Gardantè hight,
A jolly person, and of comely vew;
The second was Parlantè, a bold knight;
And next to him Jocantè did ensew;
Basciantè did him selfe most courteous shew;
But fierce Bacchantè seemd too fell and keene;
And yett in armes Noctantè greater grew:
All were faire knights, and goodly well beseene;
But to faire Britomart they all but shadowes beene.

XLVI. For shee was full of amiable grace
And manly terror mixed therewithall;
That as the one stird up affections bace,
So th' other did mens rash desires apall,
And hold them backe that would in error fall:
As hee that hath espide a vermeill Rose,
To which sharp thornes and breres the way forstall,
Dare not for dread his hardy hand expose,
But wishing it far off his ydle wish doth lose.

XLVII. Whom when the Lady saw so faire a wight,
All ignorant of her contrary sex,
(For shee her weend a fresh and lusty knight,)
Shee greatly gan enamoured to wex
And with vaine thoughts her falsed fancy vex:
Her fickle hart conceived hasty fyre,

Like sparkes of fire which fall in sclender flex,
That shortly brent into extreme desyre,
And ransackt all her veines with passion entyre.

XLVIII. Eftsoones shee grew to great impatience,
And into termes of open outrage brust,
That plaine discovered her incontinence;
Ne reckt shee who her meaning did mistrust,
For she was given all to fleshly lust,
And poured forth in sensuall delight,
That all regard of shame she had discust,
And meet respect of honor putt to flight:
So shamelesse beauty soone becomes a loathly sight.

XLIX. Faire Ladies, that to love captived arre,
And chaste desires doe nourish in your mind,
Let not her fault your sweete affections marre,
Ne blott the bounty of all womankind,
'Mongst thousands good one wanton Dame to find:
Emongst the Roses grow some wicked weeds:
For this was not to love, but lust, inclind;
For love does alwaies bring forth bounteous deeds,
And in each gentle hart desire of honor breeds.

L. Nought so of love this looser Dame did skill,
But as a cole to kindle fleshly flame,
Giving the bridle to her wanton will,
And treading under foote her honest name:
Such love is hate, and such desire is shame.
Still did she rove at her with crafty glaunce
Of her false eies, that at her hart did ayme,
And told her meaning in her countenaunce;
But Britomart dissembled it with ignoraunce.

LI. Supper was shortly dight, and downe they satt;
Where they were served with all sumptuous fare,
Whiles fruitfull Ceres and Lyæus fatt
Pourd out their plenty without spight or spare.
Nought wanted there that dainty was and rare,
And aye the cups their bancks did overflow;
And aye betweene the cups she did prepare
Way to her love, and secret darts did throw;
But Britomart would not such guilfull message know.

LII. So, when they slaked had the fervent heat
  Of appetite with meates of every sort,
  The Lady did faire Britomart entreat
  Her to disarme, and with delightfull sport
  To loose her warlike limbs and strong effort;
  But when shee mote not thereunto be wonne,
  (For shee her sexe under that straunge purport
  Did use to hide, and plaine apparaunce shonne)
  In playner wise to tell her grievaunce she begonne.

LIII. And all attonce discovered her desire
  With sighes, and sobs, and plaints, and piteous griefe,
  The outward sparkes of her inburning fire;
  Which spent in vaine, at last she told her briefe,
  That but if she did lend her short reliefe
  And doe her comfort, she mote algates dye:
  But the chaste damzell, that had never priefe
  Of such malengine and fine forgerye,
  Did easely beleeve her strong extremitye.

LIV. Full easy was for her to have beliefe,
  Who by self-feeling of her feeble sexe,
  And by long triall of the inward griefe
  Wherewith imperious love her hart did vexe,
  Could judge what paines doe loving harts perplexe.
  Who meanes no guile be guiled soonest shall,
  And to faire semblaunce doth light faith annexe:
  The bird that knowes not the false fowlers call,
  Into his hidden nett full easely doth fall.

LV. Forthy she would not in discourteise wise
  Scorne the faire offer of good will profest;
  For great rebuke it is love to despise,
  Or rudely sdeigne a gentle harts request;
  But with faire countenaunce, as beseemed best,
  Her entertaynd: nath'lesse shee inly deemd
  Her love too light, to wooe a wandring guest;
  Which she misconstruing, thereby esteemd
  That from like inward fire that outward smoke had steemd.

LVI. Therewith a while she her flit fancy fedd,
  Till she mote winne fit time for her desire;
  But yet her wound still inward freshly bledd,

And through her bones the false instilled fire
Did spred it selfe, and venime close inspire,
Tho were the tables taken all away;
And every knight, and every gentle Squire,
Gan choose his Dame with *Bascimano* gay,
With whom he ment to make his sport and courtly play.

LVII. Some fell to daunce, some fel to hazardry,
Some to make love, some to make meryment,
As diverse witts to diverse things apply;
And all the while faire Malecasta bent
Her crafty engins to her close intent.
By this th' eternall lampes, wherewith high Jove
Doth light the lower world, were halfe yspent,
And the moist daughters of huge Atlas strove
Into the Ocean deepe to drive their weary drove.

LVIII. High time it seemed then for everie wight
Them to betake unto their kindly rest:
Eftesoones long waxen torches weren light
Unto their bowres to guyden every guest.
Tho, when the Britonesse saw all the rest
Avoided quite, she gan her selfe despoile,
And safe committ to her soft fethered nest,
Wher through long watch, and late daies weary toile,
She soundly slept, and carefull thoughts did quite assoile.

LIX. Now whenas all the world in silence deepe
Yshrowded was, and every mortall wight
Was drowned in the depth of deadly sleepe;
Faire Malecasta, whose engrieved spright
Could find no rest in such perplexed plight,
Lightly arose out of her wearie bed,
And, under the blacke vele of guilty Night,
Her with a scarlott mantle covered
That was with gold and Ermines faire enveloped.

LX. Then panting softe, and trembling every joynt,
Her fearfull feete towards the bowre she mov'd,
Where she for secret purpose did appoynt
To lodge the warlike maide, unwisely loov'd;
And, to her bed approching, first she proov'd
Whether she slept or wakte: with her softe hand

She softely felt if any member moov'd,
And lent her wary eare to understand
If any puffe of breath or signe of sence shee fond.

LXI. Which whenas none she fond, with easy shifte,
For feare least her unwares she should abrayd,
Th' embroder'd quilt she lightly up did lifte,
And by her side her selfe she softly layd,
Of every finest fingers touch affrayd;
Ne any noise she made, ne word she spake,
But inly sigh'd.   At last the royall Mayd
Out of her quiet slomber did awake,
And chaunged her weary side the better ease to take.

LXII. Where feeling one close couched by her side,
She lightly lept out of her filed bedd,
And to her weapon ran, in minde to gride
The loathed leachour.   But the Dame, halfe dedd
Through suddein feare and ghastly drerihedd,
Did shrieke alowd, that through the hous it rong,
And the whole family, therewith adredd,
Rashly out of their rouzed couches sprong,
And to the troubled chamber all in armes did throng.

LXIII. And those sixe knights, that ladies Champions
And eke the Redcrosse knight ran to the stownd.
Half armd and halfe unarmd, with them attons:
Where when confusedly they came, they fownd
Their lady lying on the sencelesse grownd:
On thother side they saw the warlike Mayd
Al in her snow-white smocke, with locks unbownd,
Threatning the point of her avenging blaed;
That with so troublous terror they were all dismayd.

LXIV. About their Ladye first they flockt arownd;
Whom having laid in comfortable couch,
Shortly they reard out of her frosen swownd;
And afterwardes they gan with fowle reproch
To stirre up strife, and troublous contecke broch:
But by ensample of the last dayes losse,
None of them rashly durst to her approch,
Ne in so glorious spoile themselves embosse:
Her succourd eke the Champion of the bloody Crosse.

LXV. But one of those sixe knights, Gardantè hight,
Drew out a deadly bow and arrow keene,
Which forth he sent, with felonous despight
And fell intent, against the virgin sheene:
The mortall steele stayd not till it was seene
To gore her side; yet was the wound not deepe,
But lightly rased her soft silken skin,
That drops of purple blood thereout did weepe,
Which did her lilly smock with staines of vermeil steep.

LXVI. Wherewith enrag'd she fiercely at them flew,
And with her flaming sword about her layd,
That none of them foule mischiefe could eschew,
But with her dreadfull strokes were all dismayd:
Here, there, and every where, about her swayd
Her wrathfull steele, that none mote it abyde;
And eke the Redcrosse knight gave her good ayd,
Ay joyning foot to foot, and syde to syde;
That in short space their foes they have quite terrifyde.

LXVII. Tho, whenas all were put to shamefull flight,
The noble Britomartis her arayd,
And her bright armes about her body dight.
For nothing would she lenger there be stayd,
Where so loose life, and so ungentle trade,
Was usd of knightes and Ladies seeming gent:
So earely, ere the grosse Earthes gryesy shade
Was all disperst out of the firmament,
They tooke their steeds, and forth upon their journey
went.

CANTO II

The Redcrosse knight to Britomart
Describeth Artegall:
The wondrous myrrhour, by which she
In love with him did fall.

i. Here have I cause in men just blame to find,
   That in their proper praise too partiall bee,
   And not indifferent to woman kind,
   To whom no share in armes and chevalree
   They doe impart, ne maken memoree
   Of their brave gestes and prowesse martiall:
   Scarse do they spare to one, or two, or three,
   Rowme in their writtes; yet the same writing small
   Does all their deedes deface, and dims their glories all.

ii. But by record of antique times I finde
    That wemen wont in warres to beare most sway,
    And to all great exploites them selves inclind,
    Of wihch they still the girlond bore away;
    Till envious Men, fearing their rules decay,
    Gan coyne streight lawes to curb their liberty:
    Yet sith they warlike armes have laide away,
    They have exceld in artes and pollicy,
    That now we foolish men that prayse gin eke t' envy.

iii. Of warlike puissaunce in ages spent,
     Be thou, faire Britomart, whose prayse I wryte;
     But of all wisedom bee thou precedent,
     O soveraine Queene! whose prayse I would endyte,
     Endite I would as dewtie doth excyte;
     But ah! my rymes too rude and rugged arre,
     When in so high an object they do lyte,
     And, striving fit to make, I feare, doe marre:
     Thy selfe thy prayses tell, and make them knowen farre.

iv. She, traveiling with Guyon, by the way
    Of sondry thinges faire purpose gan to find,
    T' abridg their journey long, and lingring day;

I   M

Mongst which it fell into that Fairies mind
To aske this Briton Maid, what uncouth wind
Brought her into those partes, and what inquest
Made her dissemble her disguised kind?
Faire Lady she him seemd, like Lady drest,
But fairest knight alive, when armed was her brest.

v. Thereat she sighing softly had no powre
To speake a while, ne ready answere make;
But with hart-thrilling throbs and bitter stowre,
As if she had a fever fitt, did quake,
And every daintie limbe with horrour shake;
And ever and anone the rosy red
Flasht through her face, as it had beene a flake
Of lightning through bright heven fulmined:
At last, the passion past, she thus him answered.

vi. "Faire Sir, I let you weete, that from the howre
I taken was from nourses tender pap,
I have been trained up in warlike stowre,
To tossen speare and shield, and to affrap
The warlike ryder to his most mishap:
Sithence I loathed have my life to lead,
As Ladies wont, in pleasures wanton lap,
To finger the fine needle and nyce thread,
Me lever were with point of foemans speare be dead.

vii. "All my delight on deedes of armes is sett,
To hunt out perilles and adventures hard,
By sea, by land, where so they may be mett,
Onely for honour and for high regard,
Without respect of richesse or reward:
For such intent into these partes I came,
Withouten compasse or withouten card,
Far fro my native soyle, that is by name
The greater Brytayne, here to seek for praise and fame.

viii. "Fame blazed hath, that here in Faery lond
Doe many famous knightes and Ladies wonne,
And many straunge adventures to bee fond,
Of which great worth and worship may be wonne;
Which to prove, I this voyage have begonne.
But mote I weet of you, right courteous knight,

Tydings of one that hath unto me donne
Late foule dishonour and reprochfull spight,
The which I seeke to wreake, and Arthegall he hight."

IX. The worde gone out she backe againe would call,
As her repenting so to have missayd,
But that he, it uptaking ere the fall,
Her shortly answered: "Faire martiall Mayd,
Certes ye misavised beene t' upbrayd
A gentle knight with so unknightly blame;
For, weet ye well, of all that ever playd
At tilt or tourney, or like warlike game,
The noble Arthegall hath ever borne the name.

X. "Forthy great wonder were it, if such shame
Should ever enter in his bounteous thought,
Or ever doe that mote deserven blame:
The noble corage never weeneth ought
That may unworthy of it selfe be thought.
Therefore, faire Damzell, be ye well aware,
Least that too farre ye have your sorrow sought:
You and your countrey both I wish welfare,
And honour both; for each of other worthy are."

XI. The royall Maid woxe inly wondrous glad,
To heare her Love so highly magnifyde;
And joyd that ever she affixed had
Her hart on knight so goodly glorifyde,
How ever finely she it faind to hyde.
The loving mother, that nine monethes did beare
In the deare closett of her painefull syde
Her tender babe, it seeing safe appeare,
Doth not so much rejoyce as she rejoyced theare.

XII. But to occasion him to further talke,
To feed her humor with his pleasing style,
Her list in stryfull termes with him to balke,
And thus replyde: "How ever, Sir, ye fyle
Your courteous tongue his prayses to compyle,
It ill beseemes a knight of gentle sort,
Such as ye have him boasted, to beguyle
A simple maide, and worke so hainous tort,
In shame of knighthood, as I largely can report.

XIII. " Let bee therefore my vengeaunce to disswade,
And read where I that faytour false may find."
" Ah! but if reason faire might you perswade
To slake your wrath, and mollify your mind "
(Said he) " perhaps ye should it better find:
For hardie thing it is, to weene by might
That man to hard conditions to bind,
Or ever hope to match in equall fight,
Whose prowesse paragone saw never living wight.

XIV. " Ne soothlich is it easie for to read
Where now on earth, or how, he may be fownd;
For he ne wonneth in one certeine stead,
But restlesse walketh all the world arownd,
Ay doing thinges that to his fame redownd,
Defending Ladies cause and Orphans right,
Whereso he heares that any doth confownd
Them comfortlesse through tyranny or might:
So is his soveraine honour raisde to hevens hight."

XV. His feeling wordes her feeble sence much pleased,
And softly sunck into her molten hart:
Hart that is inly hurt is greatly eased
With hope of thing that may allegge his smart;
For pleasing wordes are like to Magick art,
That doth the charmed Snake in slomber lay.
Such secrete ease felt gentle Britomart,
Yet list the same enforce with faind gainesay;
So dischord ofte in Musick makes the sweeter lay :—

XVI. And sayd; " Sir knight, these ydle termes forbeare;
And, sith it is uneath to finde his haunt,
Tell me some markes by which he may appeare,
If chaunce I him encounter paravaunt;
For perdy one shall other slay, or daunt:
What shape, what shield, what armes, what steed,
what stedd,
And what so else his person most may vaunt? "
All which the Redcrosse knight to point aredd,
And him in everie part before her fashioned.

XVII. Yet him in everie part before she knew,
However list her now her knowledge fayne,

Sith him whylome in Britayne she did vew,
To her revealed in a mirrhour playne;
Whereof did grow her first engraffed payne,
Whose root and stalke so bitter yet did taste,
That but the fruit more sweetnes did contayne,
Her wretched dayes in dolour she mote waste,
And yield the pray of love to lothsome death at last.

XVIII. By straunge occasion she did him behold,
And much more straungely gan to love his sight,
As it in bookes hath written beene of old.
In Deheubarth, that now South-wales is hight,
What time king Ryence raign'd and dealed right,
The great Magitien Merlin had deviz'd,
By his deepe science and hell-dreaded might,
A looking glasse, right wondrously aguiz'd,
Whose vertues through the wyde worlde soone were
   solemniz'd.

XIX. It vertue had to shew in perfect sight
Whatever thing was in the world contaynd,
Betwixt the lowest earth and hevens hight,
So that it to the looker appertaynd:
Whatever foe had wrought, or frend had faynd,
Therein discovered was, ne ought mote pas,
Ne ought in secret from the same remaynd;
Forthy it round and hollow shaped was,
Like to the world itselfe, and seemd a world of glas.

XX. Who wonders not, that reades so wonderous worke?
But who does wonder, that has red the Towre
Wherein th' Aegyptian Phao long did lurke
From all mens vew, that none might her discoure,
Yet she might all men vew out of her bowre?
Great Ptolomæe it for his lemans sake
Ybuilded all of glasse, by Magicke powre,
And also it impregnable did make;
Yet when his love was false he with a peaze it brake.

XXI. Such was the glassy globe that Merlin made,
And gave unto king Ryence for his gard,
That never foes his kingdome might invade,
But he it knew at home before he hard

Tydings thereof, and so them still debar'd.
It was a famous Present for a Prince,
And worthy worke of infinite reward,
That treasons could bewray, and foes convince:
Happy this Realme, had it remayned ever since!

XXII. One day it fortuned fayre Britomart
Into her fathers closet to repayre;
For nothing he from her reserv'd apart,
Being his onely daughter and his hayre;
Where when she had espyde that mirrhour fayre,
Her selfe awhile therein she vewd in vaine:
Tho, her avizing of the vertues rare
Which thereof spoken were, she gan againe
Her to bethinke of that mote to her selfe pertaine.

XXIII. But as it falleth, in the gentlest harts
Imperious Love hath highest set his throne,
And tyrannizeth in the bitter smarts
Of them that to him buxome are and prone:
So thought this Mayd (as maydens use to done)
Whom fortune for her husband would allot:
Not that she lusted after any one,
For she was pure from blame of sinfull blott;
Yet wist her life at last must lincke in that same knot.

XXIV. Eftsoones there was presented to her eye
A comely knight, all arm'd in complete wize,
Through whose bright ventayle, lifted up on hye,
His manly face, that did his foes agrize,
And frends to termes of gentle truce entize,
Lookt foorth, as Phœbus face out of the east
Betwixt two shady mountaynes doth arize:
Portly his person was, and much increast
Through his Heroicke grace and honourable gest.

XXV. His crest was covered with a couchant Hownd,
And all his armour seemd of antique mould,
But wondrous massy and assured sownd,
And round about yfretted all with gold,
In which there written was, with cyphres old,
Achilles armes, which Arthegall did win:
And on his shield enveloped sevenfold

He bore a crowned little Ermelin,
That deckt the azure field with her fayre pouldred skin.

XXVI. The Damzell well did vew his Personage
And liked well, ne further fastned not,
But went her way; ne her unguilty age
Did weene, unwares, that her unlucky lot
Lay hidden in the bottome of the pot.
Of hurt unwist most daunger doth redound;
But the false Archer, which that arrow shot
So slyly that she did not feele the wound,
Did smyle full smoothly at her weetlesse wofull stound.

XXVII. Thenceforth the fether in her lofty crest,
Ruffed of love, gan lowly to availe;
And her prowd portaunce and her princely gest,
With which she earst tryumphed, now did quaile:
Sad, solemn, sowre, and full of fancies fraile,
She woxe; yet wist she nether how, nor why.
She wist not, silly Mayd, what she did aïle,
Yet wist she was not well at ease perdy;
Yet thought it was not love, but some melancholy.

XXVIII. So soone as Night had with her pallid hew
Defaste the beautie of the shyning skye,
And refte from men the worldes desired vew,
She with her Nourse adowne to sleepe did lye;
But sleepe full far away from her did fly:
In stead thereof sad sighes and sorrowes deepe
Kept watch and ward about her warily,
That nought she did but wayle, and often steepe
Her dainty couch with teares which closely she did
weepe.

XXIX. And if that any drop of slombring rest
Did chaunce to still into her weary spright.
When feeble nature felt her selfe opprest,
Streight-way with dreames, and with fantastick sight
Of dreadfull things, the same was put to flight;
That oft out of her bed she did astart,
As one with vew of ghastly feends affright:
Tho gan she to renew her former smart,
And thinke of that fayre visage written in her hart.

xxx. One night, when she was tost with such unrest,
Her aged Nourse, whose name was Glaucè hight,
Feeling her leape out of her loathed nest,
Betwixt her feeble armes her quickly keight,
And downe againe her in her warme bed dight:
" Ah! my deare daughter, ah! my dearest dread,
What uncouth fit," (sayd she) " what evill plight
Hath thee opprest, and with sad drearyhead
Chaunged thy lively cheare, and living made thee dead?

xxxi. " For not of nought these suddein ghastly feares
All night afflict thy naturall repose;
And all the day, when as thine equall peares
Their fit disports with faire delight doe chose,
Thou in dull corners doest thy selfe inclose;
Ne tastest Princes pleasures, ne doest spred
Abroad thy fresh youths fayrest flowre, but lose
Both leafe and fruite, both too untimely shed,
As one in wilfull bale for ever buried.

xxxii. " The time that mortall men their weary cares
Do lay away, and all wilde beastes do rest,
And every river eke his course forbeares,
Then doth this wicked evill thee infest,
And rive with thousand throbs thy thrilled brest:
Like an huge Aetn' of deepe engulfed gryefe,
Sorrow is heaped in thy hollow chest,
Whence foorth it breakes in sighes and anguish ryfe,
As smoke and sulphure mingled with confused stryfe.

xxxiii. " Ay me! how much I feare least love it bee!
But if that love it be, as sure I read
By knowen signes and passions which I see,
Be it worthy of thy race and royall sead,
Then I avow, by this most sacred head
Of my deare foster childe, to ease thy griefe
And win thy will: Therefore away doe dread
For death nor daunger from thy dew reliefe
Shall me debarre: tell me therefore, my liefest liefe!"

xxxiv. So having sayd, her twixt her armes twaine
Shee streightly straynd, and colled tenderly;
And every trembling joynt and every vaine

Shee softly felt, and rubbed busily,
To doe the frosen cold away to fly;
And her faire deawy eies with kisses deare
Shee ofte did bathe, and ofte againe did dry;
And ever her importund not to feare
To let the secret of her hart to her appeare.

xxxv. The Damzell pauzd; and then thus fearfully:
"Ah! Nurse, what needeth thee to eke my payne?
Is not enough that I alone doe dye,
But it must doubled bee with death of twaine?
For nought for me but death there doth remaine."
"O daughter deare!" (said she) "despeire no whit;
For never sore but might a salve obtaine:
That blinded God, which hath ye blindly smit,
Another arrow hath your lovers hart to hit."

xxxvi. "But mine is not" (quoth she) "like other wownd;
For which no reason can finde remedy."
"Was never such, but mote the like be fownd,"
(Said she) "and though no reason may apply
Salve to your sore, yet love can higher stye
Then reasons reach, and oft hath wonders donne."
"But neither God of love nor God of skye
Can doe" (said she) "that which cannot be donne."
"Things ofte impossible" (quoth she) "seeme, ere
begonne."

xxxvii. "These idle wordes" (said she) "doe nought aswage
My stubborne smart, but more annoiaunce breed:
For no, no usuall fire, no usuall rage
Yt is, O Nourse! which on my life doth feed,
And sucks the blood which from my hart doth bleed:
But since thy faithful zele lets me not hyde
My crime, (if crime it be) I will it reed.
Nor Prince nor pere it is, whose love hath gryde
My feeble brest of late, and launched this wound wyde.

xxxviii. "Nor man it is, nor other living wight,
For then some hope I might unto me draw;
But th' only shade and semblant of a knight,
Whose shape or person yet I never saw,
Hath me subjected to loves cruell law:

The same one day, as me misfortune led,
I in my fathers wondrous mirrhour saw,
And, pleased with that seeming goodly-hed,
Unwares the hidden hooke with baite I swallowed.

XXXIX. " Sithens it hath infixed faster hold
Within my bleeding bowells, and so sore
Now ranckleth in this same fraile fleshly mould,
That all my entrailes flow with poisnous gore,
And th' ulcer groweth daily more and more;
Ne can my ronning sore finde remedee,
Other than my hard fortune to deplore,
And languish, as the leafe faln from the tree,
Till death make one end of my daies and miseree!"

XL. " Daughter," (said she) " what need ye be dismayd?
Or why make ye such Monster of your minde?
Of much more uncouth thing I was affrayd,
Of filthy lust, contrary unto kinde;
But this affection nothing straunge I finde;
For who with reason can you aye reprove
To love the semblaunt pleasing most your minde,
And yield your heart whence ye cannot remove?
No guilt in you, but in the tyranny of love.

XLI. " Not so th' Arabian Myrrhe did set her mynd,
Nor so did Biblis spend her pining hart;
But lov'd their native flesh against al kynd,
And to their purpose used wicked art:
Yet playd Pasiphaë a more monstrous part,
That lov'd a Bul, and learnd a beast to bee.
Such shamefull lustes who loaths not, which depart
From course of nature and of modestee?
Sweete love such lewdnes bands from his faire companee.

XLII. " But thine, my Deare, (welfare thy heart, my deare!)
Though straunge beginning had, yet fixed is
On one that worthy may perhaps appeare;
And certes seemes bestowed not amis:
Joy thereof have thou and eternall blis!"
With that, upleaning on her elbow weake,
Her alablaster brest she soft did kis,

Which all that while shee felt to pant and quake,
As it an Earth-quake were: at last she thus bespake.

XLIII. " Beldame, your words doe worke me litle ease;
For though my love be not so lewdly bent
As those ye blame, yet may it nought appease
My raging smart, ne ought my flame relent,
But rather doth my helpless griefe augment;
For they, how ever shamefull and unkinde,
Yet did possesse their horrible intent;
Short end of sorrowes they therby did finde;
So was their fortune good, though wicked were their
minde.

XLIV. " But wicked fortune mine, though minde be good,
Can have no ende nor hope of my desire,
But feed on shadowes whiles I die for food,
And like a shadowe wexe, whiles with entire
Affection I doe languish and expire.
I, fonder then Cephisus foolish chyld,
Who, having vewed in a fountaine shere
His face, was with the love thereof beguyld;
I, fonder, love a shade, the body far exyld."

XLV. " Nought like," (quoth shee) " for that same wretched boy
Was of him selfe the ydle Paramoure,
Both love and lover, without hope of joy,
For which he faded to a watry flowre:
But better fortune thine, and better howre,
Which lov'st the shadow of a warlike knight;
No shadow but a body hath in powre:
That body, wheresoever that it light,
May learned be by cyphers, or by Magicke might.

XLVI. " But if thou may with reason yet represse
The growing evill, ere it strength have gott,
And thee abandond wholy do possesse,
Against it strongly strive, and yield thee nott
Til thou in open fielde adowne be smott:
But if the passion mayster thy fraile might,
So that needs love or death must bee thy lott,
Then, I avow to thee, by wrong or right
To compas thy desire, and find that loved knight."

XLVII. Her chearefull words much cheard the feeble spright
    Of the sicke virgin, that her downe she layd
    In her warme bed to sleepe, if that she might;
    And the old-woman carefully displayd
    The clothes about her round with busy ayd;
    So that at last a litle creeping sleepe
    Surprisd her sence: Shee, therewith well apayd,
    The dronken lamp down in the oyl did steepe,
    And sett her by to watch, and sett her by to weepe.

XLVIII. Earely, the morrow next, before that day
    His joyous face did to the world revele,
    They both uprose and tooke their ready way
    Unto the Church, their praiers to appele
    With great devotion, and with little zele:
    For the faire Damzel from the holy herse
    Her love-sicke hart to other thoughts did steale;
    And that old Dame said many an idle verse,
    Out of her daughters hart fond fancies to reverse.

XLIX. Retournd home, the royall Infant fell
    Into her former fitt; for-why no powre
    Nor guidaunce of herselfe in her did dwell:
    But th' aged Nourse, her calling to her bowre,
    Had gathered Rew, and Savine, and the flowre
    Of Camphora, and Calamint, and Dill;
    All which she in a earthen Pot did poure,
    And to the brim with Coltwood did it fill,
    And many drops of milk and blood through it did spill.

L. Then, taking thrise three heares from off her head,
    Them trebly breaded in a threefold lace,
    And round about the Pots mouth bound the thread;
    And, after having whispered a space
    Certein sad words with hollow voice and bace,
    Shee to the virgin sayd, thrise sayd she itt;
    " Come daughter, come; come, spit upon my face;
    Spitt thrise upon me, thrise upon me spitt;
    Th' uneven nomber for this busines is most fitt."

LI. That sayd, her rownd about she from her turnd,
    She turnd her contrary to the Sunne;
    Thrise she her turnd contrary, and returnd

All contrary; for she the right did shunne;
And ever what she did was streight undonne.
So thought she to undoe her daughters love;
But love, that is in gentle brest begonne,
No ydle charmes so lightly may remove:
That well can witnesse who by tryall it does prove.

LII. Ne ought it mote the noble Mayd avayle,
Ne slake the fury of her cruell flame,
But that shee still did waste, and still did wayle,
That, through long languour and hart-burning brame,
She shortly like a pyned ghost became
Which long hath waited by the Stygian strond.
That when old Glaucè saw, for feare least blame
Of her miscarriage should in her be fond,
She wist not how t'amend, nor how it to withstond.

CANTO III

Herein bewrayes to Britomart
The state of Arthegall;
And shews the famous Progeny,
Which from them springen shall.

I. Most sacred fyre, that burnest mightily
   In living brests, ykindled first above
   Emongst th' eternall spheres and lamping sky,
   And thence pourd into men, which men call Love!
   Not that same, which doth base affections move
   In brutish mindes, and filthy lust inflame,
   But that sweete fit that doth true beautie love,
   And choseth vertue for his dearest Dame,
   Whence spring all noble deedes and never dying fame:

II. Well did Antiquity a God thee deeme,
    That over mortall mindes hast so great might,
    To order them as best to thee doth seeme,
    And all their actions to direct aright:
    The fatall purpose of divine foresight
    Thou doest effect in destined descents,
    Through deepe impression of thy secret might,
    And stirredst up th' Heroës high intents,
    Which the late world admyres for wondrous moniments.

III. But thy dredd dartes in none doe triumph more,
     Ne braver proofe in any of thy powre
     Shewd'st thou, then in this royall Maid of yore,
     Making her seeke an unknowne Paramoure,
     From the worlds end, through many a bitter stowre:
     From whose two loynes thou afterwardes did rayse
     Most famous fruites of matrimoniall bowre,
     Which through the earth have spredd their living prayse,
     That fame in tromp of gold eternally displayes.

IV. Begin then, O my dearest sacred Dame!
    Daughter of Phœbus and of Memorye,
    That doest ennoble with immortall name

The warlike Worthies, from antiquitye,
In thy great volume of Eternitye:
Begin, O Clio! and recount from hence
My glorious Soveraines goodly auncestrye,
Till that by dew degrees, and long pretense,
Thou have it lastly brought unto her Excellence.

v. Full many wayes within her troubled mind
Old Glaucè cast to cure this Ladies griefe;
Full many waies she sought, but none could find,
Nor herbes, nor charmes, nor counsel, that is chiefe
And choicest med'cine for sick harts reliefe:
Forthy great care she tooke, and greater feare,
Least that it should her turne to fowle repriefe
And sore reproch, when so her father deare
Should of his dearest daughters hard misfortune heare.

vi. At last she her avisde, that he which made
That mirrhour, wherein the sicke Damosell
So straungely vewed her straunge lovers shade,
To weet, the learned Merlin, well could tell
Under what coast of heaven the man did dwell,
And by what means his love might best be wrought:
For, though beyond the Africk Ismael
Or th' Indian Peru he were, she thought
Him forth through infinite endevour to have sought.

vii. Forthwith them selves disguising both in straunge
And base atyre, that none might them bewray,
To Maridunum, that is now by chaunge
Of name Cayr-Merdin cald, they tooke their way:
There the wise Merlin whylome wont (they say)
To make his wonne, low underneath the ground,
In a deepe delve, farre from the vew of day,
That of no living wight he mote be found,
When he so counseld with his sprights encompast round.

viii. And, if thou ever happen that same way
To traveill, go to see that dreadful place.
It is an hideous hollow cave (they say)
Under a Rock that lyes a litle space
From the swift Barry, tombling downe apace
Emongst the woody hilles of Dynevowre:

But dare thou not, I charge, in any cace
To enter into that same baleful Bowre,
For feare the cruell Feendes should thee unwares devowre:

IX. But standing high aloft low lay thine eare,
And there such ghastly noyse of yron chaines
And brasen Caudrons thou shalt rombling heare,
Which thousand sprights with long enduring paines
Doe tosse, that it will stonn thy feeble braines;
And oftentimes great grones, and grevious stownds,
When too huge toile and labour them constraines,
And oftentimes loud strokes and ringing sowndes
From under that deepe Rock most horribly rebowndes.

x. The cause, some say, is this: A litle whyle
Before that Merlin dyde, he did intend
A brasen wall in compas to compyle
About Cairmardin, and did it commend
Unto these Sprights to bring to perfect end:
During which worke the Lady of the Lake,
Whom long he lov'd, for him in hast did send;
Who, thereby forst his workemen to forsake,
Them bownd till his retourne their labour not to slake.

XI. In the meane time, through that false Ladies traine
He was surprisd, and buried under beare,
Ne ever to his worke returnd againe:
Nath'lesse those feends may not their work forbeare,
So greatly his commandement they feare,
But there doe toyle and traveile day and night,
Untill that brasen wall they up doe reare;
For Merlin had in Magick more insight
Then ever him before, or after, living wight:

XII. For he by wordes could call out of the sky
Both Sunne and Moone, and make them him obay;
The Land to sea, and sea to maineland dry,
And darksom night he eke could turne to day:
Huge hostes of men he could alone dismay,
And hostes of men of meanest thinges could frame,
When so him list his enimies to fray;
That to this day, for terror of his fame,
The feends do quake when any him to them does name.

XIII. And, sooth, men say that he was not the sonne
Of mortall Syre or other living wight,
But wondrously begotten, and begonne
By false illusion of a guilefull Spright
On a faire Lady Nonne, that whilome hight
Matilda, daughter to Pubidius,
Who was the lord of Mathraval by right,
And coosen unto king Ambrosius;
Whence he indued was with skill so merveilous.

XIV. They, here arriving, staid awhile without,
Ne durst adventure rashly in to wend,
But of their first intent gan make new dout,
For dread of daunger which it might portend;
Untill the hardy Mayd (with love to frend)
First entering, the dreadfull Mage there fownd
Deepe busied bout worke of wondrous end,
And writing straunge characters in the grownd,
With which the stubborne feendes he to his service bownd.

XV. He nought was moved at their entraunce bold,
For of their comming well he wist afore;
Yet list them bid their businesse to unfold,
As if ought in this world in secrete store
Were from him hidden, or unknowne of yore.
Then Glaucè thus: " Let not it thee offend,
That we thus rashly through thy darksom dore
Unwares have prest; for either fatall end,
Or other mightie cause, us two did hither send."

XVI. He bad tell on; And then she thus began.
" Now have three Moones with borrowd brothers light
Thrise shined faire, and thrise seemd dim and wan,
Sith a sore evill, which this virgin bright
Tormenteth and doth plonge in dolefull plight,
First rooting tooke; but what thing it mote bee,
Or whence it sprong, I can not read aright:
But this I read, that, but if remedee
Thou her afford, full shortly I her dead shall see."

XVII. Therewith th' Enchaunter softly gan to smyle
At her smooth speeches, weeting inly well
That she to him dissembled womanish guyle,

And to her said: " Beldame, by that ye tell
More neede of leach-crafte hath your Damozell,
Then of my skill: who helpe may have elsewhere,
In vaine seekes wonders out of Magick spell."
Th' old woman wox half blanck those wordes to heare,
And yet was loth to let her purpose plaine appeare;

XVIII. And to him said: " Yf any leaches skill,
Or other learned meanes, could have redrest
This my deare daughters deepe engraffed ill,
Certes I should be loth thee to molest;
But this sad evill, which dost her infest,
Doth course of naturall cause farre exceed,
And housed is within her hollow brest,
That either seemes some cursed witches deed,
Or evill spright, that in her doth such torment breed."

XIX. The wisard could no lenger beare her bord,
But, bursting forth in laughter, to her sayd:
" Glaucè, what needes this colourable word
To cloke the cause that hath it selfe bewrayd?
Ne ye, fayre Britomartis, thus arayd,
More hidden are then Sunne in cloudy vele;
Whom thy good fortune, having fate obayd,
Hath hither brought for succour to appele;
The which the powres to thee are pleased to revele."

XX. The doubtfull Mayd, seeing her selfe descryde,
Was all abasht, and her pure yvory
Into a cleare Carnation suddeine dyde;
As fayre Aurora, rysing hastily,
Doth by her blushing tell that she did lye
All night in old Tithonus frozen bed,
Whereof she seemes ashamed inwardly:
But her olde Nourse was nought dishartened,
But vauntage made of that which Merlin had ared;

XXI. And sayd; " Sith then thou knowest all our griefe,
(For what doest not thou knowe?) of grace I pray,
Pitty our playnt, and yield us meet reliefe."
With that the Prophet still awhile did stay,
And then his spirite thus gan foorth display:
" Most noble Virgin, that by fatall lore

Hast learn'd to love, let no whit thee dismay
The hard beginne that meetes thee in the dore,
And with sharpe fits thy tender hart oppresseth sore:

XXII. " For so must all things excellent begin;
And eke enrooted deepe must be that Tree,
Whose big embodied braunches shall not lin
Till they to hevens hight forth stretched bee:
For from thy wombe a famous Progenee
Shall spring out of the auncient Trojan blood,
Which shall revive the sleeping memoree
Of those same antique Peres, the hevens brood,
Which Greeke and Asian rivers stayned with their blood.

XXIII. " Renowmed kings, and sacred Emperours,
Thy fruitfull Ofspring, shall from thee descend;
Brave Captaines, and most mighty warriours,
That shall their conquests through all lands extend,
And their decayed kingdomes shall amend:
The feeble Britons, broken with long warre,
They shall upreare, and mightily defend
Against their forren foe that commes from farre,
Till universall peace compound all civill jarre.

XXIV. " It was not, Britomart, thy wandring eye
Glauncing unwares in charmed looking glas,
But the streight course of hevenly destiny,
Led with eternall providence, that has
Guyded thy glaunce, to bring his will to pas:
Ne is thy fate, ne is thy fortune ill,
To love the prowest knight that ever was.
Therefore submit thy wayes unto his will,
And doe by all dew meanes thy destiny fulfill."

XXV. " But read," (saide Glaucè) " thou Magitian,
What meanes shall she out seeke, or what waies take?
How shall she know, how shall she finde the man?
Or what needes her to toyle, sith fates can make
Way for themselves their purpose to pertake? "
Then Merlin thus: " Indeede the fates are firme,
And may not shrinck, though all the world do shake;
Yet ought mens good endevours them confirme,
And guyde the heavenly causes to their constant terme.

XXVI. " The man, whom heavens have ordaynd to bee
The spouse of Britomart, is Arthegall:
He wonneth in the land of Fayeree,
Yet is no Fary borne, ne sib at all
To Elfes, but sprong of seed terrestriall,
And whylome by false Faries stolne away,
Whyles yet in infant cradle he did crall;
Ne other to himselfe is knowne this day,
But that he by an Elfe was gotten of a Fay:

XXVII. " But sooth he is the sonne of Gorloïs,
And brother unto Cador, Cornish king;
And for his warlike feates renowmed is,
From where the day out of the sea doth spring,
Untill the closure of the Evening:
From thence him, firmely bound with faithfull band,
To this his native soyle thou backe shalt bring,
Strongly to ayde his countrey to withstand
The powre of forreine Paynims which invade thy land.

XXVIII. " Great ayd thereto his mighty puissaunce
And dreaded name shall give in that sad day;
Where also proofe of thy prow valiaunce
Thou then shalt make, t'increase thy lover's pray.
Long time ye both in armes shall beare great sway,
Till thy wombes burden thee from them do call,
And his last fate him from thee take away;
Too rathe cut off by practise criminall
Of secrete foes, that him shall make in mischiefe fall.

XXIX. " With thee yet shall he leave, for memory
Of his late puissaunce, his ymage dead,
That living him in all activity
To thee shall represent. He, from the head
Of his coosen Constantius, without dread
Shall take the crowne that was his fathers right,
And therewith crowne himselfe in th' others stead:
Then shall he issew forth with dreadfull might
Against his Saxon foes in bloody field to fight.

XXX. " Like as a Lyon that in drowsie cave
Hath long time slept, himselfe so shall he shake;
And comming forth shall spred his banner brave

Over the troubled South, that it shall make
The warlike Mertians for feare to quake:
Thrise shall he fight with them, and twise shall win;
But the third time shall fayre accordaunce make:
And, if he then with victorie can lin,
He shall his dayes with peace bring to his earthly In.

XXXI. " His sonne, hight Vortipore, shall him succeede
In kingdome, but not in felicity:
Yet shall he long time warre with happy speed,
And with great honour many batteills try;
But at the last to th' importunity
Of froward fortune shall be forst to yield:
But his sonne Malgo shall full mightily
Avenge his fathers losse with speare and shield,
And his proud foes discomfit in victorious field.

XXXII. " Behold the man! and tell me, Britomart,
If ay more goodly creature thou didst see?
How like a Gyaunt in each manly part
Beares he himselfe with portly majestee,
That one of th' old Heroës seemes to bee!
He the six Islands, comprovinciall
In auncient times unto great Britainee,
Shall to the same reduce, and to him call
Their sondry kings to do their homage severall.

XXXIII. " All which his sonne Careticus awhile
Shall well defend, and Saxons powre suppresse:
Untill a straunger king, from unknowne soyle
Arriving, him with multitude oppresse;
Great Gormond, having with huge mightinesse
Ireland subdewd, and therein fixt his throne,
Like a swift Otter, fell through emptinesse,
Shall overswim the sea, with many one
Of his Norveyses, to assist the Britons fone.

XXXIV. " He in his furie shall overronne,
And holy Church with faithlesse handes deface,
That thy sad people, utterly fordonne,
Shall to the utmost mountaines fly apace.
Was never so great waste in any place,
Nor so fowle outrage doen by living men;

For all thy Citties they shall sacke and race,
And the greene grasse that groweth they shall bren,
That even the wilde beast shall dy in starved den.

xxxv. " Whiles thus thy Britons doe in languour pine,
Proud Etheldred shall from the North arise,
Serving th' ambitious will of Augustine,
And, passing Dee, with hardy enterprise
Shall backe repulse the valiaunt Brockwell twise,
And Bangor with massacred Martyrs fill,
But the third time shall rew his foolhardise:
For Cadwan, pittying his peoples ill,
Shall stoutly him defeat, and thousand Saxons kill.

xxxvi. " But after him, Cadwallin mightily
On his sonne Edwin all those wrongs shall wreake;
Ne shall availe the wicked sorcery
Of false Pellite his purposes to breake,
But him shall slay, and on a gallowes bleak
Shall give th' enchaunter his unhappy hire.
Then shall the Britons, late dismayd and weake,
From their long vassalage gin to respire,
And on their Paynim foes avenge their ranckled ire.

xxxvii. " Ne shall he yet his wrath so mitigate,
Till both the sonnes of Edwin he have slayne,
Offricke and Osricke, twinnes unfortunate,
Both slaine in battaile upon Layburne playne,
Together with the king of Louthiane,
Hight Adin, and the king of Orkeny,
Both joynt partakers of their fatall payne:
But Penda, fearefull of like desteny,
Shall yield him selfe his liegeman, and sweare fealty.

xxxviii. " Him shall he make his fatall Instrument
T' afflict the other Saxons unsubdewd;
He marching forth with fury insolent
Against the good king Oswald, who indewd
With heavenly powre, and by Angels reskewd,
Al holding crosses in their hands on hye,
Shall him defeate withouten blood imbrewd:
Of which that field, for endlesse memory,
Shall Hevenfield be cald to all posterity.

XXXIX. "Whereat Cadwallin wroth shall forth issew,
And an huge hoste into Northumber lead,
With which he godly Oswald shall subdew,
And crowne with martiredome his sacred head:
Whose brother Oswin, daunted with like dread,
With price of silver shall his kingdome buy;
And Penda, seeking him adowne to tread,
Shall tread adowne, and doe him fowly dye;
But shall with guifts his Lord Cadwallin pacify.

XL. "Then shall Cadwallin die; and then the raine
Of Britons eke with him attonce shall dye;
Ne shall the good Cadwallader, with paine
Or powre, be hable it to remedy,
When the full time, prefixt by destiny,
Shall be expird of Britons regiment:
For heven it selfe shall their successe envy,
And them with plagues and murrins pestilent
Consume, till all their warlike puissaunce be spent.

XLI. Yet after all these sorrowes, and huge hills
Of dying people, during eight yeares space,
Cadwallader, not yielding to his ills,
From Armoricke, where long in wretched cace
He liv'd, retourning to his native place,
Shal be by vision staide from his intent:
For th' heavens have decreëd to displace
The Britons for their sinnes dew punishment
And to the Saxons over-give their government.

XLII. "Then woe, and woe, and everlasting woe,
Be to the Briton babe that shal be borne
To live in thraldome of his fathers foe!
Late king, now captive; late lord, now forlorne;
The worlds reproch; the cruell victors scorne;
Banisht from princely bowre to wastefull wood!
O! who shal helpe me to lament and mourne
The royall seed, the antique Trojan blood,
Whose empire lenger here then ever any stood?"

XLIII. The Damzell was full deepe empassioned
Both for his griefe, and for her peoples sake,
Whose future woes so plaine he fashioned;

And, sighing sore, at length him thus bespake:
" Ah ! but will hevens fury never slake,
Nor vengeaunce huge relent it selfe at last?
Will not long misery late mercy make,
But shall their name for ever be defaste,
And quite from off the earth their memory be raste? "

XLIV. " Nay but the terme " (sayd he) " is limited,
That in this thraldome Britons shall abide;
And the just revolution measured
That they as Straungers shall be notifide:
For twise fowre hundreth yeares shal be supplide,
Ere they to former rule restor'd shal bee,
And their importune fates all satisfide:
Yet, during this their most obscuritee,
Their beames shall ofte breake forth, that men them
faire may see.

XLV. " For Rhodoricke, whose surname shal be Great,
Shall of him selfe a brave ensample shew,
That Saxon kinges his friendship shall intreat;
And Howell Dha shall goodly well indew
The salvage minds with skill of just and trew:
Then Griffyth Conan also shall upreare
His dreaded head, and the old sparkes renew
Of native corage, that his foes shall feare,
Least back againe the kingdom he from them should beare.

XLVI. " Ne shall the Saxons selves all peaceably
Enjoy the crowne, which they from Britons wonne
First ill, and after ruled wickedly;
For, ere two hundred yeares be full outronne,
There shall a Raven, far from rising Sunne,
With his wide wings upon them fiercely fly,
And bid his faithlesse chickens overronne
The fruitfull plaines, and with fell cruelty
In their avenge tread downe the victors surquedry.

XLVII. " Yet shall a third both these and thine subdew.
There shall a Lion from the sea-bord wood
Of Neustria come roring, with a crew
Of hungry whelpes, his battailous bold brood,
Whose clawes were newly dipt in cruddy blood,
That from the Daniske Tyrants head shall rend

Th' usurped crowne, as if that he were wood,
And the spoile of the countrey conquered
Emongst his young ones shall divide with bountyhed.

XLVIII. " Tho, when the terme is full accomplishid,
There shall a sparke of fire, which hath longwhile
Bene in his ashes raked up and hid,
Bee freshly kindled in the fruitfull Ile
Of Mona, where it lurked in exile;
Which shall breake forth into bright burning flame,
And reach into the house that beares the stile
Of roiall majesty and soveraine name:
So shall the Briton blood their crowne agayn reclame.

XLIX. " Thenceforth eternall union shall be made
Betweene the nations different afore,
And sacred Peace shall lovingly persuade
The warlike minds to learne her goodly lore,
And civile armes to exercise no more:
Then shall a royall Virgin raine, which shall
Stretch her white rod over the Belgicke shore,
And the great Castle smite so sore withall,
That it shall make him shake, and shortly learn to fall.

L. " But yet the end is not."—There Merlin stayd,
As overcomen of the spirites powre,
Or other ghastly spectacle dismayd,
That secretly he saw, yet note discoure:
Which suddein fitt, and halfe extatick stoure,
When the two fearefull wemen saw, they grew
Greatly confused in behaveoure.
At last, the fury past, to former hew
Hee turnd againe, and chearfull looks as earst did shew.

LI. Then, when them selves they well instructed had
Of all that needed them to be inquird,
They both, conceiving hope of comfort glad,
With lighter hearts unto their home retird;
Where they in secret counsell close conspird,
How to effect so hard an enterprize,
And to possesse the purpose they desird:
Now this, now that, twixt them they did devize,
And diverse plots did frame to maske in strange disguise.

LII. At last the Nourse in her foolhardy wit
Conceiv'd a bold devise, and thus bespake:
" Daughter, I deeme that counsel aye most fit,
That of the time doth dew advauntage take.
Ye see that good king Uther now doth make
Strong warre upon the Paynim brethren, hight
Octa and Oza, whome hee lately brake
Beside Cayr Verolame in victorious fight,
That now all Britany doth burne in armes bright.

LIII. " That, therefore, nought our passage may empeach,
Let us in feigned armes our selves disguize,
And our weake hands (need makes good schollers) teach
The dreadfull speare and shield to exercize:
Ne certes, daughter, that same warlike wize,
I weene, would you misseeme; for ye beene tall,
And large of limbe t' atchieve an hard emprize;
Ne ought ye want but skil, which practize small
Wil bring, and shortly make you a mayd Martiall.

LIV. " And, sooth, it ought your corage much inflame
To heare so often, in that royall hous,
From whence, to none inferior, ye came,
Bards tell of many wemen valorous,
Which have full many feats adventurous
Performd, in paragone of proudest men:
The bold Bunduca, whose victorious
Exployts made Rome to quake; stout Guendolen;
Renowmed Martia; and redoubted Emmilen.

LV. " And, that which more then all the rest may sway,
Late dayes ensample, which these eyes beheld:
In the last field before Menevia,
Which Uther with those forrein Pagans held,
I saw a Saxon Virgin, the which feld
Great Ulfin thrise upon the bloody playne;
And, had not Carados her hand withheld
From rash revenge, she had him surely slayne:
Yet Carados himselfe from her escapt with payne."

LVI. " Ah! read," (quoth Britomart) " how is she hight? "
" Fayre Angela " (quoth she) " men do her call,
No whit lesse fayre then terrible in fight:

She hath the leading of a Martiall
And mightie people, dreaded more then all
The other Saxons, which doe, for her sake
And love, themselves of her name *Angles* call.
Therefore, faire Infant, her ensample make
Unto thy selfe, and equall corage to thee take."

LVII. Her harty wordes so deepe into the mynd
Of the yong Damzell sunke, that great desire
Of warlike armes in her forthwith they tynd,
And generous stout courage did inspyre,
That she resolv'd, unweeting to her Syre,
Advent'rous knighthood on her selfe to don;
And counseld with her Nourse her Maides attyre
To turne into a massy habergeon,
And bad her all things put in readinesse anon.

LVIII. Th' old woman nought that needed did omit,
But all thinges did conveniently purvay.
It fortuned (so time their turne did fitt)
A band of Britons, ryding on forray
Few dayes before, had gotten a great pray
Of Saxon goods; emongst the which was seene
A goodly Armour, and full rich aray,
Which long'd to Angela, the Saxon Queene,
All fretted round with gold, and goodly wel beseene.

LIX. The same, with all the other ornaments,
King Ryence caused to be hanged hy
In his chiefe Church, for endlesse moniments
Of his successe and gladfull victory:
Of which her selfe avising readily.
In th' evening late old Glaucè thither led
Faire Britomart, and, that same Armory
Downe taking, her therein appareled
Well as she might, and with brave bauldrick garnished.

LX. Beside those armes there stood a mightie speare,
Which Bladud made by Magick art of yore,
And usd the same in batteill aye to beare;
Sith which it had beene here preserv'd in store,
For his great virtues proved long afore:
For never wight so fast in sell could sit,

But him perforce unto the ground it bore.
Both speare she tooke and shield which hong by it;
Both speare and shield of great powre, for her purpose fit.

LXI. Thus when she had the virgin all arayd,
Another harnesse which did hang thereby
About her selfe she dight, that the yong Mayd
She might in equall armes accompany,
And as her Squyre attend her carefully.
Tho to their ready Steedes they clombe full light,
And through back waies, that none might them espy,
Covered with secret cloud of silent night,
Themselves they forth convaid, and passed forward right.

LXII. Ne rested they, till that to Faery lond
They came, as Merlin them directed late:
Where, meeting with this Redcrosse Knight, she fond
Of diverse thinges discourses to dilate,
And most of Arthegall and his estate.
At last their wayes so fell, that they mote part:
Then each to other, well affectionate,
Friendship professed with unfained hart.
The Redcrosse Knight diverst, but forth rode Britomart.

CANTO IV

Bold Marinell of Britomart
Is throwne on the Rich Strond
Faire Florimell of Arthure is
Long followed, but not fond.

I. WHERE is the Antique glory now become,
That whylome wont in wemen to appeare?
Where be the brave atchievements doen by some?
Where be the batteilles, where the shield and speare,
And all the conquests which them high did reare,
That matter made for famous Poets verse,
And boastfull men so oft abasht to heare?
Beene they all dead, and laide in dolefull herse,
Or doen they onely sleepe, and shall againe reverse?

II. If they be dead, then woe is me therefore;
But if they sleepe, O let them soone awake!
For all too long I burne with envy sore
To heare the warlike feates which Homere spake
Of bold Penthesilee, which made a lake
Of Greekish blood so ofte in Trojan plaine;
But when I reade, how stout Debora strake
Proud Sisera, and how Camill' hath slaine
The huge Orsilochus, I swell with great disdaine.

III. Yet these, and all that els had puissaunce,
Cannot with noble Britomart compare,
As well for glorie of great valiaunce,
As for pure chastitee and vertue rare,
That all her goodly deedes doe well declare.
Well worthie stock, from which the branches sprong
That in late yeares so faire a blossome bare,
As thee, O Queene! the matter of my song,
Whose lignage from this Lady I derive along.

IV. Who when, through speaches with the Redcrosse Knight,
She learned had th' estate of Arthegall,
And in each point her selfe informd aright,

A friendly league of love perpetuall
She with him bound, and Congé tooke withall:
Then he forth on his journey did proceede,
To seeke adventures which mote him befall,
And win him worship through his warlike deed,
Which alwaies of his paines he made the chiefest meed.

v. But Britomart kept on her former course,
Ne ever dofte her armes, but all the way
Grew pensive through that amarous discourse,
By which the Redcrosse knight did earst display
Her lovers shape and chevalrous aray:
A thousand thoughts she fashiond in her mind,
And in her feigning fancie did pourtray
Him such as fittest she for love could find,
Wise, warlike, personable, courteous, and kind.

vi. With such selfe-pleasing thoughts her wound she fedd,
And thought so to beguile her grievous smart;
But so her smart was much more grievous bredd,
And the deepe wound more deep engord her hart,
That nought but death her dolour mote depart.
So forth she rode, without repose or rest,
Searching all lands and each remotest part,
Following the guydance of her blinded guest,
Till that to the sea-coast at length she her addrest.

vii. There she alighted from her light-foot beast,
And sitting downe upon the rocky shore,
Badd her old Squyre unlace her lofty creast:
Tho having vewd awhile the surges hore
That gainst the craggy clifts did loudly rore,
And in their raging surquedry disdaynd
That the fast earth affronted them so sore,
And their devouring covetize restraynd;
Thereat she sighed deepe, and after thus complaynd.

viii. " Huge sea of sorrow and tempestuous griefe,
Wherein my feeble barke is tossed long
Far from the hoped haven of reliefe,
Why doe thy cruell billowes beat so strong,
And thy moyst mountaines each on others throng,
Threatning to swallow up my fearefull lyfe?

O! doe thy cruell wrath and spightfull wrong
At length allay, and stint thy stormy strife,
Which in thy troubled bowels raignes and rageth ryfe.

IX. "For els my feeble vessell, crazd and crackt
Through thy strong buffets and outrageous blowes,
Cannot endure, but needes it must be wrackt
On the rough rocks, or on the sandy shallowes,
The whiles that love it steres, and fortune rowes:
Love, my lewd Pilott, hath a restlesse minde;
And fortune, Boteswaine, no assurance knowes;
But saile withouten starres against tyde and winde:
How can they other doe, sith both are bold and blinde?

X. "Thou God of windes, that raignest in the seas,
That raignest also in the Continent.
At last blow up some gentle gale of ease,
The which may bring my ship, ere it be rent,
Unto the gladsome port of her intent.
Then, when I shall my selfe in safety see,
A table, for eternall moniment
Of thy great grace and my great jeopardee,
Great Neptune, I avow to hallow unto thee!"

XI. Then sighing softly sore, and inly deepe,
She shut up all her plaint in privy griefe
For her great courage would not let her weepe,
Till that old Glaucè gan with sharpe repriefe
Her to restraine, and give her good reliefe
Through hope of those, which Merlin had her told
Should of her name and nation be chiefe,
And fetch their being from the sacred mould
Of her immortall womb, to be in heaven enrold.

XII. Thus as she her recomforted, she spyde
Where far away one, all in armour bright,
With hasty gallop towards her did ryde.
Her dolour soone she ceast, and on her dight
Her Helmet, to her Courser mounting light:
Her former sorrow into suddein wrath,
Both coosen passions of distroubled spright,
Converting, forth she beates the dusty path:
Love and despight attonce her courage kindled hath.

XIII. As, when a foggy mist hath overcast
The face of heven, and the cleare ayre engroste,
The world in darkenes dwels; till that at last
The watry Southwinde, from the seabord coste
Upblowing, doth disperse the vapour lo'ste,
And poures it selfe forth in a stormy showre:
So the fayre Britomart, having disclo'ste
Her clowdy care into a wrathfull stowre,
The mist of griefe dissolv'd did into vengeance powre.

XIV. Eftsoones, her goodly shield addressing fayre,
That mortall speare she in her hand did take,
And unto battaill did her selfe prepayre.
The knight, approching, sternely her bespake:
"Sir knight, that doest thy voyage rashly make
By this forbidden way in my despight,
Ne doest by others death ensample take,
I read thee soone retyre, whiles thou hast might,
Least afterwards it be too late to take thy flight."

XV. Ythrild with deepe disdaine of his proud threat,
She shortly thus: "Fly they, that need to fly;
Wordes fearen babes. I meane not thee entreat
To passe, but maugre thee will passe or dy."
Ne lenger stayd for th' other to reply,
But with sharpe speare the rest made dearly knowne.
Strongly the straunge knight ran, and sturdily
Strooke her full on the brest, that made her downe
Decline her head, and touch her crouper with her crown.

XVI. But she againe him in the shield did smite
With so fierce furie and great puissaunce,
That, through his three-square scuchin percing quite
And through his mayled hauberque, by mischaunce
The wicked steele through his left side did glaunce.
Him so transfixed she before her bore
Beyond his croupe, the length of all her launce;
Till, sadly soucing on the sandy shore,
He tombled on an heape, and wallowd in his gore,

XVII. Like as the sacred Oxe that carelesse stands,
With gilden hornes and flowry girlonds crownd,
Proud of his dying honor and deare bandes,

Whiles th' altars fume with frankincense arownd,
All suddeinly, with mortall stroke astownd,
Doth groveling fall, and with his streaming gore
Distaines the pillours and the holy grownd,
And the faire flowres that decked him afore:
So fell proud Marinell upon the pretious shore.

XVIII. The martiall Mayd stayd not him to lament,
But forward rode, and kept her ready way
Along the strond; which, as she over-went,
She saw bestrowed all with rich aray
Of pearles and pretious stones of great assay,
And all the gravell mixt with golden owre:
Whereat she wondred much, but would not stay
For gold, or perles, or pretious stones, an howre,
But them despised all; for all was in her powre.

XIX. Whiles thus he lay in deadly stonishment,
Tydings hereof came to his mothers eare:
His mother was the blacke-browd Cymoënt,
The daughter of great Nereus, which did beare
This warlike sonne unto an earthly peare,
The famous Dumarin; who, on a day
Finding the Nymph asleepe in secret wheare,
As he by chaunce did wander that same way,
Was taken with her love, and by her closely lay.

XX. There he this knight of her begot, whom borne
She, of his father, Marinell did name;
And in a rocky cave, as wight forlorne,
Long time she fostred up, till he became
A mighty man at armes, and mickle fame
Did get through great adventures by him donne:
For never man he suffred by that same
Rich strond to travell, whereas he did wonne,
But that he must do battail with the Sea-nymphes sonne.

XXI. An hundred knights of honorable name
He had subdew'd, and them his vassals made
That through all Faerie lond his noble fame
Now blazed was, and feare did all invade,
That none durst passen through that perilous glade:
And to advaunce his name and glory more,

Her Sea-god syre she dearely did perswade
T' endow her sonne with threasure and rich store
Bove all the sonnes that were of earthly wombes ybore.

XXII. The God did graunt his daughters deare demaund,
To doen his Nephew in all riches flow;
Eftsoones his heaped waves he did commaund
Out of their hollow bosome forth to throw
All the huge threasure, which the sea below
Had in his greedy gulfe devoured deepe,
And him enriched through the overthrow
And wreckes of many wretches, which did weepe
And often wayle their wealth, which he from them did keepe.

XXIII. Shortly upon that shore there heaped was
Exceeding riches and all pretious things,
The spoyle of all the world; that it did pas
The wealth of th' East, and pompe of Persian kings:
Gold, ambre, yvorie, perles, owches, rings,
And all that els was pretious and deare,
The sea unto him voluntary brings;
That shortly he a great Lord did appeare,
As was in all the lond of Faery, or else wheare.

XXIV. Thereto he was a doughty dreaded knight,
Tryde often to the scath of many Deare,
That none in equall armes him matchen might:
The which his mother seeing gan to feare
Least his too haughtie hardines might reare
Some hard mishap in hazard of his life.
Forthy she oft him counseld to forbeare
The bloody batteill and to stirre up strife,
But after all his warre to rest his wearie knife.

XXV. And, for his more assuraunce, she inquir'd
One day of Proteus by his mighty spell
(For Proteus was with prophecy inspir'd)
Her deare sonnes destiny to her to tell,
And the sad end of her sweet Marinell:
Who, through foresight of his eternall skill,
Bad her from womankind to keepe him well,
For of a woman he should have much ill;
A virgin straunge and stout him should dismay or kill.

XXVI. Forthy she gave him warning every day
The love of women not to entertaine;
A lesson too too hard for living clay
From love in course of nature to refraine.
Yet he his mothers lore did well retaine,
And ever from fayre Ladies love did fly;
Yet many Ladies fayre did oft complaine,
That they for love of him would algates dy:
Dy, who so list for him, he was loves enimy.

XXVII. But ah! who can deceive his destiny,
Or weene by warning to avoyd his fate?
That, when he sleepes in most security
And safest seemes, him soonest doth amate,
And findeth dew effect or soone or late;
So feeble is the powre of fleshly arme.
His mother bad him wemens love to hate,
For she of womans force did feare no harme;
So, weening to have arm'd him, she did quite disarme.

XXVIII. This was that woman, this that deadly wownd,
That Proteus prophecide should him dismay;
The which his mother vainely did expownd
To be hart-wownding love, which should assay
To bring her sonne unto his last decay.
So ticle be the termes of mortall state,
And full of subtile sophismes, which doe play
With double sences, and with false debate,
T' approve the unknowen purpose of eternall fate.

XXIX. Too trew the famous Marinell it fownd,
Who, through late triall, on that wealthy Strond
Inglorious now lies in sencelesse swownd,
Through heavy stroke of Britomartis hond.
Which when his mother deare did understond,
And heavy tidings heard, whereas she playd
Amongst her watry sisters by a pond,
Gathering sweete daffadillyes, to have made
Gay girlonds from the Sun their forheads fayr to shade;

XXX. Eftesoones both flowres and girlonds far away
Shee flong, and her faire deawy lockes yrent;
To sorrow huge she turnd her former play,

And gamesom merth to grievous dreriment:
Shee threw her selfe downe on the Continent,
Ne word did speake, but lay as in a swowne,
Whiles all her sisters did for her lament
With yelling outcries, and with shrieking sowne;
And every one did teare her girlond from her crowne.

XXXI. Soone as shee up out of her deadly fitt
Arose, shee bad her charett to be brought;
And all her sisters that with her did sitt
Bad eke attonce their charetts to be sought:
Tho, full of bitter griefe and pensife thought,
She to her wagon clombe; clombe all the rest,
And forth together went with sorrow fraught.
The waves, obedient to theyr beheast,
Them yielded ready passage, and their rage surceast.

XXXII. Great Neptune stoode amazed at their sight,
Whiles on his broad rownd backe they softly slid,
And eke him selfe mournd at their mournful plight,
Yet wist not what their wailing ment; yet did,
For great compassion of their sorrow, bid
His mighty waters to them buxome bee:
Eftesoones the roaring billowes still abid,
And all the griesly Monsters of the See
Stood gaping at their gate, and wondred them to see.

XXXIII. A teme of Dolphins raunged in aray
Drew the smooth charett of sad Cymoënt:
They were all taught by Triton to obay
To the long raynes at her commaundement:
As swifte as swallowes on the waves they went,
That their brode flaggy finnes no fome did reare
Ne bubling rowndell they behinde them sent.
The rest, of other fishes drawen weare,
Which with their finny oars the swelling sea did sheare.

XXXIV. Soone as they bene arriv'd upon the brim
Of the Rich Strond, their charets they forlore,
And let their temed fishes softly swim
Along the margent of the fomy shore,
Least they their finnes should bruze, and surbate sore
Their tender feete upon the stony grownd:

And comming to the place, where all in gore
And cruddy blood enwallowed they fownd
The lucklesse Marinell lying in deadly swownd,

XXXV. His mother swowned thrise, and the third time
Could scarce recovered bee out of her paine:
Had she not beene devoide of mortall slime,
Shee should not then have bene relyv'd againe;
But, soone as life recovered had the raine,
Shee made so piteous mone and deare wayment,
That the hard rocks could scarse from tears refraine;
And all her sister Nymphes with one consent
Supplide her sobbing breaches with sad complement.

XXXVI. "Deare image of my selfe," (she sayd) "that is
The wretched sonne of wretched mother borne,
Is this thine high advauncement? O! is this
Th' immortall name, with which thee, yet unborne,
Thy Grandsire Nereus promist to adorne?
Now lyest thou of life and honor refte;
Now lyest thou a lumpe of earth forlorne;
Ne of thy late memory is lefte,
Ne can thy irrevocable desteny bee wefte.

XXXVII. "Fond Proteus, father of false propheeis!
And they more fond that credit to thee give!
Not this the worke of womans hand ywis,
That so deepe wound through these deare members
        drive.
I feared love; but they that love doe live,
But they that dye doe nether love nor hate:
Nath'lesse to thee thy folly I forgive;
And to my selfe, and to accursed fate,
The guilt I doe ascribe: deare wisedom bought too late!

XXXVIII. "O! what availes it of immortall seed
To beene ybredd and never borne to dye?
Farre better I it deeme to die with speed
Then waste in woe and waylfull miserye:
Who dyes, the utmost dolor doth abye;
But who that lives is lefte to waile his losse:
So life is losse, and death felicity:
Sad life worse then glad death; and greater crosse
To see frends grave, then dead the grave self to engrosse.

XXXIX. " But if the heavens did his dayes envie,
And my short blis maligne, yet mote they well
Thus much afford me, ere that he did die,
That the dim eies of my deare Marinell
I mote have closed, and him bed farewell,
Sith other offices for mother meet
They would not graunt——
Yett, maulgre them, farewell, my sweetest sweet!
Farewell, my sweetest sonne, sith we no more shall
meet!"

XL. Thus when they all had sorowed their fill,
They softly gan to search his griesly wownd:
And, that they might him handle more at will,
They him disarmd; and, spredding on the grownd
Their watchet mantles frindgd with silver rownd,
They softly wipt away the gelly blood
From th' orifice; which having well upbownd,
They pourd in soveraine balme and Nectar good,
Good both for erthly med'cine and for hevenly food.

XLI. Tho when the lilly handed Liagore
(This Liagore whilome had learned skill
In leaches craft, by great Apolloes lore,
Sith her whilome upon high Pindus hill
He loved, and at last her wombe did fill
With hevenly seed, whereof wise Pæon sprong)
Did feele his pulse, shee knew there staied still
Some litle life his feeble sprites emong;
Which to his mother told, despeyre she from her flong.

XLII. Tho, up him taking in their tender hands,
They easely unto her charett beare:
Her teme at her commaundement quiet stands,
Whiles they the corse into her wagon reare,
And strowe with flowres the lamentable beare.
Then all the rest into their coches clim,
And through the brackish waves their passage sheare;
Upon great Neptunes necke they softly swim,
And to her watry chamber swiftly carry him.

XLIII. Deepe in the bottome of the sea her bowre
Is built of hollow billowes heaped hye,

Like to thicke clouds that threat a stormy showre,
And vauted all within, like to the Skye,
In which the Gods doe dwell eternally;
There they him laide in easy couch well dight,
And sent in haste for Tryphon, to apply
Salves to his wounds, and medicines of might;
For Tryphon of sea gods the soveraine leach is hight.

XLIV. The whiles the Nymphes sitt all about him rownd,
Lamenting his mishap and heavy plight;
And ofte his mother, vewing his wide wownd,
Cursed the hand that did so deadly smight
Her dearest sonne, her dearest harts delight:
But none of all those curses overtooke
The warlike Maide, th' ensample of that might;
But fairely well shee thryvd, and well did brooke
Her noble deeds, ne her right course for ought forsooke.

XLV. Yet did false Archimage her still pursew,
To bring to passe his mischievous intent,
Now that he had her singled from the crew
Of courteous knights, the Prince and Faery gent,
Whom late in chace of beauty excellent
Shee lefte, pursewing that same foster strong,
Of whose fowle outrage they impatient,
And full of firy zele, him followed long,
To reskew her from shame, and to revenge her wrong.

XLVI. Through thick and thin, through mountains and
through playns,
Those two great champions did attonce pursew
The fearefull damzell with incessant payns;
Who from them fled, as light-foot hare from vew
Of hunter swifte and scent of howndes trew.
At last they came unto a double way;
Where, doubtfull which to take, her to reskew,
Themselves they did dispart, each to assay
Whether more happy were to win so goodly pray.

XLVII. But Timias, the Princes gentle Squyre,
That Ladies love unto his Lord forlent,
And with proud envy and indignant yre
After that wicked foster fiercely went:

So beene they three three sondry wayes ybent;
But fayrest fortune to the Prince befell,
Whose chaunce it was, that sonne he did repent,
To take that way in which that Damozell
Was fledd afore, affraid of him as feend of hell.

XLVIII. At last of her far off he gained vew.
Then gan he freshly pricke his fomy steed,
And ever as he nigher to her drew,
So evermore he did increase his speed,
And of each turning still kept wary heed:
Alowd to her he oftentimes did call,
To doe away vaine doubt and needlesse dreed:
Full myld to her he spake, and oft let fall
Many meeke wordes to stay and comfort her withall.

XLIX. But nothing might relent her hasty flight,
So deepe the deadly feare of that foule swaine
Was earst impressed in her gentle spright.
Like as a fearefull Dove, which through the raine
Of the wide ayre her way does cut amaine,
Having farre off espyde a Tassell gent,
Which after her his nimble winges doth straine,
Doubleth her hast for feare to bee for-hent,
And with her pineons cleaves the liquid firmament.

L. With no lesse hast, and eke with no lesse dreed,
That fearefull Ladie fledd from him, that ment
To her no evill thought nor evill deed;
Yet former feare of being fowly shent
Carried her forward with her first intent:
And though, oft looking backward, well she vewde
Her selfe freed from that foster insolent,
And that it was a knight which now her sewde,
Yet she no lesse the knight feard then that villein rude.

LI. His uncouth shield and straunge armes her dismayd,
Whose like in Faery lond were seldom seene,
That fast she from him fledd, no lesse afrayd
Then of wilde beastes if she had chased beene:
Yet he her followd still with corage keene
So long, that now the golden Hesperus
Was mounted high in top of heaven sheene,

And warnd his other brethren joyeous
To light their blessed lamps in Joves eternall hous.

LII. All suddeinly dim wox the dampish ayre,
    And griesly shadowes covered heaven bright,
    That now with thousand starres was decked fayre:
    Which when the Prince beheld, a lothfull sight,
    And that perforce, for want of lenger light,
    He mote surceasse his suit, and lose the hope
    Of his long labour, he gan fowly wyte
    His wicked fortune that had turnd aslope,
    And cursed night that reft from him so goodly scope.

LIII. Tho, when her wayes he could no more descry,
    But to and fro at disaventure strayd;
    Like as a ship, whose Lodestar suddeinly
    Covered with cloudes her Pilott hath dismayd;
    His wearisome pursuit perforce he stayd,
    And from his loftie steed dismounting low
    Did let him forage. Downe himselfe he layd
    Upon the grassy ground to sleepe a throw:
    The cold earth was his couch, the hard steele his pillow.

LIV. But gentle Sleepe envyde him any rest:
    In stead thereof sad sorow and disdaine
    Of his hard hap did vexe his noble brest,
    And thousand Fancies bett his ydle brayne
    With their light wings, the sights of semblants vaine.
    Oft did he wish that Lady faire mote bee
    His Faery Queene, for whom he did complaine,
    Or that his Faery Queene were such as shee;
    And ever hasty Night he blamed bitterlie.

LV. " Night! thou foule Mother of annoyaunce sad,
    Sister of heavie death, and nourse of woe,
    Which wast begot in heaven, but for thy bad
    And brutish shape thrust downe to hell below,
    Where, by the grim floud of Cocytus slow,
    Thy dwelling is in Herebus black hous,
    (Black Herebus, thy husband, is the foe
    Of all the Gods,) where thou ungratious
    Halfe of thy dayes doest lead in horrour hideous.

LVI. " What had th' eternall Maker need of thee
    The world in his continuall course to keepe,
    That doest all thinges deface, ne lettest see
    The beautie of his worke?   Indeed, in sleepe
    The slouthfull body that doth love to steepe
    His lustlesse limbes, and drowne his baser mind,
    Doth praise thee oft, and oft from Stygian deepe
    Calles thee his goddesse, in his errour blind,
    And great Dame Natures handmaide chearing every
        kind.

LVII. " But well I wote, that to an heavy hart
    Thou art the roote and nourse of bitter cares,
    Breeder of new, renewer of old smarts:
    Instead of rest thou lendest rayling teares;
    Instead of sleepe thou sendest troublous feares
    And dreadfull visions, in the which alive
    The dreary image of sad death appeares:
    So from the wearie spirit thou doest drive
    Desired rest, and men of happinesse deprive.

LVIII. " Under thy mantle black there hidden lye
    Light-shonning thefte, and traiterous intent,
    Abhorred bloodshed, and vile felony,
    Shamefull deceipt, and daunger imminent,
    Fowle horror, and eke hellish dreriment:
    All these, I wote, in thy protection bee,
    And light doe shonne for feare of being shent;
    For light ylike is loth'd of them and thee;
    And all that lewdnesse love doe hate the light to see.

LIX. " For day discovers all dishonest wayes,
    And sheweth each thing as it is in deed:
    The prayses of high God he faire displayes,
    And his large bountie rightly doth areed:
    Dayes dearest children be the blessed seed
    Which darknesse shall subdue and heaven win:
    Truth is his daughter; he her first did breed
    Most sacred virgin without spot of sinne.
    Our life is day, but death with darknesse doth begin.

LX. " O! when will day then turne to me againe,
    And bring with him his long expected light?

O Titan.! hast to reare thy joyous waine;
Speed thee to spred abroad thy beames bright,
And chace away this too long lingring night;
Chace her away, from whence she came, to hell:
She, she it is, that hath me done despight:
There let her with the damned spirits dwell,
And yield her rowme to day that can it governe well."

LXI. Thus did the Prince that wearie night outweare
In restlesse anguish and unquiet paine;
And earely, ere the morrow did upreare
His deawy head out of the Ocean maine,
He up arose, as halfe in great disdaine,
And clombe unto his steed.   So forth he went
With heavy look and lumpish pace, that plaine
In him bewraid great grudge and maltalent:
His steed eke seemd t' apply his steps to his intent.

CANTO V

Prince Arthur heares of Florimell:
Three fosters Timias wound;
Belphebe findes him almost dead,
And reareth out of sownd.

I. WONDER it is to see in diverse mindes
How diversly love doth his pageaunts play,
And shewes his powre in variable kindes:
The baser wit, whose ydle thoughts alway
Are wont to cleave unto the lowly clay,
It stirreth up to sensuall desire,
And in lewd slouth to wast his carelesse day;
But in brave sprite it kindles goodly fire,
That to all high desert and honour doth aspire.

II. Ne suffereth it uncomely idlenesse
In his free thought to build her sluggish nest,
Ne suffereth it thought of ungentlenesse
Ever to creepe into his noble brest;
But to the highest and the worthiest
Lifteth it up that els would lowly fall:
It lettes not fall, it lettes it not to rest;
It lettes not scarse this Prince to breath at all,
But to his first poursuit him forward still doth call.

III. Who long time wandred through the forest wyde
To finde some issue thence; till that at last
He met a Dwarfe that seemed terrifyde
With some late perill which he hardly past,
Or other accident which him aghast;
Of whom he asked, whence he lately came,
And whither now he traveiled so fast?
For sore he swat, and, ronning through that same
Thicke forest, was bescracht and both his feet nigh lame.

IV. Panting for breath, and almost out of hart,
The Dwarfe him answerd; " Sir, ill mote I stay
To tell the same: I lately did depart

From Faery court, where I have many a day
Served a gentle Lady of great sway
And high accompt through out all Elfin land,
Who lately left the same, and tooke this way.
Her now I seeke; and if ye understand
Which way she fared hath, good Sir, tell out of hand."

v. " What mister wight," (saide he) " and how arayd? "
" Royally clad " (quoth he) " in cloth of gold,
As meetest may beseeme a noble mayd:
Her faire lockes in rich circlet be enrold,
A fayrer wight did never Sunne behold;
And on a Palfrey rydes more white then snow,
Yet she her selfe is whiter manifold.
The surest signe, whereby ye may her know,
Is that she is the fairest wight alive, I trow."

vi. " Now certes, swaine," (saide he) " such one, I weene,
Fast flying through this forest from her fo,
A foule ill-favoured foster, I have seene:
Her selfe, well as I might, I reskewd tho,
But could not stay, so fast she did foregoe,
Carried away with wings of speedy feare."
" Ah, dearest God ! " (quoth he) " that is great woe,
And wondrous ruth to all that shall it heare:
But can ye read, Sir, how I may her finde, or where? "

vii. " Perdy, me lever were to weeten that,"
(Saide he) " then ransome of the richest knight,
Or all the good that ever yet I gat:
But froward fortune, and too forward Night,
Such happinesse did, maulgre, to me spight,
And fro me reft both life and light attone.
But, Dwarfe, aread what is that Lady bright
That through this forest wandreth thus alone?
For of her errour straunge I have great ruth and mone."

viii. " That Ladie is," (quoth he) " where so she bee,
The bountiest virgin and most debonaire
That ever living eye, I weene, did see.
Lives none this day that may with her compare
In stedfast chastitie and vertue rare,
The goodly ornaments of beautie bright;

And is ycleped Florimell the fayre,
Faire Florimell belov'd of many a knight,
Yet she loves none but one, that Marinell is hight.

IX. " A Sea-nymphes sonne, that Marinell is hight,
Of my deare Dame is loved dearely well:
In other none, but him, she sets delight;
All her delight is set on Marinell,
But he sets nought at all by Florimell;
For Ladies love his mother long ygoe
Did him, they say, forwarne through sacred spell:
But fame now flies, that of a forreine foe
He is yslaine, which is the ground of all our woe.

X. " Five daies there be since he (they say) was slaine,
And fowre since Florimell the Court forwent,
And vowed never to returne againe,
Till him alive or dead she did invent.
Therefore, faire Sir, for love of knighthood gent,
And honour of trew Ladies, if ye may
By your good counsell, or bold hardiment,
Or succour her, or me direct the way,
Do one or other good, I you most humbly pray.

XI. " So may ye gaine to you full great renowme
Of all good Ladies through the worlde so wide,
And haply in her hart finde highest rowme
Of whom ye seeke to be most magnifide;
At least eternall meede shall you abide."
To whom the Prince: " Dwarfe, comfort to thee take,
For, till thou tidings learne what her betide,
I here avow thee never to forsake.
Ill weares he armes, that nill them use for Ladies sake."

XII. So with the Dwarfe he back retourn'd againe,
To seeke his Lady where he mote her finde;
But by the way he greatly gan complaine
The want of his good Squire late lefte behinde,
For whom he wondrous pensive grew in minde,
For doubt of daunger which mote him betide;
For him he loved above all mankinde,
Having him trew and faithfull ever tride,
And bold, as ever Squyre that waited by knights side:

XIII. Who all this while full hardly was assayd
    Of deadly daunger, which to him betidd;
    For, whiles his Lord pursewd that noble Mayd,
    After that foster fowle he fiercely ridd
    To bene avenged of the shame he did
    To that faire Damzell: Him he chaced long
    Through the thicke woods wherein he would have hid
    His shamefull head from his avengement strong,
    And oft him threatned death for his outrageous wrong.

XIV. Nathlesse the villein sped himselfe so well,
    Whether through swiftnesse of his speedie beast,
    Or knowledge of those woods where he did dwell,
    That shortly he from daunger was releast,
    And out of sight escaped at the least:
    Yet not escaped from the dew reward
    Of his bad deedes, which daily he increast,
    Ne ceased not, till him oppressed hard
    The heavie plague that for such leachours is prepard.

XV. For soone as he was vanisht out of sight,
    His coward courage gan emboldned bee,
    And cast t' avenge him of that fowle despight
    Which he had borne of his bold enimee:
    Tho to his brethren came, for they were three
    Ungratious children of one gracelesse syre,
    And unto them complayned how that he
    Had used beene of that foolehardie Squyre:
    So them with bitter words he stird to bloodie yre.

XVI. Forthwith themselves with their sad instruments
    Of spoyle and murder they gan arme bylive,
    And with him foorth into the forest went
    To wreake the wrath, which he did earst revive
    In their sterne brests, on him which late did drive
    Their brother to reproch and shamefull flight;
    For they had vow'd that never he alive
    Out of that forest should escape their might:
    Vile rancour their rude harts had fild with such despight.

XVII. Within that wood there was a covert glade,
    Foreby a narrow foord, to them well knowne,
    Through which it was uneath for wight to wade;

And now by fortune it was overflowne.
By that same way they knew that Squyre unknowne
Mote algates passe: forthy themselves they set
There in await with thicke woods overgrowne,
And all the while their malice they did whet
With cruell threats his passage through the ford to let.

XVIII. It fortuned, as they devised had:
The gentle Squyre came ryding that same way,
Unweeting of their wile and treason bad,
And through the ford to passen did assay;
But that fierce foster, which late fled away,
Stoutly foorth stepping on the further shore,
Him boldly bad his passage there to stay,
Till he had made amends, and full restore
For all the damage which he had him doen afore.

XIX. With that at him a quiv'ring dart he threw,
With so fell force, and villeinous despite,
That through his haberjeon the forkehead flew,
And through the linked mayles empierced quite,
But had no powre in his soft flesh to bite.
That stroke the hardy Squire did sore displease,
But more that him he could not come to smite;
For by no meanes the high banke he could sease,
But labour'd long in that deepe ford with vaine disease.

XX. And still the foster with his long bore-speare
Him kept from landing at his wished will.
Anone one sent out of the thicket neare
A cruell shaft, headed with deadly ill,
And fethered with an unlucky quill:
The wicked steele stayd not till it did light
In his left thigh, and deepely did it thrill:
Exceeding griefe that wound in him empight,
But more that with his foes he could not come to fight.

XXI. At last, through wrath and vengeaunce making way,
He on the bancke arryvd with mickle payne,
Where the third brother him did sore assay,
And drove at him with all his might and mayne
A forest-bill, which both his hands did strayne;
But warily he did avoide the blow,

And with his speare requited him againe,
That both his sides were thrilled with the throw,
And a large streame of blood out of the wound did flow.

XXII. He, tombling downe, with gnashing teeth did bite
The bitter earth, and bad to lett him in
Into the balefull house of endlesse night,
Where wicked ghosts doe waile their former sin.
Tho gan the battaile freshly to begin;
For nathemore for that spectacle bad
Did th' other two their cruell vengeaunce blin,
But both attonce on both sides him bestad,
And load upon him layd his life for to have had.

XXIII. Tho when that villayn he aviz'd, which late
Affrighted had the fairest Florimell,
Full of fiers fury and indignant hate
To him he turned, and with rigor fell
Smote him so rudely on the Pannikell,
That to the chin he clefte his head in twaine.
Downe on the ground his carkas groveling fell:
His sinfull sowle with desperate disdaine
Out of her fleshly ferme fled to the place of paine.

XXIV. That seeing, now the only last of three
Who with that wicked shafte him wounded had,
Trembling with horror, as that did foresee
The fearefull end of his avengement sad,
Through which he follow should his brethren bad,
His bootelesse bow in feeble hand upcaught,
And therewith shott an arrow at the lad;
Which, fayntly fluttering, scarce his helmet raught,
And glauncing fel to ground, but him annoyed naught.

XXV. With that he would have fled into the wood;
But Timias him lightly overhent,
Right as he entring was into the flood,
And strooke at him with force so violent,
That headlesse him into the foord he sent:
The carcas with the streame was carried downe.
But th' head fell backeward on the Continent;
So mischief fel upon the meaners crowne.
They three be dead with shame, the Squire lives with
    renowne.

XXVI. He lives, but takes small joy of his renowne;
　　　For of that cruell wound he bled so sore,
　　　That from his steed he fell in deadly swowne:
　　　Yet still the blood forth gusht in so great store,
　　　That he lay wallowd all in his owne gore.
　　　Now God thee keepe, thou gentlest squire alive,
　　　Els shall thy loving Lord thee see no more;
　　　But both of comfort him thou shalt deprive,
　　　And eke thy selfe of honor which thou didst atchive.

XXVII. Providence hevenly passeth living thought,
　　　And doth for wretched mens reliefe make way;
　　　For loe! great grace or fortune thither brought
　　　Comfort to him that comfortlesse now lay.
　　　In those same woods ye well remember may
　　　How that a noble hunteresse did wonne,
　　　Shee, that base Braggadochio did affray,
　　　And make him fast out of the forest ronne;
　　　Belphœbe was her name, as faire as Phœbus sunne.

XXVIII. She on a day, as shee pursewd the chace
　　　Of some wilde beast, which with her arrowes keene
　　　She wounded had, the same along did trace
　　　By tract of blood, which she had freshly seene
　　　To have besprinckled all the grassy greene:
　　　By the great persue which she there perceav'd,
　　　Well hoped shee the beast engor'd had beene,
　　　And made more haste the life to have bereav'd;
　　　But ah! her expectation greatly was deceav'd.

XXIX. Shortly she came whereas that wofull Squire,
　　　With blood deformed, lay in deadly swownd;
　　　In whose faire eyes, like lamps of quenched fire,
　　　The Christall humor stood congealed rownd;
　　　His locks, like faded leaves fallen to grownd,
　　　Knotted with blood in bounches rudely ran;
　　　And his sweete lips, on which before that stownd
　　　The bud of youth to blossome faire began,
　　　Spoild of their rosy red were woxen pale and wan.

XXX. Saw never living eie more heavy sight,
　　　That could have made a rocke of stone to rew,
　　　Or rive in twaine: which when that Lady bright,

Besides all hope, with melting eies did vew,
All suddeinly abasht shee chaunged hew,
And with sterne horror backward gan to start;
But when shee better him beheld shee grew
Full of soft passion and unwonted smart:
The point of pity perced through her tender hart.

XXXI. Meekely shee bowed downe, to weete if life
Yett in his frosen members did remaine;
And, feeling by his pulses beating rife
That the weake sowle her seat did yett retaine,
She cast to comfort him with busie paine.
His double folded necke she reard upright,
And rubd his temples and each trembling vaine;
His mayled haberjeon she did undight,
And from his head his heavy burganet did light.

XXXII. Into the woods thenceforth in haste shee went,
To seeke for hearbes that mote him remedy;
For shee of herbes had great intendiment,
Taught of the Nymphe which from her infancy
Her nourced had in trew Nobility:
There, whether yt divine Tobacco were,
Or Panachæa, or Polygony,
Shee fownd, and brought it to her patient deare,
Who al this while lay bleeding out his hartblood neare.

XXXIII. The soveraine weede betwixt two marbles plaine
Shee pownded small, and did in peeces bruze;
And then atweene her lilly handes twaine
Into his wound the juice thereof did scruze;
And round about, as she could well it uze,
The flesh therewith shee suppled and did steepe,
T' abate all spasme, and soke the swelling bruze;
And, after having searcht the intuse deepe,
She with her scarf did bind the wound from cold to
keepe.

XXXIV. By this he had sweet life recur'd agayne,
And, groning inly deepe, at last his eies,
His watry eies drizling like deawy rayne,
He up gan lifte toward the azure skies,
From whence descend all hopelesse remedies:
Therewith he sigh'd; and, turning him aside,

Still whenas he beheld the heavenly Mayd,
Whiles dayly playsters to his wownd she layd,
So still his Malady the more increast,
The whiles her matchlesse beautie him dismayd.
Ah God! what other could he do at least,
But love so fayre a Lady that his life releast?

XLIV. Long while he strove in his corageous brest
With reason dew the passion to subdew,
And love for to dislodge out of his nest:
Still when her excellencies he did vew,
Her soveraine bountie and celestiall hew,
The same to love he strongly was constraynd;
But when his meane estate he did revew,
He from such hardy boldnesse was restraynd,
And of his lucklesse lott and cruell love thus playnd:

XLV. "Unthankfull wretch," (said he) "is this the meed,
With which her soverain mercy thou doest quight?
Thy life she saved by her gratious deed;
But thou doest weene with villeinous despight
To blott her honour, and her heavenly light.
Dye rather, dye, then so disloyally
Deeme of her high desert, or seeme so light:
Fayre death it is, to shonne more shame, to dy:
Dye rather, dy, then ever love disloyally.

XLVI. "But if to love disloyalty it bee,
Shall I then hate her that from deathes dore
Me brought? ah, farre be such reproch fro mee!
What can I lesse doe then her love therefore,
Sith I her dew reward cannot restore?
Dye rather, dye, and dying doe her serve;
Dying her serve, and living her adore;
Thy life she gave, thy life she doth deserve:
Dye rather, dye, then ever from her service swerve.

XLVII. "But, foolish boy, what bootes thy service bace
To her to whom the hevens doe serve and sew?
Thou, a meane Squyre of meeke and lowly place;
She, hevenly borne and of celestiall hew.
How then? of all love taketh equall vew;
And doth not highest God vouchsafe to take

The love and service of the basest crew?
If she will not, dye meekly for her sake:
Dye rather, dye, then ever so faire love forsake!"

XLVIII. Thus warreid he long time against his will;
Till that through weaknesse he was forst at last
To yield himselfe unto the mightie ill,
Which, as a victour proud, gan ransack fast
His inward partes, and all his entrayles wast,
That neither blood in face nor life in hart
It left, but both did quite drye up and blast;
As percing levin, which the inner part
Of every thing consumes, and calcineth by art.

XLIX. Which seeing fayre Belphœbe gan to feare,
Least that his wound were inly well not heald,
Or that the wicked steele empoysned were:
Litle shee weend that love he close conceald.
Yet still he wasted, as the snow congeald
When the bright sunne his beames theron doth beat:
Yet never he his hart to her reveald;
But rather chose to dye for sorow great,
Then with dishonorable termes her to entreat.

L. She, gracious Lady, yet no paines did spare
To doe him ease, or doe him remedy.
Many Restoratives of vertues rare,
And costly Cordialles she did apply,
To mitigate his stubborne malady:
But that sweet Cordiall, which can restore
A love-sick hart, she did to him envy;
To him, and to all th' unworthy world forlore
She did envy that soveraine salve in secret store.

LI. That daintie Rose, the daughter of her Morne,
More deare then life she tendered, whose flowre
The girlond of her honour did adorne:
Ne suffred she the Middayes scorching powre,
Ne the sharp Northerne wind thereon to showre;
But lapped up her silken leaves most chayre,
When so the froward skye began to lowre;
But, soone as calmed was the christall ayre,
She did it fayre dispred and let to florish fayre.

LII. Eternall God, in his almightie powre,
　　To make ensample of his heavenly grace,
　　In Paradize whylome did plant this flowre;
　　Whence he it fetcht out of her native place,
　　And did in stocke of earthly flesh enrace,
　　That mortall men her glory should admyre.
　　In gentle Ladies breste and bounteous race
　　Of woman kind it fayrest Flowre doth spyre,
　　And beareth fruit of honour and all chast desyre.

LIII. Fayre ympes of beautie, whose bright shining beames
　　Adorne the world with like to heavenly light,
　　And to your willes both royalties and Reames
　　Subdew, through conquest of your wondrous might,
　　With this fayre flowre your goodly girlonds dight
　　Of chastity and vertue virginall,
　　That shall embellish more your beautie bright,
　　And crowne your heades with heavenly coronall,
　　Such as the Angels weare before Gods tribunall!

LIV. To your faire selves a faire ensample frame
　　Of this faire virgin, this Belphebe fayre;
　　To whom, in perfect love and spotlesse fame
　　Of chastitie, none living may compayre:
　　Ne poysnous Envy justly can empayre
　　The prayse of her fresh flowring Maydenhead;
　　Forthy she standeth on the highest stayre
　　Of th' honorable stage of womanhead,
　　That Ladies all may follow her ensample dead.

LV. In so great prayse of stedfast chastity
　　Nathlesse she was so courteous and kynde,
　　Tempred with grace and goodly modesty,
　　That seemed those two vertues strove to fynd
　　The higher place in her Heroick mynd:
　　So striving each did other more augment,
　　And both encreast the prayse of woman kynde,
　　And both encreast her beautie excellent:
　　So all did make in her a perfect complement.

CANTO VI

The birth of fayre Belphœbe and
Of Amorett is told:
The Gardins of Adonis fraught
With pleasures manifold.

I. WELL may I weene, faire Ladies, all this while
Ye wonder how this noble Damozell
So great perfections did in her compile,
Sith that in salvage forests she did dwell,
So farre from court and royall Citadell,
The great schoolmaistresse of all courtesy:
Seemeth that such wilde woodes should far expell
All civile usage and gentility,
And gentle sprite deforme with rude rusticity.

II. But to this faire Belphœbe in her berth
The hevens so favorable were and free,
Looking with myld aspect upon the earth
In th' Horoscope of her nativitee,
That all the gifts of grace and chastitee
On her they poured forth of plenteous horne:
Jove laught on Venus from his soverayne see,
And Phœbus with faire beames did her adorne,
And all the Graces rockt her cradle being borne.

III. Her berth was of the wombe of Morning dew,
And her conception of the joyous Prime;
And all her whole creation did her shew
Pure and unspotted from all loathly crime
That is ingenerate in fleshly slime.
So was this virgin borne, so was she bred;
So was she trayned up from time to time
In all chaste vertue and true bounti-hed,
Till to her dew perfection she were ripened.

IV. Her mother was the faire Chrysogonee,
The daughter of Amphisa, who by race
A Faerie was, yborne of high degree.

She bore Belphœbe; she bore in like cace
Fayre Amoretta in the second place:
These two were twinnes, and twixt them two did share
The heritage of all celestiall grace;
That all the rest it seemd they robbed bare
Of bounty, and of beautie, and all vertues rare.

v. It were a goodly storie to declare
By what straunge accident faire Chrysogone
Conceiv'd these infants, and how them she bare
In this wilde forrest wandring all alone,
After she had nine moneths fulfild and gone:
For not as other wemens commune brood
They were enwombed in the sacred throne
Of her chaste bodie; nor with commune food,
As other wemens babes, they sucked vitall blood:

vi. But wondrously they were begot and bred
Through influence of th' hevens fruitfull ray.
As it in antique bookes is mentioned.
It was upon a Sommers shinie day,
When Titan faire his beames did display,
In a fresh fountaine, far from all mens vew,
She bath'd her brest the boyling heat t' allay;
She bath'd with roses red and violets blew,
And all the sweetest flowers that in the forrest grew:

vii. Till faint through yrksome wearines, adowne
Upon the grassy ground her selfe she layd
To sleepe, the whiles a gentle slombring swowne
Upon her fell, all naked bare displayd.
The sunbeames bright upon her body playd,
Being through former bathing mollifide,
And pierst into her wombe, where they embayd
With so sweete sence and secret powre unspide,
That in her pregnant flesh they shortly fructifide.

viii. Miraculous may seeme to him that reades
So straunge ensample of conception;
But reason teacheth that the fruitfull seades
Of all things living, through impression
Of the sunbeames in moyst complexion,
Doe life conceive and quickned are by kynd:

So, after Nilus inundation,
Infinite shapes of creatures men doe fynd
Informed in the mud on which the Sunne hath shynd.

ix. Great father he of generation
Is rightly cald, th' authour of life and light;
And his faire sister for creation
Ministreth matter fit, which, tempred right
With heate and humour, breedes the living wight.
So sprong these twinnes in womb of Chrysogone;
Yet wist she nought thereof, but sore affright,
Wondred to see her belly so upblone,
Which still increast till she her terme had full outgone.

x. Whereof conceiving shame and foule disgrace,
Albe her guiltlesse conscience her cleard,
She fled into the wildernesse a space,
Till that unweeldy burden she had reard,
And shund dishonor which as death she feard:
Where, wearie of long traveill, downe to rest
Her selfe she set, and comfortably cheard:
There a sad cloud of sleepe her overkest,
And seized every sence with sorrow sore opprest.

xi. It fortuned, faire Venus having lost
Her little sonne, the winged god of love,
Who, for some light displeasure which him crost,
Was from her fled as flit as ayery Dove,
And left her blisfull bowre of joy above:
(So from her often he had fled away,
When she for ought him sharpely did reprove,
And wandred in the world in straunge aray,
Disguiz'd in thousand shapes, that none might him bewray.)

xii. Him for to seeke, she left her heavenly hous,
The house of goodly formes and faire aspect,
Whence all the world derives the glorious
Features of beautie, and all shapes select,
With which high God his workmanship hath deckt;
And searched everie way through which his wings
Had borne him, or his tract she mote detect:
She promist kisses sweet, and sweeter things,
Unto the man that of him tydings to her brings.

XIII. First she him sought in Court, where most he us'd
Whylome to haunt, but there she found him not;
But many there she found which sore accus'd
His falshood, and with fowle infamous blot
His cruell deedes and wicked wyles did spot:
Ladies and Lordes she everywhere mote heare
Complayning, how with his empoysned shot
Their wofull harts he wounded had whyleare
And so had left them languishing twixt hope and feare.

XIV. She then the Cities sought from gate to gate,
And everie one did aske, did he him see?
And everie one her answerd, that too late
He had him seene, and felt the crueltee
Of his sharpe dartes and whot artilleree:
And every one threw forth reproches rife
Of his mischievous deedes, and sayd that hee
Was the disturber of all civill life,
The enimy of peace, and authour of all strife.

XV. Then in the countrey she abroad him sought,
And in the rurall cottages inquir'd;
Where also many plaintes to her were brought,
How he their heedelesse harts with love had fir'd,
And his false venim through their veines inspir'd:
And eke the gentle Shepheard swaynes, which sat
Keeping their fleecy flockes as they were hyr'd,
She sweetly heard complaine, both how and what
Her sonne had to them doen; yet she did smile thereat.

XVI. But when in none of all these she him got,
She gan avize where els he mote him hyde:
At last she her bethought that she had not
Yet sought the salvage woods and forests wyde,
In which full many lovely Nymphes abyde;
Mongst whom might be that he did closely lye,
Or that the love of some of them him tyde:
Forthy she thither cast her course t' apply,
To search the secret haunts of Dianes company.

XVII. Shortly unto the wastefull woods she came,
Whereas she found the Goddesse with her crew,
After late chace of their embrewed game,

Sitting beside a fountaine in a rew;
Some of them washing with the liquid dew
From off their dainty limbs the dusty sweat
And soyle, which did deforme their lively hew;
Others lay shaded from the scorching heat,
The rest upon her person gave attendance great.

XVIII. She, having hong upon a bough on high
Her bow and painted quiver, had unlaste
Her silver buskins from her nimble thigh,
And her lanck loynes ungirt, and brests unbraste,
After her heat the breathing cold to taste:
Her golden lockes, that late in tresses bright
Embreaded were for hindring of her haste,
Now loose about her shoulders hong undight,
And were with sweet Ambrosia all besprinckled light.

XIX. Soone as she Venus saw behinde her backe,
She was asham'd to be so loose surpriz'd;
And woxe halfe wroth against her damzels slacke,
That had not her thereof before aviz'd,
But suffred her so carelessly disguiz'd
Be overtaken. Soone her garments loose
Upgath'ring, in her bosome she compriz'd
Well as she might, and to the Goddesse rose;
Whiles all her Nymphes did like a girlond her enclose.

XX. Goodly she gan faire Cytherea greet,
And shortly asked her, what cause her brought
Into that wildernesse for her unmeet,
From her sweete bowres, and beds with pleasures fraught?
That suddein chaunge she straunge adventure thought.
To whom halfe weeping she thus answered;
That she her dearest sonne Cupido sought,
Who in his frowardnes from her was fled,
That she repented sore to have him angered.

XXI. Thereat Diana gan to smile, in scorne
Of her vaine playnt, and to her scoffing sayd:
" Great pitty sure that ye be so forlorne
Of your gay sonne, that gives ye so good ayd
To your disports: ill mote ye bene apayd."
But she was more engrieved, and replide;

"Faire sister, ill beseemes it to upbrayd
A dolefull heart with so disdainfull pride:
The like that mine may be your paine another tide.

XXII. "As you in woods and wanton wildernesse
Your glory sett to chace the salvage beasts,
So my delight is all in joyfulnesse,
In beds, in bowres, in banckets, and in feasts:
And ill becomes you, with your lofty creasts,
To scorne the joy that Jove is glad to seeke:
We both are bownd to follow heavens beheasts,
And tend our charges with obeisaunce meeke.
Spare, gentle sister, with reproch my paine to eeke;

XXIII. "And tell me, if that ye my sonne have heard
To lurke emongst your Nimphes in secret wize,
Or keepe their cabins: much I am affeard
Least he like one of them him selfe disguize,
And turne his arrowes to their exercize.
So may he long him selfe full easie hide;
For he is faire and fresh in face and guize
As any Nimphe; (let not it be envide.")
So saying, every Nimph full narrowly shee eide.

XXIV. But Phœbe therewith sore was angered,
And sharply saide: "Goe, Dame; goe, seeke your boy,
Where you him lately lefte, in Mars his bed:
He comes not here; we scorne his foolish joy,
Ne lend we leisure to his idle toy:
But if I catch him in this company,
By Stygian lake I vow, whose sad annoy
The Gods doe dread, he dearly shall abye:
Ile clip his wanton wings, that he no more shall flye."

XXV. Whom whenas Venus saw so sore displeasd,
Shee inly sory was, and gan relent
What shee had said; so her she soone appeasd
With sugred words and gentle blandishment,
Which as a fountaine from her sweete lips went.
And welled goodly forth, that in short space
She was well pleasd, and forth her damzells sent
Through all the woods, to search from place to place,
If any tract of him or tidings they mote trace.

XXVI. To search the God of love her Nimphes she sent
     Throughout the wandring forest every where:
     And after them her selfe eke with her went
     To seeke the fugitive both farre and nere.
     So long they sought, till they arrived were
     In that same shady covert whereas lay
     Faire Crysogone in slombry traunce whilere;
     Who in her sleepe (a wondrous thing to say)
     Unwares had borne two babes, as faire as springing day.

XXVII. Unwares she them conceivd, unwares she bore:
      She bore withouten paine, that she conceiv'd
      Withouten pleasure; ne her need implore
      Lucinaes aide: which when they both perceiv'd,
      They were through wonder nigh of sence berev'd,
      And gazing each on other nought bespake.
      At last they both agreed her seeming griev'd
      Out of her heavie swowne not to awake
      But from her loving side the tender babes to take.

XXVIII. Up they them tooke; each one a babe uptooke,
       And with them carried to be fostered.
       Dame Phœbe to a Nymphe her babe betooke
       To be brought up in perfect Maydenhed,
       And, of her selfe, her name Belphœbe red:
       But Venus hers thence far away convayd,
       To be upbrought in goodly womanhed;
       And, in her litle loves stead, which was strayd,
       Her Amoretta cald, to comfort her dismayd.

XXIX. Shee brought her to her joyous Paradize,
      Wher most she wonnes when she on earth does dwell;
      So faire a place as Nature can devize:
      Whether in Paphos, or Cytheron hill,
      Or it in Gnidus bee, I wote not well;
      But well I wote by triall, that this same
      All other pleasaunt places doth excell,
      And called is by her lost lovers name,
      The Gardin of Adonis, far renowmd by fame.

XXX. In that same Gardin all the goodly flowres,
     Wherewith dame Nature doth her beautify,
     And decks the girlonds of her Paramoures,

Are fetcht: there is the first seminary
Of all things that are borne to live and dye,
According to their kynds. Long worke it were
Here to account the endlesse progeny
Of all the weeds that bud and blossome there;
But so much as doth need must needs be counted here.

XXXI. It sited was in fruitfull soyle of old,
And girt in with two walls on either side;
The one of yron, the other of bright gold,
That none might thorough breake, nor overstride:
And double gates it had which opened wide,
By which both in and out men moten pas:
Th' one faire and fresh, the other old and dride.
Old Genius the porter of them was,
Old Genius, the which a double nature has.

XXXII. He letteth in, he letteth out to wend
All that to come into the world desire:
A thousand thousand naked babes attend
About him day and night, which doe require
That he with fleshly weeds would them attire:
Such as him list, such as eternall fate
Ordained hath, he clothes with sinfull mire,
And sendeth forth to live in mortall state,
Till they agayn returne backe by the hinder gate.

XXXIII. After that they againe retourned beene,
They in that Gardin planted bee agayne,
And grow afresh, as they had never seene
Fleshly corruption, nor mortall payne.
Some thousand yeares so doen they there remayne,
And then of him are clad with other hew,
Or sent into the chaungefull world agayne,
Till thither they retourne where first they grew:
So, like a wheele, arownd they ronne from old to new.

XXXIV. Ne needs there Gardiner to sett or sow,
To plant or prune; for of their owne accord
All things, as they created were, doe grow,
And yet remember well the mighty word
Which first was spoken by th' Almighty Lord,
That bad them to increase and multiply:

Ne doe they need with water of the ford,
Or of the clouds, to moysten their roots dry;
For in themselves eternall moisture they imply.

XXXV. Infinite shapes of creatures there are bred,
And uncouth formes, which none yet ever knew:
And every sort is in a sondry bed
Sett by it selfe, and ranckt in comely rew;
Some fitt for reasonable sowles t' indew;
Some made for beasts, some made for birds to weare;
And all the fruitfull spawne of fishes hew
In endlesse rancks along enraunged were,
That seemd the Ocean could not containe them there.

XXXVI. Daily they grow, and daily forth are sent
Into the world, it to replenish more;
Yet is the stocke not lessened nor spent,
But still remaines in everlasting store,
As it at first created was of yore:
For in the wide wombe of the world there lyes,
In hatefull darknes and in deepe horrore,
An huge eternall Chaos, which supplyes
The substaunces of natures fruitful progenyes.

XXXVII. All things from thence doe their first being fetch,
And borrow matter whereof they are made;
Which, whenas forme and feature it does ketch,
Becomes a body, and doth then invade
The state of life out of the griesly shade.
That substaunce is eterne, and bideth so;
Ne when the life decayes and forme does fade,
Doth it consume and into nothing goe,
But chaunged is, and often altred to and froe.

XXXVIII. The substaunce is not chaungd nor altered,
But th' only forme and outward fashion;
For every substaunce is conditioned
To chaunge her hew, and sondry formes to don,
Meet for her temper and complexion:
For formes are variable, and decay
By course of kinde and by occasion;
And that faire flowre of beautie fades away,
As doth the lilly fresh before the sunny ray.

I   O

XXXIX. Great enimy to it, and to all the rest
        That in the Gardin of Adonis springs,
        Is wicked Tyme; who with his scyth addrest
        Does mow the flowring herbes and goodly things,
        And all their glory to the ground downe flings,
        Where they do wither, and are fowly mard:
        He flyes about, and with his flaggy winges
        Beates downe both leaves and buds without regard,
        Ne ever pitty may relent his malice hard.

   XL. Yet pitty often did the gods relent,
        To see so faire thinges mard and spoiled quight;
        And their great mother Venus did lament
        The losse of her deare brood, her deare delight:
        Her hart was pierst with pitty at the sight,
        When walking through the Gardin them she saw,
        Yet no'te she find redresse for such despight:
        For all that lives is subject to that law;
        All things decay in time, and to their end doe draw.

  XLI. But were it not that Time their troubler is,
        All that in this delightfull Gardin growes
        Should happy bee, and have immortall blis:
        For here all plenty and all pleasure flowes;
        And sweete love gentle fitts emongst them throwes,
        Without fell rancor or fond gealosy.
        Franckly each Paramor his leman knowes,
        Each bird his mate; ne any does envy
        Their goodly meriment and gay felicity.

 XLII. There is continuall Spring, and harvest there
        Continuall, both meeting at one tyme;
        For both the boughes doe laughing blossoms beare,
        And with fresh colours decke the wanton Pryme,
        And eke attonce the heavy trees they clyme,
        Which seeme to labour under their fruites lode:
        The whiles the joyous birdes make their pastyme
        Emongst the shady leaves, their sweet abode,
        And their trew loves without suspition tell abrode.

XLIII. Right in the middest of that Paradise
        There stood a stately Mount, on whose round top
        A gloomy grove of mirtle trees did rise,

Whose shady boughes sharp steele did never lop,
Nor wicked beastes their tender buds did crop,
But like a girlond compassed the hight;
And from their fruitfull sydes sweet gum did drop,
That all the ground, with pretious deaw bedight,
Threw forth most dainty odours and most sweet delight.

XLIV. And in the thickest covert of that shade
There was a pleasaunt Arber, not by art
But of the trees owne inclination made,
Which knitting their rancke braunches, part to part,
With wanton yvie twine entrayld athwart,
And Eglantine and Caprifole emong,
Fashiond above within their inmost part,
That nether Phœbus beams could through them throng,
Nor Aeolus sharp blast could worke them any wrong.

XLV. And all about grew every sort of flowre,
To which sad lovers were transformde of yore;
Fresh Hyacinthus, Phœbus paramoure
And dearest love;
Foolish Narcisse, that likes the watry shore;
Sad Amaranthus, made a flowre but late,
Sad Amaranthus, in whose purple gore
Me seemes I see Amintas wretched fate,
To whom sweete Poets verse hath given endlesse date.

XLVI. There wont fayre Venus often to enjoy
Her deare Adonis joyous company,
And reape sweet pleasure of the wanton boy:
There yet, some say, in secret he does ly,
Lapped in flowres and pretious spycery,
By her hid from the world, and from the skill.
Of Stygian Gods, which doe her love envy;
But she her selfe, when ever that she will,
Possesseth him, and of his sweetnesse takes her fill.

XLVII. And sooth, it seemes, they say; for he may not
For ever dye, and ever buried bee
In balefull night, where all thinges are forgot:
All be he subject to mortalitie,
Yet is eterne in mutabilitie,
And by succession made perpetuall,

Transformed oft, and chaunged diverslie;
For him the Father of all formes they call:
Therfore needs mote he live, that living gives to all.

XLVIII. There now he liveth in eternall blis,
Joying his goddesse, and of her enjoyd;
Ne feareth he henceforth that foe of his,
Which with his cruell tuske him deadly cloyd:
For that wilde Bore, the which him once annoyd,
She firmely hath emprisoned for ay,
That her sweet love his malice mote avoyd,
In a strong rocky Cave, which is, they say,
Hewen underneath that Mount, that none him losen may.

XLIX. There now he lives in everlasting joy,
With many of the Gods in company
Which thither haunt, and with the winged boy,
Sporting him selfe in safe felicity:
Who when he hath with spoiles and cruelty
Ransackt the world, and in the wofull harts
Of many wretches set his triumphes hye,
Thither resortes, and, laying his sad dartes
Asyde, with faire Adonis playes his wanton partes.

L. And his trew love faire Psyche with him playes,
Fayre Psyche to him lately reconcyld,
After long troubles and unmeet upbrayes
With which his mother Venus her revyld,
And eke himselfe her cruelly exyld:
But now in stedfast love and happy state
She with him lives, and hath him borne a chyld,
Pleasure, that doth both gods and men aggrate,
Pleasure, the daughter of Cupid and Psyche late.

LI. Hither great Venus brought this infant fayre
The yonger daughter of Chrysogonee,
And unto Psyche with great trust and care
Committed her, yfostered to bee
And trained up in trew feminitee:
Who no lesse carefully her tendered
Then her owne daughter Pleasure, to whom shee
Made her companion, and her lessoned
In all the lore of love, and goodly womanhead.

LII. In which when she to perfect ripenes grew,
Of grace and beautie noble Paragone,
She brought her forth into the worldes vew,
To be th' ensample of true love alone,
And Lodestarre of all chaste affection
To all fayre Ladies that doe live on grownd.
To Faery court she came; where many one
Admyrd her goodly haveour, and fownd
His feeble hart wide launched with loves cruel wownd.

LIII. But she to none of them her love did cast,
Save to the noble knight Sir Scudamore,
To whom her loving hart she linked fast
In faithfull love, t' abide for evermore;
And for his dearest sake endured sore
Sore trouble of an hainous enimy,
Who her would forced have to have forlore
Her former love and stedfast loialty,
As ye may elswhere reade that ruefull history.

LIV. But well I weene, ye first desire to learne
What end unto that fearefull Damozell,
Which fledd so fast from that same foster stearne
Whom with his brethren Timias slew, befell:
That was, to weet, the goodly Florimell;
Who wandring for to seeke her lover deare,
Her lover deare, her dearest Marinell,
Into misfortune fell, as ye did heare,
And from Prince Arthure fled with wings of idle feare.

CANTO VII

The witches sonne loves Florimell:
She flyes; he faines to dy.
Satyrane saves the Squyre of Dames
From Gyaunts tyranny.

I. LIKE as an Hynd forth singled from the heard,
That hath escaped from a ravenous beast,
Yet flyes away of her owne feete afeard,
And every leafe, that shaketh with the least
Murmure of winde, her terror hath encreast;
So fledd fayre Florimell from her vaine feare,
Long after she from perill was releast:
Each shade she saw, and each noyse she did heare,
Did seeme to be the same which she escapt whileare.

II. All that same evening she in flying spent,
And all that night her course continewed;
Ne did she let dull sleepe once to relent,
Nor wearinesse to slack her hast, but fled
Ever alike, as if her former dred
Were hard behind, her ready to arrest;
And her white Palfrey, having conquered
The maistring raines out of her weary wrest,
Perforce her carried where ever he thought best.

III. So long as breath and hable puissaunce
Did native corage unto him supply,
His pace he freshly forward did advaunce,
And carried her beyond all jeopardy;
But nought that wanteth rest can long aby:
He, having through incessant traveill spent
His force, at last perforce adowne did ly,
Ne foot could further move.   The Lady gent
Thereat was suddein strook with great astonishment;

IV. And, forst t' alight, on foote mote algates fare
A traveiler unwonted to such way:
Need teacheth her this lesson hard and rare,

That fortune all in equall launce doth sway,
And mortall miseries doth make her play.
So long she traveild, till at length she came
To an hilles side, which did to her bewray
A litle valley subject to the same,
All coverd with thick woodes that quite it overcame.

v. Through the tops of the high trees she did descry
A litle smoke, whose vapour thin and light
Reeking aloft uprolled to the sky:
Which chearefull signe did send unto her sight
That in the same did wonne some living wight.
Eftsoones her steps she thereunto applyd,
And came at last in weary wretched plight
Unto the place, to which her hope did guyde,
To finde some refuge there, and rest her wearie syde.

vi. There in a gloomy hollow glen she found
A little cottage, built of stickes and reedes
In homely wize, and wald with sods around;
In which a witch did dwell, in loathly weedes
And wilfull want, all carelesse of her needes;
So choosing solitarie to abide
Far from all neighbours, that her divelish deedes
And hellish arts from people she might hide,
And hurt far off unknowne whom ever she envide.

vii. The Damzell there arriving entred in;
Where sitting on the flore the Hag she found
Busie (as seem'd) about some wicked gin:
Who, soone as she beheld that suddein stound,
Lightly upstarted from the dustie ground,
And with fell looke and hollow deadly gaze
Stared on her awhile, as one astound,
Ne had one word to speake for great amaze,
But shewd by outward signes that dread her sence did daze.

viii. At last, turning her feare to foolish wrath,
She askt, what devill had her thither brought,
And who she was, and what unwonted path
Had guided her, unwelcomed, unsought?
To which the Damzell, full of doubtfull thought,
Her mildly answer'd: " Beldame, be not wroth

      With silly Virgin, by adventure brought
      Unto your dwelling, ignorant and loth,
      That crave but rowme to rest while tempest overblo'th."

IX. With that adowne out of her christall eyne
      Few trickling teares she softly forth let fall,
      That like two orient perles did purely shyne
      Upon her snowy cheeke; and therewithall
      She sighed soft, that none so bestiall
      Nor salvage hart, but ruth of her sad plight
      Would make to melt, or pitteously appall;
      And that vile Hag, all were her whole delight
      In mischiefe, was much moved at so pitteous sight;

X. And gan recomfort her in her rude wyse,
      With womanish compassion of her plaint,
      Wiping the teares from her suffused eyes,
      And bidding her sit downe, to rest her faint
      And wearie limbes awhile.   She, nothing quaint
      Nor 'sdeignfull of so homely fashion,
      Sith brought she was now to so hard constraint,
      Sate downe upon the dusty ground anon;
      As glad of that small rest as Bird of tempest gon.

XI. Tho gan she gather up her garments rent,
      And her loose lockes to dight in order dew
      With golden wreath and gorgeous ornament;
      Whom such whenas the wicked Hag did vew,
      She was astonisht at her heavenly hew,
      And doubted her to deeme an earthly wight,
      But or some Goddesse, or of Dianes crew,
      And thought her to adore with humble spright:
      T' adore thing so divine as beauty were but right.

XII. This wicked woman had a wicked sonne,
      The comfort of her age and weary dayes,
      A laesy loord, for nothing good to donne,
      But stretched forth in ydlenesse alwayes,
      Ne ever cast his mind to covet prayse,
      Or ply himselfe to any honest trade,
      But all the day before the sunny rayes
      He us'd to slug, or sleepe in slothfull shade:
      Such laesinesse both lewd and poore attonce him made.

XIII. He, comming home at undertime, there found
The fayrest creature that he ever saw
Sitting beside his mother on the ground;
The sight whereof did greatly him adaw,
And his base thought with terrour and with aw
So inly smot, that as one, which hath gaz'd
On the bright Sunne unwares, doth soone withdraw
His feeble eyne, with too much brightnes daz'd,
So stared he on her, and stood long while amaz'd.

XIV. Softly at last he gan his mother aske,
What mister wight that was, and whence deriv'd,
That in so straunge disguizement there did maske,
And by what accident she there arriv'd?
But she, as one nigh of her wits depriv'd,
With nought but ghastly lookes him answered;
Like to a ghost, that lately is reviv'd
From Stygian shores where late it wandered:
So both at her, and each at other wondered.

XV. But the fayre Virgin was so meeke and myld,
That she to them vouchsafed to embace
Her goodly port, and to their senses vyld
Her gentle speach applyde, that in short space
She grew familiare in that desert place.
During which time the Chorle, through her so kind
And courteise use, conceiv'd affection bace,
And cast to love her in his brutish mind:
No love, but brutish lust, that was so beastly tind.

XVI. Closely the wicked flame his bowels brent,
And shortly grew into outrageous fire;
Yet had he not the hart, nor hardiment,
As unto her to utter his desire;
His caytive thought durst not so high aspire:
But with soft sighes and lovely semblaunces
He ween'd that his affection entire
She should aread; many resemblaunces
To her he made, and many kinde remembraunces.

XVII. Oft from the forrest wildings he did bring,
Whose sides empurpled were with smyling red;
And oft young birds, which he had taught to sing,

His maistresse praises sweetly caroled:
Girlonds of flowres sometimes for her faire hed
He fine would dight; sometimes the squirrell wild
He brought to her in bands, as conquered
To be her thrall, his fellow-servant vild:
All which she of him tooke with countenance meeke
    and mild.

XVIII. But, past a while, when she fit season saw
To leave that desert mansion, she cast
In secret wize herselfe thence to withdraw,
For feare of mischiefe, which she did forecast
Might by the witch or by her sonne compast.
Her wearie Palfrey, closely as she might,
Now well recovered after long repast,
In his proud furnitures she freshly dight,
His late miswandred wayes now to remeasure right.

XIX. And earely, ere the dawning day appear'd,
She forth issewed, and on her journey went:
She went in perill, of each noyse affeard,
And of each shade that did it selfe present;
For still she feared to be overhent
Of that vile hag, or her uncivile sonne;
Who when, too late awaking, well they kent
That their fayre guest was gone, they both begonne
To make exceeding mone, as they had been undonne.

XX. But that lewd lover did the most lament
For her depart, that ever man did heare:
He knockt his brest with desperate intent,
And scratcht his face, and with his teeth did teare
His rugged flesh, and rent his ragged heare;
That his sad mother, seeing his sore plight,
Was greatly woe begon, and gan to feare
Least his fraile senses were emperisht quight,
And love to frenzy turnd, sith love is franticke hight.

XXI. All wayes shee sought him to restore to plight,
With herbs, with charms, with counsel, and with teares;
But tears, nor charms, nor herbs, nor counsell, might
Asswage the fury which his entrails teares:
So strong is passion that no reason heares.
Tho when all other helpes she saw to faile,

She turnd her selfe backe to her wicked leares;
And by her divelish arts thought to prevaile
To bringe her backe againe, or worke her finall bale.

XXII. Eftesoones out of her hidden cave she cald
An hideous beast of horrible aspect,
That could the stoutest corage have appald;
Monstrous, mishapt, and all his backe was spect
With thousand spots of colours queint elect,
Thereto so swifte that it all beasts did pas:
Like never yet did living eie detect;
But likest it to an Hyena was,
That feeds on wemens flesh as others feede on gras.

XXIII. It forth she cald, and gave it streight in charge
Through thicke and thin her to poursew apace,
Ne once to stay to rest, or breath at large,
Till her he had attaind and brought in place,
Or quite devourd her beauties scornefull grace.
The Monster, swifte as word that from her went,
Went forth in haste, and did her footing trace
So sure and swiftly, through his perfect sent
And passing speede, that shortly he her overhent.

XXIV. Whom when the fearefull Damzell nigh espide,
No need to bid her fast away to flie:
That ugly shape so sore her terrifide,
That it she shund no lesse then dread to die;
And her flitt palfrey did so well apply
His nimble feet to her conceived feare,
That whilest his breath did strength to him supply,
From peril free he her away did beare;
But when his force gan faile his pace gan wex areare.

XXV. Which whenas she perceiv'd, she was dismayd
At that same last extremity ful sore,
And of her safety greatly grew afrayd.
And now she gan approch to the sea shore,
As it befell, that she could flie no more,
But yield herselfe to spoile of greedinesse:
Lightly she leaped, as a wight forlore,
From her dull horse, in desperate distresse,
And to her feet betooke her doubtfull sickernesse.

XXVI. Not halfe so fast the wicked Myrrha fled
        From dread of her revenging fathers hond;
        Nor halfe so fast to save her maydenhed
        Fled fearfull Daphne on th' Ægæan strond,
        As Florimell fled from that Monster yond,
        To reach the sea ere she of him were raught:
        For in the sea to drowne herselfe she fond,
        Rather then of the tyrant to be caught:
        Thereto fear gave her wings, and need her corage taught.

XXVII. It fortuned (high God did so ordaine)
         As shee arrived on the roring shore,
         In minde to leape into the mighty maine,
         A little bote lay hoving her before,
         In which there slept a fisher old and pore,
         The whiles his nets were drying on the sand.
         Into the same shee lept, and with the ore
         Did thrust the shallop from the floting strand:
         So safety fownd at sea which she fownd not at land.

XXVIII. The Monster, ready on the pray to sease,
          Was of his forward hope deceived quight;
          Ne durst assay to wade the perlous seas,
          But greedily long gaping at the sight,
          At last in vaine was forst to turne his flight,
          And tell the idle tidings to his Dame:
          Yet, to avenge his divelish despight,
          He sett upon her Palfrey tired lame,
          And slew him cruelly ere any reskew came.

XXIX. And, after having him embowelled
        To fill his hellish gorge, it chaunst a knight
        To passe that way, as forth he traveiled:
        Yt was a goodly Swaine, and of great might,
        As ever man that bloody field did fight;
        But in vain sheows, that wont yong knights bewitch,
        And courtly services, tooke no delight;
        But rather joyd to bee then seemen sich,
        For both to be and seeme to him was labor lich.

XXX. It was to weete the good Sir Satyrane,
       That raunged abrode to seeke adventures wilde,
       As was his wont, in forest and in plaine:

He was all armd in rugged steele unfilde,
As in the smoky forge it was compilde,
And in his Scutchin bore a Satyres hedd.
He comming present, where the Monster vilde
Upon that milke-white Palfreyes carcas fedd,
Unto his reskew ran, and greedily him spedd.

XXXI. There well perceivd he that it was the horse
Whereon faire Florimell was wont to ride,
That of that feend was rent without remorse:
Much feared he least ought did ill betide
To that faire Maide, the flowre of wemens pride;
For her he dearely loved, and in all
His famous conquests highly magnifide:
Besides, her golden girdle, which did fall
From her in flight, he fownd, that did him sore apall.

XXXII. Full of sad feare and doubtfull agony
Fiercely he flew upon that wicked feend,
And with huge strokes and cruell battery
Him forst to leave his pray, for to attend
Him selfe from deadly daunger to defend:
Full many wounds in his corrupted flesh
He did engrave, and muchell blood did spend,
Yet might not doe him die: but aie more fresh
And fierce he still appeard, the more he did him thresh.

XXXIII. He wist not how him to despoile of life,
Ne how to win the wished victory,
Sith him he saw still stronger grow through strife,
And him selfe weaker through infirmity.
Greatly he grew enrag'd, and furiously
Hurling his sword away he lightly lept
Upon the beast, that with great cruelty
Rored and raged to be underkept;
Yet he perforce him held, and strokes upon him hept.

XXXIV. As he that strives to stop a suddein flood,
And in strong bancks his violence enclose,
Forceth it swell above his wonted mood,
And largely overflow the fruitfull plaine,
That all the countrey seemes to be a Maine,
And the rich furrowes flote, all quite fordonne:

The wofull husbandman doth lowd complaine
To see his whole yeares labor lost so soone,
For which to God he made so many an idle boone:

XXXV. So him he held, and did through might amate.
So long he held him, and him bett so long,
That at the last his fiercenes gan abate,
And meekely stoup unto the victor strong:
Who, to avenge the implacable wrong
Which he supposed donne to Florimell,
Sought by all meanes his dolor to prolong,
Sith dint of steele his carcas could not quell;
His maker with her charmes had framed him so well.

XXXVI. The golden ribband, which that virgin wore
About her sclender waste, he tooke in hand,
And with it bownd the beast, that lowd did rore
For great despight of that unwonted band,
Yet dared not his victor to withstand,
But trembled like a lambe fled from the pray;
And all the way him followd on the strand,
As he had long bene learned to obay;
Yet never learned he such service till that day.

XXXVII. Thus as he led the Beast along the way,
He spide far off a mighty Giauntesse
Fast flying, on a Courser dapled gray,
From a bold knight that with great hardinesse
Her hard pursewed, and sought for to suppresse.
She bore before her lap a doleful Squire,
Lying athwart her horse in great distresse,
Fast bounden hand and foote with cords of wire,
Whom she did meane to make the thrall of her desire.

XXXVIII. Which whenas Satyrane beheld, in haste
He lefte his captive Beast at liberty,
And crost the nearest way, by which he cast
Her to encounter ere she passed by;
But she the way shund nathemore forthy,
But forward gallopt fast; which when he spyde,
His mighty speare he couched warily,
And at her ran: she, having him descryde,
Her selfe to fight addrest, and threw her lode aside.

XXXIX. Like as a Goshauke, that in foote doth beare
A trembling Culver, having spide on hight
An Eagle that with plumy wings doth sheare
The subtile ayre stouping with all his might,
The quarry throwes to ground with fell despight,
And to the batteill doth her selfe prepare:
So ran the Geauntesse unto the fight;
Her fyrie eyes with furious sparkes did stare,
And with blasphemous bannes high God in peeces tare.

XL. She caught in hand an huge great yron mace,
Wherewith she many had of life depriv'd;
But, ere the stroke could seize his aymed place,
His speare amids her sun-brode shield arriv'd:
Yet nathemore the steele asonder riv'd,
All were the beame in bignes like a mast,
Ne her out of the stedfast sadle driv'd;
But, glauncing on the tempred metall, brast
In thousand shivers, and so forth beside her past.

XLI. Her Steed did stagger with that puissaunt strooke;
But she no more was moved with that might
Then it had lighted on an aged Oke,
Or on the marble Pillour that is pight
Upon the top of Mount Olympus hight,
For the brave youthly Champions to assay
With burning charet wheeles it nigh to smite;
But who that smites it mars his joyous play,
And is the spectacle of ruinous decay.

XLII. Yet, therewith sore enrag'd, with sterne regard
Her dreadfull weapon she to him addrest,
Which on his helmet martelled so hard
That made him low incline his lofty crest,
And bowd his battred visour to his brest:
Wherewith he was so stund that he n'ote ryde,
But reeled to and fro from east to west.
Which when his cruell enimy espyde,
She lightly unto him adjoyned syde to syde;

XLIII. And, on his collar laying puissaunt hand,
Out of his wavering seat him pluckt perforse,
Perforse him pluckt, unable to withstand

Or helpe himselfe; and laying thwart her horse,
In loathly wise like to a carrion corse,
She bore him fast away.   Which when the knight
That her pursewed saw, with great remorse
He nere was touched in his noble spright,
And gan encrease his speed as she encreast her flight.

XLIV. Whom when as nigh approching she espyde,
She threw away her burden angrily;
For she list not the batteill to abide,
But made her selfe more light away to fly:
Yet her the hardy knight pursewd so nye
That almost in the backe he oft her strake;
But still, when him at hand she did espy,
She turnd, and semblaunce of faire fight did make,
But, when he stayd, to flight againe she did her take.

XLV. By this the good Sir Satyrane gan awake
Out of his dreame that did him long entraunce,
And, seeing none in place, he gan to make
Exceeding mone, and curst that cruell chaunce
Which reft from him so faire a chevisaunce.
At length he spyde whereas that wofull Squyre,
Whom he had reskewed from captivaunce
Of his strong foe, lay tombled in the myre,
Unable to arise, or foote or hand to styre.

XLVI. To whom approching, well he mote perceive
In that fowle plight a comely personage
And lovely face, made fit for to deceive
Fraile Ladies hart with loves consuming rage,
Now in the blossome of his freshest age.
He reard him up and loosd his yron bands,
And after gan inquire his parentage,
And how he fell into the Gyaunts hands,
And who that was which chaced her along the lands.

XLVII. Then trembling yet through feare the Squire bespake:
"That Geauntesse Argantè is behight,
A daughter of the Titans which did make
Warre against heven, and heaped hils on hight
To scale the skyes and put Jove from his right:
Her syre Typhoeus was; who, mad through merth,

And dronke with blood of men slaine by his might,
Through incest her of his owne mother Earth
Whylome begot, being but halfe twin of that berth:

XLVIII. " For at that berth another Babe she bore;
To weet, the mightie Ollyphant, that wrought
Great wreake to many errant knights of yore,
And many hath to foule confusion brought.
These twinnes, men say, (a thing far passing thought)
While in their mothers wombe enclosd they were,
Ere they into the lightsom world were brought,
In fleshly lust were mingled both yfere,
And in that monstrous wise did to the world appere.

XLIX. " So liv'd they ever after in like sin,
Gainst natures law and good behaveoure;
But greatest shame was to that maiden twin,
Who, not content so fowly to devoure
Her native flesh and staine her brothers bowre,
Did wallow in all other fleshly myre,
And suffred beastes her body to deflowre,
So whot she burned in that lustfull fyre;
Yet all that might not slake her sensuall desyre:

L. " But over all the countrie she did raunge
To seeke young men to quench her flaming thrust,
And feed her fancy with delightfull chaunge:
Whom so she fittest findes to serve her lust,
Through her maine strength, in which she most doth trust,
She with her bringes into a secret Ile,
Where in eternall bondage dye he must,
Or be the vassall of her pleasures vile,
And in all shamefull sort him selfe with her defile.

LI. " Me, seely wretch, she so at vauntage caught,
After she long in waite for me did lye,
And meant unto her prison to have brought,
Her lothsom pleasure there to satisfye;
That thousand deathes me lever were to dye
Then breake the vow that to faire Columbell
I plighted have, and yet keepe stedfastly.
As for my name, it mistreth not to tell:
Call me the Squyre of Dames; that me beseemeth well.

LII. " But that bold knight, whom ye pursuing saw
　　　That Geauntesse, is not such as she seemd,
　　　But a faire virgin that in martiall law
　　　And deedes of armes above all Dames is deemd,
　　　And above many knightes is eke esteemd
　　　For her great worth: She Palladine is hight.
　　　She you from death, you me from dread, redeemd;
　　　Ne any may that Monster match in fight,
　　　But she, or such as she, that is so chaste a wight."

LIII. " Her well beseemes that Quest," (quoth Satyrane)
　　　" But read, thou Squyre of Dames, what vow is this,
　　　Which thou upon thy selfe hast lately ta'ne?"
　　　" That shall I you recount," (quoth he) " ywis,
　　　So be ye pleasd to pardon all amis.
　　　That gentle Lady whom I love and serve,
　　　After long suit and wearie servicis,
　　　Did aske me, how I could her love deserve,
　　　And how she might be sure that I would never swerve?

LIV. " I, glad by any meanes her grace to gaine,
　　　Badd her commaund my life to save or spill.
　　　Eftsoones she badd me, with incessaunt paine
　　　To wander through the world abroad at will,
　　　And every where, where with my power or skill
　　　I might doe service unto gentle Dames,
　　　That I the same should faithfully fulfill;
　　　And at the twelve monethes end should bring their names
　　　And pledges, as the spoiles of my victorious games.

LV. " So well I to faire Ladies service did,
　　　And found such favour in their loving hartes,
　　　That ere the yeare his course had compassid,
　　　Thre hundred pledges for my good desartes,
　　　And thrice three hundred thanks for my good partes,
　　　I with me brought, and did to her present:
　　　Which when she saw, more bent to eke my smartes
　　　Then to reward my trusty true intent,
　　　She gan for me devise a grievous punishment

LVI. " To weet, that I my traveill should resume,
　　　And with like labour walke the world arownd,
　　　Ne ever to her presence should presume,

Till I so many other Dames had fownd,
The which, for all the suit I could propownd,
Would me refuse their pledges to afford,
But did abide for ever chaste and sownd."
" Ah! gentle Squyre," (quoth he) " tell at one word,
How many fownd'st thou such to put in thy record? "

LVII. " Indeed, Sir knight," (said he) " one word may tell
All that I ever fownd so wisely stayd,
For onely three they were disposd so well;
And yet three yeares I now abrode have strayd,
To fynd them out." " Mote I," (then laughing sayd
The knight) " inquire of thee what were those three,
The which thy proffred curtesie denayd?
Or ill they seemed sure avizd to bee,
Or brutishly brought up, that nev'r did fashions see."

LVIII. " The first which then refused me," (said hee)
" Certes was but a common Courtisane;
Yet flat refusd to have adoe with mee,
Because I could not give her many a Jane."
(Thereat full hartely laughed Satyrane.)
" The second was an holy Nunne to chose,
Which would not let me be her Chappellane,
Because she knew, she said, I would disclose
Her counsell, if she should her trust in me repose.

LIX. " The third a Damzell was of low degree,
Whom I in countrey cottage fownd by chaunce:
Full litle weened I that chastitee
Had lodging in so meane a maintenaunce;
Yet was she fayre, and in her countenaunce
Dwelt simple truth in seemely fashion.
Long thus I woo'd her with due observaunce,
In hope unto my pleasure to have won;
But was as far at last, as when I first begon.

LX. " Safe her, I never any woman found
That chastity did for it selfe embrace,
But were for other causes firme and sound;
Either for want of handsome time and place,
Or else for feare of shame and fowle disgrace.
Thus am I hopelesse ever to attaine

Where she was wont her Sprightes to entertaine,
The maisters of her art: there was she faine
To call them all in order to her ayde,
And them conjure, upon eternall paine,
To counsell her, so carefully dismayd,
How she might heale her sonne whose senses were decayd.

v. By their advice, and her owne wicked wit,
She there deviz'd a wondrous worke to frame,
Whose like on earth was never framed yit;
That even Nature selfe envide the same,
And grudg'd to see the counterfet should shame
The thing it selfe: In hand she boldly tooke
To make another like the former Dame,
Another Florimell, in shape and looke
So lively and so like, that many it mistooke.

vi. The substance, whereof she the body made,
Was purest snow in massy mould congeald,
Which she had gathered in a shady glade
Of the Riphœan hils, to her reveald
By errant Sprights, but from all men conceald:
The same she tempred with fine mercury
And virgin wex that never yet was seald,
And mingled them with perfect vermily;
That like a lively sanguine it seemd to the eye.

vii. Instead of eyes two burning lampes she set
In silver sockets, shyning like the skyes,
And a quicke moving Spirit did arret
To stirre and roll them like to womens eyes:
Instead of yellow lockes she did devyse
With golden wyre to weave her curled head;
Yet golden wyre was not so yellow thryse
As Florimells fayre heare: and, in the stead
Of life, she put a Spright to rule the carcas dead;

viii. A wicked Spright, yfraught with fawning guyle
And fayre resemblance above all the rest,
Which with the Prince of Darkenes fell somewhyle
From heavens blis and everlasting rest:
Him needed not instruct which way were best
Him selfe to fashion likest Florimell,

Ne how to speake, ne how to use his gest;
For he in counterfesaunce did excell,
And all the wyles of wemens wits knew passing well.

IX. Him shaped thus she deckt in garments gay,
Which Florimell had left behind her late;
That who so then her saw would surely say
It was her selfe whom it did imitate,
Or fayrer then her selfe, if ought algate
Might fayrer be.   And then she forth her brought
Unto her sonne that lay in feeble state;
Who seeing her gan streight upstart, and thought
She was the Lady selfe whom he so long had sought.

X. Tho fast her clipping twixt his armes twayne,
Extremely joyed in so happy sight,
And soone forgot his former sickely payne:
But she, the more to seeme such as she hight,
Coyly rebutted his embracement light;
Yet still, with gentle countenaunce, retain'd
Enough to hold a foole in vaine delight.
Him long she so with shadowes entertain'd,
As her Creatresse had in charge to her ordain'd.

XI. Till on a day, as he disposed was
To walke the woodes with that his Idole faire,
Her to disport and idle time to pas
In th' open freshnes of the gentle aire,
A knight that way there chaunced to repaire;
Yet knight he was not, but a boastfull swaine
That deedes of armes had ever in despaire,
Proud Braggadocchio, that in vaunting vaine
His glory did repose, and credit did maintaine.

XII. He, seeing with that Chorle so faire a wight,
Decked with many a costly ornament,
Much merveiled thereat, as well he might,
And thought that match a fowle disparagement:
His bloody speare eftesoones he boldly bent
Against the silly clowne, who dead through feare
Fell streight to ground in great astonishment.
"Villein," (sayd he) "this Lady is my deare;
Dy, if thou it gainesay: I will away her beare."

XIII. The fearefull Chorle durst not gainesay nor dooe,
    But trembling stood, and yielded him the pray;
    Who, finding litle leasure her to wooe
    On Tromparts steed her mounted without stay,
    And without reskew led her quite away.
    Proud man himselfe then Braggadochio deem'd,
    And next to none after that happy day,
    Being possessed of that spoyle, which seem'd
    The fairest wight on ground, and most of men esteem'd.

XIV. But, when hee saw him selfe free from poursute,
    He gan make gentle purpose to his Dame
    With termes of love and lewdnesse dissolute;
    For he could well his glozing speaches frame
    To such vaine uses that him best became:
    But she thereto would lend but light regard,
    As seeming sory that she ever came
    Into his powre, that used her so hard
    To reave her honor, which she more then life prefard.

XV. Thus as they two of kindnes treated long,
    There them by chaunce encountred on the way
    An armed knight upon a courser strong,
    Whose trampling feete upon the hollow lay
    Seemed to thunder, and did nigh affray
    That Capons corage: yet he looked grim,
    And faynd to cheare his lady in dismay,
    Who seemd for feare to quake in every lim,
    And her to save from outrage meekely prayed him.

XVI. Fiercely that straunger forward came: and, nigh
    Approching, with bold words and bitter threat
    Bad that same boaster, as he mote, on high,
    To leave to him that lady for excheat,
    Or bide him batteill without further treat.
    That challenge did too peremptory seeme,
    And fild his senses with abashment great;
    Yet seeing nigh him jeopardy extreme,
    He it dissembled well, and light seemd to esteeme

XVII. Saying, " Thou foolish knight, that weenst with words
    To steale away that I with blowes have wonne,
    And brought through points of many perilous swords:

But if thee list to see thy Courser ronne,
Or prove thy selfe, this sad encounter shonne,
And seeke els without hazard of thy hedd."
At those prowd words that other knight begonne
To wex exceeding wroth, and him aredd
To turne his steede about, or sure he should be dedd.

xviii. " Sith then," (said Braggadochio) " needes thou wilt
Thy daies abridge through proofe of puissaunce,
Turne we our steeds; that both in equall tilt
May meete againe, and each take happy chaunce."
This said, they both a furlongs mountenaunce
Retird their steeds, to ronne in even race;
But Braggadochio, with his bloody launce,
Once having turnd, no more returnd his face,
But lefte his love to losse, and fled him selfe apace.

xix. The knight, him seeing flie, had no regard
Him to poursew, but to the lady rode;
And having her from Trompart lightly reard,
Upon his Courser sett the lovely lode,
And with her fled away without abode.
Well weened he, that fairest Florimell
It was with whom in company he yode,
And so her selfe did alwaies to him tell;
So made him thinke him selfe in heven that was in hell.

xx. But Florimell her selfe was far away,
Driven to great distresse by fortune straunge,
And taught the carefull Mariner to play,
Sith late mischaunce had her compeld to chaunge
The land for sea, at randon there to raunge:
Yett there that cruell Queene avengeresse,
Not satisfyde so far her to estraunge
From courtly blis and wonted happinesse,
Did heape on her new waves of weary wretchednesse.

xxi. For being fled into the fishers bote
For refuge from the Monsters cruelty,
Long so she on the mighty maine did flote,
And with the tide drove forward carelessly;
For th' ayre was milde and cleared was the skie,
And all his windes Dan Aeolus did keepe

From stirring up their stormy enmity,
As pittying to see her waile and weepe:
But all the while the fisher did securely sleepe.

XXII. At last when droncke with drowsinesse he woke,
And saw his drover drive along the streame,
He was dismayd; and thrise his brest he stroke,
For marveill of that accident extreame:
But when he saw that blazing beauties beame,
Which with rare light his bote did beautifye,
He marveild more, and thought he yet did dreame
Not well awakte; or that some extasye
Assotted had his sence, or dazed was his eye.

XXIII. But when her well avizing hee perceiv'd
To be no vision nor fantasticke sight,
Great comfort of her presence he conceiv'd,
And felt in his old corage new delight
To gin awake, and stir his frosen spright:
Tho rudely askte her, how she thither came?
"Ah!" (sayd she) "father, I note read aright
What hard misfortune brought me to this same;
Yet am I glad that here I now in safety ame.

XXIV. "But thou, good man, sith far in sea we bee,
And the great waters gin apace to swell,
That now no more we can the mayn-land see,
Have care, I pray, to guide the cock-bote well,
Least worse on sea then us on land befell."
Thereat th' old man did nought but fondly grin,
And saide his boat the way could wisely tell;
But his deceiptfull eyes did never lin
To looke on her faire face and marke her snowy skin.

XXV. The sight whereof in his congealed flesh
Infixt such secrete sting of greedy lust,
That the drie withered stocke it gan refresh,
And kindled heat that soone in flame forth brust:
The driest wood is soonest burnt to dust.
Rudely to her he lept, and his rough hond
Where ill became him rashly would have thrust;
But she with angry scorne did him withstond,
And shamefully reproved for his rudenes fond.

XXVI. But he, that never good nor maners knew,
      Her sharpe rebuke full litle did esteeme;
      Hard is to teach an old horse amble trew:
      The inward smoke, that did before but steeme,
      Broke into open fire and rage extreme;
      And now he strength gan adde unto his will,
      Forcyng to doe that did him fowle misseeme.
      Beastly he threwe her downe, ne car'd to spill
      Her garments gay with scales of fish that all did fill.

XXVII. The silly virgin strove him to withstand
      All that she might, and him in vaine revild:
      Shee strugled strongly both with foote and hand
      To save her honor from that villaine vilde,
      And cride to heven, from humane help exild.
      O! ye brave knights, that boast this Ladies love,
      Where be ye now, when she is nigh defild
      Of filthy wretch? well may she you reprove
      Of falsehood or of slouth, when most it may behove.

XXVIII. But if that thou, Sir Satyran, didst weete,
      Or thou, Sir Peridure, her sory state,
      How soone would yee assemble many a fleete,
      To fetch from sea that ye at land lost late!
      Towres, citties, kingdomes, ye would ruinate
      In your avengement and despiteous rage,
      Ne ought your burning fury mote abate;
      But if Sir Calidore could it presage,
      No living creature could his cruelty asswage.

XXIX. But sith that none of all her knights is nye,
      See how the heavens, of voluntary grace
      And soveraine favor towards chastity,
      Doe succor send to her distressed cace;
      So much high God doth innocence embrace.
      It fortuned, whilest thus she stifly strove,
      And the wide sea importuned long space
      With shrilling shriekes, Proteus abrode did rove,
      Along the fomy waves driving his finny drove.

XXX. Proteus is Shepheard of the seas of yore,
      And hath the charge of Neptunes mighty heard;
      An aged sire with head all frory hore,

And sprinckled frost upon his deawy beard:
Who when those pittifull outcries he heard
Through all the seas so ruefully resownd,
His charett swifte in hast he thither steard,
Which with a teeme of scaly Phocas bownd
Was drawne upon the waves that fomed him arownd.

XXXI. And comming to that Fishers wandring bote,
That went at will withouten card or sayle,
He therein saw that yrkesome sight, which smote
Deepe indignation and compassion frayle
Into his hart attonce: streight did he hayle
The greedy villein from his hoped pray,
Of which he now did very litle fayle,
And with his staffe, that drives his heard astray,
Him bett so sore, that life and sence did much dismay.

XXXII. The whiles the pitteous Lady up did ryse,
Ruffled and fowly raid with filthy soyle,
And blubbred face with teares of her faire eyes:
Her heart nigh broken was with weary toyle,
To save her selfe from that outrageous spoyle;
But when she looked up, to weet what wight
Had her from so infamous fact assoyld,
For shame, but more for feare of his grim sight,
Downe in her lap she hid her face, and lowdly shright.

XXXIII. Her selfe not saved yet from daunger dredd
She thought, but chaung'd from one to other feare:
Like as a fearefull partridge, that is fledd
From the sharpe hauke which her attached neare,
And fals to ground to seeke for succor theare,
Whereas the hungry Spaniells she does spye
With greedy jawes her ready for to teare:
In such distresse and sad perplexity
Was Florimell, when Proteus she did see her by.

XXXIV. But he endevored with speaches milde
Her to recomfort, and accourage bold,
Bidding her feare no more her foemen vilde,
Nor doubt himselfe; and who he was her told:
Yet all that could not from affright her hold,
Ne to recomfort her at all prevayld;

For her faint hart was with the frosen cold
Benumbd so inly, that her wits nigh fayld,
And all her sences with abashment quite were quayld.

XXXV. Her up betwixt his rugged hands he reard,
And with his frory lips full softly kist,
Whiles the cold ysickles from his rough beard
Dropped adowne upon her yvory brest:
Yet he him selfe so busily addrest,
That her out of astonishment he wrought;
And out of that same fishers filthy nest
Removing her, into his charet brought,
And there with many gentle termes her faire besought.

XXXVI. But that old leachour, which with bold assault
That beautie durst presume to violate,
He cast to punish for his hainous fault:
Then tooke he him, yet trembling sith of late,
And tyde behind his charet, to aggrate
The virgin whom he had abusde so sore;
So drag'd him through the waves in scornfull state,
And after cast him up upon the shore;
But Florimell with him unto his bowre he bore.

XXXVII. His bowre is in the bottom of the maine,
Under a mightie rocke, gainst which doe rave
The roring billowes in their proud disdaine,
That with the angry working of the wave
Therein is eaten out an hollow cave,
That seemes rough Masons hand with engines keene
Had long while laboured it to engrave:
There was his wonne; ne living wight was seene
Save one old Nymph, hight Panopè, to keepe it cleane.

XXXVIII. Thither he brought the sory Florimell,
And entertained her the best he might,
And Panopè her entertaind eke well,
As an immortall mote a mortall wight,
To winne her liking unto his delight:
With flattering wordes he sweetly wooed her,
And offered faire guiftes t' allure her sight;
But she both offers and the offerer
Despysde, and all the fawning of the flatterer.

XXXIX. Dayly he tempted her with this or that,
  And never suffred her to be at rest;
  But evermore she him refused flat,
  And all his fained kindnes did detest,
  So firmely she had sealed up her brest.
  Sometimes he boasted that a God he hight,
  But she a mortall creature loved best:
  Then he would make him selfe a mortall wight;
  But then she said she lov'd none, but a Faery knight.

 XL. Then like a Faerie knight him selfe he drest,
  For every shape on him he could endew;
  Then like a king he was to her exprest,
  And offred kingdoms unto her in vew,
  To be his Leman and his Lady trew:
  But when all this he nothing saw prevaile,
  With harder meanes he cast her to subdew,
  And with sharpe threates her often did assayle;
  So thinking for to make her stubborne corage quayle.

 XLI. To dreadfull shapes he did him selfe transforme;
  Now like a Gyaunt; now like to a feend;
  Then like a Centaure; then like to a storme
  Raging within the waves: thereby he weend
  Her will to win unto his wished eend;
  But when with feare, nor favour, nor with all
  He els could doe, he saw him selfe esteemd,
  Downe in a Dongeon deepe he let her fall,
  And threatned there to make her his eternall thrall.

 XLII. Eternall thraldome was to her more liefe
  Than losse of chastitie, or chaunge of love:
  Dye had she rather in tormenting griefe
  Then any should of falsenesse her reprove,
  Or loosenes, that she lightly did remove.
  Most vertuous virgin! glory be thy meed,
  And crowne of heavenly prayse with Saintes above,
  Where most sweet hymmes of this thy famous deed
  Are still emongst them song, that far my rymes exceed.

 XLIII. Fit song of Angels caroled to bee!
  But yet whatso my feeble Muse can frame
  Shal be t' advance thy goodly chastitee

And to enroll thy memorable name
In th' heart of every honourable Dame,
That they thy vertuous deedes may imitate,
And be partakers of thy endlesse fame.
Yt yrkes me leave thee in this wofull state,
To tell of Satyrane where I him left of late.

XLIV. Who having ended with that Squyre of Dames
A long discourse of his adventures vayne,
The which himselfe then Ladies more defames,
And finding not th' Hyena to be slayne,
With that same Squyre retourned back againe
To his first way. And, as they forward went,
They spyde a knight fayre pricking on the playne,
As if he were on some adventure bent,
And in his port appeared manly hardiment.

XLV. Sir Satyrane him towardes did addresse,
To weet what wight he was, and what his quest;
And, comming nigh, eftsoones he gan to gesse,
Both by the burning hart which on his brest
He bare, and by the colours in his crest,
That Paridell it was. Tho to him yode,
And him saluting as beseemed best,
Gan first inquire of tydinges farre abrode,
And afterwardes on what adventure now he rode.

XLVI. Who thereto answering said: "The tydinges bad,
Which now in Faery court all men doe tell,
Which turned hath great mirth to mourning sad,
Is the late ruine of proud Marinell,
And suddein parture of faire Florimell
To find him forth: and after her are gone
All the brave knightes that doen in armes excell
To saveguard her ywandred all alone:
Emongst the rest my lott (unworthy') is to be one."

XLVII. "Ah! gentle knight," (said then Sir Satyrane)
"Thy labour all is lost, I greatly dread,
That hast a thanklesse service on thee ta'ne,
And offrest sacrifice unto the dead:
For dead, I surely doubt, thou maist aread
Henceforth for ever Florimell to bee;

That all the noble knights of Maydenhead,
Which her ador'd, may sore repent with mee,
And all faire Ladies may for ever sory bee."

XLVIII. Which wordes when Paridell had heard, his hew
Gan greatly chaunge and seemd dismaid to bee;
Then said: "Fayre Sir, how may I weene it trew,
That ye doe tell in such uncerteintee?
Or speake ye of report, or did ye see
Just cause of dread, that makes ye doubt so sore?
For, perdie, elles how mote it ever bee,
That ever hand should dare for to engore
Her noble blood? The hevens such crueltie abhore."

XLIX. "These eyes did see that they will ever rew
T' have seene," (quoth he) "when as a monstrous
beast
The Palfrey whereon she did travell slew,
And of his bowels made his bloody feast:
Which speaking token sheweth at the least
Her certeine losse, if not her sure decay:
Besides, that more suspicion encreast,
I found her golden girdle cast astray,
Distaynd with durt and blood, as relique of the
pray."

L. "Ay me!" (said Paridell) "the signes be sadd;
And, but God turne the same to good sooth-say,
That Ladies safetie is sore to be dradd.
Yet will I not forsake my forward way,
Till triall doe more certeine truth bewray."
"Faire Sir," (quoth he) "well may it you succeed!
Ne long shall Satyrane behind you stay,
But to the rest, which in this Quest proceed,
My labour adde, and be partaker of their speed."

LI. "Ye noble knights," (said then the Squyre of Dames)
"Well may yee speede in so praiseworthy payne!
But sith the Sunne now ginnes to slake his beames
In deawy vapours of the westerne mayne,
And lose the teme out of his weary wayne,
Mote not mislike you also to abate
Your zealous hast, till morrow next againe

Both light of heven and strength of men relate:
Which if ye please, to yonder castle turne your gate.''

LII. That counsell pleased well: so all yfere
Forth marched to a Castle them before;
Where soone arryving they restrained were
Of ready entraunce, which ought evermore
To errant knights be commune: wondrous sore
Thereat displeasd they were, till that young Squyre
Gan them informe the cause, why that same dore
Was shut to all which lodging did desyre:
The which to let you weet will further time requyre.

CANTO IX

Malbecco will no straunge knights host,
For peevish gealousy.
Paridell giusts with Britomart:
Both shew their auncestry.

I. REDOUBTED knights, and honorable Dames,
To whom I levell all my labours end,
Right sore I feare, least with unworthie blames
This odious argument my rymes should shend,
Or ought your goodly patience offend,
Whiles of a wanton Lady I doe write,
Which with her loose incontinence doth blend
The shyning glory of your soveraine light;
And knighthood fowle defaced by a faithlesse knight.

II. But never let th' ensample of the bad
Offend the good; for good, by paragone
Of evill, may more notably be rad,
As white seemes fayrer macht with blacke attone;
Ne all are shamed by the fault of one:
For lo! in heven, whereas all goodnes is,
Emongst the Angels, a whole legione
Of wicked Sprightes did fall from happy blis;
What wonder then if one, of women all, did mis?

III. Then listen, Lordings, if ye list to weet
The cause why Satyrane and Paridell
Mote not be entertaynd, as seemed meet,
Into that Castle, (as that Squyre does tell.)
" Therein a cancred crabbed Carle does dwell,
That has no skill of Court nor courtesie,
Ne cares what men say of him, ill or well;
For all his dayes he drownes in privitie,
Yet has full large to live and spend at libertie.

IV. " But all his minde is set on mucky pelfe,
To hoord up heapes of evill gotten masse,
For which he others wrongs, and wreckes himselfe:

Yet is he lincked to a lovely lasse,
Whose beauty doth her bounty far surpasse;
The which to him both far unequall yeares,
And also far unlike conditions has;
For she does joy to play amongst her peares,
And to be free from hard restraynt and gealous feares.

v. " But he is old, and withered like hay,
Unfit faire Ladies service to supply;
The privie guilt whereof makes him alway
Suspect her truth, and keepe continuall spy
Upon her with his other blincked eye;
Ne suffreth he resort of living wight
Approch to her, ne keepe her company,
But in close bowre her mewes from all mens sight,
Depriv'd of kindly joy and naturall delight.

vi. " Malbecco he, and Hellenore she hight;
Unfitly yokt together in one teeme.
That is the cause why never any knight
Is suffred here to enter, but he seeme
Such as no doubt of him he neede misdeeme."
Thereat Sir Satyrane gan smyle, and say;
" Extremely mad the man I surely deeme,
That weenes with watch and hard restraynt to stay
A womans will, which is disposed to go astray.

vii. " In vaine he feares that which he cannot shonne;
For who wotes not, that womans subtiltyes
Can guylen Argus, when she list misdonne?
It is not yron bandes, nor hundred eyes,
Nor brasen walls, nor many wakefull spyes,
That can withhold her wilfull wandring feet;
But fast goodwill, with gentle courtesyes,
And timely service to her pleasures meet,
May her perhaps containe, that else would algates fleet."

viii. " Then is he not more mad," (sayd Paridell)
" That hath himselfe unto such service sold,
In dolefull thraldome all his dayes to dwell?
For sure a foole I doe him firmely hold,
That loves his fetters, though they were of gold.
But why doe wee devise of others ill,

Whyles thus we suffer this same dotard old
To keepe us out in scorne, of his owne will,
And rather do not ransack all, and him selfe kill?"

IX. "Nay, let us first" (sayd Satyrane) "entreat
The man by gentle meanes to let us in,
And afterwardes affray with cruell threat,
Ere that we to efforce it doe begin:
Then, if all fayle, we will by force it win,
And eke reward the wretch for his mesprise,
As may be worthy of his haynous sin."
That counsell pleasd: then Paridell did rise
And to the Castle gate approcht in quiet wise.

X. Whereat soft knocking entrance he desyrd.
The good man selfe, which then the Porter playd,
Him answered, that all were now retyrd
Unto their rest, and all the keyes convayd
Unto their maister, who in bed was layd,
That none him durst awake out of his dreme;
And therefore them of patience gently prayd.
Then Paridell began to chaunge his theme,
And threatned him with force and punishment extreme:

XI. But all in vaine, for nought mote him relent.
And now so long before the wicket fast
They wayted, that the night was forward spent,
And the faire welkin fowly overcast
Gan blowen up a bitter stormy blast,
With showre and hayle so horrible and dred,
That this faire many were compeld at last
To fly for succour to a little shed,
The which beside the gate for swyne was ordered.

XII. It fortuned, soone after they were gone,
Another knight, whom tempest thither brought,
Came to that Castle, and with earnest mone,
Like as the rest, late entrance deare besought:
But, like so as the rest, he prayd for nought;
For flatly he of entrance was refusd.
Sorely thereat he was displeased, and thought
How to avenge himselfe so sore abusd,
And evermore the Carle of courtesie accusd.

XIII. But, to avoyde th' intollerable stowre,
 He was compeld to seeke some refuge neare,
 And to that shed, to shrowd him from the showre,
 He came, which full of guests he found whyleare,
 So as he was not let to enter there:
 Whereat he gan to wex exceeding wroth,
 And swore that he would lodge with them yfere,
 Or them dislodge, all were they liefe or loth;
And so defyde them each, and so defyde them both.

XIV. Both were full loth to leave that needfull tent,
 And both full loth in darkenesse to debate;
 Yet both full liefe him lodging to have lent,
 And both full liefe his boasting to abate:
 But chiefely Paridell his hart did grate
 To heare him threaten so despightfully,
 As if he did a dogge in kenell rate
 That durst not barke; and rather had he dy
Then, when he was defyde, in coward corner ly.

XV. Tho hastily remounting to his steed
 He forth issew'd: like as a boystrous winde,
 Which in th' earthes hollow caves hath long ben hid
 And shut up fast within her prisons blind,
 Makes the huge element, against her kinde,
 To move and tremble as it were aghast,
 Untill that it an issew forth may finde:
 Then forth it breakes, and with his furious blast
Confounds both land and seas, and skyes doth overcast.

XVI. Their steel-hed speares they strongly coucht, and met
 Together with impetuous rage and forse,
 That with the terrour of their fierce affret
 They rudely drove to ground both man and horse,
 That each awhile lay like a sencelesse corse.
 But Paridell sore brused with the blow
 Could not arise the counterchaunge to scorse,
 Till that young Squyre him reared from below;
Then drew he his bright sword, and gan about him throw.

XVII. But Satyrane forth stepping did them stay,
 And with faire treaty pacifide their yre.
 Then, when they were accorded from the fray,

Against that Castles Lord they gan conspire,
To heape on him dew vengeaunce for his hire.
They beene agreed; and to the gates they goe
To burn the same with unquenchable fire,
And that uncurteous Carle, their commune foe,
To doe fowle death to die, or wrap in grievous woe.

XVIII. Malbecco, seeing them resolvd indeed
To flame the gates, and hearing them to call
For fire in earnest, ran with fearfull speed,
And to them calling from the castle wall,
Besought them humbly him to beare withall,
As ignorant of servants bad abuse
And slacke attendaunce unto straungers call.
The knights were willing all things to excuse,
Though nought belev'd, and entraunce late did not refuse.

XIX. They beene ybrought into a comely bowre,
And servd of all things that mote needfull bee;
Yet secretly their hoste did on them lowre,
And welcomde more for feare then charitee;
But they dissembled what they did not see,
And welcomed themselves.   Each gan undight
Their garments wett, and weary armour free,
To dry them selves by Vulcanes flaming light,
And eke their lately bruzed parts to bring in plight.

XX. And eke that straunger knight emongst the rest
Was for like need enforst to disaray:
Tho, whenas vailed was her lofty crest,
Her golden locks, that were in trammells gay
Upbounden, did them selves adowne display
And raught unto her heeles; like sunny beames,
That in a cloud their light did long time stay,
Their vapour vaded, shewe their golden gleames,
And through the persant aire shoote forth their azure
    streames.

XXI. Shee also dofte her heavy haberjeon,
Which the faire feature of her limbs did hyde;
And her well-plighted frock, which she did won
To tucke about her short when she did ryde,
Shee low let fall, that flowd from her lanck syde
Downe to her foot with carelesse modestee.

Then of them all she plainly was espyde
To be a woman-wight, unwist to bee,
The fairest woman-wight that ever eie did see.

XXII. Like as Bellona (being late returnd
From slaughter of the Giaunts conquered;
Where proud Encelade, whose wide nosethrils burnd
With breathed flames, like to a furnace redd,
Transfixed with her speare downe tombled dedd
From top of Hemus by him heaped hye:)
Hath loosd her helmet from her lofty hedd,
And her Gorgonian shield gins to untye
From her lefte arme, to rest in glorious victorye.

XXIII. Which whenas they beheld, they smitten were
With great amazement of so wondrous sight;
And each on other, and they all on her,
Stood gazing, as if suddein great affright
Had them surprized.   At last, avizing right
Her goodly personage and glorious hew,
Which they so much mistooke, they tooke delight
In their first error, and yett still anew
With wonder of her beauty fed their hongry vew.

XXIV. Yet note their hongry vew be satisfide,
But seeing still the more desir'd to see,
And ever firmely fixed did abide
In contemplation of divinitee:
But most they mervaild at her chevalree
And noble prowesse, which they had approv'd,
That much they faynd to know who she mote bee;
Yet none of all them her thereof amov'd
Yet every one her likte, and every one her lov'd.

XXV. And Paridell, though partly discontent
With his late fall and fowle indignity,
Yet was soone wonne his malice to relent,
Through gratious regard of her faire eye,
And knightly worth which he too late did try,
Yet tried did adore.   Supper was dight;
Then they Malbecco prayd of courtesy,
That of his lady they might have the sight
And company at meat, to doe them more delight.

xxvi. But he, to shifte their curious request,
    Gan causen why she could not come in place;
    Her crased helth, her late recourse to rest,
    And humid evening ill for sicke folkes cace;
    But none of those excuses could take place,
    Ne would they eate till she in presence came.
    Shee came in presence with right comely grace,
    And fairely them saluted, as became,
    And shewd her selfe in all a gentle courteous Dame.

xxvii. They sat to meat; and Satyrane his chaunce
    Was her before, and Paridell beside;
    But he him selfe sate looking still askaunce
    Gainst Britomart, and ever closely eide
    Sir Satyrane, that glaunces might not glide:
    But his blinde eie, that sided Paridell,
    All his demeasnure from his sight did hide:
    On her faire face so did he feede his fill,
    And sent close messages of love to her at will.

xxviii. And ever and anone, when none was ware,
    With speaking lookes, that close embassage bore,
    He rov'd at her, and told his secret care
    For all that art he learned had of yore;
    Ne was she ignoraunt of that leud lore,
    But in his eye his meaning wisely redd,
    And with the like him aunswerd evermore.
    Shee sent at him one fyrie dart, whose hedd
    Empoisned was with privy lust and gealous dredd.

xxix. He from that deadly throw made no defence,
    But to the wound his weake heart opened wyde:
    The wicked engine through false influence
    Past through his eies, and secretly did glyde
    Into his heart, which it did sorely gryde.
    But nothing new to him was that same paine,
    Ne paine at all; for he so ofte had tryde
    The powre thereof, and lov'd so oft in vaine,
    That thing of course he counted love to entertaine.

xxx. Thenceforth to her he sought to intimate
    His inward griefe, by meanes to him well knowne:
    Now Bacchus fruit out of the silver plate

He on the table dasht, as overthrowne,
Or of the fruitfull liquor overflowne;
And by the dauncing bubbles did divine,
Or therein write to lett his love be showne;
Which well she redd out of the learned line;
A sacrament prophane in mistery of wine.

XXXI. And, when so of his hand the pledge she raught,
The guilty cup she fained to mistake,
And in her lap did shed her idle draught,
Shewing desire her inward flame to slake.
But such close signes they secret way did make
Unto their wils, and one eies watch escape:
Two eies him needeth, for to watch and wake,
Who lovers will deceive.   Thus was the ape,
By their faire handling, put into Malbeccoes cape.

XXXII. Now, when of meats and drinks they had their fill,
Purpose was moved by that gentle Dame
Unto those knights adventurous, to tell
Of deeds of armes which unto them became,
And every one his kindred and his name.
Then Paridell, in whom a kindly pride
Of gratious speach and skill his words to frame
Abounded, being glad of so fitte tide
Him to commend to her, thus spake, of al well eide.

XXXIII. " Troy, that art now nought but an idle name,
And in thine ashes buried low dost lie,
Though whilome far much greater then thy fame,
Before that angry Gods and cruell skie
Upon thee heapt a direfull destinie;
What boots it boast thy glorious descent,
And fetch from heven thy great genealogie,
Sith all thy worthie prayses being blent
Their ofspring hath embaste, and later glory shent?

XXXIV. " Most famous Worthy of the world, by whome
That warre was kindled which did Troy inflame,
And stately towres of Ilion whilome
Brought unto balefull ruine, was by name
Sir Paris far renowmd through noble fame;
Who, through great prowesse and bold hardinesse,

From Lacedæmon fetcht the fayrest Dame
That ever Greece did boast, or knight possesse,
Whom Venus to him gave for meed of worthinesse;

xxxv. " Fayre Helene, flowre of beautie excellent,
And girlond of the mighty Conquerours,
That madest many Ladies deare lament
The heavie losse of their brave Paramours,
Which they far off beheld from Trojan toures,
And saw the fieldes of faire Scamander strowne
With carcases of noble warrioures
Whose fruitlesse lives were under furrow sowne,
And Xanthus sandy bankes with blood all overflowne.

xxxvi. " From him my linage I derive aright,
Who long before the ten yeares siege of Troy,
Whiles yet on Ida he a shepeheard hight,
On faire Oenone got a lovely boy,
Whom, for remembrance of her passed joy,
She, of his Father, Parius did name;
Who, after Greekes did Priams realme destroy,
Gathred the Trojan reliques sav'd from flame,
And with them sayling thence to th' isle of Paros came.

xxxvii. " That was by him cald Paros, which before
Hight Nausa: there he many yeares did raine,
And built Nausicle by the Pontick shore;
The which he dying lefte next in remaine
To Paridas his sonne,
From whom I Paridell by kin descend:
But, for faire ladies love and glories gaine,
My native soile have lefte, my dayes to spend
In seewing deeds of armes, my lives and labors end."

xxxviii. Whenas the noble Britomart heard tell
Of Trojan warres and Priams citie sackt,
The ruefull story of Sir Paridell,
She was empassiond at that piteous act,
With zelous envy of Greekes cruell fact
Against that nation, from whose race of old
She heard that she was lineally extract;
For noble Britons sprong from Trojans bold,
And Troynovant was built of old Troyes ashes cold.

xxxix. Then, sighing soft awhile, at last she thus:
    " O lamentable fall of famous towne!
    Which raignd so many yeares victorious,
    And of all Asie bore the soveraine crowne,
    In one sad night consumd and throwen downe:
    What stony hart, that heares thy haplesse fate,
    Is not empierst with deepe compassiowne,
    And makes ensample of mans wretched state,
    That floures so fresh at morne, and fades at evening
        late?

xl. " Behold, Sir, how your pitifull complaint
    Hath fownd another partner of your payne;
    For nothing may impresse so deare constraint
    As countries cause, and commune foes disdayne.
    But if it should not grieve you backe agayne
    To turne your course, I would to heare desyre
    What to Aeneas fell; sith that men sayne
    He was not in the cities wofull fyre
    Consum'd, but did him selfe to safety retyre."

xli. " Anchyses sonne, begott of Venus fayre,"
    Said he, " out of the flames for safegard fled,
    And with a remnant did to sea repayre;
    Where he through fatall errour long was led
    Full many yeares, and weetlesse wandered
    From shore to shore emongst the Lybick sandes,
    Ere rest he fownd.   Much there he suffered,
    And many perilles past in forreine landes,
    To save his people sad from victours vengefull handes.

xlii. " At last in Latium he did arryve,
    Where he with cruell warre was entertaind
    Of th' inland folke, which sought him backe to drive,
    Till he with old Latinus was constraind
    To contract wedlock, (so the fates ordaind)
    Wedlocke contract in blood, and eke in blood
    Accomplished, that many deare complaind:
    The rivall slaine, the victour, through the flood
    Escaped hardly, hardly praisd his wedlock good.

xliii. " Yet, after all, he victour did survive,
    And with Latinus did the kingdom part;

But after, when both nations gan to strive
Into their names the title to convart,
His sonne Iülus did from thence depart
With all the warlike youth of Trojans bloud,
And in long Alba plast his throne apart;
Where faire it florished and long time stoud,
Till Romulus, renewing it, to Rome remoud."

XLIV. "There; there," (said Britomart) "afresh appeard
The glory of the later world to spring,
And Troy againe out of her dust was reard
To sitt in second seat of soveraine king
Of all the world, under her governing.
But a third kingdom yet is to arise
Out of the Trojans scattered ofspring,
That in all glory and great enterprise,
Both first and second Troy shall dare to equalise.

XLV. "It Troynovant is hight, that with the waves
Of wealthy Thamis washed is along,
Upon whose stubborne neck, (whereat he raves
With roring rage, and sore him selfe does throng)
That all men feare to tempt his billowes strong,
She fastned hath her foot; which stands so hy,
That it a wonder of the world is song
In forreine landes; and all which passen by,
Beholding it from farre, doe thinke it threates the skye.

XLVI. "The Trojan Brute did first that citie fownd,
And Hygate made the meare thereof by West,
And Overt gate by North: that is the bownd
Toward the land; two rivers bownd the rest.
So huge a scope at first him seemed best,
To be the compasse of his kingdomes seat:
So huge a mind could not in lesser rest,
Ne in small meares containe his glory great,
That Albion had conquered first by warlike feat."

XLVII. "Ah! fairest Lady knight," (said Paridell)
"Pardon, I pray, my heedlesse oversight,
Who had forgot that whylome I heard tell
From aged Mnemon; for my wits beene light.
Indeed he said, (if I remember right)

CANTO X

Paridell rapeth Hellenore:
Malbecco her poursewes:
Fynds emongst Satyres, whence with him
To turne she doth refuse.

I. THE morow next, so soone as Phœbus Lamp
   Bewrayed had the world with early light,
   And fresh Aurora had the shady damp
   Out of the goodly heven amoved quight,
   Faire Britomart and that same Faery knight
   Uprose, forth on their journey for to wend:
   But Paridell complaynd, that his late fight
   With Britomart so sore did him offend,
   That ryde he could not, till his hurts he did amend.

II. So foorth they far'd; but he behind them stayd,
    Maulgre his host, who grudged grievously
    To house a guest that would be needes obayd,
    And of his owne him lefte not liberty:
    Might wanting measure moveth surquedry.
    Two things he feared, but the third was death;
    That fiers youngmans unruly maystery;
    His money, which he lov'd as living breath;
    And his faire wife, whom honest long he kept uneath.

III. But patience perforce, he must abie
     What fortune and his fate on him will lay;
     Fond is the feare that findes no remedie:
     Yet warily he watcheth every way,
     By which he feareth evill happen may;
     So th' evill thinkes by watching to prevent:
     Ne doth he suffer her, nor night nor day,
     Out of his sight her selfe once to absent:
     So doth he punish her, and eke him selfe torment.

IV. But Paridell kept better watch then hee,
    A fit occasion for his turne to finde.
    False love! why do men say thou canst not see,

And in their foolish fancy feigne thee blinde,
That with thy charmes the sharpest sight doest binde,
And to thy will abuse?   Thou walkest free,
And seest every secret of the minde;
Thou seest all, yet none at all sees thee:
All that is by the working of thy Deitee.

v. So perfect in that art was Paridell,
That he Malbeccoes halfen eye did wyle;
His halfen eye he wiled wondrous well,
And Hellenors both eyes did eke beguyle,
Both eyes and hart attonce, during the whyle
That he there sojourned his woundes to heale;
That Cupid selfe, it seeing, close did smyle
To weet how he her love away did steale,
And bad that none their joyous treason should reveale.

vi. The learned lover lost no time nor tyde
That least avantage mote to him afford,
Yet bore so faire a sayle, that none espyde
His secret drift, till he her layd abord.
When so in open place and commune bord
He fortun'd her to meet, with commune speach
He courted her; yet bayted every word,
That his ungentle hoste n'ote him appeach
Of vile ungentlenesse, or hospitages breach.

vii. But when apart (if ever her apart)
He found, then his false engins fast he plyde,
And all the sleights unbosomd in his hart:
He sigh'd, he sobd, he swownd, he perdy dyde,
And cast himselfe on ground her fast besyde:
Tho, when againe he him bethought to live,
He wept, and wayld, and false laments belyde,
Saying, but if she Mercie would him give,
That he mote algates dye, yet did his death forgive.

viii. And otherwhyles with amorous delights
And pleasing toyes he would her entertaine;
Now singing sweetly to surprize her sprights,
Now making layes of love and lovers paine,
Bransles, Ballads, virelayes, and verses vaine;
Oft purposes, oft riddles, he devysd,

And thousands like which flowed in his braine,
With which he fed her fancy, and entysd
To take to his new love, and leave her old despysd.

IX. And every where he might, and everie while,
He did her service dewtifull, and sewd
At hand with humble pride and pleasing guile;
So closely yet, that none but she it vewd,
Who well perceived all, and all indewd.
Thus finely did he his false nets dispred,
With which he many weake harts had subdewd
Of yore, and many had ylike misled:
What wonder then, if she were likewise carried?

X. No fort so fensible, no wals so strong,
But that continuall battery will rive,
Or daily siege, through dispurvayaunce long
And lacke of reskewes, will to parley drive;
And Peece, that unto parley eare will give,
Will shortly yield it selfe, and will be made
The vassall of the victors will bylive:
That stratageme had oftentimes assayd
This crafty Paramoure, and now it plaine display'd:

XI. For through his traines he her intrapped hath,
That she her love and hart hath wholy sold
To him, without regard of gaine or scath,
Or care of credite, or of husband old,
Whom she hath vow'd to dub a fayre Cucquold.
Nought wants but time and place, which shortly shee
Devized hath, and to her lover told.
It pleased well: So well they both agree:
So readie rype to ill ill wemens counsels bee!

XII. Darke was the Evening, fit for lovers stealth,
When chaunst Malbecco busie be elsewhere,
She to his closet went, where all his wealth
Lay hid; thereof she countlesse summes did reare,
The which she meant away with her to beare;
The rest she fyr'd, for sport, or for despight:
As Hellene, when she saw aloft appeare
The Trojane flames and reach to hevens hight,
Did clap her hands, and joyed at that dolefull sight.

XIII. This second Helene, fayre Dame Hellenore,
    The whiles her husband ran with sory haste
    To quench the flames which she had tyn'd before,
    Laught at his foolish labour spent in waste,
    And ran into her lovers armes right fast;
    Where streight embraced she to him did cry
    And call alowd for helpe, ere helpe were past;
    For lo! that Guest did beare her forcibly,
    And meant to ravish her, that rather had to dy.

XIV. The wretched man hearing her call for ayd,
    And ready seeing him with her to fly,
    In his disquiet mind was much dismayd:
    But when againe he backeward cast his eye,
    And saw the wicked fire so furiously
    Consume his hart, and scorch his Idoles face,
    He was therewith distressed diversely,
    Ne wist he how to turne, nor to what place:
    Was never wretched man in such a wofull cace.

XV. Ay when to him she cryde, to her he turnd,
    And left the fire; love money overcame:
    But, when he marked how his money burnd,
    He left his wife; money did love disclame:
    Both was he loth to loose his loved Dame,
    And loth to leave his liefest pelfe behinde;
    Yet, sith he n'ote save both, he sav'd that same
    Which was the dearest to his dounghill minde,
    The God of his desire, the joy of misers blinde.

XVI. Thus whilest all things in troublous uprore were,
    And all men busie to suppresse the flame,
    The loving couple neede no reskew feare,
    But leasure had and liberty to frame
    Their purpost flight, free from all mens reclame;
    And Night, the patronesse of love-stealth fayre,
    Gave them safe conduct, till to end they came.
    So beene they gone yfere, a wanton payre
    Of lovers loosely knit, where list them to repayre.

XVII. Soone as the cruell flames yslaked were,
    Malbecco, seeing how his losse did lye,
    Out of the flames which he had quencht whylere,

Into huge waves of griefe and gealosye
Full deepe emplonged was, and drowned nye
Twixt inward doole and felonous despight:
He rav'd, he wept, he stampt, he lowd did cry,
And all the passions that in man may light
Did him attonce oppresse, and vex his caytive spright.

XVIII. Long thus he chawd the cud of inward griefe,
And did consume his gall with anguish sore:
Still when he mused on his late mischiefe,
Then still the smart thereof increased more,
And seemd more grievous then it was before.
At last when sorrow he saw booted nought,
Ne griefe might not his love to him restore,
He gan devise how her he reskew mought:
Ten thousand wayes he cast in his confused thought.

XIX. At last resolving, like a Pilgrim pore,
To search her forth where so she might be fond,
And bearing with him treasure in close store,
The rest he leaves in ground: So takes in hond
To seeke her endlong both by sea and lond.
Long he her sought, he sought her far and nere,
And every where that he mote understond
Of knights and ladies any meetings were;
And of each one he mett he tidings did inquere.

XX. But all in vaine: his woman was too wise
Ever to come into his clouch againe,
And hee too simple ever to surprise
The jolly Paridell, for all his paine.
One day, as hee forpassed by the plaine
With weary pace, he far away espide
A couple, seeming well to be his twaine,
Which hoved close under a forest side,
As if they lay in wait, or els them selves did hide.

XXI. Well weened hee that those the same mote bee;
And as he better did their shape avize,
Him seemed more their maner did agree;
For th' one was armed all in warlike wize,
Whom to be Paridell he did devize;
And th' other, al yclad in garments light

Discolourd like to womanish disguise,
He did resemble to his lady bright;
And ever his faint hart much earned at the sight:

XXII. And ever faine he towards them would goe,
But yet durst not for dread approchen nie,
But stood aloofe, unweeting what to doe;
Till that prickt forth with loves extremity
That is the father of fowle gealosy,
He closely nearer crept the truth to weet:
But, as he nigher drew, he easily
Might scerne that it was not his sweetest sweet,
Ne yet her Belamour, the partner of his sheet:

XXIII. But it was scornefull Braggadochio,
That with his servant Trompart hoverd there,
Sith late he fled from his too earnest foe:
Whom such whenas Malbecco spyed clere,
He turned backe, and would have fled arere,
Till Trompart, ronning hastely, him did stay,
And bad before his soveraine Lord appere.
That was him loth, yet durst he not gainesay,
And comming him before low louted on the lay.

XXIV. The boaster at him sternely bent his browe,
As if he could have kild him with his looke,
That to the ground him meekely made to bowe,
And awfull terror deepe into him strooke,
That every member of his body quooke.
Said he, " Thou man of nought, what doest thou here
Unfitly furnisht with thy bag and booke,
Where I expected one with shield and spere
To prove some deeds of armes upon an equall pere? "

XXV. The wretched man at his imperious speach
Was all abasht, and low prostrating said:
" Good Sir, let not my rudenes be no breach
Unto your patience, ne be ill ypaid;
For I unwares this way by fortune straid,
A silly Pilgrim driven to distresse,
That seeke a Lady "—There he suddein staid,
And did the rest with grievous sighes suppresse,
While teares stood in his eies, few drops of bitternesse.

XXVI. "What Lady, man?" (said Trompart) "take good hart,
And tell thy griefe, if any hidden lye:
Was never better time to shew thy smart
Then now that noble succor is thee by,
That is the whole worlds commune remedy."
That chearful word his weak heart much did cheare,
And with vaine hope his spirits faint supply,
That bold he sayd; "O most redoubted Pere!
Vouchsafe with mild regard a wretches cace to heare."

XXVII. Then sighing sore, "It is not long," (saide hee)
"Sith I enjoyd the gentlest Dame alive;
Of whom a knight, no knight at all perdee,
But shame of all that doe for honor strive,
By treacherous deceipt did me deprive:
Through open outrage he her bore away,
And with fowle force unto his will did drive;
Which al good knights, that armes doe bear this day,
Are bownd for to revenge, and punish if they may.

XXVIII. "And you, most noble Lord, that can and dare
Redresse the wrong of miserable wight,
Cannot employ your most victorious speare
In better quarell then defence of right,
And for a Lady gainst a faithlesse knight:
So shall your glory bee advaunced much,
And all faire Ladies magnify your might,
And eke my selfe, albee I simple such,
Your worthy paine shall wel reward with guerdon rich."

XXIX. With that out of his bouget forth he drew
Great store of treasure, therewith him to tempt;
But he on it lookt scornefully askew,
As much disdeigning to be so misdempt,
Or a war-monger to be basely nempt;
And sayd; "Thy offers base I greatly loth,
And eke thy words uncourteous and unkempt:
I tread in dust thee and thy money both,
That, were it not for shame"—So turned from him
        wroth.

XXX. But Trompart, that his maistres humor knew
In lofty looks to hide an humble minde,
Was inly tickled with that golden vew.

And in his eare him rownded close behinde:
Yet stoupt he not, but lay still in the winde,
Waiting advauntage on the pray to sease,
Till Trompart, lowly to the grownd inclinde,
Besought him his great corage to appease,
And pardon simple man that rash did him displease.

XXXI. Big looking like a doughty Doucepere,
At last he thus; "Thou clod of vilest clay,
I pardon yield, and with thy rudenes beare;
But weete henceforth, that all that golden pray,
And all that els the vaine world vaunten may,
I loath as doung, ne deeme my dew reward:
Fame is my meed, and glory vertues pay:
But minds of mortall men are muchell mard
And mov'd amisse with massy mucks unmeet regard.

XXXII. "And more: I graunt to thy great misery
Gratious respect; thy wife shall backe be sent:
And that vile knight, who ever that he bee,
Which hath thy lady reft and knighthood shent,
By Sanglamort my sword, whose deadly dent
The blood hath of so many thousands shedd,
I sweare, ere long shall dearely it repent;
Ne he twixt heven and earth shall hide his hedd,
But soone he shal be fownd, and shortly doen be dedd."

XXXIII. The foolish man thereat woxe wondrous blith,
As if the word so spoken were halfe donne,
And humbly thanked him a thousand sith
That had from death to life him newly wonne,
Tho forth the Boaster marching brave begonne
His stolen steed to thunder furiously,
As if he heaven and hell would over-ronne,
And all the world confound with cruelty;
That much Malbecco joyed in his jollity.

XXXIV. Thus long they three together traveiled,
Through many a wood and many an uncouth way,
To seeke his wife that was far wandered:
But those two sought not but the present pray,
To weete, the treasure which he did bewray,
On which their eies and harts were wholly sett,

With purpose how they might it best betray;
For, sith the howre that first he did them lett
The same behold, therwith their keene desires were
    whett.

xxxv. It fortuned, as they together far'd,
They spide where Paridell came pricking fast
Upon the plaine; the which him selfe prepar'd
To guist with that brave straunger knight a cast,
As on adventure by the way he past,
Alone he rode without his Paragone;
For, having filcht her bells, her up he cast
To the wide world, and lett her fly alone:
He nould be clogd. So had he served many one.

xxxvi. The gentle Lady, loose at randon lefte,
The greene-wood long did walke, and wander wide
At wilde adventure, like a forlorne wefte;
Till on a day the Satyres her espide
Straying alone withouten groome or guide:
Her up they tooke, and with them home her ledd,
With them as housewife ever to abide,
To milk their gotes, and make them cheese and bredd;
And every one as commune good her handeled

xxxvii. That shortly she Malbecco has forgott,
And eke Sir Paridell, all were he deare;
Who from her went to seeke another lott,
And now by fortune was arrived here,
Where those two guilers with Malbecco were.
Soone as the old man saw Sir Paridell,
He fainted, and was almost dead with feare,
Ne word he had to speake his griefe to tell,
But to him louted low, and greeted goodly well;

xxxviii. And, after, asked him for Hellenore:
" I take no keepe of her," (sayd Paridell)
" She wonneth in the forrest there before."
So forth he rode as his adventure fell;
The whiles the Boaster from his loftie sell
Faynd to alight, something amisse to mend;
But the fresh Swayne would not his leasure dwell,
But went his way: whom when he passed kend,
He up remounted light, and after faind to wend.

XXXIX. " Perdy, nay," (said Malbecco) " shall ye not;
But let him passe as lightly as he came:
For litle good of him is to be got,
And mickle perill to bee put to shame.
But let us goe to seeke my dearest Dame,
Whom he hath left in yonder forest wyld;
For of her safety in great doubt I ame,
Least salvage beastes her person have despoyld:
Then all the world is lost, and we in vaine have toyld."

XL. They all agree, and forward them addresse:
" Ah! but," (said crafty Trompart) " weete ye well,
That yonder in that wastefull wildernesse
Huge monsters haunt, and many dangers dwell;
Dragons, and Minotaures, and feendes of hell,
And many wilde woodmen which robbe and rend
All traveilers: therefore advise ye well
Before ye enterprise that way to wend:
One may his journey bring too soone to evill end."

XLI. Malbecco stopt in great astonishment,
And with pale eyes fast fixed on the rest,
Their counsell crav'd in daunger imminent.
Said Trompart; " You, that are the most opprest
With burdein of great treasure, I thinke best
Here for to stay in safetie behynd:
My Lord and I will search the wide forest."
That counsell pleased not Malbeccoes mynd,
For he was much afraid him selfe alone to fynd.

XLII. " Then is it best," (said he) " that ye doe leave
Your treasure here in some security,
Either fast closed in some hollow greave,
Or buried in the ground from jeopardy,
Till we returne againe in safety:
As for us two, least doubt of us ye have,
Hence farre away we will blyndfolded ly,
Ne privy bee unto your treasures grave."
It pleased; so he did. Then they march forward brave.

XLIII. Now, when amid the thickest woodes they were,
They heard a noyse of many bagpipes shrill,
And shrieking Hububs them approching nere,
Which all the forest did with horrour fill.

That dreadfull sound the bosters hart did thrill
With such amazment, that in hast he fledd,
Ne ever looked back for good or ill;
And after him eke fearefull Trompart spedd:
The old man could not fly, but fell to ground half dedd.

XLIV. Yet afterwardes, close creeping as he might,
He in a bush did hyde his fearefull hedd.
The jolly Satyres, full of fresh delight,
Came dauncing forth, and with them nimbly ledd
Faire Helenore with girlonds all bespredd,
Whom their May-lady they had newly made:
She, proude of that new honour which they redd,
And of their lovely fellowship full glade,
Daunst lively, and her face did with a Lawrell shade.

XLV. The silly man that in the thickett lay
Saw all this goodly sport, and grieved sore;
Yet durst he not against it doe or say,
But did his hart with bitter thoughts engore,
To see th' unkindnes of his Hellenore.
All day they daunced with great lusty-hedd,
And with their horned feet the greene gras wore,
The whiles their Gotes upon the brouzes fedd,
Till drouping Phœbus gan to hyde his golden hedd.

XLVI. Tho up they gan their mery pypes to trusse,
And all their goodly heardes did gather rownd;
But every Satyre first did give a busse
To Hellenore; so busses did abound.
Now gan the humid vapour shed the grownd
With perly deaw, and th' Earthes gloomy shade
Did dim the brightnesse of the welkin rownd,
That every bird and beast awarned made
To shrowd themselves, whiles sleepe their sences did invade.

XLVII. Which when Malbecco saw, out of the bush
Upon his handes and feete he crept full light,
And like a Gote emongst the Gotes did rush;
That, through the helpe of his faire hornes on hight,
And misty dampe of misconceyving night,
And eke through likenesse of his gotish beard,
He did the better counterfeite aright:
So home he marcht emongst the horned heard,
That none of all the Satyres him espyde or heard.

XLVIII. At night, when all they went to sleepe, he vewd
    Whereas his lovely wife emongst them lay,
    Embraced of a Satyre rough and rude,
    Who all the night did minde his joyous play:
    Nine times he heard him come aloft ere day,
    That all his hart with gealosy did swell;
    But yet that nights ensample did bewray
    That not for nought his wife them loved so well,
    When one so oft a night did ring his matins bell.

XLIX. So closely as he could he to them crept,
    When wearie of their sport to sleepe they fell,
    And to his wife, that now full soundly slept,
    He whispered in her eare, and did her tell
    That it was he which by her side did dwell;
    And therefore prayd her wake to heare him plaine.
    As one out of a dreame not waked well
    She turnd her, and returned back againe;
    Yet her for to awake he did the more constraine.

L. At last with irkesom trouble she abrayd;
    And then perceiving that it was indeed
    Her old Malbecco, which did her upbrayd
    With loosenesse of her love and loathly deed,
    She was astonisht with exceeding dreed,
    And would have wakt the Satyre by her syde;
    But he her prayd, for mercy or for meed,
    To save his life, ne let him be descryde,
    But hearken to his lore, and all his counsell hyde.

LI. Tho gan he her perswade to leave that lewd
    And loathsom life, of God and man abhord,
    And home returne, where all should be renewd
    With perfect peace and bandes of fresh accord,
    And she receivd againe to bed and bord,
    As if no trespas ever had beene donne:
    But she it all refused at one word,
    And by no meanes would to his will be wonne,
    But chose emongst the jolly Satyres still to wonne.

LII. He wooed her till day-spring he espyde,
    But all in vaine; and then turnd to the heard,
    Who butted him with hornes on every syde,

And trode downe in the durt, where his hore beard
Was fowly dight, and he of death afeard.
Early, before the heavens fairest light
Out of the ruddy East was fully reard,
The heardes out of their foldes were loosed quight,
And he emongst the rest crept forth in sory plight.

LIII. So soone as he the Prison-dore did pas,
He ran as fast as both his feet could beare,
And never looked who behind him was,
Ne scarsely who before: like as a Beare,
That creeping close amongst the hives to reare
An hony-combe, the wakefull dogs espy,
And him assayling sore his carkas teare,
That hardly he with life away does fly,
Ne stayes, till safe him selfe he see from jeopardy.

LIV. Ne stayd he, till he came unto the place
Where late his treasure he entombed had;
Where when he found it not, (for Trompart bace
Had it purloyned for his maister bad)
With extreme fury he became quite mad,
And ran away, ran with him selfe away;
That who so straungely had him seene bestadd,
With upstart haire and staring eyes dismay,
From Limbo lake him late escaped sure would say.

LV. High over hilles and over dales he fledd,
As if the wind him on his winges had borne;
Ne banck nor bush could stay him, when he spedd
His nimble feet, as treading still on thorne:
Griefe, and despight, and gealosy, and scorne,
Did all the way him follow hard behynd;
And he himselfe himselfe loath'd so forlorne,
So shamefully forlorne of womankynd,
That, as a Snake, still lurked in his wounded mynd.

LVI. Still fled he forward, looking backward still;
Ne stayd his flight nor fearefull agony,
Till that he came unto a rocky hill
Over the sea suspended dreadfully,
That living creature it would terrify
To looke adowne, or upward to the hight:

From thence he threw him selfe despiteously,
All desperate of his fore-damned spright,
That seemd no help for him was left in living sight.

LVII. But through long anguish and selfe-murdring thought,
He was so wasted and forpined quight,
That all his substance was consum'd to nought,
And nothing left but like an aery Spright,
That on the rockes he fell so flit and light,
That he thereby receiv'd no hurt at all;
But chaunced on a craggy cliff to light,
Whence he with crooked clawes so long did crall,
That at the last he found a cave with entrance small.

LVIII. Into the same he creepes, and thenceforth there
Resolv'd to build his balefull mansion
In drery darkenes and continuall feare
Of that rocks fall, which ever and anon
Threates with huge ruine him to fall upon,
That he dare never sleepe, but that one eye
Still ope he keepes for that occasion;
Ne ever rests he in tranquillity,
The roring billowes beat his bowre so boystrously.

LIX. Ne ever is he wont on ought to feed
But todes and frogs, his pasture poysonous,
Which in his cold complexion doe breed
A filthy blood, or humour rancorous,
Matter of doubt and dread suspitious,
That doth with curelesse care consume the hart,
Corrupts the stomacke with gall vitious,
Cros-cuts the liver with internall smart,
And doth transfixe the soule with deathes eternall dart

LX. Yet can he never dye, but dying lives,
And doth himselfe with sorrow new sustaine,
That death and life attonce unto him gives,
And painefull pleasure turnes to pleasing paine.
There dwels he ever, miserable swaine,
Hatefull both to him selfe and every wight;
Where he, through privy griefe and horrour vaine,
It woxen so deform'd that he has quight
Forgot he was a man, and Gelosy is hight.

CANTO XI

Britomart chaceth Ollyphant;
Findes Scudamour distrest:
Assayes the house of Busyrane,
Where loves spoyles are exprest.

I. O HATEFULL hellish Snake! what furie furst
Brought thee from balefull house of Proserpine,
Where in her bosome she thee long had nurst,
And fostred up with bitter milke of tine,
Fowle Gealosy! that turnest love divine
To joylesse dread, and mak'st the loving hart
With hatefull thoughts to languish and to pine,
And feed it selfe with selfe-consuming smart?
Of all the passions in the mind thou vilest art!

II. O! let him far be banished away,
And in his stead let Love for ever dwell;
Sweete Love, that doth his golden wings embay
In blessed Nectar and pure Pleasures well,
Untroubled of vile feare or bitter fell.
And ye, faire Ladies, that your kingdomes make
In th' harts of men, them governe wisely well,
And of faire Britomart ensample take,
That was as trew in love as Turtle to her make.

III. Who with Sir Satyrane, as earst ye red,
Forth ryding from Malbeccoes hostlesse hous,
Far off aspyde a young man, the which fled
From an huge Geaunt, that with hideous
And hatefull outrage long him chaced thus;
It was that Ollyphant, the brother deare
Of that Argantè vile and vitious,
From whom the Squyre of Dames was reft whylere
This all as bad as she, and worse, if worse ought were.

IV. For as the sister did in feminine
And filthy lust exceede all womankinde,
So he surpassed his sex masculine,

In beastly use, all that I ever finde:
Whom when as Britomart beheld behinde
The fearefull boy so greedily poursew,
She was emmoved in her noble minde,
T' employ her puissaunce to his reskew,
And pricked fiercely forward where she did him vew.

v. Ne was Sir Satyrane her far behinde,
But with like fiercenesse did ensew the chace.
Whom when the Gyaunt saw, he soone resinde
His former suit, and from them fled apace:
They after both, and boldly bad him bace,
And each did strive the other to outgoe;
But he them both outran a wondrous space,
For he was long, and swift as any Roe,
And now made better speed t' escape his feared foe.

vi. It was not Satyrane, whom he did feare,
But Britomart the flowre of chastity;
For he the powre of chaste hands might not beare,
But alwayes did their dread encounter fly:
And now so fast his feet he did apply,
That he has gotten to a forrest neare,
Where he is shrowded in security.
The wood they enter, and search everie where;
They searched diversely, so both divided were.

vii. Fayre Britomart so long him followed,
That she at last came to a fountaine sheare,
By which there lay a knight all wallowed
Upon the grassy ground, and by him neare
His haberjeon, his helmet, and his speare:
A little off his shield was rudely throwne,
On which the winged boy in colours cleare
Depeincted was, full easie to be knowne,
And he thereby, where ever it in field was showne.

viii. His face upon the grownd did groveling ly,
As if he had beene slombring in the shade;
That the brave Mayd would not for courtesy
Out of his quiet slomber him abrade,
Nor seeme too suddeinly him to invade.
Still as she stood, she heard with grievous throb

Him grone, as if his hart were peeces made,
And with most painefull pangs to sigh and sob,
That pitty did the Virgins hart of patience rob.

IX. At last forth breaking into bitter plaintes
He sayd; "O soverayne Lord! that sit'st on hye
And raignst in blis emongst thy blessed Saintes,
How suffrest thou such shamefull cruelty
So long unwreaked of thine enimy?
Or hast thou, Lord, of good mens cause no heed?
Or doth thy justice sleepe and silent ly?
What booteth then the good and righteous deed,
If goodnesse find no grace, nor righteousnes no meed?

X. "If good find grace, and righteousnes reward,
Why then is Amoret in caytive band,
Sith that more bounteous creature never far'd
On foot upon the face of living land?
Or if that hevenly justice may withstand
The wrongfull outrage of unrighteous men,
Why then is Busirane with wicked hand
Suffred, these seven monethes day, in secret den
My Lady and my love so cruelly to pen!

XI. "My Lady and my love is cruelly pend
In dolefull darkenes from the vew of day,
Whilest deadly torments doe her chast brest rend,
And the sharpe steele doth rive her hart in tway,
All for she Scudamore will not denay.
Yet thou, vile man, vile Scudamore, art sound,
Ne canst her ayde, ne canst her foe dismay;
Unworthy wretch to tread upon the ground,
For whom so faire a Lady feeles so sore a wound!"

XII. There an huge heape of singults did oppresse
His strugling soule, and swelling throbs empeach
His foltring toung with pangs of drerinesse,
Choking the remnant of his plaintife speach,
As if his dayes were come to their last reach:
Which when she heard, and saw the ghastly fit
Threatning into his life to make a breach,
Both with great ruth and terrour she was smit,
Fearing least from her cage the wearie soule would flit.

XIII. Tho stouping downe she him amoved light;
Who, therewith somewhat starting, up gan looke,
And seeing him behind a stranger knight,
Whereas no living creature he mistooke,
With great indignaunce he that sight forsooke,
And, downe againe himselfe disdainfully
Abjecting, th' earth with his faire forhead strooke:
Which the bold Virgin seeing gan apply
Fit medcine to his griefe, and spake thus courtesly:—

XIV. " Ah gentle knight! whose deepe conceived griefe
Well seemes t' exceed the powre of patience,
Yet, if that hevenly grace some goode reliefe
You send, submit you to high providence;
And ever in your noble hart prepense,
That all the sorrow in the world is lesse
Then vertues might and values confidence:
For who nill bide the burden of distresse,
Must not here thinke to live; for life is wretchednesse.

XV. " Therefore, faire Sir, doe comfort to you take,
And freely read what wicked felon so
Hath outrag'd you, and thrald your gentle make.
Perhaps this hand may helpe to ease your woe,
And wreake your sorrow on your cruell foe; ·
At least it faire endevour will apply."
Those feeling words so neare the quicke did goe,
That up his head he reared easily,
And, leaning on his elbowe, these few words lett fly.

XVI. " What boots it plaine that cannot be redrest,
And sow vaine sorrow in a fruitlesse eare,
Sith powre of hand, nor skill of learned brest,
Ne worldly price, cannot redeeme my deare
Out of her thraldome and continuall feare:
For he, the tyrant, which her hath in ward
By strong enchauntments and blacke Magicke leare,
Hath in a dungeon deepe her close embard,
And many dreadfull feends hath pointed to her gard.

XVII. " There he tormenteth her most terribly
And day and night afflicts with mortall paine,
Because to yield him love she doth deny,

Once to me yold, not to be yolde againe:
But yet by torture he would her constraine
Love to conceive in her disdainfull brest;
Till so she doe, she must in doole remaine,
Ne may by living meanes be thence relest:
What boots it then to plaine that cannot be redrest?"

XVIII. With this sad hersall of his heavy stresse
The warlike Damzell was empassiond sore,
And sayd; "Sir knight, your cause is nothing lesse
Then is your sorrow certes, if not more;
For nothing so much pitty doth implore
As gentle Ladyes helplesse misery:
But yet, if please ye listen to my lore,
I will, with proofe of last extremity,
Deliver her fro thence, or with her for you dy.

XIX. "Ah! gentlest knight alive," (sayd Scudamore)
"What huge heroicke magnanimity
Dwells in thy bounteous brest! what couldst thou more,
If shee were thine, and thou as now am I?
O! spare thy happy daies, and them apply
To better boot; but let me die that ought:
More is more losse; one is enough to dy."
"Life is not lost," (said she) "for which is bought
Endlesse renowm, that, more then death, is to be sought."

XX. Thus shee at length persuaded him to rise,
And with her wend to see what new successe
Mote him befall upon new enterprise.
His armes, which he had vowed to disprofesse,
She gathered up and did about him dresse,
And his forwandred steed unto him gott:
So forth they forth yfere make their progresse,
And march not past the mountenaunce of a shott,
Till they arriv'd whereas their purpose they did plott.

XXI. There they dismounting drew their weapons bold,
And stoutly came unto the Castle gate,
Whereas no gate they found them to withhold,
Nor ward to waite at morne and evening late;
But in the Porch, that did them sore amate,
A flaming fire, ymixt with smouldry smoke

I   Q

And stinking sulphure, that with griesly hate
And dreadfull horror did all entraunce choke,
Enforced them their forward footing to revoke.

XXII. Greatly thereat was Britomart dismayd,
Ne in that stownd wist how her selfe to beare;
For daunger vaine it were to have assayd
That cruell element, which all things feare,
Ne none can suffer to approchen neare:
And, turning backe to Scudamour, thus sayd:
"What monstrous enmity provoke we heare?
Foolhardy as th' Earthes children, the which made
Batteill against the Gods, so we a God invade.

XXIII. "Daunger without discretion to attempt
Inglorious, beastlike is: therefore, Sir knight,
Aread what course of you is safest dempt,
And how he with our foe may come to fight."
"This is" (quoth he) "the dolorous despight,
Which earst to you I playnd: for neither may
This fire be quencht by any witt or might,
Ne yet by any meanes remov'd away;
So mighty be th' enchauntments which the same do stay.

XXIV. "What is there ells but cease these fruitlesse paines,
And leave me to my former languishing?
Faire Amorett must dwell in wicked chaines,
And Scudamore here die with sorrowing."
"Perdy not so," (saide shee) "for shameful thing
Yt were t' abandon noble chevisaunce
For shewe of perill, without venturing:
Rather let try extremities of chaunce,
Then enterprised praise for dread to disavaunce."

XXV. Therewith, resolv'd to prove her utmost might,
Her ample shield she threw before her face,
And her swords point directing forward right
Assayld the flame; the which eftesoones gave place,
And did it selfe divide with equall space,
That through she passed, as a thonder bolt
Perceth the yielding ayre, and doth displace
The soring clouds into sad showres ymolt;
So to her yold the flames, and did their force revolt.

XXVI. Whom whenas Scudamour saw past the fire
      Safe and untoucht, he likewise gan assay
      With greedy will and envious desire,
      And bad the stubborne flames to yield him way:
      But cruell Mulciber would not obay
      His threatfull pride, but did the more augment
      His mighty rage, and with imperious sway
      Him forst, (maulgre) his fercenes to relent,
      And backe retire, all scorcht and pittifully brent.

XXVII. With huge impatience he inly swelt,
       More for great sorrow that he could not pas
       Then for the burning torment which he felt;
       That with fell woodnes he effierced was,
       And wilfully him throwing on the gras
       Did beat and bounse his head and brest ful sore:
       The whiles the Championesse now entred has
       The utmost rowme, and past the foremost dore;
       The utmost rowme abounding with all precious store:

XXVIII. For round about the walls yclothed were
        With goodly arras of great majesty,
        Woven with gold and silke, so close and nere
        That the rich metall lurked privily,
        As faining to be hidd from envious eye;
        Yet here, and there, and every where, unwares
        It shewd it selfe and shone unwillingly;
        Like a discoloured Snake, whose hidden snares
        Through the greene gras his long bright burnisht back
              declares.

XXIX. And in those Tapets weren fashioned
      Many faire pourtraicts, and many a faire feate;
      And all of love, and al of lusty-hed,
      As seemed by their semblaunt, did entreat:
      And eke all Cupids warres they did repeate,
      And cruell battailes, which he whilome fought
      Gainst all the Gods to make his empire great;
      Besides the huge massacres, which he wrought
      On mighty kings and kesars into thraldome brought.

XXX. Therein was writt how often thondring Jove
     Had felt the point of his hart-percing dart,
     And, leaving heavens kingdome, here did rove

I   Q 2

In straunge disguize, to slake his scalding smart;
Now, like a Ram, faire Helle to pervart,
Now, like a Bull, Europa to withdraw:
Ah! how the fearefull Ladies tender hart
Did lively seeme to tremble, when she saw
The huge seas under her t' obay her servaunts law.

XXXI. Soone after that, into a golden showre
Him selfe he chaung'd, faire Danaë to vew;
And through the roofe of her strong brasen towre
Did raine into her lap an hony dew;
The whiles her foolish garde, that litle knew
Of such deceipt, kept th' yron dore fast bard,
And watcht that none should enter nor issew:
Vaine was the watch, and bootlesse all the ward,
Whenas the God to golden hew him selfe transfard.

XXXII. Then was he turnd into a snowy Swan,
To win faire Leda to his lovely trade:
O wondrous skill! and sweet wit of the man,
That her in daffadillies sleeping made
From scorching heat her daintie limbes to shade;
Whiles the proud Bird, ruffing his fethers wyde
And brushing his faire brest, did her invade:
She slept; yet twixt her eielids closely spyde
How towards her he rusht, and smiled at his pryde.

XXXIII. Then shewd it how the Thebane Semelee,
Deceivd of gealous Juno, did require
To see him in his soverayne majestee
Armd with his thunderbolts and lightning fire,
Whens dearely she with death bought her desire.
But faire Alcmena better match did make,
Joying his love in likenes more entire:
Three nights in one, they say, that for her sake
He then did put, her pleasures lenger to partake.

XXXIV. Twise was he seene in soaring Eagles shape,
And with wide winges to beat the buxome ayre:
Once, when he with Asterie did scape;
Againe, when as the Trojane boy so fayre
He snatcht from Ida hill, and with him bare:
Wondrous delight it was there to behould

How the rude Shepheards after him did stare,
Trembling through feare least down he fallen should,
And often to him calling to take surer hould.

XXXV. In Satyres shape Antiopa he snatcht;
And like a fire, when he Aegin' assayd:
A shepeheard, when Mnemosyne he catcht;
And like a Serpent to the Thracian mayd.
Whyles thus on earth great Jove these pageaunts playd,
The winged boy did thrust into his throne,
And scoffing thus unto his mother sayd:
" Lo! now the hevens obey to me alone,
And take me for their Jove, whiles Jove to earth is
        gone."

XXXVI. And thou, faire Phœbus, in thy colours bright
Wast there enwoven, and the sad distresse
In which that boy thee plonged, for despight
That thou bewray'dst his mothers wantonnesse,
When she with Mars was meynt in joyfulnesse:
Forthy he thrild thee with a leaden dart
To love faire Daphne, which thee loved lesse;
Lesse she thee lov'd then was thy just desart,
Yet was thy love her death, and her death was thy
        smart.

XXXVII. So lovedst thou the lusty Hyacinct;
So lovedst thou the faire Coronis deare;
Yet both are of thy haplesse hand extinct,
Yet both in flowres doe live, and love thee beare,
The one a Paunce, the other a sweet-breare:
For griefe whereof, ye mote have lively seene
The God himselfe rending his golden heare,
And breaking quite his garlond ever greene,
With other signes of sorrow and impatient teene.

XXXVIII. Both for those two, and for his owne deare sonne,
The sonne of Climene, he did repent;
Who, bold to guide the charet of the Sunne,
Himselfe in thousand peeces fondly rent,
And all the world with flashing fire brent;
So like, that all the walles did seeme to flame:
Yet cruell Cupid, not herewith content,

Forst him eftsoones to follow other game,
And love a Shephards daughter for his dearest Dame.

XXXIX. He loved Isse for his dearest Dame,
And for her sake her cattell fedd awhile,
And for her sake a cowheard vile became
The servant of Admetus, cowheard vile,
Whiles that from heaven he suffered exile.
Long were to tell each other lovely fitt;
Now, like a Lyon hunting after spoile;
Now, like a stag; now, like a faulcon flit:
All which in that faire arras was most lively writ.

XL. Next unto him was Neptune pictured,
In his divine resemblance wondrous lyke:
His face was rugged, and his hoarie hed
Dropped with brackish deaw: his threeforkt Pyke
He stearnly shooke, and therewith fierce did stryke
The raging billowes, that on every syde
They trembling stood, and made a long broad dyke,
That his swift charet might have passage wyde
Which foure great Hippodames did draw in temewise
    tyde.

XLI. His seahorses did seeme to snort amayne,
And from their nosethrilles blow the brynie streame,
That made the sparckling waves to smoke agayne,
And flame with gold; but the white fomy creame
Did shine with silver, and shoot forth his beame.
The God himselfe did pensive seeme and sad,
And hong adowne his head as he did dreame;
For privy love his brest empierced had,
Ne ought but deare Bisaltis ay could make him glad.

XLII. He loved eke Iphimedia deare,
And Aeolus faire daughter, Arnè hight,
For whom he turned him selfe into a Steare,
And fedd on fodder to beguile her sight.
Also to win Deucalions daughter bright,
He turned him selfe into a Dolphin fayre;
And like a winged horse he tooke his flight
To snaky-locke Medusa to repayre,
On whom he got faire Pegasus that flitteth in the ayre.

XLIII. Next Saturne was, (but who would ever weene
      That sullein Saturne ever weend to love?
      Yet love is sullein, and Saturnlike seene,
      As he did for Erigone it prove)
      That to a Centaure did him selfe transmove.
      So proov'd it eke that gratious God of wine,
      When for to compasse Philliras hard love,
      He turnd himselfe into a fruitfull vine,
      And into her faire bosome made his grapes decline.

XLIV. Long were to tell the amorous assayes,
      And gentle pangues, with which he maked meeke
      The mightie Mars, to learne his wanton playes;
      How oft for Venus, and how often eek
      For many other Nymphes, he sore did shreek,
      With womanish teares, and with unwarlike smarts,
      Privily moystening his horrid cheeke:
      There was he painted full of burning dartes,
      And many wide woundes launched through his inner partes.

XLV. Ne did he spare (so cruell was the Elfe)
      His owne deare mother, (ah! why should he so?)
      Ne did he spare sometime to pricke himselfe,
      That he might taste the sweet consuming woe,
      Which he had wrought to many others moe.
      But, to declare the mournfull Tragedyes
      And spoiles wherewith he all the ground did strow,
      More eath to number with how many eyes
      High heven beholdes sad lovers nightly theeveryes.

XLVI. Kings, Queenes, Lords, Ladies, knights, and Damsels gent,
      Were heap'd together with the vulgar sort,
      And mingled with the raskall rablement,
      Without respect of person or of port,
      To shew Dan Cupids powre and great effort:
      And round about a border was entrayld
      Of broken bowes and arrowes shivered short;
      And a long bloody river through them rayld,
      So lively and so like that living sence it fayld.

XLVII. And at the upper end of that faire rowme
      There was an Altar built of pretious stone
      Of passing valew and of great renowme,

On which there stood an Image all alone
Of massy gold, which with his owne light shone;
And winges it had with sondry colours dight,
More sondry colours then the proud Pavone
Beares in his boasted fan, or Iris bright,
When her discolourd bow she spreds through hevens hight.

XLVIII. Blyndfold he was; and in his cruell fist
A mortall bow and arrowes keene did hold,
With which he shot at randon, when him list,
Some headed with sad lead, some with pure gold;
(Ah man! beware how thou those dartes behold.)
A wounded Dragon under him did ly,
Whose hideous tayle his lefte foot did enfold,
And with a shaft was shot through either eye,
That no man forth might draw, ne no man remedye.

XLIX. And underneath his feet was written thus,
Unto the Victor of the Gods this bee :
And all the people in that ample hous
Did to that image bowe their humble knee,
And oft committed fowle Idolatree.
That wondrous sight faire Britomart amazd,
Ne seeing could her wonder satisfie,
But ever more and more upon it gazd,
The whiles the passing brightnes her fraile sences dazd.

L. Tho, as she backward cast her busie eye
To search each secrete of that goodly sted,
Over the dore thus written she did spye,
Bee bold : she oft and oft it over-red,
Yet could not find what sence it figured:
But what so were therein or writ or ment,
She was no whit thereby discouraged
From prosecuting of her first intent,
But forward with bold steps into the next roome went.

LI. Much fayrer then the former was that roome,
And richlier by many partes arayd;
For not with arras made in painefull loome,
But with pure gold it all was overlayd,
Wrought with wilde Antickes, which their follies playd
In the rich metall as they living were.

A thousand monstrous formes therein were made,
Such as false love doth oft upon him weare;
For love in thousand monstrous formes doth oft appeare.

LII. And all about the glistring walles were hong
With warlike spoiles and with victorious prayes
Of mightie Conquerours and Captaines strong,
Which were whilome captived in their dayes
To cruell love, and wrought their owne decayes.
Their swerds and speres were broke, and hauberques rent,
And their proud girlonds of tryumphant bayes
Troden in dust with fury insolent,
To shew the victors might and mercilesse intent.

LIII. The warlike Mayd, beholding earnestly
The goodly ordinaunce of this rich Place,
Did greatly wonder; ne could satisfy
Her greedy eyes with gazing a long space:
But more she mervaild that no footings trace
Nor wight appeard, but wastefull emptinesse
And solemne silence over all that place:
Straunge thing it seem'd, that none was to possesse
So rich purveyaunce, ne them keepe with carefulnesse.

LIV. And, as she lookt about, she did behold
How over that same dore was likewise writ,
Be bolde, be bolde, and every where, *Be bold ;*
That much she muz'd, yet could not construe it
By any ridling skill, or commune wit.
At last she spyde at that rowmes upper end
Another yron dore, on which was writ,
Be not too bold ; whereto though she did bend
Her earnest minde, yet wist not what it might intend.

LV. Thus she there wayted untill eventyde,
Yet living creature none she saw appeare,
And now sad shadowes gan the world to hyde
From mortall vew, and wrap in darkenes dreare;
Yet nould she d'off her weary armes, for feare
Of secret daunger, ne let sleepe oppresse
Her heavy eyes with natures burdein deare,
But drew her selfe aside in sickernesse,
And her wel-pointed wepons did about her dresse.

CANTO XII

The maske of Cupid, and th enchant-
ed Chamber are displayd;
Whence Britomart redeemes faire A-
moret through charmes decayd.

I. Tho, whenas chearelesse Night ycovered had
Fayre heaven with an universall clowd,
That every wight dismayd with darkenes sad
In silence and in sleepe themselves did shrowd,
She heard a shrilling Trompet sound alowd,
Signe of nigh battaill, or got victory:
Nought therewith daunted was her courage prowd,
But rather stird to cruell enmity,
Expecting ever when some foe she might descry.

II. With that an hideous storme of winde arose,
With dreadfull thunder and lightning atwixt,
And an earthquake, as if it streight would lose
The worlds foundations from his centre fixt:
A direfull stench of smoke and sulphure mixt
Ensewd, whose noyaunce fild the fearefull sted
From the fourth howre of night untill the sixt;
Yet the bold Britonesse was nought ydred,
Though much emmov'd, but stedfast still persevered.

III. All suddeinly a stormy whirlwind blew
Throughout the house, that clapped every dore,
With which that yron wicket open flew,
As it with mighty levers had bene tore,
And forth yssewd, as on the readie flore
Of some Theatre, a grave personage
That in his hand a braunch of laurell bore,
With comely haveour and count'nance sage,
Yclad in costly garments fit for tragicke Stage.

IV. Proceeding to the midst he stil did stand,
As if in minde he somewhat had to say;
And to the vulgare beckning with his hand,

In signe of silence, as to heare a play,
By lively actions he gan bewray
Some argument of matter passioned:
Which doen, he backe retyred soft away,
And, passing by, his name discovered,
Ease, on his robe in golden letters cyphered.

v. The noble Mayd still standing all this vewd,
And merveild at his straunge intendiment.
With that a joyous fellowship issewd
Of Minstrales making goodly meriment,
With wanton Bardes, and Rymers impudent;
All which together song full chearefully
A lay of loves delight with sweet concent:
After whom marcht a jolly company,
In manner of a maske, enranged orderly.

vi. The whiles a most delitious harmony
In full straunge notes was sweetly heard to sound,
That the rare sweetnesse of the melody
The feeble sences wholly did confound,
And the frayle soule in deepe delight nigh drownd:
And, when it ceast, shrill trompets lowd did bray,
That their report did far away rebound;
And, when they ceast, it gan againe to play,
The whiles the maskers marched forth in trim aray.

vii. The first was Fansy, like a lovely Boy
Of rare aspect, and beautie without peare,
Matchable ether to that ympe of Troy,
Whom Jove did love and chose his cup to beare;
Or that same daintie lad, which was so deare
To great Alcides, that, when as he dyde,
He wailed womanlike with many a teare,
And every wood and every valley wyde
He filled with Hylas name; the Nymphes eke Hylas cryde.

viii. His garment nether was of silke nor say,
But paynted plumes in goodly order dight,
Like as the sunburnt Indians do aray
Their tawney bodies in their proudest plight:
As those same plumes so seemd he vaine and light,
That by his gate might easily appeare;

For still he far'd as dauncing in delight,
And in his hand a windy fan did beare,
That in the ydle ayre he mov'd still here and theare.

IX. And him beside marcht amorous Desyre,
Who seemd of ryper yeares then th' other Swayne,
Yet was that other swayne this elders syre,
And gave him being, commune to them twayne:
His garment was disguysed very vayne,
And his embrodered Bonet sat awry:
Twixt both his hands few sparks he close did strayne,
Which still he blew and kindled busily,
That soone they life conceiv'd, and forth in flames did fly.

X. Next after him went Doubt, who was yclad
In a discolour'd cote of straunge disguyse,
That at his backe a brode Capuccio had,
And sleeves dependaunt Albanesè-wyse:
He lookt askew with his mistrustfull eyes,
And nycely trode, as thornes lay in his way,
Or that the flore to shrinke he did avyse;
And on a broken reed he still did stay
His feeble steps, which shrunck when hard thereon he lay.

XI. With him went Daunger, cloth'd in ragged weed
Made of Beares skin, that him more dreadfull made;
Yet his owne face was dreadfull, ne did need
Straunge horrour to deforme his griesly shade:
A net in th' one hand, and a rusty blade
In th' other was; this Mischiefe, that Mishap:
With th' one his foes he threatned to invade,
With th' other he his friends ment to enwrap;
For whom he could not kill he practizd to entrap.

XII. Next him was Feare, all arm'd from top to toe,
Yet thought himselfe not safe enough thereby,
But feard each shadow moving too or froe;
And, his owne armes when glittering he did spy
Or clashing heard, he fast away did fly,
As ashes pale of hew, and winged heeld,
And evermore on Daunger fixt his eye,
Gainst whom he alwayes bent a brasen shield,
Which his right hand unarmed fearefully did wield.

XIII. With him went Hope in rancke, a handsome Mayd,
Of chearefull looke and lovely to behold:
In silken samite she was light arayd,
And her fayre lockes were woven up in gold:
She alway smyld, and in her hand did hold
An holy-water-sprinckle, dipt in deowe,
With which she sprinckled favours manifold
On whom she list, and did great liking sheowe,
Great liking unto many, but true love to feowe.

XIV. And after them Dissemblaunce and Suspect
Marcht in one rancke, yet an unequall paire;
For she was gentle and of milde aspect,
Courteous to all and seeming debonaire,
Goodly adorned and exceeding faire:
Yet was that all but paynted and pourloynd,
And her bright browes were deckt with borrowed haire;
Her deeds were forged, and her words false coynd,
And alwaies in her hand two clewes of silke she twynd.

XV. But he was fowle, ill favoured, and grim,
Under his eiebrowes looking still askaunce;
And ever, as Dissemblaunce laught on him,
He lowrd on her with daungerous eyeglaunce,
Shewing his nature in his countenaunce:
His rolling eies did never rest in place,
But walkte each where for feare of hid mischaunce,
Holding a lattis still before his face,
Through which he stil did peep as forward he did pace.

XVI. Next him went Griefe and Fury, matcht yfere;
Griefe all in sable sorrowfully clad,
Downe hanging his dull head with heavy chere,
Yet inly being more then seeming sad:
A paire of Pincers in his hand he had,
With which he pinched people to the hart,
That from thenceforth a wretched life they ladd,
In wilfull languor and consuming smart,
Dying each day with inward wounds of dolours dart.

XVII. But Fury was full ill appareiled
In rags, that naked nigh she did appeare,
With ghastly looks and dreadfull drerihed;

And from her backe her garments she did teare,
And from her head ofte rente her snarled heare:
In her right hand a firebrand shee did tosse
About her head, still roming here and there;
As a dismayed Deare in chace embost,
Forgetfull of his safety, hath his right way lost.

XVIII. After them went Displeasure and Pleasaunce,
He looking lompish and full sullein sad,
And hanging downe his heavy countenaunce;
She chearfull, fresh, and full of joyaunce glad,
As if no sorrow she ne felt ne drad;
That evill matched paire they seemd to bee:
An angry Waspe th' one in a viall had,
Th' other in hers an hony-laden Bee.
Thus marched these six couples forth in faire degree.

XIX. After all these there marcht a most faire Dame,
Led of two grysie Villeins, th' one Despight,
The other cleped Cruelty by name:
She, dolefull Lady, like a dreary Spright
Cald by strong charmes out of eternall night,
Had Deathes owne ymage figurd in her face,
Full of sad signes, fearfull to living sight;
Yet in that horror shewd a seemely grace,
And with her feeble feete did move a comely pace.

XX. Her brest all naked, as nett yvory
Without adorne of gold or silver bright,
Wherewith the Craftesman wonts it beautify,
Of her dew honour was despoyled quight;
And a wide wound therein (O ruefull sight!)
Entrenched deep with knyfe accursed keene,
Yet freshly bleeding forth her fainting spright,
(The worke of cruell hand) was to be seene,
That dyde in sanguine red her skin all snowy cleene.

XXI. At that wide orifice her trembling hart
Was drawne forth, and in silver basin layd,
Quite through transfixed with a deadly dart,
And in her blood yet steeming fresh embayd:
And those two villeins, which her steps upstayd,
When her weake feete could scarcely her sustaine,

And fading vitall powres gan to fade,
Her forward still with torture did constraine,
And evermore encreased her consuming paine.

XXII. Next after her, the winged God him selfe
Came riding on a Lion ravenous,
Taught to obay the menage of that Elfe
That man and beast with powre imperious
Subdeweth to his kingdome tyrannous.
His blindfold eies he bad awhile unbinde,
That his proud spoile of that same dolorous
Faire Dame he might behold in perfect kinde;
Which seene, he much rejoyced in his cruell minde.

XXIII. Of which ful prowd, him selfe up rearing hye
He looked round about with sterne disdayne,
And did survay his goodly company;
And, marshalling the evill-ordered trayne,
With that the darts which his right hand did straine
Full dreadfully he shooke, that all did quake,
And clapt on hye his coulourd winges twaine,
That all his many it affraide did make:
Tho, blinding him againe, his way he forth did take.

XXIV. Behinde him was Reproch, Repentaunce, Shame;
Reproch the first, Shame next, Repent behinde:
Repentaunce feeble, sorrowful, and lame;
Reproch despightfull, carelesse, and unkinde;
Shame most ill-favourd, bestiall, and blinde:
Shame lowrd, Repentaunce sighd, Reproch did scould;
Reproch sharpe stings, Repentaunce whips entwinde,
Shame burning brond-yrons in her hand did hold:
All three to each unlike, yet all made in one mould.

XXV. And after them a rude confused rout
Of persons flockt, whose names is hard to read:
Emongst them was sterne Strife, and Anger stout;
Unquiet Care, and fond Unthriftyhead;
Lewd Losse of Time, and Sorrow seeming dead;
Inconstant Chaunge, and false Disloyalty;
Consuming Riotise, and guilty Dread
Of heavenly vengeaunce; faint Infirmity;
Vile Poverty; and, lastly, Death with infamy.

XXVI. There were full many moe like maladies,
Whose names and natures I note readen well;
So many moe, as there be phantasies
In wavering wemens witt, that none can tell,
Or paines in love, or punishments in hell:
All which disguized marcht in masking wise
About the chamber by the Damozell;
And then returned, having marched thrise,
Into the inner rowme from whence they first did rise.

XXVII. So soone as they were in, the dore streightway
Fast locked, driven with that stormy blast
Which first it opened, and bore all away.
Then the brave Maid, which al this while was plast
In secret shade, and saw both first and last,
Issewed forth, and went unto the dore
To enter in, but fownd it locked fast:
It vaine she thought with rigorous uprore
For to efforce, when charmes had closed it afore.

XXVIII. Where force might not availe, there sleights and art
She cast to use, both fitt for hard emprize:
Forthy from that same rowme not to depart
Till morrow next shee did her selfe avize,
When that same Maske againe should forth arize.
The morrowe nexte appeard with joyous cheare,
Calling men to their daily exercize:
Then she, as morrow fresh, her selfe did reare
Out of her secret stand that day for to outweare.

XXIX. All that day she outwore in wandering
And gazing on that Chambers ornament,
Till that againe the second evening
Her covered with her sable vestiment,
Wherewith the worlds faire beautie she hath blent:
Then, when the second watch was almost past,
That brasen dore flew open, and in went
Bold Britomart, as she had late forecast,
Nether of ydle showes, nor of false charmes aghast.

XXX. So soone as she was entred, rownd about
Shee cast her eies to see what was become
Of all those persons which she saw without:

But lo! they streight were vanisht all and some;
Ne living wight she saw in all that roome,
Save that same woefull Lady, both whose hands
Were bounden fast, that did her ill become,
And her small waste girt rownd with yron bands
Upon a brasen pillour, by the which she stands.

XXXI. And her before the vile Enchaunter sate,
Figuring straunge characters of his art:
With living blood he those characters wrate,
Dreadfully dropping from her dying hart,
Seeming transfixed with a cruell dart;
And all perforce to make her him to love.
Ah! who can love the worker of her smart?
A thousand charmes he formerly did prove,
Yet thousand charmes could not her stedfast hart
    remove.

XXXII. Soone as that virgin knight he saw in place,
His wicked bookes in hast he overthrew,
Not caring his long labours to deface;
And, fiercely running to that Lady trew,
A murdrous knife out of his pocket drew,
The which he thought, for villeinous despight,
In her tormented bodie to embrew:
But the stout Damzell, to him leaping light,
His cursed hand withheld, and maistered his might.

XXXIII. From her, to whom his fury first he ment,
The wicked weapon rashly he did wrest,
And, turning to herselfe, his fell intent,
Unwares it strooke into her snowie chest,
That litle drops empurpled her faire brest.
Exceeding wroth therewith the virgin grew,
Albe the wound were nothing deepe imprest,
And fiercely forth her mortall blade she drew,
To give him the reward for such vile outrage dew.

XXXIV. So mightily she smote him, that to ground
He fell halfe dead: next stroke him should have slaine,
Had not the Lady, which by him stood bound,
Dernly unto her called to abstaine
From doing him to dy. For else her paine

Should be remedilesse; sith none but hee
Which wrought it could the same recure againe.
Therewith she stayd her hand, loth stayd to bee;
For life she him envyde, and long'd revenge to see:

xxxv. And to him said: " Thou wicked man, whose meed
For so huge mischiefe and vile villany
Is death, or if that ought doe death exceed;
Be sure that nought may save thee from to dy
But if that thou this Dame do presently
Restore unto her health and former state:
This doe, and live, els dye undoubtedly."
He, glad of life, that lookt for death but late,
Did yield him selfe right willing to prolong his date:

xxxvi. And, rising up, gan streight to over-looke
Those cursed leaves, his charmes back to reverse.
Full dreadfull thinges out of that balefull booke
He red, and measur'd many a sad verse,
That horrour gan the virgins hart to perse,
And her faire locks up stared stiffe on end,
Hearing him those same bloody lynes reherse;
And, all the while he red, she did extend
Her sword high over him, if ought he did offend.

xxxvii. Anon she gan perceive the house to quake,
And all the dores to rattle round about:
Yet all that did not her dismaied make,
Nor slack her threatfull hand for daungers dout:
But still with stedfast eye and courage stout
Abode, to weet what end would come of all.
At last that mightie chaine, which round about
Her tender waste was wound, adowne gan fall,
And that great brasen pillour broke in peeces small.

xxxviii. The cruell steele, which thrild her dying hart,
Fell softly forth, as of his owne accord,
And the wyde wound, which lately did dispart
Her bleeding brest, and riven bowels gor'd,
Was closed up, as it had not beene bor'd,
And every part to safety full sownd,
As she were never hurt, was soone restord.
Tho, when she felt her selfe to be unbownd
And perfect hole, prostrate she fell unto the grownd.

XXXIX. Before faire Britomart she fell prostrate,
          Saying; "Ah noble knight! what worthy meede
          Can wretched Lady, quitt from wofull state,
          Yield you in lieu of this your gracious deed?
          Your vertue selfe her owne reward shall breed,
          Even immortall prayse and glory wyde,
          Which I your vassall, by your prowesse freed,
          Shall through the world make to be notifyde,
          And goodly well advaunce that goodly well was tryde."

XL. But Britomart, uprearing her from grownd,
          Said: "Gentle Dame, reward enough I weene,
          For many labours more then I have found,
          This, that in safetie now I have you seene,
          And meane of your deliverance have beene.
          Henceforth, faire Lady, comfort to you take,
          And put away remembrance of late teene;
          Insted thereof, know that your loving Make
          Hath no lesse griefe endured for your gentle sake."

XLI. She much was cheard to heare him mentiond,
          Whom of all living wightes she loved best.
          Then laid the noble Championesse strong hond
          Upon th' enchaunter which had her distrest
          So sore, and with foule outrages opprest.
          With that great chaine, wherewith not long ygoe
          He bound that pitteous Lady prisoner, now relest,
          Himselfe she bound, more worthy to be so,
          And captive with her led to wretchednesse and wo.

XLII. Returning back, those goodly rowmes, which erst
          She saw so rich and royally arayd,
          Now vanisht utterly and cleane subverst
          She found, and all their glory quite decayd;
          That sight of such a chaunge her much dismayd
          Thence forth descending to that perlous porch
          Those dreadfull flames she also found delayd
          And quenched quite like a consumed torch,
          That erst all entrers wont so cruelly to scorch.

XLIII. More easie issew now then entrance late
          She found; for now that fained dreadfull flame,
          Which chokt the porch of that enchaunted gate

And passage bard to all that thither came,
Was vanisht quite, as it were not the same,
And gave her leave at pleasure forth to passe.
Th' Enchaunter selfe, which all that fraud did frame
To have efforst the love of that faire lasse,
Seeing his worke now wasted, deepe engrieved was.

XLIV. But when the Victoresse arrived there
Where late she left the pensife Scudamore
With her own trusty Squire, both full of feare,
Neither of them she found where she them lore:
Thereat her noble hart was stonisht sore;
But most faire Amoret, whose gentle spright
Now gan to feede on hope, which she before
Conceived had, to see her own deare knight,
Being thereof beguyld, was fild with new affright.

XLV. But he, sad man, when he had long in drede
Awayted there for Britomarts returne,
Yet saw her not, nor signe of her good speed,
His expectation to despaire did turne,
Misdeeming sure that her those flames did burne;
And therefore gan advize with her old Squire,
Who her deare nourslings losse no lesse did mourne,
Thence to depart for further aide t' enquire:
Where let them wend at will, whilest here I doe respire.

THE
TEMPLE PRESS   LETCHWORTH
ENGLAND

1. XXI · XXIII 3. 31. 5. 18

EVERYMAN,
I WILL GO WITH
THEE,
& BE THY GVIDE
IN THY MOST NEED
TO GO BY THY SIDE